Effective Techniques for Application Development with Visual FoxPro©

Hentzenwerke Publishing

Published by:
Hentzenwerke Publishing
980 East Circle Drive
Whitefish Bay, WI 53217

Hentzenwerke Publishing books are available through booksellers and directly from the publisher. Contact Hentzenwerke Publishing at:
414.332.9876
414.332.9463 (fax) or
www.hentzenwerke.com

Effective Techniques for Application Development with Visual FoxPro
By Jim Booth & Steve Sawyer
      Technical Editor: Steven P. Dingle
      Copy Editor: Jeana Randell
      Cover Art: "Welder" by Todd Gnacinski, Milwaukee, WI

ISBN: 0-96550-937-0

Manufactured in the United States of America

My work on this book is dedicated to my wife Carole, my three boys Vincent, Louis and Edward, and to my wife's friend Judy Rado. Without their encouragement my work on this book could not have been completed.

- Jim Booth

I would like to dedicate this book to my family.
To Marcia, my lovely wife, for her unfailing love, patience and encouragement.
To Lee, my eldest son, who often makes me feel like I might really
know something worthwhile, instead of being a complete idiot.
Most of all, this book is dedicated to my younger son Dylan,
who watched Dad work in his office every weekend this summer.
*It's **done**, Dylan, it's **done**!*

- Steve Sawyer

"This book was written in the summer and fall of 1998, while the current version of Visual FoxPro was 6.0. Since then, new service packs for Visual Studio and new releases of Visual Studio may have become available. Based on our understanding of the direction that Microsoft is taking with future products, the information in this book should be completely relevant for later versions."

Table of Contents

Chapter 6: Rules, Triggers and Referential Integrity 67

Chapter 7: Data Manipulation Classes   93

Chapter 13: Manager Objects,the Non-Visible Application Objects   261

Chapter 14: Developer Tools   309

Acknowledgements

I would like to acknowledge the assistance I have received from the FoxPro electronic community on the Universal Thread (www.universalthread.com), CompuServe, and the Microsoft newsgroups.

Special thanks goes to John Petersen for his help in understanding ADO, RDO, and all that other three-letter stuff. Steven Black deserves my thanks for his undying dedication to effective use of Object Orientation development techniques. Steve has been a helpful "thorn in my side" making me pay attention to the effective use of Object Orientation.

Also, a special thanks to our publisher, Hentzenwerke Publishing. The folks at Hentzenwerke are among the best in the world.

- Jim Booth

There are two groups of people that I must thank, and who deserve partial credit for any positive contribution I have made to this work. There are those that have, with patience and endless kindness, helped me learn what I know, through their writing, their service in online forums, and through personal mentoring. There are others that have allowed me the opportunity to pass what I have learned to others through articles and books. Many of these people have served in both capacities. The following list is by no means complete. Space does not permit me to list everyone from whom I've learned. However, the following people, at one time or another, have all had a tremendous influence on my skills and my career as a developer.

Lisa Slater Nicholls, Tamar Granor, Jim Booth, Whil Hentzen, Steven Black, Doug Hennig, Y. Alan Griver, Ken Levy, Pat Adams, Ted Roche, and in fond memory, Tom Rettig and Glenn Hart.

Special thanks to Steven P. Dingle, our technical editor, who asks the best damn questions.

-Steve Sawyer

Chapter 1
Introduction

Any journey is best begun with a roadmap.

When Whil approached us to do this book, the most significant feature that he wanted us to include was "wisdom." We immediately wondered why he would use such a word in the context of recruiting us to do a book. However, after a moment's reflection (and much to our relief— we thought we were really going to be on the spot!), we realized that wisdom is not the same as intelligence, nor is it the same as knowledge. Wisdom is acquired only through experience. Usually that experience is painful, because valuable experience involves making decisions that later turn out to be mistakes. After making mistakes on a development project, we're faced with another decision—to either live with and work around the mistakes, or to back up and redo a great deal of work to correct the mistake.

We have made our fair share of mistakes over the three years we've worked with Visual FoxPro, and in the process have come to an understanding of what does and does not work well in solving certain problems that confront us when creating applications. The purpose of this book is to share with you some of the things we have learned.

One challenge of learning to be an effective Visual FoxPro developer is wading through the multiplicity of available choices when you're confronted with a particular problem that needs to be solved in the context of a particular application. Visual FoxPro's Xbase heritage means that almost every feature, command and function that has been added to any Xbase dialect from the early '80s to the present has found its way into the product. Add to that the features, commands and functions appropriate to an object-oriented language, and you have three Thanksgiving dinners worth of stuff.

It isn't easy to whittle down the commands, functions and features by eliminating those that the documentation claims are for "backward compatibility" only. In many cases these items have, indeed, been replaced by better, more appropriate techniques. But the fact remains that some are unique in their functionality and in certain circumstances cannot be duplicated using any other feature. As an example, ON KEY LABEL and VARREAD() have certainly been well replaced by KeyPress and ActiveControl. However, TAGNO() and PCOUNT(), included in FoxPro 2.6 to provide dBase compatibility, have no other equivalent function or technique. Fortunately, in the case of PCOUNT(), Microsoft has acknowledged that this function provides functionality unique from that provided by PARAMETERS(), and has begun fully documenting this function.

Beyond the sheer number of commands and functions, the complexity of some of the objects that we have to work with can be very intimidating. The combo box has 143 different properties, events and methods. 143! Sheesh! In FoxBASE+, a table field had a data type (one of five—character, numeric, logical, date and memo), a size, and a position within the table. In VFP6.0, we have a choice of 11 different data types (the original five, plus general, currency, datetime, double, float and integer, plus two variants of these, the character binary and memo binary). We also have a choice of whether the field accepts null values, and nine different properties for each field if the table is included in a database—Caption, Comment, DefaultValue, DisplayClass, DisplayClassLibrary, Format, InputMask, RuleExpression and RuleText.

The developer has so many different features to choose from that it can become difficult to decide exactly which ones to use, which ones to pass by, and which ones to avoid at all costs. Further, there are almost always two ways of doing *anything* in Visual FoxPro, and frequently more than that. Given such a surfeit of choice, opportunities abound for doing things the hard way—or in a manner inappropriate to the situation—and causing a lot of frustration, to say nothing of creating an application that may be well nigh unto unmaintainable.

Hence this book. We've tried to put together a list of what we feel are the most important issues facing the Visual FoxPro developer, and to show you how we've chosen to deal with these issues.

Who this book is for

This book is intended for developers who are fairly familiar with Visual FoxPro. If you're looking for a good introduction to Visual FoxPro, we highly recommend Whil Hentzen's *Programming Visual FoxPro 3.0*, and his contribution to this series, *The Fundamentals: Building Visual Studio Applications on a Visual FoxPro 6.0 Foundation*. If the material in either or both of these books is familiar to you, then you're ready for this book.

To get the most out of this book, you should be able to put together a simple application; hopefully you've already created an application or two. These don't necessarily have to be production applications, but the simple kind of thing we all create when we're learning a new language—with a database, a menu, a couple of forms and a report.

This book is *not* for those who are brand new to Visual FoxPro. If your experience is entirely with FoxPro 2.x, dBase, Delphi, C++, Visual Basic, PowerBuilder or any other language, you need to get up to speed with one of Whil's books mentioned above, or an equivalent.

Neither is this book for those looking for information about how to implement an application framework. We both strongly believe in using a framework of some kind, but creating a robust framework suitable for use in a multi-programmer shop is beyond the scope of this book. We do discuss many of the issues that must be addressed in a framework, but the focus is on resolving these issues in a logical and design-influenced manner.

Likewise, if you're already into your second or third production Visual FoxPro application, and have a fairly well-developed framework in use, this book should serve as an interesting discussion of issues you've probably already resolved, and an opportunity to see how others have approached the same problems.

The *right* way to do things

It's important to understand that we're not necessarily trying to tell you the *right* way to do things; we just want to share the ways that have worked well for us. We will discuss the issues that have influenced our design decisions, so you can decide for yourself how best to create your applications. This is not to say that we don't have some strong opinions about how applications should be created, and we'll try to make sure that we offer some rationale for those opinions. Many people trying to come to grips with the Brave New World that Visual FoxPro represents are a bit intimidated by the "purist" attitude displayed by more experienced Visual FoxPro developers, which can very easily sound condescending. We are both very pragmatic developers, but have learned the value of what some of the purists have advocated. If we sound "purist" on some issues, please understand that we've painted ourselves into many a corner by ignoring some of that purist hogwash; we've lived to regret it and to "tell the tale." Then again, sometimes even we don't agree on the best approach to a particular issue!

Good design has always been important to producing quality, maintainable, scalable software. It assumes a much greater importance in an object-oriented programming language because the consequences of a design decision are much greater in an object-oriented system. This is a two-edged sword. The very thing that can make our lives easier, speed the assembly of the application and improve the maintainability and consistency of the code, can also make our lives a living hell, and make our applications a virtually unmaintainable mess.

This is not a book about object-oriented design. However, as we discuss the various areas of building an application we will by the very nature of the book, discuss how design decisions affect the implementations currently being discussed.

How this book is organized

This book is organized around several issues that we feel present the greatest difficulty to folks who are ready to begin their first production applications, or who have already embarked on or even completed a production application, and are finding it harder than they think it should be.

We have decided not to present a complete, functioning application as part of this book. We made this decision for several reasons. First, it frees us from having to create a single, monolithic application framework; we can instead explore different ways of getting the job done, without regard to how we did things in another part of the book. Second, you're probably aware of the old saying that the last 10 percent of an application takes 90 percent of the time and effort, and we wanted to devote more time and effort to discussion and demonstration of how to create applications, rather than putting the finishing touches on a demonstration app.

As a result, each chapter centers on a different piece of application construction, and explores that issue in the context of creating a portion of an application. All demonstration code is designed to work with modified versions of the "Time and Data" data set that ships with Visual FoxPro 6.0.

Copies of the database as used in these examples, as well as our sample apps, are available from the Developer's Download Files from the Hentzenwerke Publishing website **www.hentzenwerke.com.**

A note about the Source Code

Developer's
Download
Files Icon

For a book, as with software, "shipping is a feature". Because the two authors of this book were most comfortable working with their own foundation classes and database features, we decided to include source code in two separate directories of the Developer's Download Files, rather than spending the time collaborating on a single database and set of foundation classes. Each chapter with source code will refer you to the directory where the example code is located.

The authors and our technical editor have tested all example code. This does not mean that it is completely bullet-proof. As you well know, only rigorous field testing can completely wring the bugs out of a piece of code. There hasn't been time or personnel for this level of testing, nor is it our intention to create robust code that you can cut and paste into your own applications. Many of the foundation class features are in use in production applications, but the example code is intended as just that – examples of ideas that have worked for us, and that would be refined, alpha- and beta- tested if they were going to be used in a production application.

As a result, do not be too dismayed if you find a bug in our code. We do it all the time. We would expect that any bugs that remain in the code at this point will not detract from the ideas that the text and the sample code are presenting.

Take note

Then there are times when we have something of special interest, or maybe a related topic, or maybe two different opinions to present. We've offset that in the text and slapped a "Note" icon on it.

Note Icon

Chapter 2
In The Beginning

Everything in life has a beginning—a point where the details are ill defined. Application development is not any different. All projects have a beginning; the actions we take and decisions we make at the beginning will heavily influence the rest of the project. In this chapter we'll look into the beginning of application projects and find some ideas on how to make them work for us instead of against us. This chapter is not a treatise on Object Oriented Analysis and Design, but rather a pragmatic discussion of some ideas that can help that process to be more fruitful.

Finding out what needs to be done

The first order of business is to get a clue! Get some idea what the project is about. This may seem obvious, but it isn't. There are two sets of ideas about the project: the developer's and the client's. These two views are seldom the same.

We are developers so we can understand the developer's need to gather details about the functional requirements, how many forms there will be, how many data tables are needed, how the tables relate to each other, and all those other things developers need to know.

However, clients often see the project in a very different way. A client has pain! Something is wrong in their business. Perhaps a competitor is beating them in the marketplace, or they're losing inventory through shrinkage and can't track it down. Maybe the cost of sales is too high and profits are being hurt. Or it may even be that the company is growing at a very rapid rate and they sense a loss of control over their costs.

Whatever it is, the client has a problem that is causing them pain. They aren't hiring us to build great software; they are hiring us to relieve their pain. If we want to succeed with the project, then we must focus on relieving the client's pain. To do that we must understand the pain and where it's coming from.

What do we know?

We know about building applications. We know how to make computers sing. We can tweak the last nanosecond out of those SQL queries. We know how to protect the referential integrity and enforce the domain constraints. We can validate fields, rows, and even whole tables.

All of these things are important to a successful project; however, we're totally off base thinking that the client cares about these issues at all. The client cares about finding the shortest route to pain relief.

What does the client know?

The client knows that they are in pain; they may or may not know the exact cause of their pain. They know how they run their business. They know their market and their customers. They know what their customers want. They know how to build their product or provide their service.

The client is human and likes to feel important and intelligent. If we start out by forcing them into a structured analysis of their business, we're putting them into an uncomfortable situation where they don't know the jargon and they're unfamiliar with the processes. Human nature says they'll do everything in their power to shorten that experience as much as they can.

Herein lies the conflict

We have been told time and again that solid analysis and design are critical to a solid application. This is simply a truth of nature. We also know that clients see the analysis and design phases as wasted time. They see it that way because nothing new is showing up on their computers. They also see it that way because the process is a nightmare for them. They feel inadequate and unintelligent.

What can we do to change this? How can we get the client to buy into good analysis and design? We can do it by not telling them that's what we're doing, by dumping the jargon and the fancy forms and checklists (oh, we'll use them, but not in front of the client—at least not at first).

Start the analysis by saying something like, "This system is going to need to work well within your business and I'm not anywhere near knowledgeable enough about your business to accomplish that. I'll need your help and your expertise to deal with the business side of this project. Can you describe the nature of your business for me?"

Let these early conversations be loose and descriptive of the client's overall business. Take copious notes. Retire from these early meetings and analyze your notes. Then write a few pages of summary, in English, describing what you understand. Return to the client and ask them to read the summary and let you know what you've got right and, more importantly, what you've got wrong.

After one or two go-arounds with this, you can start bringing out the checklists and the other fancy charts and diagrams. Introduce these documents slowly and explain their structure. Work slowly into the details of the information contained within the documents.

By following these few ideas at the very beginning, you'll be better able to get the client to buy into the analysis phase (without them even knowing that's what they did) and you'll probably get much better and more complete information from them.

Having a plan

Once the analysis is fairly complete and you have a good, solid foundation of understanding both the project requirements and the business in general, you can begin to make a plan for the project. The early design is that plan.

You wouldn't consider leaving on a two-week vacation without having any idea of where you were going or how to get there. A vacation that starts that way is surely going to have problems. No, you would select a destination or two and then review the maps to plan the best route. You might vary from your plan during the vacation, but you wouldn't start without a plan.

Project development is the same way. You don't want to start without a plan—some kind of map of where you're headed and how you intend to get there. Without a plan, you'll likely travel down many dead-end roads and have to dump the work and start again.

Having a design doesn't mean that you won't alter it during the development; you most certainly will. You'll discover information or learn something new about your tools that will cause you to alter your plan. That's fine. It even has a name: it's called *iterative development*.

Your plan should include class designs for those objects that you'll be using, your data design with the persistent relations defined, user interface design, report design, and other things. There is no law that says you cannot use Visual FoxPro to accomplish these designs. You can use the form designer to lay out the forms and the user interface, the database designer to lay out the tables and relations, and the report designer to lay out the reports. The issue is that you don't want to spend a lot of time filling in the details at this stage. Why not? Because things will change. It is much easier to redo a form that has little or no code in it, than to feel the cramps of throwing away two days of work on a form that just does not fit.

Iterative development

The processes of Analysis, Design and Implementation are almost always shown as a timeline, where one process does not begin until the previous one is completed. This isn't how it works in the real world. We analyze the information until we have a degree of understanding; then we begin to design the application. Often during the design, questions will arise that cause us to go back to the analysis and get the answers.

When our design is fairly well laid out, we begin building the components that will comprise the application. This process inevitably will uncover weakness, omissions, or outright errors in our design, which cause us to stop and return to the design to alter it.

The one mortal sin for any developer is pride of authorship. Pride of authorship will cause us to resist scrapping something that isn't quite right. We'll twist, pry, sweat, hammer, squeeze, push, pull, bend, spindle and mutilate that thing to try to get it to work. The longer we beat on it, the higher the degree of pride of authorship and the more difficult it becomes to finally let go, scrap it, and start over again.

Whenever you find yourself even remotely considering starting something over, remember this: **IT WILL NEVER GET EASIER TO START OVER THAN IT IS RIGHT NOW; IT WILL ONLY GET HARDER.**

Chapter 3
The Application

An application is greater than the sum of its parts. Good application development requires an appreciation and understanding of the idea of application services and ensuring that each component is available to the rest of the system.

Forms or objects created for some specific purpose do much of the actual "work" of an application. It is possible to accomplish some meaningful task by running a form from the command window or by instantiating some object and calling its methods. However, doing so does not demonstrate the functioning of an *application*.

An application needs to expose all of the functionality of the system through a seamlessly integrated user interface that addresses many more issues than simply insulating the user from the DO FORM command.

System-level services

Each component of an application provides services to the user or to another component of the application—or some combination of both. A form in a database application (assuming it's visible) provides a service to users; it allows them to enter, view, or alter data stored in the database. A command button on that form also provides a service, allowing users to communicate their wishes, and provides a service to the rest of the form by passing along user input to the appropriate method. A menu likewise serves the user's need to launch a particular form, and may carry out that wish by passing it along to a form manager.

Some components exist only to provide system-level services—that is, their responsibility is to manage or facilitate some aspect of the application internally. A method of a form may provide a service to the form by disabling the Save button until the user has modified the current record. However, in this book, we'll refer to system-level services as those that apply system-wide, meaning "global to the application" rather than the usual connotation of "on the level of the operating system." System-level services transform individual components such as data tables, forms, reports, and menus into a complete application.

System-level services can include some or all of the following functions. This list is by no means exhaustive. Individual applications may require additional services, and you may decide to provide—or a particular application may need—additional system-level services.

- **Application launching.** "Kicking off" the entire process—setting the path, loading the class libraries, procedure files and runtime libraries, starting the menu or other component launcher, issuing the "READ EVENTS," and so on.
- **User identification and security.** Restricting or allowing access to the system or certain portions of the system, and making the identity of the current user globally available to the system.

- **Forms management.** Limiting instances of certain forms, instantiating necessary tool-bars, closing forms programmatically, arranging forms on the user's desktop, and coordinating active forms with toolbars, menus and other interface elements.
- **Menu management.** Encapsulating code necessary to implement dynamic menu behavior, such as changing menu prompts, adding or removing menu pads or menu bars, and so on.
- **Report management.** Encapsulating all reporting processes in a single component to facilitate maintenance (for the developer) and access (for the user).
- **Saving and restoring user preferences.** Form sizes, toolbar buttons, grid arrangements, default search values, and so on.
- **Global configuration.** System-wide settings to determine default system behaviors, settings, and assumptions, including network and drive layout, pathing, and business rules.
- **Error handling.** Informing users of unexpected error conditions, and recording error information for debugging and troubleshooting.
- **Services not elsewhere specified.** Establishing environment-specific settings (SET TALK, SET DELETED, SET STATUS BAR ad nauseum), the removal and restoration (for the developer's benefit during development) of the system menu and toolbars as well as other services that may be required.

How these services (and other services that are provided on a smaller scope, usually at the form level) are provided represents a significant part of the "under the hood" design of an application, and not surprisingly, an important part of any application framework. Services that are built into the classes and code libraries used to build system-level components, or into the foundation class hierarchy, will unavoidably place the application somewhere on an important continuum that the developer must keep in mind as design decisions are made. The extremes of this continuum represent maximal and minimal flexibility and abstraction. The more abstract these services, the more easily they can be adapted to specific needs of the application; the more concrete, the more they will dictate how specific needs of the application are met. Abstract services are highly generic and reusable. Concrete services are tailored to meet more specific application needs.

One way that a compromise can be reached between these two design extremes is to provide global, system-level services through a multitude of individual components, each instantiated from object classes, or object subclasses. This makes it easier to substitute different components when the need arises, or to subclass certain components while leaving others intact. However, there is no rule that says they can't be provided by a single, monolithic application object. That decision will be influenced by the specifics of the application and your own preferences or style of work. Chapter 10 will discuss objects for providing many of these system-level services in greater detail. For the remainder of this chapter, however, we will that the application object is the only system-level object that we need be concerned about. We can assume that this object either provides all global system-level services directly, or is responsible for instantiating all subsidiary system-level objects such as form and menu managers or error handlers.

The Kickoff

In common with any other programming language, Visual FoxPro 6 must have a program module identified as "Main" in the project manager. This program module contains the first lines of code that are executed when the application is started. In a Visual FoxPro 6 application, this is usually a program (.PRG) file, which performs the most rudimentary steps necessary to get the application going.

At the bare minimum, this "main" program (often called, not surprisingly, MAIN.PRG), must perform the following tasks:

1.   Set the correct default directory.
2.   Issue a SET PATH command to enable the application to find all the components necessary to the application's operation.
3.   Load the minimum necessary class and code API libraries and procedure files.
4.   Set the working environment to a state necessary to get the rest of the application up and running.
5.   Instantiate the application object.
6.   Issue the READ EVENTS command.

Let's consider each of these items in more detail.

SET DEFAULT TO

While it's possible to set the default or working directory to the application in the property sheet of the Start menu shortcut, it can also be set incorrectly. Thus, it's important to *ensure* that the program is running from the correct directory.

The most common practice is to place the program file itself into the same directory that you wish to make the default directory. This eliminates many pathing problems in trying to locate external program elements and data files. This also makes it extremely easy to set the default directory without having to store this information in the registry or a configuration file. The SYS(16) function (when used with the optional argument of 0: SYS(16,0)) returns the drive and full path and filename of the "top level" program that is currently executing. This, together with the JUSTPATH() function that is now a native Visual FoxPro 6 function, can be used to determine where the application is installed:

```
lcHomeDirectory = JUSTPATH(SYS(16,0))
SET DEFAULT TO (lcHomeDirectory)
```

SET PATH TO

Here we come up against an issue that is related to the highly interactive mode in which Visual FoxPro applications are written. In conventional programming languages that use native-code compilers, the testing environment is not significantly different from the production environment. However, when running a program module, whether it be a form, a program, or a report, if not doing so from within a compiled application, the program module has to be in the Visual FoxPro path, or the name of the program must include its relative path in order to be located and executed.

One of the great advantages of Visual FoxPro's highly interactive development environment is the ability to test a program module or the entire application without having to go through an edit/save/compile/run cycle. To fully exploit this, our MAIN.PRG has to be able to set the path so that all program components can be found.

However, while it is necessary to have MAIN.PRG issue a SET PATH to allow the production application to locate the database files, most program modules are compiled into the application (whether compiled to an .APP or .EXE). Thus, it isn't necessary for the path to be set to the directories containing these module's source files in the production environment, where the development directory structure doesn't usually exist. But it is very handy to be able to run and test the entire application by issuing the command DO MAIN (or whatever you call your "main" program) in the command window, in which case all of the directories in the development directory tree need to be in the search path.

The solution is to maintain, during development, a program in the project directory that is also included in the project, and is called by MAIN.PRG. This program determines whether the application is running in "development mode"—that is, by issuing DO MAIN in the command window—or whether we're running a compiled .APP or .EXE. Then, based on this determination, this program sets the path appropriately:

```
* Partial Program Listing LocalPath.PRG
SET PATH TO LocalData;RemoteData
IF RIGHT(SYS(16,0),3) = "FXP"
   SET PATH TO SET("PATH") +
";..\COMMON\LIBS;..\COMMON\PROGS;FORMS;PROGS;INCLUDE"
ENDIF
```

Note that the way LocalPath.PRG works is to identify if the "top level" program has an extension of .FXP, indicating that we're running MAIN.PRG (automatically compiled to an .FXP file). If this is the case, then it isn't sufficient to simply include the data directories in the search path, but we must include all directories containing source code

.   In production, SYS(16,0) will return a filename with an extension of .APP or .EXE, and therefore won't bother including the development directories in the SET PATH command.

As the application progresses, the directory structure may change, and it is necessary to keep LocalPath.PRG up to date with these changes. An additional advantage of keeping LocalPath.PRG in the application directory is that by simply issuing DO LocalPath.PRG in the command window, all of the development directories are placed into our search path during development.

SET CLASSLIB TO/SET PROCEDURE TO/SET LIBRARY TO

The next task that MAIN.PRG must accomplish is to ensure that all necessary class and API libraries and procedure files are loaded into memory. MAIN.PRG will have to instantiate the application object, so at the very minimum its class library must be included. It also may call functions and procedures in either API libraries or procedure files, or instantiate objects whose class definitions reside in other class libraries. Thus, it is best to make no distinction about what may or may not be needed *at the moment*, and simply load all procedure files and libraries that are used in the application.

We can rely again on our LocalPath.PRG file to take care of this task. During development, these libraries and procedure files are added to the list of SET commands in Local-

Path.PRG as they are created or employed in some part of the application. In addition to its function within the context of the application, again as with the pathing, this is handy during development; issuing **DO LocalPath.PRG** in the command window puts all of our resources at our immediate disposal.

Here is another section of LocalPath.PRG:

```
SET PROCEDURE TO proclib ADDITIVE
SET PROCEDURE TO applib ADDITIVE
SET CLASSLIB TO ccontrls ADDITIVE
SET CLASSLIB TO cenviron ADDITIVE
SET CLASSLIB TO cforms ADDITIVE
```

SET TALK/SET EXCLUSIVE

There are more than 100 SET commands in Visual FoxPro 6. (I don't know how many there are exactly—I got tired of counting at 100). In the development environment, we usually prefer to have many of these options set a particular way, yet prefer (and indeed rely on) them to be set differently in our applications. Thus the need, in development mode, to be able to change these settings for testing our application, and to restore them to the settings preferred by the developer when the application terminates.

SET TALK is probably the best example of this situation, because most developers prefer to have TALK set ON during interactive work at the command window, but there are very few situations (other than running a query) in which TALK is set ON in an application. In fact, to avoid any cryptic messages on the desktop or in the status bar, it is important to record the current setting of SET TALK (so it can be restored when the application exits), and issue SET TALK OFF as soon as possible.

Likewise, the developer may operate with SET EXCLUSIVE ON, but an application may very quickly access a shared table for the purpose of executing a login procedure, so it's likewise important to save the current SET EXCLUSIVE setting for later restoration, and to SET EXCLUSIVE OFF.

Including the TALK and EXCLUSIVE settings, we have thus far talked about seven environmental settings that MAIN.PRG directly or indirectly must fiddle with, and may be different than what the developer prefers. So it is necessary for MAIN.PRG to save the current settings for TALK, EXCLUSIVE, DEFAULT, PATH, CLASSLIB, LIBRARY and PROCEDURE, and provide some way of restoring them after the application has terminated.

One really handy behavior associated with the creation and destruction of objects is that the Init() event (and its associated method code) fires once each time an object is instantiated, and the Destroy() event (and *its* associated code) fires once each time an object is destroyed. This arrangement is tailor-made for saving and restoring a state or condition. As a result, most developers use a couple of objects for setting such environmental settings, and optionally, restoring them when the objects are destroyed. Such an object can be instantiated by MAIN.PRG, but this would require that the class library in which the environment-setting object is defined be loaded into memory with a SET CLASSLIB command. To get around this chicken-and-egg situation, we store the current settings for these six values to memory variables that are then transferred to our environment setting object after it has been instantiated. This object can be instantiated by MAIN.PRG or as part of the instantiation of the application object.

oApp = CREATEOBJECT()

After storing the current environmental settings that get changed almost immediately, setting the default directory, setting the path, and loading the necessary libraries, we're all set to instantiate the application object. By instantiating the application object as a private or public memory variable, it is scoped to the entire application, and is therefore visible, and all of its properties and services are available to all other components and modules in the system. These services may include, but are not limited to, any or all of the system-level services discussed above.

READ EVENTS

Some application frameworks and some developers place the READ EVENTS command in a method of the application object that is called by MAIN.PRG. However, it facilitates error handling if the RETURN TO MASTER command can be used to return control to MAIN.PRG; thus, it is better to issue the READ EVENTS in MAIN.PRG.

Also by keeping the READ EVENTS in MAIN.PRG, we have the added ability to avoid issuing that command when we are running in the development mode, thus leaving the command window and the ability to edit forms and programs available to the developer while the application is running. This is accomplished by allowing MAIN.PRG to accept a parameter that indicates that the system is being run in development mode and controlling the creation of oApp and the issuing of READ EVENTS according to this parameter. The following code shows how this might be done.

```
* MAIN.PRG
LPARAMETERS plDevMode
* Other setup code as described above
...

IF plDevMode
    IF TYPE("oApp") <> "U"
        RELEASE oApp
    ENDIF
    PUBLIC oApp
ENDIF
oApp = CreateObject("ApplicationClass")
IF NOT plDevMode
    READ EVENTS
ENDIF
```

Before MAIN.PRG

I know, you thought I said that MAIN.PRG is the first thing that gets executed. Well, yes, but there is something that comes into play *before* MAIN.PRG, and that's the CONFIG.FPW file.

This file can be stored external to the application, or it can be compiled into the application itself. When running the compiled application, it is often preferred to delay the appearance of the Visual FoxPro main screen until after the program is loaded, a splash screen has been displayed, the caption and icon have been set, and so on. This is also important in an application that uses a single SDI form as the user interface, where the Visual FoxPro main screen is never made visible. The single line in the CONFIG.FPW file that allows all of this to be accomplished is the command SCREEN=OFF.

If you use this technique, be aware that your application object will need to make the _SCREEN or _VFP object visible at the appropriate time.

To summarize, **Listing 3-1** illustrates a typical minimal MAIN.PRG.

Listing 3-1. An example of MAIN.PRG, the startup program.

```
* MAIN.PRG
LPARAMETERS plDevMode
IF SET("TALK") = "ON"
   SET TALK OFF
   LcOldTalk = "ON"
ENDIF
pcOldExclusive = SET("EXCLUSIVE")
pcOldDefault = SET("DEFAULT")
pcOldPath = SET("PATH")
pcOldClassLib = SET("CLASSLIB")
pcOldProc = SET("PROCEDURE")
pcOldLib = SET("LIBRARY")
DO localpath.PRG
IF plDevMode
   IF TYPE("oApp") <> "U"
      RELEASE oApp
   ENDIF
   PUBLIC oApp
ENDIF
oApp = CREATEOBJECT("aApplication")
IF TYPE("oApp") = "O" ;
      AND !ISNULL(oApp)
   * If the application object has successfully
   * instantiated, it will store the private
   * memvars holding the environmental settings
   * created above
   RELEASE LIKE p*
ENDIF
IF NOT plDevMode
   READ EVENTS
   RELEASE ALL EXTENDED
   CLEAR ALL
   CLOSE ALL
ENDIF
```

Note that this is an example of a *minimal* MAIN.PRG. Typically, MAIN.PRG would immediately use the system services of the application object to put up a system menu, clear a splash screen, run a logon procedure, and so on. All this would be done before issuing READ EVENTS.

Note, too, that the menu—or more likely the application object—must be responsible for issuing the CLEAR EVENTS command to terminate the application.

A function launching mechanism

The most basic of the components that begin to integrate an application, referred to only in passing above, but worthy of separate consideration, is some kind of mechanism to allow the user to launch forms, reports, and other processes. While this component also provides a significant service to the user, its role in integrating the other components of the application makes it worthy of consideration as a system-level service provider. In addition, the level of cooperation between various function-launching mechanisms and the rest of the system often requires a high degree of integration between these components at a system level.

Unfortunately, Microsoft continues to drag its feet in giving us a menu *object.* As a result, the menu is not discussed much in the context of Visual FoxPro applications, but this service is still usually performed by way of a menu system. However, we're increasingly seeing tool-bars (some that can be user-configurable) as a launching mechanism, and in the good old DOS days, hotkeys or keystroke commands were common.

With Visual FoxPro 6, it's possible to employ any combination of these techniques to allow the user to access an order-entry form or a report of customer contacts. The choice of which methods will be employed is primarily of importance to the end user, and must be de-cided with a great deal of user input. While some methods such as using function keys may seem archaic, they may be perfectly reasonable in keyboard-centric applications. An applica-tion that is a rewrite of an existing application, which has a large number of current users, will be adapted to more easily if familiar interface elements are preserved. If the user interface on the old system made extensive use of function keys, preserving this as an interface element in the rewrite makes perfect sense.

There is also no requirement that there must be only one way of interfacing with the ap-plication. Allowing the user to decide between using keystrokes or a mouse, or between a toolbar and a menu, shows a great deal of sensitivity to the fact that different users have dif-ferent ways of working. While Microsoft may like to make high-handed assumptions about how we interact with our computers, there is no reason why we should perpetuate this behav-ior.

Flexibility during development

During development, being forced to compile and run the entire application every time we test a component can be a real impediment to the entire process. If, for (an extreme) example, we're working on a method or procedure that will end up being 100 lines of code, and em-bodies some rather tricky logic, it's usually best to write it incrementally, testing each stage of the algorithm before proceeding to the next. Sometimes I actually write the method as a .PRG, substituting memory variables for object properties, write a little, test a little, write a little, and then cut and paste it into the object method. Then I search and replace to change the memory variables to object properties.

Sometimes this technique can't be used, especially if we're working with visible form components. In this case, it is preferable to add a control, or add a bit of code to a method, set a property or two, and then run the form. Fix any problems discovered, add another control or set another property, then re-run the form. If we are forced to compile and run the entire appli-cation to test each component, then we're going to be much less inclined to introduce new code and components incrementally. We're going to try to make the most of each compile/run cycle by writing as much code, setting as many properties, and adding as many objects as we can manage before each test run. This has the potential to make the debugging process a nightmare, because the number of changes we make before each test run makes it very diffi-cult to zero in on the particular change that has introduced the error, particularly in a scenario in which there are complex algorithms in code or heavy interaction between objects.

I'm actually discussing two issues here. The first is to avoid having to test components only within the context of the entire application, and the second is to make such testing easier when desired. What is desirable is the ability to both test components individually, and (when desired) to easily run the entire application without having to rebuild and recompile.

Maintaining the LocalPath.PRG file mentioned earlier will make it possible to have an application that you can run and test without being forced to recompile the entire application. With this program called by your MAIN.PRG, all the source code is accessible, API class and procedure libraries are loaded, and paths are set. It's then possible to run your entire application by simply issuing DO MAIN in the command window with it running as it would if you had compiled it. It will still be necessary to occasionally rebuild the application, checking the "Recompile all files" option in the Build... dialog, particularly if you make use of include files, which are only incorporated into object classes and program files when the files are compiled.

To explore the issue of being able to run most components individually, outside the context of the application, it's helpful to consider a principle in programming known as "loose coupling" of program components. This means reducing the interdependency of program elements, so that each is a "black box" that is familiar to the rest of the system only insofar as the rest of the system is familiar with its interface. The "interface" here, of course, refers not to a user interface, but the interface that the component presents to the rest of the system, the methods, exposed properties, method or function arguments, and return value data types. The simpler this interface (the fewer the exposed methods and properties, and the fewer the arguments passed to methods or functions), the more the coupling of the component can be described as "loose." This makes components interchangeable as long as they present a consistent interface. Loose coupling also allows components to function to some extent without depending on the presence of other components or objects, or depending on a certain system state (like having certain tables open, or certain work areas selected, or certain objects instantiated). Adhering to high standards of loose coupling will make it easier to develop and test program components. Let's consider this idea by example.

Consider a form that uses a grid to display some information to the user. The grid's Column Count property is 40, the grid columns' Movable and Resizable properties and the grid's AllowHeaderSizing and AllowRowSizing properties are all set .T. Clearly, the user could spend considerable time customizing the appearance of this grid, with the columns sized and ordered, and the headers and rows sized as desired. One way to save these settings, allowing them to be restored the next time the user runs this particular form is to write the user's preferences to the system registry, and then read them from the registry when the form is next instantiated. There are numerous examples of object classes that define objects designed to accomplish this task, one of which ships with Visual FoxPro 6 (REGISTRY.VCX). It's possible to make a design decision that such an object will be added to any form that required its services, so that this feature of the form could be easily tested. On the other hand, another design decision could be made that such an object really provides a system-level service, and as a result, the registry-interfacing object should be instantiated as a child object of the application object, named for example "oRegistry", available for use by any form in the system.

In this situation, if the form is run during development using DO FORM <formName> in the command window, and it attempts to restore the grid's settings from the registry by referencing the oRegistry object, we're going to get an error, and the form may not run at all. To enable us to run this form during development in this scenario, we need to make some more design decisions.

- Check for the existence of the oRegistry object. Save or restore the grid settings only if the object is found, and use default values for the various settings if the object isn't available.
- Check for the existence of the oRegistry object. If it exists, store a reference to the object to a form property, and make all calls to this object by referencing the form property rather than the object directly. If the oRegistry object doesn't exist, create an instance of this object's class stored to the same form property.

By implementing either of these techniques, the form can be run and tested by itself from the command window, or in the context of the running application. The second technique's advantage: not only can the form run, but the behavior of saving and restoring the grid settings can be tested when the form is run in stand-alone mode.

Loose coupling of program elements is a programming principle that promotes flexibility and maintainability, but the principle of "loose coupling" can make each program component more manageable during development and testing as well. Whenever possible, you should be able to run any form or any other program module as a stand-alone module for testing purposes. Clearly, this may be completely impossible for some forms, objects and functions, depending on their roles in the system, but making your program modules independent of other program elements will improve your application overall, and will make development and testing easier.

With the ideas in this chapter behind us, we can proceed to talk more about the process of developing the application. We'll delve more deeply into how to put the rest of the pieces together within this framework to get a database application up and running. The next few chapters start with the stuff underlying almost all applications created with Visual FoxPro: the data that the application maintains and manipulates.

Chapter 4
Data - Keys and Indexes

Indexes have been part of the Xbase arena since the beginning. As newer versions of the various products were introduced, the indexing capabilities were expanded. Visual FoxPro gives us all of the original index types and then adds some new things. In this chapter we will explore the area of indexes and the benefits they provide. We will also explore the area of relational keys. We'll see the differences between relational keys and indexes and how indexes can help us in implementing our relational designs.

What are keys?

The term *key* is used in many different contexts in our work; there are key expressions for indexes, primary keys, foreign keys and candidate keys. Let's catalog all these differing meanings for the term *key* and expand our understanding of the whole key mess.

One simplified definition for a relational database is this: "A database that is comprised of multiple tables, which each store information about a single person, place, thing or concept. These tables can be related to each other, through the use of shared values, to produce information that none of the tables can provide alone." The *shared values*, referred to in that definition, are relational keys. There are two types of relational keys: primary and foreign. See **Figure 1**.

- A **primary key** is defined as "a field or group of fields that unambiguously identifies a specific record within a table. The primary key, or any part, may not have a value of NULL."

- A **foreign key** is defined as "a field or group of fields in one table that identifies a record in another table."

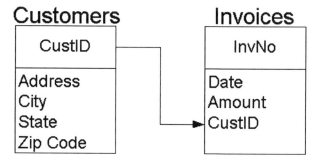

Figure 1. A diagram showing primary and foreign keys and the relation derived with them.

Figure 1 shows a customer and invoice table. You can see that the customer table has CustID as its primary key and the invoice table has InvNo as its primary key. In the invoice table you see a field named CustID—this is a foreign key connecting an invoice to a customer record. The line shows that relationship.

One absolute rule for relational databases is that every table *must* have a primary key. If a table does not include any one field or combination of more than one field that can perform the role of primary key, you must add another field to that table to perform that role. Failing to do this will render the table unstable in terms of data integrity. This means that eventually you'll have data problems that can be directly attributed to the lack of a primary key.

There can be more than one candidate for the primary key in a table design. For example, consider an employee table that has Employee Number and Social Security Account fields. Either of these fields could be designated as the primary key. They are both unique for each employee, and they are both required for all employees, so either one will do. These two fields would be referred to as *candidate keys* because they are both candidates for being the primary key. We need to select one of them to perform the role of primary key; when we do, the other one will continue to be called a candidate key.

> *There are cases in which use of a Social Security Number as a primary key can cause problems. Social security numbers are supposed to be unique, but as with all other absolutes, it isn't so. There have been numerous cases of duplicate social security numbers being issued, and not everyone has one (such as infants and non-citizens). Any system using a social security number as a primary or candidate key should take this possibility into account.*

Primary and candidate indexes

Visual FoxPro has index types named *primary* and *candidate*. Are these the same as what we just discussed? Not exactly. The relational terms of primary and candidate key are referring to the roles that certain fields will play in terms of your data design. The Visual FoxPro index types are implementation tools that you can use after the roles have been determined.

You can have a primary key in a table without using a primary index (you could use a regular index instead) and you can create a candidate index on a field that isn't a candidate for the primary key. So you can see that these aren't exactly the same things. We'll discuss the indexes a little later in this chapter.

Compound primary keys

According to our earlier definition of "primary key," it can be comprised of more than one field. When a primary key is comprised of more than one field it is called a *compound primary key*. Compound primary keys are perfectly valid within the realm of relational design. However, they present a set of complexities that you should be aware of before you decide to use them.

The first issue with compound primary keys is that they're more complex than a single field primary key. Applying the KISS principle (Keep It Simple, Stupid) dictates that you select the more simple primary key to use. You'll be able to manage these primary keys much easier if they are single fields.

Another issue isn't directly related to the complexity of the compound primary key. One of the things you must manage related to primary keys is a change in value. Whenever this occurs you must deal with all of those records in other tables that are pointing to the primary key that changed. This is called *managing referential integrity*, which will be covered in detail in a later chapter. So what does this have to do with compound primary keys?

A compound primary key is comprised of more than one field, and the fields comprising the compound primary key have meaning to the user outside their roles as primary keys. If a field has meaning to a person, that person will eventually want to change that field. When they do change a field that is part of the primary key, you must deal with the fallout in the referential integrity.

What do you do if the only possible primary key is a compound one?

Surrogate primary keys

Enter the *surrogate primary key*. A surrogate key is a field added to the table's structure that has no meaning or purpose other than being the primary key. These surrogate keys can be completely hidden from the users. Because the users never see the surrogate key and it has no meaning other than its role as primary key, it's highly unlikely that its value will be changed. Because its value won't change, you don't have to deal with the referential integrity issue related to a change in the value.

The appendix of this book contains a section on *data normalization*. Data normalization is a process through which you validate your table designs and eliminate problems. There are six steps in the normalization process; however, the last two apply only when there is a compound primary key. That means that if you use surrogate primary keys (which are always single fields) you eliminate the need to apply the last two normalization steps, thus simplifying your work. Hey, we're definitely in favor of anything that makes our workload lighter.

Also, because surrogate keys are meaningless, there's no need for the user to provide the key value. You can generate surrogate keys programmatically without any difficulty.

When you use surrogate primary keys, there's usually one or more other candidates in the table structure. For example, consider a customer table. The user will require some kind of customer identification for printing on invoices and so forth. You might name this field CustomerNumber. Let's assume that the user assigns alphanumeric values to the customer number (for example, ACME Corporation is assigned ACME01). This is helpful to the user because the customer number is indicative of the customer's name. For the surrogate primary key, you add a field named CustomerID, which is an integer field that holds a unique number. All of the related tables store your CustomerID value for referencing the customer record.

Let's say that one day, ACME gets bought out by Zenith and suddenly the customer number of ACME01 is no longer indicative of the customer's name. The user wants to change the customer number to ZENI01. Because you're using a surrogate primary key, you can allow the user to change the customer number and not be concerned with the change. Why? Because that field's value does not appear anywhere else in the system. All of the historic related data will remain connected to the customer's record because your surrogate key has not changed its value.

Using surrogate primary keys is a good thing! Okay, so how do you implement them? How do you generate new keys for new records?

Implementing surrogate primary keys

Our recommendation for surrogate primary keys is to use the integer data type. We suggest this data type for two reasons: first, integers can store more than 4 billion unique values in just four bytes if you allow negative values. That number is reduced to just over 2 billion if you use only positive values. Two billion is a pretty large number and four bytes isn't very much space at all.

The second reason for using integers for the surrogate keys is that testing indicates that integers are handled faster by Visual FoxPro than any other data type. This is probably related to the fact that integers are stored on disk exactly the same way they are used in memory, thus eliminating the need for conversion between storage formats.

We will use integer surrogate keys. How do we assign the keys during record creation? The Visual FoxPro database container provides field properties that we can use. One of those properties is the Default Value. This default value is used to populate a field when a new record is appended and no value is specified for the field. For our surrogate key field we can specify the default value as a user-defined function call, which will return the next primary key value.

You can handle the problem of generating unique values for the surrogate key by using a table that holds the next key value to be used for each table in your database. The structure for this table is described in **Table 1**.

 Table 1. The structure for the primary key table named NextKey.dbf.

Field Name	Data Type	Size	Comment
IIdKey	Integer	4	The primary key for this table
CTableName	Character	128	The table's name, stored in uppercase
INextKey	Integer	4	The next value for the primary key for this table

The next issue is the code that will return the primary keys for you. The following program listing below shows one approach.

Listing 1. An example of a GetKey program.

```
* GetKey.prg
LPARAMETERS pcTableName
* pcTableName is the name of the table that we want a PK for
* Check for a character parameter
IF TYPE("pcTableName") <> "C"
  * Invalid parameter
  RETURN 0
ENDIF
pcTableName = UPPER(pcTableName)
* Save the environment
LOCAL lcAlias, liReturn
lcAlias = ALIAS()
IF NOT USED("NextKey")
  SELECT 0
  USE NextKey
ELSE
  SELECT NextKey
```

```
ENDIF
LOCATE FOR cTableName = pcTableName
IF NOT FOUND()
 * No record for this table
 APPEND BLANK
 REPLACE iNextKey WITH 1, ;
 cTableName WITH pcTableName
 liReturn = 0
ENDIF
* Lock the record
DO WHILE NOT RLOCK()
 * Short delay
 INKEY(.02,"H")
ENDDO
* Get the PK
liReturn = iNextKey
* Update the iNextKey field
REPLACE iNextKey WITH iNextKey + 1
UNLOCK
IF NOT EMPTY( lcAlias )
 SELECT ( lcAlias )
ELSE
 SELECT 0
ENDIF
RETURN liReturn
```

The previous program will get the next key for a particular table. You'll notice that the locking method in this code isn't very robust. You can get away with this approach because this table's record will only be locked for a very short period of time by any station.

In a later chapter we will examine the stored procedures for a database. You might choose to place this code in the database's stored procedures. The only problem with doing so is that the stored procedures are only visible to the tables that are part of the database. This means that you'd need to duplicate this code in every database you created. If you make this code a program file of its own, then all tables in all databases could use the same code. We will create this program as a .prg file and not store it in the database's stored procedures.

How do you reference this program from the default value property of the surrogate key? For each table's surrogate key field, you'll put GetKey("TableName") in the default value property. Now, whenever you issue an APPEND BLANK for a table, you'll get the next primary key automatically assigned to the record.

Visual FoxPro indexes

In the first part of this chapter we discussed the relational keys that you'll be using in your databases. Visual FoxPro has the ability to provide indexes that can assist in managing those keys, as well as provide other benefits to your applications. This section of the chapter will present the various types of indexes that are available in Visual FoxPro and some of the pros and cons about using them.

Indexes in Visual FoxPro are files that are independent of the actual data files that provide for a sorting of the records in the data file. Compound index files (CDX) are capable of storing more than one ordering of the data in a single index file. Each ordering is called a *tag* and each tag has an *index expression*. The index expression defines the ordering of the records.

Index expressions can be a single field reference or complex expressions comprised of the concatenation of multiple fields. The expression may even contain references to variables that aren't part of the table structure.

Index types defined

Visual FoxPro has four available index types: Regular, Unique, Primary and Candidate. Definitions of each index type follow.

Regular indexes

Regular indexes are the simplest type available. There is no uniqueness enforcement, allowing multiple entries in the index for the same index expression value. These are the most common indexes used.

Unique indexes

Unique indexes are similar to regular indexes, in that they don't enforce uniqueness on the expression. However, they do store only one reference in the index for each unique value of the expression. These indexes are the cause of many misunderstandings on the part of developers. You can depend on a unique index accuracy only immediately after it is created.

Let's look at an example to understand the problems. You have a customer table that stores the state in which the customer is located. You'd like to know in which states you have customers. Because you don't want to see the same state listed for every customer you have in that state, use a unique index on state to provide this listing. Create the index as shown in the following code:

```
INDEX ON State TAG CustState UNIQUE
```

Using the UNIQUE keyword in the INDEX command creates the unique index for you.

Now imagine that you have 25,000 customers in the state of New York. Your unique index shows you that you have customers in New York. However, the unique index is referring to only one of the 25,000 customers in New York because there is only one entry in the index for New York. If you now edit that one customer and change its state to New Jersey, the reference to that customer record for New York will be removed from the unique index (and a reference may be added for New Jersey if you had no other New Jersey customer already there). The problem is that Visual FoxPro will update the unique index only in reference to the one record that was edited. Visual FoxPro does not check all the other records to see if there is any other record for New York. This means that there is no reference to New York in your index. This is in spite of the fact that you have 24,999 more customers in New York. The index will remain this way until you either re-create it or edit one of those New York customer records.

Consider another situation. The unique index creates an index entry for the *first* occurrence of a key value. If you have a unique index on your state field, and the record for the first customer in the table whose state field is "NY" is deleted, this entry still appears in the index. If SET DELETED is ON, you can't "see" this record, and it will appear as though you have no customers in New York.

You can see that the unique index isn't being maintained the way you might expect it to be, but there is also no bug in the way it is being maintained. Our conclusion is that if you need a unique index, create it when you're going to use it and delete it when you're through with it. This is the only way you can be assured that the index accurately reflects the data in the table. Also make sure that you include a FOR NOT DELETED() statement in the INDEX command when you create a temporary unique index to insure that SET DELETED does not interfere with the accuracy of your results.

Candidate and primary indexes

Candidate and primary indexes have one thing in common: They restrict the values of their expressions to being unique within the table's data. If you attempt to add a record to a table that duplicates the value of a candidate or primary index expression, Visual FoxPro will generate an error indicating that the uniqueness of the index was violated.

You can use these two index types to prevent duplicate values from getting into a table and enforcing the integrity of the primary or candidate keys for that table. The difference between primary and candidate indexes is that there can be only one primary index on a table but any number of candidate indexes. Primary indexes can exist only for tables that are part of a database, while candidate indexes can be created on free tables.

Using a primary or candidate index is an absolute enforcement of uniqueness on the index expression. There is no way to get around it. This is because the design goal of these two index types is to provide the constraints for candidate and primary keys—and those constraints require absolute uniqueness.

This uniqueness includes the consideration of deleted records, because in the field of relational theory, there is no concept of a deleted record. Either the record is in the table or it isn't. Visual FoxPro uses the concept of a record being in the table but marked as deleted. This can cause a problem if you aren't aware of it and don't plan ahead for it.

For example, consider the customer table we mentioned earlier. It had a customer number field that was alphanumeric and was a candidate key for the table. If you create a candidate index on that field, it will enforce uniqueness. However, what happens if you delete a customer record and then try to add a new one that uses the same customer number as the deleted record? The candidate index won't allow the new record into the table because the deleted record causes a violation of the uniqueness of the candidate key.

How can you get around this so that deleted records are not considered by the candidate index? You can put a filter on the candidate index on the DELETED() function. This will eliminate the deleted records from the candidate index; thus, those deleted records won't be considered in the uniqueness of the index's expression. Likewise, if it's necessary to create a temporary unique index, and if the table is likely to have deleted records, then including FOR NOT DELETED() in the index expression will address the issue of a unique-indexed deleted record.

Filtering indexes

As stated in the previous paragraph, filtered indexes can be of value. Filtered indexes use the FOR option of the INDEX command (in the visual designers, you can use the Filter column of the designer to specify a FOR clause).

Filtering an index can be helpful in providing a rapid method of seeing only a subset of the records in a table. These indexes also can help with the candidate and primary index and deleted record problem described earlier. However, adding a filter to an index will remove the ability of Rushmore to use that index for optimization. You would need to maintain a duplicate to the filtered index, without the filter, to allow Rushmore to optimize expressions matching the filtered index's expression.

In the earlier example of the candidate index on CustomerNumber, you would add the FOR condition of NOT DELETED() to the candidate index and create an additional regular index on CustomerNumber with no filter to be used by Rushmore.

The roles that indexes play

Now that you understand various types of indexes, you need to figure out what these indexes can do for you, and how to use them to your best advantage. An index can fill some very specific roles in your system design—including ordering the data records, managing relations between tables, optimizing performance of various data-access processes, and filtering the records you see in a table. Let's look at these roles individually.

Ordering the records in a table

The most common reason to create an index is to provide an order to the records in a table that is based on some expression. Indexes allow you to have more than one record order without needing to physically sort the table for each order.

The obvious use for ordering records is to use one or more fields in the table to provide a sequence for the records, and then simply create an index on that field or the concatenation of more than one field. What happens if you have a character field and a numeric field and you want an order on the combination of those two? Visual FoxPro has a number of data type conversion functions that you can use to accomplish this. Remember that the key for any index is an expression, and an expression can use Visual FoxPro functions and even User Defined Functions (UDF).

For example, assume you have a table of customers that lists the city and the credit limit for each customer. You want a listing of customers alphabetically by city and numerically by credit limit within the cities. You could index this table like so:

```
INDEX ON City + STR(CreditLimit) TAG CityCred
```

What if you wanted the CreditLimit in descending order within city so that the customer with the highest credit limit was first in any given city? Try this:

```
INDEX ON City + STR(999999999999-CreditLimit) TAG CityCred
```

Okay, you're saying, so this stuff works with numbers and characters, but what about characters and dates? Assume that your customer table has a field named CustomerSince, which holds the date that any given customer first did business with you. You want the city order and the CustomerSince within the city, and the dates in descending order. Here's the code:

```
INDEX ON City + STR({12/31/9999} - CustomerSince) TAG CitySinc
```

For simple date concatenations, you can use the DTOS() function to convert the date to a character string that preserves the chronological ordering for the date.

How about using UDF in an index expression? Yes, this can be done. You simply use the UDF as you would anywhere else. However, we recommend against it for the following reasons:

- It will slow down performance of your application, because Visual FoxPro has to evaluate the UDF call every time anything happens.

- It will render your table unusable whenever the UDF isn't available to the index. This means that the table cannot be opened if Visual FoxPro can't "see" the UDF. Trying to open the table will result in an error.

In rare situations where the use of a UDF in an index expression might be unavoidable, do what needs to be done. Just make sure it isn't an easy decision to use a UDF in an index expression.

Index expressions can refer to fields in tables other than the one for which the index is being made.

For example, you might want to see invoices in order by customer name and invoice date within the customer names. The Name field is in the Customer table and the Invoice Date field is in the Invoice table, meaning you'd need to create the index like so:

```
USE Invoice
USE Customer ORDER CustID IN 0
SET RELATION TO CustID INTO Customer
INDEX ON Customer.Name + STR({12/31/9999}-Invoice.InvDate) TAG CustDate
```

Again, although this type of index can be built, it's a very bad idea. One reason is that the invoice table can no longer be open unless the customer table is already open and the order is set correctly in the customer table. Also, whenever the invoice table may be edited, it's required that the relation be set into the customer table. Otherwise, this index will become inaccurate, referring to the wrong customer name. If a customer record is edited, whether or not the invoice table is open, this index won't be updated to reflect any change in a customer's name. When you need to see data with this type of ordering, use a view or an SQL SELECT command to get the data and order it (see chapter 3).

Notice in the previous code that the alias names are used in the index expression. This is necessary because of the two-table issue. Using an alias within an index expression can cause problems; for example:

```
USE Invoice
INDEX ON Invoice.InvNo TAG InvNo
USE

USE Invoice ALIAS MyInvoices && errors will follow
```

Errors will occur here because Visual FoxPro stored the exact expression that you typed in the index header. This means the index expression in the index file's header is "Invoice.InvNo". On the fourth line, you open the invoice table and assign it an alias of MyInvoices. What happened when Visual FoxPro tried to update the index tag? An *alias not found* error! Why? Because Visual FoxPro is looking for the alias *Invoice* and it doesn't exist. Avoid the use of aliases in index expressions. Remember that alias names are volatile and exist only at run time. It might help if you keep this in mind: Tables don't have alias names; work areas do. A work area doesn't always have an alias name that is identical to the name of the table that is open in it.

Data filtering

Using the FOR clause of the INDEX ON command allows you to filter the records included in an index. When you set the order for the table to a filtered index, you see only the records that are included in the index. This means that in certain situations an index can provide very fast filtering of a table.

For example, imagine a table of customers that includes the CreditLimit field described earlier. In this application it's necessary to see these customers in three groups: those with a credit limit between $0 and $1,000; those with a credit limit between $1,001 and $100,000; and those with a credit limit over $100,000. You could open the customer table and then set a filter on it, but this would be relatively slow even if the filter was optimized. The following code shows how you could create three indexes to handle this:

```
USE Customer
INDEX ON Name FOR CreditLimit <= 1000 TAG CustLow
INDEX ON Name FOR CreditLimit > 1000 AND CreditLimit <=100000 TAG CustMed
INDEX ON Name FOR CreditLimit > 100000 TAG CustHigh
```

Now, if you want to see the low-limit customers, simply SET ORDER TO CustLow on the Customer table; to see the high-limit customers, you'd SET ORDER TO CustHigh. The filtering with these indexes is nearly instantaneous and the navigation between records would be virtually no slower than without the filter.

You also can use this filtering index technique for dynamic filters. Under certain circumstances it may be faster to build a temporary index than to deal with the performance hit caused by a SET FILTER.

Optimizing performance

Visual FoxPro's optimization technology is named "Rushmore." This technology uses indexes to increase the speed of resolving filters and queries. Rushmore can optimize the expressions associated with the FOR clause and the WHERE clause.

Rushmore does its optimization by using existing (and open) indexes to resolve the conditions in a FOR clause or a WHERE clause, rather than looking at the data in the DBF file itself. Because indexes are smaller than the DBF, more of the index can be held in memory, which speeds up processing. Furthermore, indexes are binary tree structures, so searching for a specific value in an index is much faster than reading each record from a table and checking it for the expression.

An optimizable expression uses one of these four formats:

```
<Index Key Expression> <Comparison Operator> <Exp>
<Exp> <Comparison Operator> <Index Key Expression>
BETWEEN(<Index Key Expression>, <Exp1>, <Exp2>)
INLIST(<Index Key Expression>, <Exp1>, <Exp2>, ...)
```

Here, the <Index Key Expression> must be an exact match with the key expression for an open index. <Exp> and <Exp#> are any expression. The optimizable Comparison operators are <, >, <=, >=, <>, !=, #, =, and ==.

This code shows some examples of optimizable and non-optimizable expressions:

```
USE Customer
INDEX ON UPPER(LastName) + UPPER(FirstName) TAG Name

* Not optimizable because the index expression is not exactly matched
LOCATE FOR LastName + FirstName = "SMITH"

* Optimizable
LOCATE FOR UPPER(LastName) + UPPER(FirstName) = "SMITH"

* Not optimizable
LOCATE FOR UPPER(LastName) = "SMITH"
```

Rushmore will *not* use an index that has a FOR condition (Ex. INDEX ON Name FOR Balance > 1000 TAG BigName will not be used). Also, Rushmore doesn't use indexes created with the UNIQUE option (Ex. INDEX ON State TAG States UNIQUE will not be used). An index with a NOT in its expression will not be used by Rushmore (Ex. INDEX ON NOT Active TAG Inactive will not be used).

Because of Rushmore's inability to use filtered indexes, it's advisable to create an unfiltered version of any filtered index you may have. Due to the use of indexes for optimization, it's advisable to identify the fields that are very likely to be used in selecting records and create indexes on those fields even though you may not use those indexes for ordering records.

It's important to carefully phrase your FOR and WHERE clauses to take advantage of Rushmore so you can get the highest possible performance from your applications.

The DELETED() index

One of the most commonly overlooked selection criterion that is a candidate for having an index is the deleted status of a record. We tend to forget that the command SET DELETED ON is really equivalent to SET FILTER TO DELETED() = .F. When SET DELETED is ON, it's irrelevant whether or not there are any deleted records; the filter must be checked by Visual FoxPro.

Because the DELETED ON setting causes the deleted status of records to be checked, having an index on DELETED() will make this test optimizable. We advise that every table have an index on the expression DELETED() in order to fully optimize your queries.

Managing relations

Indexes are required for relations between tables. The syntax of the SET RELATION command demands that the target of the relation be indexed on the expression of the relation. This code shows the syntax of the SET RELATION command:

```
SET RELATION TO <Expression> INTO <Alias>
```

Notice that in the syntax of this command there is no statement of what should be matched in the target alias. The target alias must have an index order set that has a key expression matching the expression of the relation. In fact, the SET RELATION command sets up an automatic SEEK to be executed in the target whenever the record pointer is moved in the source alias. The only time an index order is not required in the target is when the expression is numeric. When the expression is numeric and no index order is set in the target, the record number will be used to resolve the relationship.

We have visual mechanisms for setting up relationships, but they're just faces put on top of the SET RELATION command.

Persistent relations

In a database, you're able to establish relations between tables. These relations are called *persistent relations* because they persist beyond a given work session. Their general purposes are to set the default for your visual data environment setups and to be used by your referential integrity enforcement code.

Persistent relations are established by dragging a primary or candidate index of one table to an index of another table. These relations are based on an index's relation to another index. If the target index is regular, the relation will be one-to-many; if the target index is primary or candidate, the relation will be one-to-one.

You can create a persistent relation that has the same table as source and target; this is called a *self-relation*. When would you ever want to do this? One example would be an employee table where one of the fields was Manager and it contained the EmployeeID of the person's boss. In this case you might want a persistent relation from the Manager index to the EmployeeID index on the Employee table.

Because persistent relations are based entirely on indexes, the existence of the proper indexes to build these relations is critical.

Temporal relations

You create *temporal relations* in your form and report data environments, as well as in your program code. These relations are called *volatile* because any trace of their existence disappears when the work session ends. There is no persistence to these relations.

Temporal relations are created based on an expression in the source table being related to an index in the target table. Visually (in a form or report data environment) you can base these relations only on single fields, but by using the SET RELATION command you can use complex expressions for them.

There is no requirement that the temporal relations must match any persistent relations in the database. The persistent relations will be set up as defaults when tables are dragged and dropped to a data environment, but you can delete those relations from the data environment and set other relations.

Indexing views

Yes, you can create indexes on views. You can't store them in any permanent form, so you have to create them every time you open the view. Indexing views can be very beneficial in providing varied sort orders for the data in the view, and in speeding the location of specific records by allowing you to use SEEK.

To create an index on a view, you simply need to select the view and issue an INDEX ON command. If these indexes are created as a structural CDX file, Visual FoxPro will erase them when the view is closed. If they're created in separate IDX files, then you must erase them yourself.

The only caveat to indexing views is that table buffering will preclude the creation of an index. This is easily handled, though, as follows:

```
LOCAL lnBuffering
lnBuffering = CursorGetProp( "BUFFERING", "TheView" )
CursorSetProp( "BUFFERING", 5, "TheView" )
INDEX ON Name TAG Name
CursorSetProp( "BUFFERING", lnBuffering, "TheView" )
```

You can even improve the speed of indexing views by taking advantage of the NODATA option. If you USE a view with the NODATA option, then there will be no records in the view while you create the indexes. In a visual data environment, you can set the NoDataOnLoad property for the cursor to .T. and get the same effect. Look for more information on using indexes with views in Chapter 5.

Chapter 5
Data - Views

Views, a new feature introduced with Visual FoxPro 3.0, provide a way to take a new approach to many aspects of our applications. At the simplest, views represent a way of storing queries within the Visual FoxPro database container. They can, if desired, be used exclusively to provide the interface between forms, code and the data tables.

The term "view" is used interchangeably to identify two different but related things. The first is the entity that is stored in the Visual FoxPro database—that is, the SQL-Select statement and related properties that define the view— and the second is the temporary cursor that is created when the view is opened. There is virtually no difference between opening a view with USE <ViewName> and executing a query using the INTO CURSOR <cursorName> clause. The difference lies in the behavior of a cursor created using a simple SELECT…INTO statement when compared with one created by opening a view.

Views vs. queries
The following features compare and contrast views and queries:

* A view is opened just as a table is—by issuing the USE <ViewName> command; a query is executed by issuing the SELECT…FROM…INTO command in code, or by executing a query stored as a .QPR file. Opening a view requires that the database containing the view definition is open and is currently selected (which can be accomplished with the SET DATABASE TO command).
* Views do not support the TO, INTO ARRAY and INTO TABLE options of a SELECT-SQL statement. While the output from queries can be directed to a table or array, or to a text file, a printer or the screen, views direct their output only to cursors, and the cursor alias is the same as the name used to identify the view.
* Views can be constructed with runtime parameter variables. These parameter variables can be pre-populated, or they'll generate a runtime prompt for a value if the view is opened without establishing a value for the parameter prior to opening the view.
* Cursors resulting from opening views can be modified. A cursor resulting from an SQL-SELECT is opened as a read-only file.
* View fields share all of the properties belonging to table fields, including Caption, Comment, DefaultValue, DisplayClass, DisplayClassLibrary, Format, InputMask, RuleExpression, and RuleText.
* Views share some properties with tables, such as RuleExpression and RuleText.
* Changes made to a view-based cursor can (conditionally) be written back to the tables on which the view is based.

The last four items in the above list—the "writability" of views, the table-like properties for views and view fields, and the fact that changes made to views can affect the underlying tables—represent the real significance of views for application development.

A read-only view—that is, a view that is intended only to display, not update, our table data—is not much different from a query. A query can incorporate memory variables in its WHERE clause that can be assigned values programmatically, join tables, create "virtual" or "calculated" columns, and so on. The fact that it is more convenient to store views in the database instead of queries in code or .QPR files has caused queries to be used somewhat less often than was the case with versions of FoxPro prior to version 3. However, this doesn't differentiate the *function* of these views within an application—merely the way in which they are *packaged*.

The remainder of this chapter will focus on the utility of views for manipulating the data in our applications.

How views work in an application

The short answer to the question "How do we use views in our applications?" is "Just like we use tables." In every case, any technique, feature or syntax used with a table can also be used, 100 percent unchanged, with a view. Well, almost.

- If you want a form control to update a field in a table, you specify Alias.FieldName as the control's ControlSource property. If you're working with a view, you use (again) Alias.FieldName.
- If you want to programmatically change a field in a table, you use REPLACE <Alias.FieldName> WITH <value>. For a view, you still use REPLACE <Alias.FieldName> WITH <value>—no difference. In fact, most commands in the Xbase language, such as SCAN...ENDSCAN, SET FILTER, SCATTER/GATHER, COPY TO, and so on, work on views just as they do on tables.
- If you want to move to the next record, you use the SKIP command; to skip to the first record, use the LOCATE command; to skip to the last record, use the GOTO BOTTOM command. Same for views. If you want to change the order of the items in a table, you SET ORDER TO <index tag>. To change the order of items in a view, you SET ORDER TO <index tag>.
- When you're through editing records in a buffered table and want to commit the changes to the tables, you use the TableUpdate() function. When working with views, you use the TableUpdate() function.

With the last two items in the list above, we begin to get into a couple of areas in which working with views is a little different than working with tables, and you've probably noticed that we haven't made any reference to relations or parent/child tables.

We'll get to these aspects of working with views a little later. For now, the important thing to be aware of is that working with views differs *very little* from working directly against tables.

That little something extra

Note that, in the list presented above comparing views and queries, a view's fields share all the properties of table fields. This allows the view fields to operate interchangeably with table fields within an application. As mentioned in the previous section, all commands and functions or techniques that we might use with table fields will work just as well with view fields.

However, view fields have a whole stack of new properties that are not shared by table fields; and a bunch of properties are unique to views and not shared by tables. Most of these relate to the fact that we can update the tables on which the view is based. Some of these properties are useful only when the view is a *remote view*, that is, a view that draws records not directly from Visual FoxPro tables, but from an ODBC data source, usually an SQL database. SQL databases can include SQL Server or Oracle or an Access .MDB file or even VFP tables if you access them using ODBC. The other properties are of interest in all updateable views.

The first of these properties we need to be aware of is the SendUpdates property of the view. If .T., this indicates that changes made to the view can be sent back to the underlying table. In order for this to happen, VFP requires a critical piece of information: It must have some way of matching up a particular record in our view with the corresponding record in the underlying table. It does so by matching up (at minimum) the *key fields* that, individually or collectively, uniquely identify each record. In a properly designed database, each record in every table has a primary key value. This key can be determined by the value of a single field, or can be a "composite key" that is made up of the values of more than one field (see the previous chapter on indexes and keys). From this, it follows that we must use the KeyField property of the view fields to indicate those fields that represent the primary key value of the underlying table.

The next piece of information needed to make an updateable view "work" is which fields we want to be updated when we commit changes made to the view. This can include any number of the fields in the view, although if the view includes "calculated" or "virtual" fields, these exist only in the view, and cannot be marked as "updateable."

In the View Designer, these two properties are set by using the "Key" and "Updateable" columns, and the "Send SQL updates" on the "Update criteria" page.

Finally, we must specify exactly how modifications to the view are sent to the underlying tables. This involves two different properties: the WhereType property and the UpdateType property. You will notice option buttons to select these options are also on the "Update criteria" page of the view designer. In the view designer, these properties are set by setting the options for "SQL WHERE clause includes" and "Update Using."

The WhereType property specifies how a record in our view is "matched" with a record in the underlying table. For local views, we have three choices: use the key field(s) only, the key field(s) along with any modified fields, or the key field(s) and any updateable fields. There is a fourth choice for remote views that uses the key field(s) and the timestamp placed on the table by the database server.

From a practical standpoint, the WhereType is actually specifying the answer to the question, "How are we to detect an update conflict?" If the WhereType is set to "1–Key Fields Only," the update will be made if there is a record in the underlying table that has the same key value, *without regard to the fact that another user may have made changes to the record since the record was retrieved.* At the other extreme, if we specify a value of "2–Key and updatable" for the WhereType property, an update conflict will be reported (and the update will fail) if any updateable field in the underlying table has changed between the time the view is opened and the time the user tries to commit his changes. In other words, Visual FoxPro looks for a matching record in the underlying table based on the key field(s) and all of the updatable fields. If one of these fields has changed, Visual FoxPro will *not* be able to find the matching record, and the update will fail. This most closely emulates the behavior of Visual FoxPro tables when working directly against the tables—if two users update the same record, the last one to attempt to save her changes gets an update conflict error.

An intermediate choice (and one of the coolest things about using views) is that if we specify a WhereType of "3–Key and Modified Fields," then Visual FoxPro examines only the fields that the user has changed, along with the key field, to find a matching record in the underlying tables. This means that if Bullwinkle modifies only field "A", and Rocky modifies only field "B" on the same record, and they both commit their changes, no update conflict occurs—both edits are saved without error.

Buffering and views

There are only two buffering options for views: optimistic row buffering (the default) and optimistic table buffering. There is no option for pessimistic buffering (views can't place a lock on the underlying tables while open) and there is no way to disable buffering for views. Since some type of data buffering is the norm for production applications, and since optimistic buffering is preferred in the majority of situations, this does not usually present a significant limitation. If a particular application requires pessimistic buffering, then views may not be appropriate.

While views do not natively provide the ability to pessimistically lock a record, this does not mean that a situation in which an application requires pessimistic locking (the record is locked when it is opened for editing) cannot consider using views. Views can still be employed in this situation, but some other mechanism must be employed to determine whether a particular record can be edited, or if it is already in use by another user. This can be accomplished by using a "semaphore" locking scheme, in which a shared table is used to keep track of tables and records open for editing. This table can additionally store information concerning the user, and the date and time the record was locked. One of the slickest ways of implementing such a semaphore-locking scheme I've heard of is to actually get a lock on the semaphore table record. If another user needs to access the record and cannot lock the corresponding semaphore record, then the user is either locked out, or the record is opened "read only". The advantage of this approach is that if a user who has a lock on the record experiences a crash or a power failure, the server automatically removes the lock, making the record available to other users on the system without the need for an administrative utility to "unlock" the record.

When a query is executed in Visual FoxPro, all tables named in the query's FROM clause are automatically opened. This is also true when using local views. These tables are not buffered, so when a TableUpdate() is issued on a local view, the modifications are written immediately to the underlying table. While it is possible to explicitly open each of the underlying tables, either in code using the USE command or by placing them in a form's DataEnvironment and employing some kind of buffering scheme on them, there is no benefit in doing so. Indeed, this requires that a TableUpdate() be issued first on each view, and then a second time on each of the underlying tables in order to commit the changes the user has made to the view. As in running a query, the underlying tables remain open. Closing the cursor holding the result set does not close the underlying tables. Thus there is no difference (with one exception) between allowing a view to open its underlying tables automatically or by placing those tables in the DataEnvironment—tables added to the DataEnvironment use the form's buffering setting (none by default). The exception is when you're using the Default Data Session. The view will be closed when the DataEnvironment is destroyed (if AutoCloseTables is .T.), but the underlying tables are left open. If you add the tables to the DataEnvironment, *before adding the views,* they will be closed when the form is closed. Adding the tables *first* to get this behavior is important. The tables and views are opened in the order in which their associated cursor objects are added to the DataEnvironment. If you add the views first, the tables will be opened automatically, and will be left open when the form is destroyed. If the tables are opened before the views, then the DataEnvironment takes responsibility for closing them when the DataEnvironment is destroyed.

For more information on buffering, see Chapter 7.

Indexing views

Indexing is not a core technique to using views, but it can lend so much to your applications that it deserves some discussion.

Yes, you can index a view. After the view is opened, you simply execute INDEX ON <view_name> TAG <tag_name> and you're all set. You can do this in the Init() method of the form, or in any other method. However, I've found that the best place to perform this task is in the Init() of the DataEnvironment. This event occurs before any other control is initialized, so the views are indexed and ready for use by any control. If you're opening the views with the NoDataOnLoad property set to .T., then the views contain no records when the DataEnvironment.Init() fires, so the indexes are created almost instantaneously and are then automatically updated when you execute a REQUERY() on the view. Remember that the result set for a view is stored in a cursor. When a cursor is closed, the disk-based table associated with it is deleted from your disk, and likewise any .CDX files containing indexes.

Why would you want to index a view? Here are some reasons:

- To set a relation between two views at runtime. This isn't something that you need every day, but put this idea in your bag of tricks—it might come in handy.
- To allow the user to change the order of multiple records in a grid or list box.
- To enable incremental searching in a grid, or on a column other than the first column in a list box.

For whatever reason you decide to index a view, you need to be aware of some traps for the unwary involving indexing a view:

- You cannot index a table-buffered view. You must first set the buffering to row buffering, create the index, then set the buffering to table buffering. No big deal, but you just need to be aware of the limitation.

```
* DataEnvironment.Init()
CURSORSETPROP('buffering',3,<view_alias>) && row buffered
SELECT <view_Alias>
INDEX ON <expression> TAG <tag name>
* back to table buffered
CURSORSETPROP('buffering',5,<view_Alias>)
```

- You cannot create more than one index tag on a read-only view (the ReadOnly property is .T.). The .CDX file gets flagged as ReadOnly also, and creating a second index tag attempts to write to the .CDX file.
- REQUERY() or SELECT stores the number of records in the result set to the _TALLY system memory variable. If TALK is set OFF, INDEX and REINDEX do not update _TALLY, and it is reset to 0. If you're running with TALK set OFF (the usual situation) and index a view after opening it, _TALLY will contain 0, without regard to how many records were in the result set. If you REQUERY() an indexed view, _TALLY will be also be reset to 0 because the table is REINDEX()ed after the SELECT is re-executed, resetting _TALLY to 0. In these situations you'll need to use RECCOUNT() or some other technique to determine how many records are in the result set.

Parameterized views

Let's assume we create a view on our 25,000-record customer table, named "v_customer", that uses the following query expression:

```
SELECT * FROM customer
```

All of the fields are updateable, and the primary key field is flagged as the key field.

Opening this query by issuing the **USE v_customer** command, or by placing this view into the DataEnvironment of a form and running the form, will retrieve all 25,000 client records. We can then locate the customer record we want to work with, make changes, and then issue a TableUpdate() command to commit the changes.

You're absolutely right if you're thinking that all of this doesn't sound very efficient. First, the query executes and grabs all 25,000 records. Then, we have an unindexed cursor in which we'll have to issue a non-optimized LOCATE command to find a particular customer record (SEEK() requires an index). This is not normally the way in which updateable views are employed in an application. Instead, the views are *parameterized*, that is, a filter condition is established in the view that determines which subset of records are retrieved, using a special memory variable that establishes the filter at runtime.

A view parameter is established by specifying a memory variable as the comparison value in a WHERE clause, and preceding the name of that memory variable with a question mark, as in the following example:

```
CREATE SQL VIEW v_customer AS ;
  SELECT * FROM customer WHERE cCust_ID = ?vp_cCust_ID
```

Many developers are familiar with specifying a memory variable in a WHERE clause. The difference between doing this and creating a parameterized view is that if the memory variable does not exist when the view is opened, an error will occur. On the other hand, in a parameterized view, if the memory variable does not exist, a dialog pops up, prompting you for the value of the variable. However, these types of views aren't usually used this way in a production application. The usual practice is to either open the view using the USE command, but with the NODATA clause, or more commonly, to place the view into the DataEnvironment of a form, and set the NoDataOnLoad property to .T.

Here are the effects of establishing a view parameter and opening the view in this way:

- No error is triggered because the memory variable specified in the WHERE clause doesn't exist.
- The dialog prompting the user for a parameter value is *not* triggered.
- The view is opened without any records, so it appears exactly like a newly defined table does before any records have been added.

After the view is opened using the NODATA keyword, a value can be assigned to the parameter variable and the REQUERY() function can be called. This will cause the SELECT command to be re-executed, retrieving all records that match the condition specified by the WHERE clause and the value of the parameter.

For example, look at the v_Employees view established in the Time and Billing sample database. All fields are selected, and the WHERE clause (as shown on the FILTER page in the view designer) is:

```
WHERE Employees.cEmployeeNumber = ?vp_cEmployeeNumber
```

Make sure that you SET STATUS BAR ON, and from the command window, issue the following commands:

```
USE v_Employees NODATA
vp_cEmployeeNumber = "5"
? REQUERY()
```

Note that after issuing the USE command, the status bar briefly showed "Selected 0 records in .02 seconds", and then showed "v_employees Record: None", indicating that we have a data entity with the alias "v_employees" open in the current work area, and that it contains no records. After assigning the character value of 5 to the memory variable vp_cEmployeeNumber, and calling the REQUERY() function, the value of 1 was displayed on the Visual FoxPro desktop, and status bar briefly displayed "Selected 1 record in .03 seconds" (your machine may execute the query faster or slower than mine does), then displayed "v_employees Record: 1/1". If you browse the result set, you will see that we've selected the record for Laura Callahan.

In general, the parameter for an updateable view will specify a value for one of three things:

- A primary key value—often for retrieving a parent table record

- A candidate key value—a non-surrogate alternative to a surrogate primary key
- A foreign key value—often for retrieving child table records

In the case of the v_Employees view, the view parameter specifies a value for the cEmployeeNumber field, a candidate key. We could just as easily establish a view parameter on the primary key value, which is an integer value found in the iEmployeeID field. However, this database uses *surrogate* keys as primary and foreign keys. Surrogate key values are system-generated and contain no business data. Surrogate keys are established strictly for maintaining a link between tables, and are seldom, if ever, revealed to the user. As a result of this, and the fact that the Employees table has no parent table, it is unlikely that the user would know the integer primary key value, but it's very likely to know the employee's employee number. Hence the logical decision to select records based on the candidate key value.

There is a little gotcha lurking with regard to parameterized views. It is always necessary to REQUERY() a parameterized view after setting the value of the parameter. Because of this, be aware that you should not flag a parameterized view as ReadOnly, even if the SendUpdates property of the view is .F. or if you have no intention of modifying it. The reason is that re-querying a view attempts to write to the table associated with the cursor, and a "Cannot update the cursor" error will result.

> When working with parameterized views, it's sometimes helpful to re-member some "tricks" with regard to the WHERE clause.

1. BETWEEN(), which is Rushmore optimizable, can be used not just to select multiple records that fall within a range of values, but also to select records that match a single value. This is particularly useful when working with integer surrogate keys.

```
SELECT *;
    FROM <table> ;
    WHERE <primary key> BETWEEN ?vp_LowPK and ?vp_HIPk
```

   If you set liLowPK and lnHIPk to the same value you get one record. If you instead set it to:

```
liLowPK = -2147483647
lnHIPk  =  2147483646
```

   ... you'd get all the records

2. If exact is set OFF and you have a character key value or a filter condition applied to a character field, the empty string ("") will match all records.
3. If you prefer to not be dependent on the status of SET EXACT, or want to up-size to SQL Server (which behaves as if EXACT is set ON), you can use LIKE and "pad" a view parameter with "%" which is a wildcard character, analogous to the "*" used in file masks. For example:

```
SELECT * ;
    FROM <table> ;
    WHERE UPPER(cLastName) LIKE ?vp_cLastName
```

If "SM%" is stored to vp_cLastName, the view will retrieve records for last names Smith, Smythe, Small, Smeed, and so on.

So what's the point?

If you haven't previously worked with views (or thought about them very much), you might be wondering what advantages views provide.

One very important advantage doesn't really apply to *local* views, that is, views that execute queries against tables in a native Visual FoxPro database. However, this advantage is of critical importance when using a *remote* view, which executes a query against a database server, such as SQL Server, Sybase or Oracle. With remote views, instead of your workstation examining 100,000 records on the server to determine which ones meet the filter conditions (as specified in the WHERE clause), the request is processed at the server, and only those records that meet the filter criteria are returned to the workstation. The end result is that network traffic is greatly reduced, which is a major benefit of using client/server architecture. The "searching" is done by the server when opening a remote view, but performed by the client when working with a local view. Note that, when opening a local view, all of the underlying tables are also opened to allow the workstation to determine which records meet the selection criteria.

However, many developers have discovered that there are other wonderful advantages in using local views instead of working directly against the Visual FoxPro tables. I first began using views in Visual FoxPro 3.0, simply as an exercise to check out this new feature. This "exercise" quickly evolved into my preferred method of interacting with data, so that I now use views exclusively for all database interactions. We'll come back to these specific issues later in the chapter. But for now, let me simply say that I have discovered that views are a much simpler and cleaner way to interact with data. They require a little more up-front design and implementation work, but the additional effort is leveraged mightily throughout the development process.

Views in action

Enough talk. Let's look at a form that actually uses views exclusively to interact with the database. You can examine the demonstration code by opening the CHAP5 project (Chap5.pjx) from the download files.

The form that illustrates use of views in data entry and maintenance is TIMECARD.SCX. Before proceeding further, let me stress that the sample form is "demoware." It isn't completely bullet-proof, and is not intended to be so. For instance, it's possible to add a new time card without associating it with any employee. With books, as with software, shipping is a feature, OK? Also, if you've been examining the tables and views up to this point and run with EXCLUSIVE set ON during development (as I think most of us do), remember to CLOSE TABLES ALL before trying to run the form, or you'll get "Error loading file—record number 7. cDmForm <or one of its members>. Loading form or the data environment: Error loading the data environment: Table is in use." Boy, do I *hate* that error—I must see it 20 times a day!

The form allows you to examine any time card for any employee, or create a new time card. The time card contains a reference to the employee and the date the time card was recorded, and is implemented as a single record in the table Time_Cards. The form also displays the child records stored in the Time_Card_Hours table, which represents the detail of the time card. This detail includes the date worked, start and ending times, the project worked on, and the nature of the work performed, stored both as a code in an integer field and as free-form text in a memo field.

An existing time card is selected by first selecting an employee via a drop-down list, which in turn populates another drop-down list with a list of time cards on file for that employee, listed by date. Selecting one date causes a set of detail records to be displayed in a grid. The grid displays the project and work code for each detail record using a drop-down list. For cosmetic reasons, the memo field for each record is not displayed in the grid, but in an edit box immediately below the grid. The form has Add, Save, Cancel, Delete and Close command buttons.

Field rules prevent empty values for the line item start and end times, and a table rule prevents entering an end time before a start time. Violation of these rules will prevent saving a record, and the form gives appropriate error messages.

Adding a record allows selection of an employee using a drop-down list, entry of a date for the time card, and entry of line-item details. Line-item details are not required to save a record. AllowAddNew is set to .T. on the grid, allowing the user to add new records simply by pressing the down arrow while in the grid. Extraneous detail records (determined by seeing a newly appended record without a value for the date worked) are automatically TableRevert()ed prior to saving the record.

Before getting into the specifics of the example form, we should take a quick look at the code in the foundation form class that is used to create the form. Note that these data manipulation methods, while in use in production applications, are expanded upon and made more flexible by the data handling objects and techniques discussed in Chapter 7.

cDMForm methods

The form for this chapter's example is based on a foundation form class, cDMForm, designed to be data-aware, and capable of manipulation of updateable cursors. Most (though not all) methods of this form class are not in any way specific to the use of views. However, making a design decision to use views exclusively has allowed some simplification of these methods. For instance, you won't see any code checking to see if buffering is in effect for any cursor, because optimistic buffering is *always* active for a view. Likewise, it isn't necessary to check to see if we're working with a view or a table when using a function like CURSORGETPROP('SendUpdates'), which applies only to views.

Init()

The Init() event method is set up to accept an argument containing a reference to an application object, and to pass this object reference to the basic form class from which cDMForm is subclassed. More important to this example is the call to the classes' BuildCursorArray() method.

BuildCursorArray()

In order to write reusable code to manipulate the cursors that may be opened by a form, it is necessary to maintain a list of the cursors with which we need to be concerned. This means that when checking for changes to data, saving changes to data, discarding changes to data, and so on, we need to concern ourselves with a subset of all tables and views that might be open while a form is running. The Chapter 5 demonstration form TIMECARD.SCX has 11 tables and views open while running. Only two of these are actually updateable views that the form is intended to manipulate.

Unlike many other container objects in Visual FoxPro, the DataEnvironment object does not have a collection property for its contained cursor objects. It's necessary to build and maintain our own collection of cursors. While we're at it, as suggested in the previous paragraph, we might as well create our collection with only those cursor objects that represent updateable views. This makes further checks for the updateability of a cursor in other methods unnecessary. BuildCursorArray() stores to a form array property, a reference to each Cursor object in the DataEnvironment that represents an updateable view.

When committing changes, the order in which the various cursors are updated is often very important. Consider the situation in which you are adding a new set of records that includes a parent record and a set of child records. If there is an insert trigger on the child table that prevents insertion of child records without a corresponding parent record, it will be necessary to commit the new parent record first, and then the child records. To enable this behavior, there must be some way, at design time, to specify this update order. The BuildCursorArray() method relies on a design decision to always have a numeric digit as the last one or two characters of the cursor object's name, and contains an ASSERT to enforce this. This allows the developer to specify, by way of the last characters of the cursor names, what order is to be used when updating the cursors. This makes it possible for BuildCursorArray() to sort the array of cursors in the order in which they are to be updated.

The view-specific part of this method is the check for whether the view is updateable, using the CURSORGETPROP('SendUpdates') function. There is also an interesting bit of code that stores a connection handle to the form if the view is a remote view. Limiting connections in a client/server application is highly desirable (it minimizes the chances of running out of resources on the server) so all remote views should be established using the SHARE clause. This, together with using an existing connection handle for any SQL pass-through commands, means that your entire application can run using only a single connection to the SQL server (see **Listing 5-1**).

Listing 5-1. The BuildCursorArray() method.

```
* BuildCursorArray() Method
LOCAL lnCursors, ;
   lcReference, ;
   loReference, ;
   lcAlias, ;
   x, ;
   lcCursorName

LOCAL ARRAY laCursors[1]
* Create an array of all objects in the
* form's DataEnvironment. Since we will eventually
```

```
* be winnowing this list down to only the cursors
* we might as well start out calling the array laCursors
* and the number thereof lnCursors
lnCursors = AMEMBERS(laCursors, THISFORM.DATAENVIRONMENT, 2)
IF lnCursors = 0
   THISFORM.nCursors = 0
   RETURN
ENDIF


* Swap the name stored in each element
* with the object that the name refers to
FOR x = 1 TO lnCursors
   IF VARTYPE(laCursors[x]) = "L"
      EXIT
   ENDIF
   lcReference = "THISFORM.DataEnvironment." + laCursors[x]
   loReference = EVALUATE(lcReference)
   * just in case someone sneaks in a relation on
   * us, we'll get rid of it
   IF LOWER(loReference.BASECLASS) = "relation"
      ADEL(laCursors,x)
      lnCursors = lnCursors - 1
      x = x - 1
      LOOP
   ENDIF
   laCursors[x] = loReference
ENDFOR


* Eliminate from the array any references to
* cursor objects that represent an updateable
FOR x = 1 TO lnCursors
   IF VARTYPE(laCursors[x]) = "L"
      EXIT
   ENDIF
   lcAlias = laCursors[x].ALIAS
   IF x = 1 AND THISFORM.nConnectHandle = 0
      * Nothing has established a connection handle
      IF CURSORGETPROP("Sourcetype",lcAlias) = 2
         * This is a remote view, so we'll grab the
         * connection handle for this view so it's
         * available for the use of any SQL pass-through
         * commands we may need to execute
         THISFORM.nConnectHandle = CURSORGETPROP("ConnectHandle",lcAlias)
      ENDIF
   ENDIF
   IF CURSORGETPROP("SendUpdates",lcAlias) = .F. OR laCursors[x].READONLY
      * This cursor represents a read-only entity,
      * so we'll get rid of it
      ADEL(laCursors,x)
      lnCursors = lnCursors - 1
      x = x - 1
      LOOP
   ENDIF
ENDFOR
* Transfer the array of cursors and the
* number thereof to the form
THISFORM.nCursors = lnCursors
DIMENSION THISFORM.aCursors(THISFORM.nCursors, 2)
FOR x = 1 TO THISFORM.nCursors
```

```
      THISFORM.aCursors[x,1] = laCursors[x]
ENDFOR

* Store the 'number' of the cursor object
* to the second column of the form array property
FOR x = 1 TO THISFORM.nCursors
   lcCursorName = THISFORM.aCursors[x,1].NAME
   ASSERT ISDIGIT(RIGHT(lcCursorName,1))
   * If this assert fails, the developer didn't
   * follow the  practice of ending each cursor
   * name with a 1 or 2-digit numeric value
   IF ISDIGIT(LEFT(RIGHT(lcCursorName,2),1))
      THISFORM.aCursors[x,2] = VAL(RIGHT(lcCursorName,2))
   ELSE
      THISFORM.aCursors[x,2] = VAL(RIGHT(lcCursorName,1))
   ENDIF
ENDFOR
* Now, sort the aCursors array according to
* the 'number' of the cursor
ASORT(THISFORM.aCursors, 2)
```

Our technical editor has pointed out that the BuildCursorArray() method in Listing 5-1 makes an assumption that we won't be mixing local and remote views, hence the check for a connection handle only when encountering the first view. You'll need to modify this bit of code if you have a database that does indeed mix the two view types, because the first view encountered may not be remote.

Changed()

An important service that the form needs to provide is the ability to detect if the data being displayed by the form has been changed. This is needed when the user is in mid-edit and tries to close the form, or if the application tries to close the form programmatically. We want to allow the user to save his changes before the form is closed, discard the changes, or cancel whatever operation is closing the form. This whole mechanism for the cDMForm class is handled by the QueryUnload(), Close() and OkToClose() methods. However, they all rely on the Changed() method to determine the situation with regard to the form.

This method works by detecting "dirty" buffers, or data buffers in which some value has been changed since the data was retrieved from the disk where it is stored. To do this, it relies on the GETFLDSTATE() function. GETFLDSTATE() does a good job of distinguishing between the following four conditions:

- A newly appended record, unchanged
- An existing record, unchanged
- A newly appended record, changed
- An existing record, changed

A shortcoming of GETFLDSTATE(), and therefore a shortcoming of this method, is that it cannot distinguish between a value that was changed by the user but was later changed back to its original value, nor can it distinguish between a modification that was initiated by the user and a modification that was triggered in a newly appended record by a default value or the execution of a rule.

You will note the comment in this code that all views should be table buffered, even if you have only one record. This is because of the fact (discovered and documented by our able technical editor) that certain operations, contrary to expectation, will attempt to move the record pointer. If the view is row buffered, this will cause an automatic TableUpdate(), which is to be avoided at all costs. The update can fail, especially since the user hasn't finished with his data entry. And without the code written in the Save() method (discussed below), the user could be faced with a cryptic Visual FoxPro-generated error dialog, rather than the user-friendly and informative message that the HandleError() method will present. However, the Changed() method is bracketed to handle either type of buffering, so it won't inadvertently trigger an update if the cursor, for some reason, isn't table buffered.

One significant advantage of using local views is that you have in your possession only a subset of records. This means that you can act (when appropriate) on all records, rather than trying to restrict any operation to a subset of the records of a table using SCAN FOR or filters or some other mechanism. This gives rise to a view-specific behavior of this method, which is that there is no limitation on the SCAN...ENDSCAN applied on table-buffered views. If this code were to be executed on a million-record, table-buffered table, this could have a noticeable impact on performance.

One might suggest, instead of relying on GETFLDSTATE() to detect changes, to use the GETNEXTMODIFIED() function instead. However, GETNEXTMODIFIED() considers a newly appended blank record to be a modified record, whether or not it contains any data, and it is still necessary to use GETFLDSTATE() to determine if the record can be discarded. Also, because of Visual FoxPro's near-light-speed handling of its native cursors, the SCAN...ENDSCAN executes in the blink of an eye, even with thousands of records to examine. Finally, the SCAN...ENDSCAN loop terminates immediately if it detects a changed record. See **Listing 5-2**.

Listing 5-2. The Changed() method.

```
* Changed() method
LOCAL lcStatus, ;
   lcAlias , ;
   lcOldAlias, ;
   lnCurrentRecord, ;
   llRetVal, ;
   x
lcOldAlias = ALIAS()
* Loop through our collection
* of updateable cursors
FOR x = 1 TO THISFORM.nCursors
   lcAlias = THISFORM.aCursors[x,1].ALIAS
   * Check to see if the cursor is table buffered
   * (they should all be table buffered)
   IF CURSORGETPROP('buffering',lcAlias) = 5
      * Store the current record
      * Change to the work area of the cursor
      SELECT (lcAlias)
      * The following line deals successfully with empty cursors
      lnCurrentRecord = ;
IIF(EOF(lcAlias),RECCOUNT(lcAlias),RECNO(lcAlias))
      * Check all records to see if they've changed
      SCAN
```

```
            lcStatus = GETFLDSTATE (-1,lcAlias)
            * Note - GETFLDSTATE() returns .NULL.
            * if at EOF()
            IF !ISNULL(lcStatus) ;
                  AND ("2" $ lcStatus ;
                  OR "4" $ lcStatus)
               llRetVal = .T.
               * If this record has changed
               * proceed no further
               EXIT
            ENDIF
         ENDSCAN
         * Don't position the record pointer
         * if we're dealing with an empty cursor
         IF lnCurrentRecord > 0
            GOTO lnCurrentRecord
         ENDIF
         IF llRetVal = .T.
            EXIT
         ENDIF
      ELSE
         * Yadda, yadda, yadda....
         lcStatus = GETFLDSTATE(-1,lcAlias)
         IF !ISNULL(lcStatus) ;
                  AND ("2" $ lcStatus ;
                  OR "4" $ lcStatus)
            llRetVal = .T.
            EXIT
         ENDIF
      ENDIF
ENDFOR
IF ! EMPTY(lcOldAlias)
   SELECT (lcOldAlias)
ENDIF
RETURN llRetVal
```

Cancel()

The Cancel() method (see **Listing 5-3**) allows you to execute the TABLEREVERT() function on all updateable cursors, and uses the cursors collection created by the BuildCursorArray() method. While it seems that many developers believe forms should always be in "edit mode," there are circumstances, and sometimes entire applications, that require the user to explicitly put the form into an "edit mode" before he can modify the data. Hence the inclusion of a reset of the form's lEditMode property in the Cancel() method. If interested, you can examine the lEditWatch property and the Refresh() method of the foundation control classes in the cContrls.VCX class library that is included in the CHAP5 project.

Listing 5-3. The Cancel() method.

```
* Cancel() method
LOCAL lcAlias , ;
   x
* Loop through the cursors collection
* and execute a TableRevert() on each
FOR x = 1 TO THISFORM.nCursors
   lcAlias = THISFORM.aCursors[x,1].ALIAS
```

```
    TABLEREVERT(.T.,lcAlias)
ENDFOR
THISFORM.lEditMode = .F.
THISFORM.REFRESH()
```

Delete()

The foundation classes used in this example are based on a production application currently in development. In the past, it has been my practice to leave this method empty in the foundation class, and write form-specific delete method code in the form instance. Thus far, in the application we're developing, the assumptions inherent in this foundation class code have stood up well. The assumptions are:

- If only one table is updateable, it will be the table indicated by the InitialSelectedAlias property of the DataEnvironment object. If there is more than one updateable cursor, there will be a familial (parent/child/grandchild/great-grandchild) relationship between the updateable cursors, and the parent table will be the one indicated by the InitialSelectedAlias property of the DataEnvironment object.
- Deletion of a parent record will never require interaction with child records at the level of the form; that is, any interaction with child records is handled by the database via delete triggers.
- The interface standard for deletion is to immediately commit the change and "clear" the display of the current record, hence the call to the form's Save() and ClearCursors() methods. A confirmation ("do you really want to delete…") dialog is an option that can be implemented in the form instance, and can execute the foundation class Delete() method conditionally.

The foregoing assumptions (note the ASSERT in **Listing 5-4** below) allow the Delete() method to concern itself only with the alias specified in the InitialSelectedAlias property. The ClearCursors() method is empty at the level of the foundation cDMForm class, and is discussed later in the context of the Time Card form.

Listing 5-4. The Delete() method.

```
* Delete() method
WITH THISFORM
   ASSERT ! EMPTY(.DATAENVIRONMENT.INITIALSELECTEDALIAS)
   SELECT (.DATAENVIRONMENT.INITIALSELECTEDALIAS)
   DELETE
   IF .SAVE()
     .ClearCursors()
     .REFRESH()
   ENDIF
ENDWITH
```

Save()

The Save() method does all the things that a good Save() method should:

- Provides a "hook" via a call to an empty method (BeforeSave()) that allows last-minute actions to be executed just before committing changes. Typical and form-specific actions that this method could perform are updating child records with foreign-key values, deleting extraneous records, modifying cursors based on calculated values, such as storing a total to a parent record based on a total of child record fields, and so on.
- Wraps all TableUpdate() commands in a transaction, ensuring all-or-nothing commitment of a multiple-table update.
- Calls the TableUpdate() function for each cursor in the cursors collection, in the order specified by the cursors collection.
- Executes an END TRANSACTION if all updates were successful.
- Executes a ROLLBACK if all updates were not successful, and stores all error information to a form array.
- Calls other form methods conditionally depending on success or failure of the updates: AfterSuccessfulSave() in the case of successful updates, and HandleError() and After-FailedSave() if the saves fail.

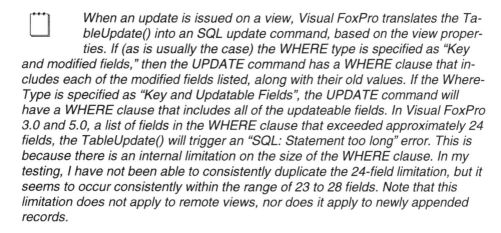

When an update is issued on a view, Visual FoxPro translates the TableUpdate() into an SQL update command, based on the view properties. If (as is usually the case) the WHERE type is specified as "Key and modified fields," then the UPDATE command has a WHERE clause that includes each of the modified fields listed, along with their old values. If the Where-Type is specified as "Key and Updatable Fields", the UPDATE command will have a WHERE clause that includes all of the updateable fields. In Visual FoxPro 3.0 and 5.0, a list of fields in the WHERE clause that exceeded approximately 24 fields, the TableUpdate() will trigger an "SQL: Statement too long" error. This is because there is an internal limitation on the size of the WHERE clause. In my testing, I have not been able to consistently duplicate the 24-field limitation, but it seems to occur consistently within the range of 23 to 28 fields. Note that this limitation does not apply to remote views, nor does it apply to newly appended records.

I must admit that I've never triggered this error in a production application. However, it would be irresponsible for Microsoft to leave this situation unaddressed. With the release of Visual FoxPro 6, this limitation has been increased to 40 fields, and the VFP development team have given us yet another SYS() function, SYS(3055) that allows us to further increase this limit, albeit with some performance penalty. Should you run up against this scenario, you can look to SYS(3055) as a way of selectively changing the limit when necessary

Listing 5-5. *The Save() method.*

```
* Save() method
LOCAL lcAlias , ;
   llSuccess, ;
   x
THISFORM.BeforeSave()
BEGIN TRANSACTION
```

```
* Use the cursors collection
FOR x = 1 TO THISFORM.nCursors
   * determine the cursor alias
   lcAlias = THISFORM.aCursors[x,1].ALIAS
   * Update all rows, don't force the update
   llSuccess = TABLEUPDATE(1,.F.,lcAlias)
   IF !llSuccess
      ROLLBACK
      AERROR(THISFORM.aErrorInfo)
      EXIT
   ENDIF
ENDFOR
IF llSuccess
   END TRANSACTION
   THISFORM.AfterSuccessfulSave()
   THISFORM.lEditMode = .F.
   THISFORM.REFRESH()
ELSE
   THISFORM.HandleError()
   THISFORM.AfterFailedSave()
ENDIF
RETURN llSuccess
```

uKeyValue property, uKeyValue_Assign() and Requery() methods

The vast majority of forms have a single key value that determines the set of records that are retrieved. A primary key value for a parent table is also the foreign key value for the child records. This value is often needed by various methods of the form; rather than passing it around as method arguments and storing it using local memory variables, it's much more convenient to store it to a form property. Because this key value can be of any data type, the property in the foundation class for storing this value is uKeyValue, and has "u" (for "unknown") as its initial character.

Forms that use parameterized views in their DataEnvironment will have the cursor's No-DataOnLoad property set to .T. This allows the view to open without having to first establish and assign a value to the view parameter variable. After the views are open and the form is up and running, it is then possible to programmatically establish the proper value for the view parameter, and then call the REQUERY() function to retrieve the records that the user wants to work with. In the foundation cDMForm class, there is an empty Requery() method that is populated with form-specific code in each instance of the form.

In versions of Visual FoxPro prior to version 6, a call to the form's Requery() method immediately followed the line that stored the key value to the form property. VFP 6.0 now has something called an ASSIGN method, which is triggered whenever its associated property is modified. The ASSIGN method can be used to change the value that actually gets assigned, prevent assignment of certain values, take some action depending on the old and new values of the property, or simply execute some code in response to the changed value. This last function is the one that is intended for the uKeyValue_Assign() method. Note that the default code for an ASSIGN method accepts a parameter that holds the new value for the property being modified, and the method then stores this value to the property. As you will see, in the form instance it is important to call the DODEFAULT() function and pass the new property value before calling the form's Requery() method, because the Requery() method will expect the new value to be stored in the uKeyValue property.

Before proceeding with a detailed discussion of the sample form, take a moment to go back over the preceding methods, and notice how little difference there is from the same methods that you might write to work with tables directly. The only new method is the Requery() method, which would likely be replaced by a Lookup() method in a table-based form.

The views used by the Time Card form

The Time Card form uses six views, as illustrated in **Table 1**.

Table 1. *Views used by the Time Card form.*

View name	Param-eterized	Updateable	Comments
V_Time_Cards	Yes	Yes	The view of the parent table being updated—one record by primary key value.
V_Time_Card_Hours	Yes	Yes	The view of the child table being updated—multiple records by foreign key.
V_EmployeeListRO	No	No	A list of all employees.
V_TimeCardsByEmpID_RO	Yes	No	A list of time cards on file for a particular employee.
V_SystemCodesRO	Yes	No	A list of codes—parameter specifies which type of code is retrieved.
V_ProjectListRO	No	No	A list of all current projects.

Some views are opened by being placed into the DataEnvironment of the form, while others are opened programmatically at runtime.

Views in the DataEnvironment

Opening TIMECARD.SCX in the form designer and opening the DataEnvironment, you will see four views. You can immediately tell that they're views because they all begin with "v_", my naming convention for views. You'll notice that two of the views end with the letters "RO". This is another convention that I employ to indicate that these views are "read only," that is, their SendUpdates property is set to .F. These views are present only for the purpose of populating two drop-down lists. v_EmployeeListRO supports a drop-down list (actually, two—cboEmployeeLookup and cboEmployee), and v_Time_Cards_ByEmpID_RO supports another—cboTimeCards.

The v_EmployeeListRO view is not parameterized. It simply pulls up a list of employee names (a virtual field concatenating first and last names) along with their last names (for sorting purposes), their employee number and their surrogate employee ID values. The last is important because the employee number is not stored in any other table other than the employee table. If we need to retrieve other sets of records based on a selected employee (and we do), we'll need the surrogate key, not the employee number. The drop-down list class that uses this view is cboEmployees and is stored in the CHAP5.VCX class library.

The important properties of the ComboBox class are:

- BoundColumn = 3
- ColumnCount = 2 (allows the Employee number to display when dropped down)
- RowSourceType = 2—Alias
- RowSource = "v_EmployeeListRO"
- Style = 2—drop-down list
- BoundTo = .T. (the bound column is an integer type)

There is also an ASSERT in the Init() to make sure that the developer remembered to add the view named in the RowSource to the DataEnvironment.

The v_TimeCardsByEmpID_RO view is parameterized, allowing it to retrieve only those records that correspond to a particular employee. The field being matched is iEmployeeID, and the view parameter is ?vp_iEmployeeID. I think you can detect another naming convention here, related to **V**iew **P**arameters. The fields in the view are simply the date of the time card, and the primary key value for that record, which is found in the iTimeCardID field. This is the foreign key value in the Time_Card_Hours table, and will be used to establish a view parameter for that view also.

The combo box that uses this view, cboTimeCards, is also stored in CHAP5.VCX. The following are the important properties for this ComboBox:

- BoundColumn = 2
- ColumnCount = 1
- RowSourceType = 2—Alias
- RowSource = "v_time_cardsByEmpID_RO"
- Value = 0
- Style = 2—drop-down list
- BoundTo = .T. (the bound column is an integer)

The other two views are the "meat" of the form. These are the two updateable views that are actually being manipulated. v_Time_Cards duplicates the structure of the Time_Cards table, and v_Time_Card_Hours duplicates the structure of the Time_Card_Hours table. All fields are updateable, and the primary key field for both views has a default value of NEWID("<tableName>").

You might be wondering why I'm establishing the primary key value in the view rather than at the database level. First, there's no rule that says you can't do both (which is the case here.) Unlike the behavior in VFP 3, a default value dirties the buffer. Thus, if it's established in the view, the TableUpdate() doesn't cause a second primary key value to be generated in the table; but it will accept and store the value generated in the view. However, the advantage with establishing the default value in the view (beyond just being able to do so) is that it's then available to use in populating the foreign key value of any child table records that have been added. SQL Server has a feature whereby you can establish an integer column as an identity column, which is automatically incremented, and can be determined after a TableUpdate() using SQL pass-through to retrieve the @@identity value. However, if you plan on upsizing an application to client/server, or (the gods forbid!) you have to create an application that can work with either local *or* remote data, it's a good idea to establish a method that won't have to be bracketed or rewritten to work in a client/server environment. Establishing the PK value in the views works in either environment.

As long as we're on the subject of primary key values, **Listing 5-6** shows the NEWID() function that is kept in the database's stored procedures for calculating new PK values. Chapter 4 presented a GetKey() function that serves the same purpose. However, if the PK table is stored in a remote database, we don't have access to the Xbase functions like SEEK() and LOCATE, so I came up with a NEWID() function that will again work seamlessly across a local data and client/server environment. It uses the same table structure for the NextKey table as is used in Chapter 4.

Listing 5-6. *A NEWID() function that relies on views and SQL rather than Xbase.*

```
* NEWID() Function
FUNCTION NewID(tcTable)
ASSERT VARTYPE(tcTable) = "C" ;
    AND ! EMPTY(tcTable)
LOCAL lnRetVal, ;
    lcOldAlias, ;
    llSuccess
lcOldAlias = ALIAS()
lnRetVal = 0
vp_cTableName = UPPER(tcTable)
IF ! USED("v_NextKey")
    USE "time and billing!v_NextKey" IN 0
ELSE
    REQUERY("v_NextKey")
ENDIF
IF _TALLY = 1
    SELECT v_NextKey
    llSuccess = .F.
    DO WHILE ! llSuccess
        lnRetVal = v_NextKey.iNextKey
        REPLACE v_NextKey.iNextKey WITH v_NextKey.iNextKey + 1
        llSuccess = TABLEUPDATE(1)
        * If the TABLEUPDATE() fails, it means that some other
        * user grabbed the key value we were about to use
        * and replaced it with an incremented value
        * so we just grab the one the other user placed in
        * the NextKey table and try again
        IF ! llSuccess
            REQUERY("v_NextKey")
        ENDIF
    ENDDO
ENDIF
IF ! EMPTY(lcOldAlias)
    SELECT (lcOldAlias)
ENDIF
RETURN lnRetVal
```

The v_Time_Cards view also has a default value of DATE() for its tDateEntered field, and there is a rule on the tDateWorked field of the v_Time_Card_Hours view. The rule is a function in the database's stored procedures, and is shown in **Listing 5-7**.

Listing 5-7. A field-level rule to facilitate data entry.

```
FUNCTION time_card_date_rule()
   REPLACE tStart WITH tDateWorked + 9*3600
   REPLACE tEnd WITH tDateWorked + 16*3600
ENDFUNC
```

This rule simply "roughs in" a start time of 9:00 a.m. and an end time of 4:00 p.m. based on the date entered for the tDateWorked field. This illustrates one of the slickest aspects of using local views. You can use two entirely different sets of rules—one set for the tables in the database that enforce data integrity, and a second set in the views that facilitate data entry. Using a field or row-level rule on a view is often much easier than trying to write code in a grid's When(), AfterRowColChange(), BeforeRowColChange() and Delete() events, or in the LostFocus(), Valid() or InteractiveChange() events of its contained controls!

Runtime views

By running TIMECARD.SCX and opening the Data Sessions window, you can quickly see the tables and views that are in use by the form at runtime. You'll notice that the following views are not opened by the DataEnvironment:

- v_SystemCodesRO
- v_ProjectListRO

Listing 5-8 shows the commands that create these two views (this is just for illustration; both views can be created in the View Designer).

Listing 5-8. Read-only views for project and system codes picklists.

```
CREATE SQL VIEW v_ProjectListRO AS ;
   SELECT Projects.cprojectname, ;
         Projects.iprojectid;
      FROM "time and billing!projects";
      ORDER BY Projects.cprojectname

CREATE SQL VIEW v_SystemCodesRO AS ;
   SELECT Systemcodes.cdescription, ;
         Systemcodes.icode_id;
      FROM "time and billing!systemcodes";
      WHERE Systemcodes.ctype = ?vp_cType;
      ORDER BY Systemcodes.cdescription
```

The drop-down-list picklists that use these views work a little differently than the two discussed above. First, they are a little more "encapsulated." They use a RowSourceType of 5–Array, and have their own array property to hold the contents of the two views above. Also, they open the views if they're not already open, so the views they use don't have to be added to the DataEnvironment. They work by calling their Requery() method from their Init() event. This is also convenient if these picklists need to be refreshed as a result of opening another form, adding a new project or code, and then returning to the time card form. A call to the

Requery() methods of these two controls does the trick. **Listing 5-9** shows the code in the cboProjects class:

Listing 5-9. The Requery() method of the object cboProjects.

```
LOCAL lcOldAlias ;
    lnTally ;
    lnRowCount

lcOldAlias = ALIAS()
* Make sure the database is open
* and currently active, otherwise
* the view can't be found
IF !DBUSED("time and billing")
    OPEN DATABASE "time and billing"
ENDIF
SET DATABASE TO "time and billing"
IF ! USED("v_ProjectListRO")
    USE v_ProjectListRO NODATA IN 0
ENDIF
* Make sure we have the latest version
REQUERY("v_ProjectListRO")
lnTally = _TALLY
IF lnTally = 0
    DIMENSION THIS.alist[1,2]
    STORE "" TO THIS.alist
ELSE
    DIMENSION THIS.alist[lnTally,2]
ENDIF
SELECT v_ProjectListRO
lnRowCount = 1
SCAN
    THIS.alist[lnRowCount,1] = v_ProjectListRO.cProjectName
    THIS.alist[lnRowCount,2] = v_ProjectListRO.iProjectID
    lnRowCount = lnRowCount + 1
ENDSCAN

IF !EMPTY(lcOldAlias)
    SELECT (lcOldAlias)
ENDIF
```

> *If you're used to saving and restoring environmental settings in your code, you may wonder about the SET DATABASE command. You need to be concerned about the currently selected database when a) programmatically opening a view, b) calling a function/procedure in the stored procedures, or c) retrieving a property using DBGETPROP(). If you don't SET DATABASE TO prior to issuing any of those commands, you'll get hosed eventually, even if you only have one database opened, because it isn't necessarily currently selected. Thus, the proper defensive programming practice is not to save and restore the currently selected database, but to make sure that you have the database (or the correct database, if you are dealing with more than one) currently selected before issuing a command that works on the currently selected database. Not having an open database selected as the current database poses no problem in other situations.*

Similarly, with private data sessions, bound form controls, and the addition of alias clauses to most commands and functions that act on a cursor, the need to save and restore the current work area is greatly reduced, even though many of us—out of habit—continue to do so. I have adopted the practice of never using a command or function without explicitly specifying an alias for the appropriate work area when the command or function supports an alias or work area argument. As a result, as with SET DATABASE, I program defensively by never assuming the state of the environment, and always select the proper work area for those few commands (like APPEND FROM or LOCATE or SCAN...ENDSCAN) that do not accept an argument to specify an alias or work area.

As you can see from the code in Listing 5-9, the cboProjects control has two columns (but only displays the first), with the names of the projects in the first column, and the second with the surrogate primary key value for each project.

CHAP5.VCX contains two other combo boxes that are both subclassed from cboSystemCodes. cboSystemCodes uses v_SystemCodesRO, which is parameterized as shown in Listing 5-8. The SystemCodes table is an "overloaded" table. If you browse it, you'll see that it contains two different kinds of codes: work codes and expense codes. cboSystemCodes calls its Requery() method just as does cboProjects. However, its Requery() method has to establish a view parameter to retrieve only one type of code from the SystemCodes table. This value is stored in the cType property of cboSystemCodes. The Requery() method for cboSystemCodes is shown in **Listing 5-10**.

Listing 5-10. The Requery() method for cboSystemCodes.

```
LOCAL lcOldAlias ;
   lnTally ;
   lnRowCount

lcOldAlias = ALIAS()

IF !DBUSED("time and billing")
   OPEN DATABASE "time and billing"
ENDIF
SET DATABASE TO "time and billing"
IF !USED("v_SystemCodesRO")
   USE v_SystemCodesRO NODATA IN 0
ENDIF
* Here's where we establish the view
* parameter
vp_cType = THIS.cType
REQUERY("v_SystemCodesRO")
lnTally = _TALLY
IF lnTally = 0
   DIMENSION THIS.alist[1,2]
   STORE "" TO THIS.alist
ELSE
   DIMENSION THIS.alist[lnTally,2]
ENDIF
SELECT v_SystemCodesRO
lnRowCount = 1
SCAN
```

```
    THIS.alist[lnRowCount,1] = v_SystemCodesRO.cDescription
    THIS.alist[lnRowCount,2] = v_SystemCodesRO.iCode_ID
    lnRowCount = lnRowCount + 1
ENDSCAN

IF !EMPTY(lcOldAlias)
    SELECT (lcOldAlias)
ENDIF
```

The two classes subclassed from cboSystemCodes are cboWorkCodes and cboExpen-seCodes, and each has its cType property set accordingly.

Our ever-vigilant technical editor was wondering about my use of SCAN...ENDSCAN to transfer information from cursors into the arrays used by the combo box picklists. One of the powerful aspects of views is that they are data-source independent. All views are stored as a local cursor. Thus, a view is a view as far as VFP is concerned. It doesn't matter whether the view is drawing from a VFP database, a FoxPro 2.x database, an Access .MDB file or a SQL Server database. As long as the view definition is what the code expects it to be, it doesn't care (or know, usually) where the data actually comes from. However, unlike the situation where we know that the data will only come from a Visual FoxPro table, and can use a SELECT...INTO ARRAY, views cannot be directed into arrays. Even if we use ODBC and SQL pass-through, the results of a query executed with SQLEXEC() are placed into a cursor. By using a view and SCAN...ENDSCAN to transfer view contents to the array, we can freely change the source of the data without having to change the code.Depending on the situation, COPY TO ARRAY can be used, but SCAN...ENDSCAN provides a little more flexibility to concatenate or otherwise modify the cursor contents. For a lot more information on these techniques, refer to Chapter 11

The grid

The grid in the time card form contains an instance of cboProjects and an instance of cboWorkCodes, so the description of the codes is displayed, rather than the code itself. To allow these codes to be displayed all the time, the Sparse property of the columns is set to .F. For cosmetic purposes, the SpecialEffect property of the lists is set to "1–Plain" and the Bor-derStyle is set to "0–None".

The old swaperoo

When the form is first run, two drop-down-list-style picklists are visible at the top of the form—one for employees and the other for time cards by date. When the Add() button is clicked, the employee drop-down list is made invisible, and another is made visible, in the same position and identical to the first. The difference is that the "add mode" drop-down list is bound to the iEmployeeID field of the v_Time_Cards view, and the "edit mode" drop-down list is not. The cboEmployeeLookup control is used only for specifying an employee whose time cards you want to edit. The cboEmployee control is used to modify the employee ID of a new record.

Also, when the form goes into "add mode," the drop-down list that shows time cards for specific dates for the selected employee is made invisible, and a text box bound to the v_Time_Cards.tDateEntered field is made visible. The process of toggling these four controls is performed by the Add() method, the Cancel() method and the AfterSuccessfulSave() method.

Cut to the chase

Now that we've gotten the mundane stuff out of the way, let's concentrate on the real work of the form.

In order to work with views, a form performs two basic functions that distinguish them from forms working directly against Visual FoxPro tables. It stores user-determined key values to view parameters and calls the REQUERY() function on each updateable view. Beyond that, there isn't much that is really different from how a form would handle the tables directly.

In practice, the only features of a view-form that are different from a table-form are how it accesses an existing record, and that it follows a slightly different procedure before adding new records.

Selecting a time card—accessing an existing record

To select a time card for viewing or editing, the user first selects an employee. The InteractiveChange of the cboEmployeeLookup control stores its value to the form's iEmployeeID property. An iEmployeeID_Assign method is thus triggered. This method, shown in part in **Listing 5-11**, establishes the view parameter and executes the REQUERY() on the v_Time_CardsByEmpID_RO view and calls cboTimeCards.Requery() to update it with the new list of time cards for the selected employee.

Listing 5-11. Part of the iEmployeeID_Assign method.

```
vp_iEmployeeID = ThisForm.iEmployeeID
REQUERY("v_time_CardsByEmpID_RO")
ThisForm.cboTimeCards.Requery()
```

Control returns to the InteractiveChange event method of cboEmployeeLookup, which then sets the value of cboTimeCards to 0, to reflect that none of the time cards for this employee are selected. At this point, the list property of cboTimeCards has been populated with the records from v_Time_CardsByEmpID_RO, which is a list of all the time cards, ordered by date, that are on file for the selected employee.

The act of storing 0 to the value property of cboTimeCards causes its ProgrammaticChange event to fire, which calls the method code for the InteractiveChange event. This is primarily for the purpose of "clearing" the display when the user is already viewing a time card and wants to view a different time card. We'll see how this is accomplished in a moment.

The next thing the user does, after selecting an employee, is select which time card he wishes to view by making a selection from the cboTimeCards drop-down list. The InteractiveChange() event method of cboTimeCards stores the drop-down's value (the iTimeCardID of the selected time card) to the uKeyValue property of the form. There is an assign method associated with the uKeyValue property. This method calls the form's Requery() method. The code for the uKeyValue_Assign and the Requery() method are shown in **Listing 5-12**.

Listing 5-12. *The uKeyValue_Assign() and Requery() methods.*

```
* uKeyValue_Assign
LPARAMETERS vnewval
DoDefault(vnewval) && Stores the iTimeCardID value to the form's uKeyValue
property
ThisForm.Requery()

* Requery() Method
vp_iTimeCardID = ThisForm.uKeyValue
REQUERY("v_Time_Card_Hours")
REQUERY("v_Time_Cards")
ThisForm.Refresh()
```

As you can see from Listing 5-12, four lines of code take the form's uKeyValue property (which is a primary key value for the Time_Cards table, and a foreign key value for the Time_Card_Hours table) and retrieve the corresponding records from each table by calling the REQUERY() function for each view, then refreshing the form.

Adding a new time card

Adding a new time card requires two steps. The first is "blanking," "clearing" or "purging" the cursors. This means requerying the updateable views in such a way that they contain no records—they're ready to have a new, empty record appended. This is what differentiates adding records in a form that uses views from one that works with tables. The second step is the same step necessary when working with tables—appending blank records to the cursors, ready to accept the data that the user wants to enter.

Clearing cursors is important, because when working with views it is imperative that you never have records "in hand," other than those you intend to work with. Simply doing an APPEND BLANK on v_Time_Cards when viewing another record would give you two records—one for the new one you are adding, and another for the one you were just viewing. Because of this, when adding a new record (or deleting an existing record), it is necessary to do something that will result in a RECCOUNT() of 0 for all updateable views.

Logically, simply executing a query using a view parameter value that has no corresponding records in the table will do the trick. If you're using integer surrogate keys, and are retrieving records by the key values (and have a rule that says the primary keys can't be 0) then you're all set. Storing a 0 to the view parameters and calling REQUERY() will have the desired result—views with empty result sets.

If, on the other hand, you're using character surrogate keys, things become a little trickier. If you're doing the filter comparison using "=" and EXACT is set OFF, or if you use the LIKE operator, then you have to ensure that the character string that you specify does not, and will never, exist in the table, nor will it ever appear as a subset of the key values in the table. If you are using a base 62 scheme (which uses all uppercase and lowercase letters as well as the digits 0–9), you can never guarantee that you won't someday match an existing record. If you run with EXACT ON, or use the "==" operator, you can clear the cursor by using the empty string for the view parameter.

If the view uses a non-surrogate character field for the view parameter comparison, it may be easy to select an expression that will never show up in the table. For instance, if the filter comparison is being performed on the cInvoiceNo field, and the invoice numbers are six characters consisting only of the digits 0–9, then you can use a parameter value of "XXXXXX" (or any other string of alpha characters) to clear the cursors.

In the case of the Time Card form, the key values are indeed integers, and there is a rule on the primary key field prohibiting 0 values. Storing a value of 0 to the view parameters for both v_Time_Cards and v_Time_Card_Hours and requerying both views will yield an empty result set for both views.

Recognizing the need for this functionality, the cDMForm contains an empty ClearCursors() method. In the Time Card form, this method has only a single line of code:

```
ThisForm.cboEmployeeLookup.Value = 0
```

Executing this line of code will initiate the following cascade of events, courtesy of control events and the new assign methods. Note that nothing in this cascade of events is anything different than what has already been coded to allow the user to display an existing time card. The user cannot (by selecting an employee from the list) select an iEmployeeID value of 0, so the ClearCursors() method takes care of this:

- Changing the value property of cboEmployeeLookup to 0 triggers CboEmployee-Lookup.ProgrammaticChange().
- CboEmployeeLookup.ProgrammaticChange() calls CboEmployee-Lookup.InteractiveChange().
- CboEmployeeLookup.InteractiveChange() stores 0 to the form's iEmployeeID property.
- Storing 0 to the form's iEmployeeID property triggers the iEmployeeID_Assign method.
- The iEmployeeID_Assign method stores 0 to the view parameter and calls REQUERY() for v_Time_CardsByEmpID_RO, which clears that view.
- CboEmployeeLookup.InteractiveChange() also stores 0 to cboTimeCards.Value, which triggers cboTimeCards.ProgrammaticChange().
- cboTimeCards.ProgrammaticChange() calls cboTimeCards.InteractiveChange().
- cboTimeCards.InteractiveChange() stores 0 to the form's uKeyValue property.
- Storing 0 to the form's uKeyValue property triggers the uKeyValue_Assign() method.
- uKeyValue_Assign() calls the form's Requery() method, which calls REQUERY() for v_Time_Cards and v_Time_Card_Hours, which clears both views.

Before leaving the example form, I'd like to call your attention to the BeforeSave() method, which does something that might look a bit unusual in the case of a deleted time-card record. This database has a delete trigger on the Time_Cards table, which causes all related child records in Time_Card_Hours to be deleted if the Time_Cards record is deleted. If the user has modified any records in v_Time_Card_Hours before deleting the time card, the update of the v_Time_Cards view (which, you'll recall, occurs first because the cursor name for this view ends in "1") will delete the related Time_Card_Hours records. Then, the update of the v_Time_Card_Hours view takes place, and it will detect that the underlying tables have been changed (they've been deleted!) and the update will fail because of an update conflict.

To avoid this, the BeforeSave() method checks to see if the parent record in v_Time_Cards has been deleted, and if so, it reverts any changes made to the child view.

The View/Query Designer

Within a typical application, views will fall into one of two groups: one group of views designed as updateable views that are used to modify the data, and another group designed as *non*-updateable views, to support reports, on-screen inquires, picklists and validation queries. In general, updateable views are almost always parameterized and usually incorporate fields from only a single table.

Although you can feel extremely clever constructing a single view that joins three tables and performs updates on all three, I've found that the KISS (Keep It Simple, Stupid!) principle applies as well to the creation of updateable views as it does to almost any other aspect of application development. When creating updateable views, adhere to the following three rules of thumb:

1. The SQL property of the view should look like this: SELECT * FROM <table_name> WHERE <field_name> = <view_parameter> — note only one table, no joins.
2. A single field should be flagged as the key field. If you're using integer surrogate keys, you're home free.
3. All fields should be flagged as updateable.

Save your cleverness for adding some useful "virtual" fields to your updateable views or creating rules that facilitate data entry … and save a *lot* of cleverness for those thorny reporting requirements that the client has in the specifications!

From the previous couple of paragraphs, you can see that the View Designer does a good job meeting all your needs for creating updateable views. But the View Designer really falls down in some of the complex queries required for some lists and reports. Let's take a moment to understand why the View Designer is so limited in this area.

There are two types of join syntax that are permitted under the ANSI '92 SQL standard. Many have come to describe the two types of syntax as the "nested" and the "sequential" syntax. The following listings show only the FROM clause of a SELECT command to illustrate the differences.

Listing 5-13. *An example of "nested" join syntax.*

```
1.   FROM <table_1> ;
2.      JOIN <table_2> ;
3.         JOIN <table_3> ;
4.            JOIN <table_4> ;
5.            ON <table_4_expression> = <table_3_expression> ;
6.         ON <table_3_expression> = <table_2_expression> ;
7.      ON <table_2_expression> = <table_1_expression> ;
```

In **Listing 5-13**, line 6 shows an expression joining table_3 with table_2, but it could just as well join table_4 with table_3, or any other table within the "nest."

Listing 5-14. *An example of "sequential" join syntax.*

```
1.  FROM <table_1> JOIN <table_2> ;
        ON <table_1_expression> = <table_2_expression> ;
2.      JOIN <table_3> ;
3.          ON <table_3_expression> = <table_2_expression> ;
4.      JOIN <table_4> ;
5.          ON <table_4_expression> = <table_3_expression>
```

In **Listing 5-14**, line 6 could join table_4 with table_3, table_2 or table_1; this fact seems readily apparent and quite intuitive. In general, I strongly believe that anyone who tries to create a complex query using the "nested" syntax, as shown in Listing 5-13, is a confirmed masochist, and should be kept away form sharp objects. The reason becomes apparent when trying to create a join as illustrated in **Figure 1**.

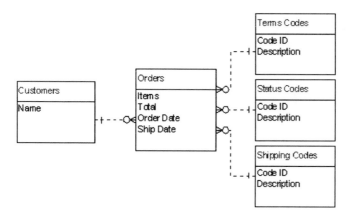

Figure 1. *A join scenario suspected to be impossible using the "nested" join syntax.*

Figure 1 illustrates a view that has, as a requirement, the customer name, order items, total amount, order date and ship date, as well as the description associated with the terms code, status code, and the shipping code on each order. Using the "sequential" syntax, it's a walk in the park. Using the "nested" syntax … well, call me when you have it done—meanwhile, I'm going on a two-month vacation.

Even if we simplify the query illustrated in Figure 1 by eliminating the need for descriptions from two of the three code tables, the nested syntax is still somewhat cumbersome, requiring us to be very careful with the *order* in which the joins are made to get the desired results. Matters get even worse when you introduce outer joins into the equation. To be fair, there might be some unique capabilities inherent in the nested syntax, but I have yet to discover them.

So what does this have to do with the Visual FoxPro View Designer? The view designer stores the join conditions using the nested syntax. As a result, it becomes either very difficult to use, or downright useless when creating a complex view.

All is not lost, however. Most experienced developers include a file that ends up being called something like VIEWSCRIPT.PRG (see **Listing 5-15**) in which these complex views can be maintained in code. If you're not already comfortable with writing SQL code, I strongly encourage you to develop that skill as soon as possible. Many skills we acquire eventually become obsolete. However, I think the ability to easily write SQL query syntax is one that really has some "legs," and will be useful for many years to come.

The big drawback in maintaining a view in code is that we have no easy way to set the properties for the various view fields, such as which field is the key field, what fields are up-dateable, and what UpdateType and WhereType are to be used. Establishing these rules in code requires a long sequence of DBSETPROP() commands. However, as mentioned above, most (if not all) of the updateable views you will be using involve no joins, and as a result can be handled very nicely using the View Designer. The views that you will most likely be creating and maintaining in code are used for reports and for creating on-screen queries and form picklists. This type of view is not an updateable view, but a "read–only" view, as shown in the Chapter 5 example form, and exists only to conveniently store a scheme for extracting and presenting some information from the database. A view is by default *not* updateable. So creating a complex view in code doesn't have to do anything other than specify the name under which the view is stored, and the SELECT statement with the view parameters (if any). Using the example illustrated in Figure 1, you might see a developer use the code in Listing 5-15 to support this particular report.

Listing 5-15. *An example of a "read-only" view that would be maintained in code in a VIEWSCRIPT.PRG file.*

```
PROCEDURE Create_V_Order_Status_RO
   CREATE SQL VIEW v_Order_Status_RO AS ;
      SELECT customers.cName, ;
             orders.iItems, ;
             orders.dordered, ;
             orders.dshipped, ;
             orders.ytotal, ;
             termscodes.cDescription AS terms, ;
             statusCodes.cDescription AS status, ;
             shippingCodes.cDescription AS via, ;
      FROM customers JOIN orders ;
            ON customers.cCust_ID = orders.cCust_ID ;
         JOIN systemcodes termsCodes;
            ON orders.iTerms_Ref = termsCodes.iCode_ID ;
         JOIN systemcodes statusCodes ;
            ON orders.iStatus_Ref = statusCodes.iCode_ID ;
         JOIN systemcodes shippingCodes ;
            On orders.iShip_Ref = shippingCodes.iCode_ID ;
         WHERE orders.cCust_ID = ?vp_cCust_ID
ENDPROC
```

Once this procedure is written, it can be executed as shown in **Listing 5-16**.

Listing 5-16. *Executing the view-maintenance routine in Listing 5-15.*

```
IF NOT DBUSED("<target_database>")
   OPEN DATABASE <target_database>
ENDIF
SET DATABASE TO <target_database>
```

```
SET PROCEDURE TO viewscript ADDITIVE
DO create_v_order_status_RO
```

However, my preferred method is to open the target database and make it the currently selected database with SET DATABASE (this is important!). Then, open the VIEWSCRIPT.PRG in the Visual FoxPro editor, highlight everything *within* the procedure, right-click with the mouse and choose "Execute selection" from the shortcut menu. This is particularly convenient when it's necessary to modify the view. You modify, select and run the CREATE SQL VIEW command, then close and save the VIEWSCRIPT.PRG.

The case for updateable views

Let me clearly state that I in no way want to try to convince anyone that views are the only way, or even the "right" way, to interact with data. There is no principle, or best practice, or even a rule of thumb that will dictate when/if you should use updateable views. There is no rule (or even a school of thought) that says you're a dummy if you don't use views, and there is certainly no rule that says you can't use a mixture of updateable views and direct table manipulation. However, in my life as a developer, certain things have come down the pike that have resonated with my soul in some way—things that make me say to myself, "This is Right; This is Good." Procedural programming, naming conventions, black-box routines, reusable code and object-oriented programming were all concepts that "clicked" when I began to understand how they worked. Each new approach or idea brought me a big step closer to some kind of programmer's Nirvana, where the DoWhatIMean() function is a reality! Once I started using updateable views, I experienced the same feeling of "Wow" that I did with some of the earlier concepts. I hope that more folks give views a spin, and find themselves closer to Programming Perfection as I did.

Why would you exclusively use views?

First, I've found that working with views is a very easy way to interact with data. The whole process has a very "clean" feel to it. This is not a factor to be discounted—how much of what we do in our development practices do we do simply because "it feels right"?

There are no indexes, relations or filters that have to be maintained at runtime to ensure that we're only modifying the data that we intend to modify. With the exception of occasionally restoring the record pointer to its original position after moving it when doing some kind of processing, and checking for an EOF() condition when appropriate, the record pointer can be ignored. Views can be indexed if it's necessary to allow the user to control the order in which records are displayed, and the index order can be changed without concern for "breaking" an established relation.

Then there are field-level rules. Work with tables and you really don't want to enforce field-level rules; violating a rule means the user absolutely *cannot* leave a field or control until the rule is satisfied. Likewise, a row-level rule must be satisfied before moving the record pointer to another record (See Chapter 6 for more information on rules). With views, field-level and row-level rules can be used freely because they aren't evaluated until the TableUpdate() is executed.

While on the subject of rules, we can establish two completely different sets of rules: one at the table level to enforce data integrity, and one at the view level to facilitate data entry.

I've spent days trying to accomplish the most god-awful things using the myriad of grid events and other form controls, that were suddenly a piece of cake when I called a stored procedure from a view field- or row-level rule. (Refer to Chapters 11 and 12 for some important views on using Grids).

Server-based SQL databases are increasingly popular, and being able to interact with them effectively is a valuable skill. Acquiring this skill requires that we begin to think entirely within the constraints of SQL commands. You can't perform a SEEK on a SQL Server table to validate a user's input. However, you can create a lookup table on the fly using a view, index that view, and use that for validation. You can also use a view and dispense with Xbase syntax almost entirely, as shown in **Listing 5-17**.

Listing 5-17. *A sample data-validation function using a view.*

```
FUNCTION ValidatePartNumber(tcPartNumber)
   vp_cPartNumber = tcPartNumber
   IF ! USED("v_ValidatePart")
      USE v_ValidatePart IN 0
   ELSE
      REQUERY("v_ValidatePart")
   ENDIF
   IF _TALLY = 0
      llReturnValue = .F.
   ELSE
      llReturnValue = .T.
   ENDIF
   RETURN llReturnValue
ENDFUNC
```

Note that the foregoing function works equally well with remote views as it does with local views.

Designing Visual FoxPro applications using views exclusively helps you to begin thinking more in terms of pure SQL, which not only influences how you implement the application, but with how you design the database!

Jim : Steve and I agree about a lot of things, but exclusive use of views isn't one of them. Views, both local and remote, are very powerful tools and they should not be dismissed from our collection of weapons. However, exclusively doing anything in application development leaves the possibility of missing a mechanism of solving a problem simply because it doesn't fit our exclusive vision of things.
The design of the data access mechanisms should be part of the analysis and design of the overall application, and it should consider all of the issues involved. Using views for data access exclusively is one of many options available to the developer, and it should be considered as such: one of the possibilities.
Data-aware form classes should be capable of handling views and tables in the data for the form. Not doing this simply creates a form class that fails under certain conditions.
There are times when the extra overhead of views is not necessary—for example, in a small departmental system where using tables directly is fine. Also, using

views can seriously complicate development of real-time systems. The level of indirection that is the very power of a view causes an inherent problem in real-time applications.

So, I say, keep things in perspective. Views are powerful and they offer certain advantages. However, nothing is just advantages; all things also carry disadvantages. To blindly go forward without acknowledgement of the disadvantages of a certain path is giving those disadvantages absolute power over your work.

Now that I've said all of this, I have to agree with Steve that, in most cases, using views exclusively for data management is a very good approach to development.

Steve replies:
I agree with Jim's points in general. However, my experience is that the "extra overhead" that Jim speaks of isn't really worth worrying about. In fact, making a design decision to use views lends a simplicity and clarity to the development process that is really quite surprising once you get involved with it. Believe me when I say that I'm probably one of the world's laziest developers, and if something is a lot of extra work or headache, I'm quick to dump it. I agree that few things in life consist only of advantages, but updateable views are one of the things that seem a little thin on the downside.

Performance considerations

A concern I frequently hear from developers when I talk about using views is that using views will slow down the application. Consider that Visual FoxPro is (and long has been) the fastest database management tool in the known universe. Views are simply one way of retrieving data, and retrieving data is what FoxPro does best, right?

Just to provide a couple of examples, I have a view in a production application that uses a complex series of outer joins to extract 1163 records from four tables containing 51, 117, 1223 and 1229 records. This view executes (starting with all tables closed) in 0.45 seconds on a 200 MHz laptop with a run-of-the-mill IDE drive. I also have a view that extracts 5100 records from a single table of 126,000 records in 0.43 seconds on the same machine. Remember that virtually every updateable view you are likely to use will be indexed on the primary or foreign key, and that this is the field that is used in the WHERE clause in the query. Rushmore kicks in every time, and you get the records fast-fast-fast!

If you take the time to give views a try, you'll find just how easy they are to use, and how in many ways they'll make your life much easier. They do require some up-front time and effort to get comfortable with the ideas and techniques, and perhaps a little more design work at the database level, but it's effort that pays off handsomely in the long run.

Chapter 6
Rules, Triggers and
Referential Integrity

Developers have gotten along just fine for many years without having rules, triggers and referential integrity code built into their databases. As a result, it's easy to think that this set of Visual FoxPro features can be ignored. Even though we've done without these particular tools, we *have* been enforcing rules and referential integrity all along. In the past we had no choice but to enforce rules and protect the integrity of our data in our forms or procedural code. Now, we have some options that are worth considering; when judiciously applied, they can save us some work and improve the quality of our applications.

Rule and trigger functions

Many lines of code have been written to protect the integrity of our databases. Consider the following issues that are probably representative of issues you've encountered:

- Deletion of the last line-item of an invoice
- Entering a client without a case number
- Entering a line-item on an invoice for an item that is only returned, never sold (like an empty acetylene tank)
- Entering a purchase order with a specified shipping method of "UPS" when only "Motor Carrier" and "Air Freight" are valid shipping methods for this vendor
- Changing an invoice number
- Deletion of a customer when there is active or inactive historical information related to this customer
- Entering a quantity of 2 items that sell for $5 each, and showing the extension correctly as $10
- Deletion of an invoice with 112 line items
- Entering a birth date of 12/15/1928 for a 6-year-old child

Much of what we do to protect the integrity of our systems' data falls into one of three categories:

- Domain constraints—Limiting field values to those permitted for the type of data that the field represents.
- Internal consistency—Ensuring that no two fields contain logically inconsistent data.
- Referential integrity—Limiting the occurrence of "orphan" records.

Let's consider a few examples based on the preceding list.

If the user chooses to delete an invoice, it would be nice if all we had to do was to issue the DELETE command on the invoice record and commit the change. However, in the real world, we really should also delete those 112 line items. This is an example of a referential integrity function. We are eliminating the possibility of "orphan" records in the line-items table.

A customer ordered three $5 widgets for a total of $15, but because the stock was short, one of the three items was backordered and only two were shipped. The user edits the order prior to invoicing, changing the quantity shipped to 2. The total needs to be changed from $15 to $10. This is an example of an internal consistency function. The unit price, the quantity sold and the extended amount must be logically consistent and mathematically correct.

If the user enters a birth date of 12/15/1928 into a patient record in a pediatric medical practice management program, we might have some code to check the age of the patient. If the calculation results in an age greater than 18 (or whatever criteria the practice has for its clientele), we could present the user with a message indicating that this value is not appropriate, and requiring that it be corrected before committing changes to the record. This represents a domain constraint function.

Thus, the question is not *whether* our applications need to deal with these situations; it's *how*. The rules, triggers and referential integrity code that we build into the database can be part of your strategy for addressing these needs.

In addition to the basic requirements with regard to data integrity, we can use rules and triggers in other ways to enhance our applications or make them easier to implement. We saw one example of this in Chapter 5, in which a rule was used to perform a calculation that was much more easily implemented as a field-level rule on a view than it was using control events in a grid.

What are rules and triggers?

Visual FoxPro internally detects when changes are made to the data contained in tables in a database. The developer has the option of evaluating a logical expression in response to these changes. The expression can be, or incorporate any native Visual FoxPro function, like EMPTY() or ISNULL() or a user-defined function (UDF). Usually any UDF called by a rule or trigger is stored in the .DBC as a stored procedure. Because the .DBC is automatically opened when one of its tables is opened, this ensures that the UDF will always be available when called by a rule or trigger. As pointed out in Chapter 4, however, if it's necessary to share UDF's across multiple databases, you can (in order to ease maintenance) store them in a shared procedure file or as independent .PRG's. Note that if you intend to access your Visual FoxPro database via ODBC, that the ODBC driver has certain limitations on what can and cannot be accomplished in a stored procedure.

> *More recent versions of the Visual FoxPro ODBC driver (since version 5) improve on support for stored procedures. Keep in mind that, in order to provide complete, 100 percent support for any stored procedures you might write, the ODBC driver would need to incorporate the entire VFP runtime library, which just isn't practical. However, if it's expected that applications other than VFP must be able to modify data contained in a VFP database, then careful attention to the commands that are and are not supported by ODBC will*

minimize unnecessary rule and trigger failure as a result of the use of unsupported commands and functions. For the current state of the ODBC driver, consult the DRVVFP.HLP file for a complete list of supported and unsupported commands and functions. As of this writing, this file is installed with VFP 6.0 under the VFP home directory, in Distrib.src\System.

When a table belonging to a Visual FoxPro database is opened, that database is automatically opened, but it is not selected as the current database. This is a concern when calling a UDF programmatically, since it's necessary to issue a SET DATABASE TO <database name> in order for the UDF to be in the calling stack. However, this is not a concern when considering rule and trigger code. Rule and trigger code knows what database the table or view is associated with, and will automatically search the stored procedures for the UDF whenever a rule or trigger is fired. With rule and trigger code, there's no need to make the associated database the currently selected database with SET DATABASE TO.

Any change to existing data will execute field-rule code associated with the modified field, the table or row rule associated with the table, and the update trigger. When a record is deleted, the delete trigger is fired. If a new record is inserted into the table, or if a deleted record is recalled, the insert trigger fires.

Let's look at some of the basic behaviors of rules and triggers.

Rule behavior

There are two types of rules in Visual FoxPro, and they can be applied to either tables or views. There are field rules and table rules. The table rules are also commonly referred to as "row" rules. Both types of rules display certain behaviors:

- They fire when data is changed. They're optionally non-retroactive (can be added to an existing table without being applied to existing records).
- They prevent shifting focus to another row or field if the rule is violated; that is, if the rule evaluates to .F.
- They fire when a new row is inserted. A rule will fail if default field values violate the rules, preventing the insertion of a new record.
- They aren't affected by buffering; that is, they cannot be "turned off."
- They cannot move the record pointer *for the current table* during rule-code execution.
- Code executed by a rule or trigger allows use of the OLDVAL() and GETFLDSTATE() functions but doesn't require buffering to be in effect.

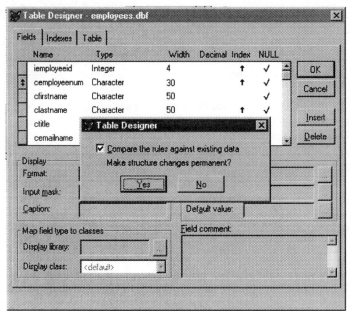

Figure 1. *The Table Designer prompting to apply rules to existing records*

One limitation of some Visual FoxPro form controls is that there is no native technique for determining if a control's value has been changed. The InteractiveChange event fires for every keystroke, or every increment of a spinner, and as a result is often too "granular" in its response. As a result, many developers perform some evaluation in the LostFocus( ) method of the control to determine if the user has made any change.

Such an evaluation is not needed when establishing rules. The rule fires only when the value of the field or fields to which the rule is bound changes. And this is true of *any* change, including inserting a new row or appending a blank row. Because the failure of a rule (that is, the rule evaluates to .F.) prevents the user from shifting the focus to another field or moving the record pointer, this behavior suggests that it is very important to ensure that the default field values do not violate a rule. Such a situation would forever prevent insertion of a blank row.

When establishing a rule for an existing table, the rule is applied by default to all existing records. However, you have the option of adding a new rule, *without* applying the rule to the existing records. If modifying the table using the Table Designer (as seen in **Figure 1**), this can be accomplished by clearing the check box labeled "Compare the rules against existing data" in the Save dialog. If establishing the rule in code using the ALTER TABLE command, use the NOVALIDATE clause. Note that this prevents applying the rule to existing records *at the time the rule is established*, but if the user subsequently modifies an existing field or record, the rule will be applied.

When working directly against tables, there is no way of temporarily "turning off" rules during data entry. Buffering has no effect. A row or table-buffered table will not prevent a field-level rule from firing as soon as the field loses focus, and a table-buffered table will not prevent a row-level rule from firing when the user moves the record pointer.

If you execute a UDF from a rule, you cannot move the record pointer in the table executing the UDF as a rule, but you can change work areas and navigate through another table.

Here is one of the more interesting (and surprising) behaviors of code that is called from a rule or trigger: Two functions that normally require table buffering to be in effect when called, GETFLDSTATE() and OLDVAL(), work just fine within rule and trigger code. This implies that there is a level of internal buffering to which we don't normally have access, and which allows us to determine the state of the "dirty buffer" flags and the value of each field prior to modification in rule and trigger code, even if buffering isn't in effect.

Field and row rule behavior

In addition to all the behaviors mentioned above, field rules display the following properties:

- They fire as soon as the modified field loses focus.
- Failure (returning .F.) absolutely prevents moving off the field, or any control bound to the field.
- Field-rule code can modify fields on the current record, except the one firing the trigger.

By contrast, table or "row-level" rules include these properties:

- They fire only when the record pointer is moved.
- Row-rule code can modify any field in the modified record.

Data validation

Because rules can be used to validate user-entered data, we should examine data-validation techniques in general for a moment, and then assess rules as a tool to use for data validation in the larger context.

Data validation is usually of concern in the context of end-user data entry. This is where the developer loses some control over the application. As a result, the developer must program defensively, but in a user-friendly manner that facilitates data entry and protects the integrity of the data. In this context, data validation can be handled in one or a combination of several ways. Deciding how to handle data-entry data validation requires answering two questions: First, when is the user informed about unacceptable data? Second, how is the user prevented from putting the unacceptable data into the database? Unfortunately, there are no hard and fast rules that can be used to answer either question.

As a general rule of thumb, it's best to inform a user as soon as possible that some piece of data is unacceptable. On the other hand, you want users to be free to enter data in any order they find convenient, and not interrupt the flow of their work with message boxes and beeps. There is also the matter of performance and efficiency. If we call some kind of validation routine or method for every keystroke, this could have a noticeable impact on the application's performance. It is possible to eliminate the need for data validation in the first place by limiting the user's ability to enter data to only those values that are permissible, via some kind of picklist control, or by enabling or disabling, as appropriate, various options on a form.

A very basic validation technique is to use the Valid() EventMethod of a control, returning a value of 0 if the data entered is not acceptable. This prevents the user from shifting focus from the control until he enters an acceptable value. To many developers, this is one of the worst ways to enforce data validation. In the worst case, it forces the user to enter an acceptable value even if all he wants to do is click the Cancel button.

Another basic technique, but one which works at the extreme opposite end of the spectrum, is one in which the form's Save() method is executed conditionally, depending on the validity of all data entered. This confronts the user with an informational message after he completes data entry and asks to save all entries.

A middle-ground approach taken by some developers is that the validation is done periodically during data entry, possibly triggered by the LostFocus() events of the various controls, or via a Timer object, which enables or disables the Save button depending on the validity of the user's entries. This technique can be very effective, especially if there is some mechanism (via the status bar, for instance) to inform the user as to why the Save button is disabled.

One inherent weakness of performing data validation at the user-interface level of an application is that the rules are often hard-coded. This might be perfectly acceptable in some situations, and less so in others. Consider the rule, used as an example above, that considers a patient's birth date to be invalid if it yields an age over 18. What if the pediatrician decides that she will no longer treat adolescents, and the age limit needs to be lowered to 12? Or perhaps the age limit varies by the patient's insurance plan? A data-driven rule would be preferable in this case. In fact, this particular rule is really a *business* rule, and some would argue that such a rule should *not* be enforced in the database itself.

Rules can play a role in all three approaches. The problem with allowing the user to actually violate a rule on a table interactively is that a FoxPro-generated dialog is presented to the user, displaying the message text that is stored in the RuleText property associated with the rule. While this behavior by itself does not present a problem, the ultimate effect on the user is the same as returning a value of 0 from a Valid() EventMethod – they are forced to satisfy the rule before they are allowed to shift focus to any other control, including the close box or "Exit" command button.

> *A Valid method can return a logical or numeric value. If a logical .F. is returned, the effect is to produce an audible "beep" and a wait window that says "Invalid input", and if the user then presses the <Enter> key, the control's previous value is restored. This behavior can be avoided if desired, giving the developer more control over the response to the invalid input by returning a value of 0. This simply prevents the control from losing focus; no automatic error indicator is triggered. A value of other than 0 moves focus to a subsequent or prior control on the form, depending on the value returned. A 1 moves focus to the next control, while a –2 moves focus back two controls in the tab order.*

Thus, performing data validation by table and field rules represents a rather draconian extreme. However, when table or field rules are in place on a table, they aren't triggered by data entered into an updateable view, at least not until the data modifications are committed using TableUpdate(). If the TableUpdate() fails due to a rule violation, the value of the RuleText property gets stored in the array created with the AERROR() function, and can be used to present the user with an informative message box.

When using views, it is even possible to employ the database rules without ever triggering them, using them instead to enable or disable a Save button, and displaying useful information to the user. The following lines of code will retrieve the field-rule expression and the field-rule text from an open database:

```
DBGETPROP("<Table.FieldName>","Field","RuleExpression")
DBGETPROP("<Table.FieldName>","Field","RuleText")
```

Given that it's easy to determine the ControlSource property of any given control, the name of the underlying table's field can be determined by the following line of code:

```
DBGETPROP("<View.FieldName>","Field","UpdateName")
```

Another way of giving the user immediate feedback about a domain constraint violation, but absolutely preventing the violation in the database, involves using a single stored procedure for both views and tables, but responding differently depending on whether the rule is being called from the table or the view. The following stored procedure is used to validate the tDateWorked field of both the v_Time_Card_Hours view and the Time_Card_Hours table. The code in **Listing 6-1** gives the user an error message that doesn't interrupt the flow of data entry when using a view, but will not allow the invalid data to be inserted into the database when the TableUpdate() is called.

Listing 6-1. *A dual-purpose, field-validation stored procedure.*

```
FUNCTION ValidateDateWorked()
    LOCAL llValid
    #DEFINE LOCALVIEW 1

    IF EMPTY(tDateWorked) OR tDateWorked > DATE()
       llValid = .F.
    ELSE
       llValid = .T.
    ENDIF
    IF CURSORGETPROP("SourceType") = LOCALVIEW ;
          AND ! llValid
       ?? CHR(7)
       SET MESSAGE TO "Invalid Date"
       WAIT "Invalid date" WINDOW NOWAIT
       llValid = .T.
    ENDIF
    RETURN llValid
ENDFUNC
```

This function uses the CURSORGETPROP() function to determine whether the field is being changed in a view or in the table directly. If in a view, it simply beeps, displays a WAIT WINDOW NOWAIT and puts a message on the status bar to alert the user that something needs to be corrected before she can commit her changes. If the user is updating the table directly (or initiates a Save() despite the error), the function returns a value of .F. and the update is rejected.

Note that this function is triggered (as are all rules) when a new record is appended, and the rule is triggered subsequently only when the user makes a change to the tDateWorked field. Establishing an appropriate default value could address this issue.

Data modification using rules

If you're familiar with the various normalization rules for database design, you're probably familiar with the most common rules corresponding to what is known as first, second and third normal forms. (See Appendix Two for an explanation of Data Normalization) Part of the third normal form specifies that there shouldn't be any redundant calculated data in a record—that is, you shouldn't include a column that contains values that can be calculated from the values contained in two or more other fields. For instance, third normal form argues against having an "extension" column when you have quantity and price fields; the extension can be determined from these two fields and doesn't need to be stored in the table.

However, in even the most carefully designed and rigorously implemented database, this is the rule that is most commonly deliberately violated. Sometimes it allows certain application features to be implemented more easily, or perhaps the clients or users prefer that such calculated fields be included. Once this decision is made, it then becomes necessary to accurately maintain the values stored in these fields. If the calculated fields are not displayed during data entry, they can be "batch" updated prior to committing the user's modifications. However, if the calculated fields need to be displayed and updated in "real time" during data entry, rules can come to the rescue here, simply replacing the calculated value based on the contents of other fields.

You can see an example of this application in the Time_Card_Hours_Rule() that is fired in response to a change to either the tStart or tEnd fields of the v_Time_Card_Hours view. Changing either value results in a recalculation of the value stored in the bBillableHours field. Note that because it was preferred that this synchronization be "real-time" and visible to the user, it was implemented in the view. It could also be implemented in the table itself. This would guarantee that no further code would be required in the application to ensure that bBillableHours was always consistent with the start and end times entered.

Another self-modification rule is evident in the v_Time_Card_Hours view. Note that there are *two* functions called in the rule for the tDateWorked field. One is the one discussed earlier, validating this field, but the other was demonstrated in Chapter 5 and is used to establish default values for the tStart and tEnd fields, making the data-entry process a little more efficient.

Trigger behavior

Triggers display somewhat different behaviors than do rules, owing to their different function and usage within an application. As with rules, triggers fire in response to changes made to the tables in our database. We can then decide to evaluate one or more expressions in response to these events. The following points summarize trigger behaviors:

- Triggers fire on TABLEUPDATE(), or on modification if the table is not buffered. Thus, you can delay evaluation of any trigger expression or execution of any trigger code by using buffering.
- UPDATE occurs when any field is changed.

- INSERT occurs when a new record is added, *or* when a deleted record is recalled.
- DELETE occurs when the delete flag is set.
- Delete code can change work areas and modify other tables.
- Code executed in response to a trigger cannot modify the record that is firing the trigger.
- OLDVAL() and GETFLDSTATE() can be used even if the table is not buffered.

As with table and view rules, we use properties for each table in the database to specify what action is to be performed when any of these three triggers are fired. Note that, unlike rules, which can work on fields or tables, there exist only *table* triggers. Modifying a view alone will not fire a trigger; a trigger will be fired only when the changes in a view are used to modify the underlying table by calling the TableUpdate() function.

While table and field rules often can be a single expression (like NOT EMPTY(cCase_No)), the expressions evaluated in response to a trigger are usually user-defined functions. Such functions are usually maintained in the database's stored procedures. There is no requirement that trigger code be kept in the database's stored procedures. As with any other UDF, as long as Visual FoxPro can find the code, it'll be executed. However, unlike a key-value-generating function, trigger functions are most often very database-specific, and therefore less likely to be shared between databases. Thus, there isn't usually much to be gained by storing trigger functions in a separate procedure file.

In putting together a comprehensive system that employs rules and triggers, it's important to understand the normal sequence of events between the user changing a field value in a form and the change being recorded on disk:

1. Data is modified in a view or buffered table.
2. We attempt to commit the modifications by issuing a TableUpdate().
3. Rules (if any) are fired.
4. If a rule does not fail, any applicable triggers are fired.
5. Modifications are accepted/rejected (equivalent to TableRevert() at the table level).

So what can you do with triggers? The most common use for triggers, in part because Microsoft supplies a spiffy tool that supports it, is building referential integrity rules into our databases. Later we'll discuss other interesting things that can be done with triggers, but we'll start with a discussion of referential integrity.

Referential integrity

Referential integrity is a fancy word for avoiding "orphan" records, or child records with no corresponding parent records. Orphan records are created by:

- Inserting a child record when no corresponding parent record exists
- Deleting a parent record, leaving the corresponding child records intact
- Changing a parent record's primary key value, so that the child record's foreign key value no longer points to a valid parent record

As you can see, each of these three actions corresponds to one of the three available triggers. In the case of an INSERT, we can respond in one of two ways: we can either ignore the insertion of an orphan record, or we can *restrict* (prohibit) the insertion if no parent record exists. In the case of a DELETE, we can ignore the deletion, allowing the orphan records; we can *cascade* the deletion to any child records, deleting them along with their parent; or we can restrict the deletion, prohibiting it if any child records exist. Similarly, we have the same options when the primary key value of a parent record is changed; we can ignore the change, cascade the change to the child records, or restrict the change if child records exist.

Referential integrity rules apply to *relations*, not to tables. As a result, a delete or update rule applies to the deletion or modification of the *parent* table, and an insertion to the *child* table. The role of a particular table changes depending on which relationship we're referring to. Thus, while we assign code to be executed in response to a trigger for a particular table, the action of that code will vary depending on the nature of the relationship. We may require deletion of a record in table A to cascade to table B, but be restricted if there are child records in table C. If you're unfamiliar with referential integrity rules and this seems a bit unclear, it should click into place as this chapter progresses. See **Table 1**.

Table 1. *Available referential integrity options.*

	Cascade	Restrict	Ignore
Delete	●	●	●
Update	●	●	●
Insert		●	●

Keep in mind that these options are not exhaustive. They are simply the most common way of enforcing referential integrity, and they are the options provided by the Visual FoxPro Referential Integrity builder. You could respond to a deletion, for instance, by changing the foreign key value of the child records to a default value, preserving their contents, and changing their reference to another "utility" parent record that allows them to be accessed, but in a different context. For example, imagine that a salesperson is leaving a company, and the sales manager wants to remove his record from the salesperson table but reassign his accounts to another salesperson (or perhaps, by default, to the sales manager). Another alternative is to change the foreign key to .NULL. or some other value that indicates that the parent records have been removed. Finally, there is one issue that referential integrity and orphan records fail to address: the case in which a parent without children is meaningless—a purchase order or invoice without line items is a good example. All of these issues can be addressed through properly crafted code that is executed in response to a trigger.

Remember, too, that no rule says that there is anything inherently wrong with orphan records. Whether orphan records are acceptable or not can be decided only within the context of a particular database design. For instance, Microsoft SQL Server has a feature called "Declarative Referential Integrity," in which each declared relation cascades deletions and updates, and restricts insertions. This is a shotgun approach, and *does* imply that orphan records are to be avoided. This is not necessarily the case. The best example of the permissibility of orphan records is a codes table. A codes table is a parent table, and the tables that use those codes are the child tables. If a code field is a required field in the child table, then putting a restriction on the insertion of the child records will enforce this. However, if the code field is not required, then there should be no restriction on the insertion; orphan child records are permitted.

Now that we have some idea of what referential integrity is all about, let's take a look at the sample database in the \SAS\LocalData\ folder of the download files.

Figure 2 shows all of the table relations along with their associated referential integrity rules.

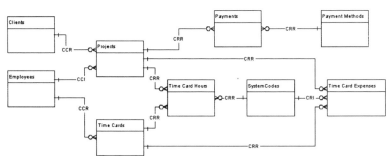

Figure 2. *Relations and referential integrity rules from \SAS\LocalData\Time and Billing.DBC. Rules are stated in Update/Delete/Insert order and indicate* C̲*ascade,* R̲*estrict or* I̲*gnore.*

The referential integrity rules for each relation are shown in **Figure 2**. The first letter indicates the rule for updates, the second for deletions, and the third for insertions. For example, the rules for the relation between employees and time_cards is "CCR", indicating that changes (updates) to the primary key of the employee record are cascaded to the time_cards table, preserving the link. Deletion of an employee record is cascaded to related records in the time_cards table, and inserts to the time_cards table are restricted to only records that have a corresponding employee record.

Contrast the deletion rule between the employees table and the time_cards table, with that between the time_cards table and the time_card_hours table. Deletions in employees are cascaded to time_cards, but deletions in time_cards are *restricted* if corresponding records exist in time_card_hours. Note that insertions to the time_card_hours table are restricted and prohibited unless a parent record exists in the projects table. Thus, the existence of a time_card_hours record implies that some work has been done on a project, and deletion of a record in the time_card_hours table could result in the loss of a record of billable hours on a current project. Thus, the rule permits removal of an employee, and will automatically delete the employee's time_card records. However, time_card records cannot be deleted if billable hours are associated with the time_card. The end result of this set of rules is that the delete trigger on the employee table should succeed as long as there are no billable hours on one of the employee's time cards, but fail if there are billable hours associated with one of his time cards.

Consider one more example.

The rules on the relation between systemCodes and time_card_expenses prohibits deletion of a systemCode record if its code is in use in the time_card_expenses table. However, an expense may be incurred for which there exists (as yet) no expense code, so insertion of a time_card_expenses record is permitted, even though there may be no corresponding record in the systemCodes table. Thus, the user can enter an expense record without having to provide an expense code. The presence of a memo field would allow the user to log an unusual or one-time expense in a timely fashion without having to create a new expense code.

Implementing referential integrity rules

In the Visual FoxPro Database Container (the .DBC file), the referential integrity rules are stored in a field called "RIINFO", using the same three-character code used in Figure 2, which indicates the rules to be enforced on updates, deletions and insertions. If you open the sample \SAS\LocalData\Time and Billing.DBC as a table and browse it, you will see that all of the RIINFO fields are empty except for those records whose object type is "Relation." It is possible to manipulate this field directly, but it isn't convenient. Note that the name of the child table in the relation is found by referring to the record with the objectid indicated by the parentid field of the relation record. Even worse, the parent table's name is buried in the binary data in the Property field of the .DBC! Not really optimal for setting these values.

Note, too, that setting these values only indicates the rules that you would *like* to have enforced, but does nothing (by themselves) to *enforce* these rules. The RIINFO field in the .DBC is simply a convenient repository for the rules that we want to enforce.

Because this sample database uses surrogate primary and foreign keys, we could easily indicate "Ignore" for all updates. This is because the user never sees the primary key field in the application, and therefore has no opportunity to change it; nor is there any reason to want to change any of the primary keys. They have no meaning in and of themselves, which is why they're called "surrogate." (See Chapter 4 for more information.) The user can change the employee number (which is not a primary key) without having to worry about changing its value in any child tables, because the employee number (not the employee ID) doesn't appear in any child tables. However, I've included both cascade and restrict rules on updates for demonstration purposes. It's kinda neat to browse the employee and time_cards tables at the same time, and watch the employee ID change in the time_cards table in response to changing it in the employee table!

The VFP Referential Integrity Builder

Microsoft includes, as part of the Visual FoxPro package, a Referential Integrity Builder that both allows you to manipulate the values in the RIINFO field, and from these values, generate referential integrity code that is stored in the stored procedures of the database. The good news: the RI code generated by this utility works pretty well. The bad news is that there's no way to set the RIINFO field values *without* generating the RI code, and the code that the RI builder generates is so voluminous and verbose that it's very difficult to trace or understand. This code can (in fairly complex systems) generate an object file that exceeds the Visual FoxPro limit of 64K on compiled program modules. A project I'm currently working on has more than 270 relations—as a result of this and the fact that RI rules were established on deletions and insertions of all tables, the builder-generated RI code did indeed hit this limit.

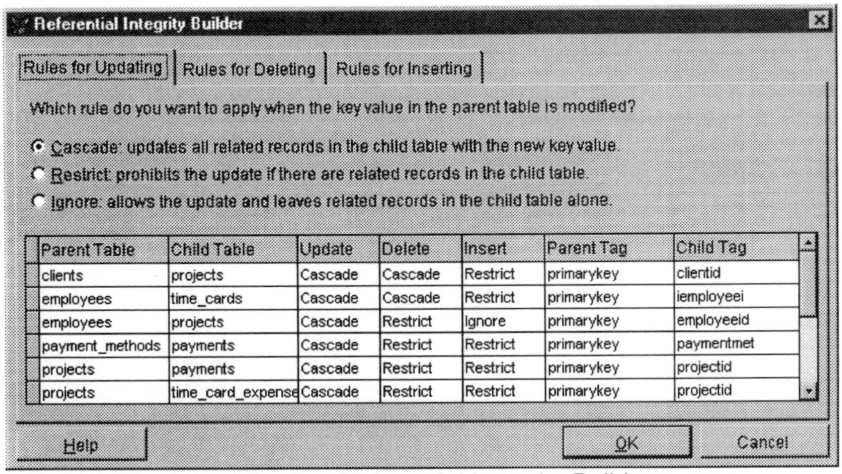
Referential Integrity Builder
Rules for Updating
Rules for Deleting
Rules for Inserting
Which rule do you want to apply when the key value in the parent table is modified?
Cascade: updates all related records in the child table with the new key value.
Restrict: prohibits the update if there are related records in the child table.
Ignore: allows the update and leaves related records in the child table alone.
Parent Table | Child Table | Update | Delete | Insert | Parent Tag | Child Tag
clients | projects | Cascade | Cascade | Restrict | primarykey | clientid
employees | time_cards | Cascade | Cascade | Restrict | primarykey | iemployeei
employees | projects | Cascade | Restrict | Ignore | primarykey | employeeid
payment_methods | payments | Cascade | Restrict | Restrict | primarykey | paymentmet
projects | payments | Cascade | Restrict | Restrict | primarykey | projectid
projects | time_card_expense | Cascade | Restrict | Restrict | primarykey | projectid
Help
OK
Cancel

Figure 3. The Visual FoxPro Referential Integrity Builder

In Visual FoxPro 3.0, a limitation on the RI builder required that it couldn't handle compound primary or foreign keys—that is, keys that were determined by the values of more than one field, as in cInvoice + cCust_ID or cPart + PADL(LTRIM(STR(iLine_No)),10). This was corrected in Visual FoxPro 5.0, but to be honest I've long had a strong aversion to compound primary and foreign keys (that's *keys*, not *indexes*). Since my adoption of integer surrogate keys, this limitation became even less of a concern.

The only remaining problem with the RI builder-generated code, as far as I'm concerned, is that many developers are forced to accept its efficacy on faith, or if they have the patience, they must test the code repeatedly, and verify empirically that it indeed works as it's supposed to. Given the complexity that can exist in even a fairly simple relational database model, it isn't unusual to be confronted unexpectedly with a failed trigger. Until you become comfortable with your own RI rules and the code that implements them, you'll find yourself tracing the RI code to find out what trigger is failing and why. If you do this repeatedly (as I have) with the RI builder-generated code, you'll eventually come to have a high degree of confidence in its operation.

However, many developers will take one look at the RI builder-generated code and say (with a great deal of justification), "I don't have time to figure out how this works, and determine if it works, and I'm not going to make my users/clients test this stuff!"

Sadly, referential integrity code does *not* have to be this ugly.

Referential integrity logic

If we are to consider only the five different situations that basic RI logic needs to handle, the logic is extremely simple, as shown in Table 2.

Table 2. *Basic referential integrity logic.*

Case	Action
Cascaded Update	Change the foreign key value in the child table from its present value to the new value just established for the parent table's primary key
Restricted Update	Check to see if there are any child records, and if so, prohibit the update
Cascaded Delete	Delete all child records with a foreign key value matching the primary key value of the parent record
Restricted Delete	Check to see if there are any child records, and if so, prohibit the deletion
Restricted Insert	Check to see if there is a record in the parent table whose primary key value is the same as the foreign key value for the record being inserted. If there is, allow the insert, if not, prohibit the insert

Using a product like Visual FoxPro, we have two basic choices on how to implement this logic.

We can (as the RI builder-generated code does) rely on Xbase commands and procedural coding to set the appropriate indexes, establish the key values of the tables being modified, SEEK the values of interest in the related tables, and take the appropriate actions. As an alternative, we can take advantage of the more powerful and concise SQL techniques that we have at our disposal.

> *While Microsoft SQL Server, as mentioned previously, provides a facility for "Declarative" referential integrity, if you need more control over how RI rules are applied, you must write trigger code that looks suspiciously like what you'll see in this chapter. Because the only way to modify the data in a SQL database is via SQL commands, there is no option to use Xbase syntax. However, as you can see from the code shown in this chapter, SQL makes this type of code much simpler, makes it easier to follow and debug, and requires a lot less typing! I've often wondered why the RI builder uses procedural Xbase code to do the job. Considering that this tool was created for VFP 3.0, it's likely that a decision was made to go for tried-and-true techniques rather than rely on SQL commands that were newly introduced with VFP 3.0.*

Before looking at how we can accomplish this, let's examine a couple of issues that the RI builder-generated code deals with, and see if we can't simplify this part of our implementation.

Of the five different types of procedures that we'll need to perform the five different cases listed above, only two of them involve modifying data – The operations that implement cascading rules. Operations that implement restriction rules do not modify any data outside the table that is currently firing a trigger.

When considering the cascading operations, there are two important things that need to be accomplished. We need to be able to "undo" anything that is done. A cascaded change implies the possibility of a change in table A cascading to table B. The change in B cascades to table C. However, there is no guarantee that *every* relation in such a chain has a cascading rule. If table C has a child table D, and the relation between tables C and D carries a restrictive rule, then updating or deleting records in table C would fail (it has child records in D and therefore prohibits the change). At this point, related records in table B have already been changed to reflect the change made to table A. What if the cascaded change between B and C fails because of the restrictive rule between C and D? Another possible scenario is if table A is related to two child tables, B1 and B2. There is a cascading rule between A and B1, but a restrictive rule between A and B2. It can happen that the cascade between A and B1 occurs first, but table B2 has child records that cause the trigger to fail.

In either of these scenarios, do we go back and "undo" the change made to the tables already modified as a result of a cascading rule? We sure do, and in fact Visual FoxPro has this neat thing called a TRANSACTION that allows us to very easily do just that.

A table is often a child of some tables and a parent to others. Because of this, we can never be certain whether the trigger is firing because the user is making a change to a table, or whether a table is being modified in response to a trigger firing on a parent table. Because it's important for all cascading operations to be wrapped in a single transaction, only the code fired by the first trigger in a chain reaction of triggers needs to BEGIN TRANSACTION, END TRANSACTION if the cascades are successful, and ROLLBACK if any of the triggers fails. Fortunately, someone at Microsoft anticipated this need and provided the _TRIGGERLEVEL system memory variable that can be used to determine when we are in a "top-level" trigger, and not someplace else further down the chain of triggers. _TRIGGERLEVEL is 0 when trigger code is not executing, 1 when the first level trigger is executing, and increments by 1 for each subsequent trigger that is fired.

The other, related issue that we need to address with regard to cascading RI functions is that our top-level function needs to determine whether some other RI function caused a trigger to fail, so it knows whether to END TRANSACTION or ROLLBACK. The way in which a UDF called by a trigger "fails" is to return a value of .F. However, the RI code we write doesn't call a UDF (which would allow it to check the value returned by the UDF), it simply performs the appropriate modifications to a child table. As you might expect, the failure of a trigger puts Visual FoxPro into an error condition. Thus, by simply executing a command that will cause a private memory variable to be set in the event of an error, we can detect a failure of another trigger, or indeed, any other type of error that occurs as a result of the execution of our trigger code.

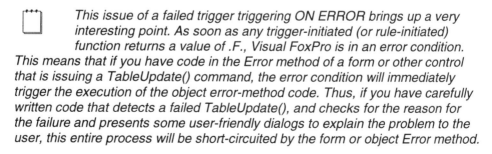

This issue of a failed trigger triggering ON ERROR brings up a very interesting point. As soon as any trigger-initiated (or rule-initiated) function returns a value of .F., Visual FoxPro is in an error condition. This means that if you have code in the Error method of a form or other control that is issuing a TableUpdate() command, the error condition will immediately trigger the execution of the object error-method code. Thus, if you have carefully written code that detects a failed TableUpdate(), and checks for the reason for the failure and presents some user-friendly dialogs to explain the problem to the user, this entire process will be short-circuited by the form or object Error method.

If you examine the RI builder-generated code, you'll see that this business of setting the ON ERROR and beginning a transaction is performed for all RI procedures, not just those involving cascading changes. This isn't necessary for restricted changes. A change is either restricted at the top-level trigger code, in which case there is no need to detect an error at a subsequent trigger level; or the current trigger was initiated by a cascading change at a higher trigger level. Therefore, only cascading code needs to take responsibility for wrapping things in a transaction, and checking for errors further up the line.

Algorithms for cascading and restricting changes

Let's put together all of the ideas we've discussed so far, using some pseudo-code to get a feel for how we will implement our referential integrity rules. **Listing 6-2** shows the pseudo-code for a cascading change, and illustrates how the top-level call wraps subsequent triggers in a transaction and can detect if some other trigger fails. **Listing 6-3** shows the steps in restricting a change, depending on the presence or absence of related records.

Listing 6-2. Pseudo-code for a cascading RI function.

```
Check if _TRIGGERLEVEL is 1
   Save old ON ERROR setting
   Tell ON ERROR to set a private memvar .T.
   BEGIN TRANSACTION
Determine primary key value for record being changed
Perform necessary action on child table
Check again if _TRIGGERLEVEL is 1
   Check to see if our private error memvar is .T.
      ROLLBACK
   Else
      END TRANSACTION
   Restore old ON ERROR
RETURN .T. as long as no error occurred
```

Listing 6-3. Pseudo-code for a restricting RI function.

```
Determine value of key field for modified record
Check for matching records in the related table
Set the return value depending on the presence or absence of related records
RETURN the return value
```

The "perform necessary action" referred to in Listing 6-2 is either a DELETE-SQL command or an UPDATE-SQL command, depending on whether we are cascading a delete or an update.

In Listing 6-3 the "matching records" are either child records in the case of a restricted DELETE or UPDATE, or parent records in the case of a restricted INSERT. The presence or absence of matching records is accomplished by issuing a SELECT-SQL command that counts the related records. The return value is .T. if no related records are found on a restricted DELETE or UPDATE, but .F. if no related records are found on a restricted insert.

Before proceeding with closer examination of the actual code, let's look at the information that the RI functions need to perform. In the RI builder-generated code, this information is hard-coded, which requires each RI rule to be implemented as a separate code block. However, you'll note that the RI builder code repeats the same pattern of commands over and over, and that the information needed to create each code block is:

- The name of the parent table
- The name of the child table
- The name of the parent's primary key field
- The name of the child's foreign key field

Could we write a single reusable block of code for each of the five RI situations, and simply pass these four pieces of information as arguments? We could, indeed. Imagine for a moment that we have an array that contains not only the four pieces of information listed above for each relation in the database, but also the type of rules to apply to each of the three different types of triggers. If we know what table is being modified, and how it's being modified, we could use this array as a lookup to determine which function to call and what arguments to pass.

The whole enchilada - a universal referential integrity function

As mentioned in the previous section, we need several pieces of information before we can hope to act appropriately in response to a trigger.

It's easy to determine the table being modified, because we know that a trigger is being executed, so the table being modified is open in the currently selected work area. We can determine the table name by using CURSORGETPROP("SourceName") so we don't need to be confused by aliases. However, it's trickier to determine what kind of modification is being made.

I am grateful to Jim Duffy of TakeNote Computer Consulting for asking a very interesting question awhile back on CompuServe's VFOX forum. Jim asked if there was any way to determine, within a piece of trigger code, what trigger was being fired. I'm *extremely* grateful to Michael Colbert of Intelligent Computer Solutions, who, after a bunch of us dummies replied to Jim with "Duh, I don't think you can do that, Jim," came back with a supremely elegant solution to the problem. Michael figured out that because GETFLDSTATE() works within trigger code even if the table isn't buffered, you can use this to figure out what trigger is being fired. If the record is DELETED() and GETFLDSTATE() indicates that the deletion flag has changed, a delete trigger is firing. If GETFLDSTATE() indicates that the deletion flag has changed, but the record is *not* DELETED(), then an insert trigger is firing. If there are one or more 2's in the string returned by GETFLDSTATE(-1), then the record is being modified and an update trigger is firing. If there are 3's and/or 4's in the string returned by GETFLDSTATE(-1), then we're dealing with a new record, and an insert trigger is being fired. What could be simpler?

So, one last piece of pseudo-code and we'll take a look at the real thing. **Listing 6-4** represents the function (yes, a single function) that is specified for every update, delete and insert trigger for every table in the system.

Listing 6-4*. Pseudo-code for a universal RI function.*

```
Determine whose trigger code is being fired
Determine what kind of trigger is being fired
```

```
Establish a lookup array with referential integrity specifications
Based on the table, and the type of trigger, search the lookup array
Determine from the lookup array if an RI rule is to be enforced
Call the appropriate RI function, passing the necessary 4 values from the
lookup array
Return the value returned by the RI function
```

Examination of this pseudo-code should make it obvious that the only thing that's going to change in this function is the array referred to in the third line. If we can establish an easy way to set up this array, we'll be much closer to having a reliable, maintainable, and most of all *understandable* and *verifiable* referential integrity system. There are many times when a trigger will fail unexpectedly, and you'll find yourself tracing this code to make sure it's working right. There are so few lines involved that doing so won't be much of a chore. The RI builder-generated code is such a convoluted mess that you need the patience of Job to trace it through much more than a single level of triggers.

Listing 6-5 shows the NewRI() function as implemented in the sample database for this chapter, with an abbreviated version of the lookup array.

Listing 6-5. The NewRI() universal referential integrity function.

```
FUNCTION NewRI()
  LOCAL lcRecordState, ;
    lcTriggerType, ;
    lcTable, ;
    llRetVal, ;
    lcParentKey, ;
    lcChildKey, ;
    lnRelations, ;
    i
  LOCAL ARRAY laRelations[1]

  #DEFINE CHILDCOL 1
  #DEFINE PARENTCOL 2
  #DEFINE CHILDKEYCOL 3
  #DEFINE PARENTKEYCOL 4
  #DEFINE UPDATECOL 5
  #DEFINE DELETECOL 6
  #DEFINE INSERTCOL 7

  lcTable = CURSORGETPROP("SourceName")
  * Determine what type of trigger is firing
  lcRecordState = GETFLDSTATE(-1)
  DO CASE
    CASE LEFT(lcRecordState,1) = "2" AND DELETED()
      lcTriggerType = "DELETE"
    CASE LEFT(lcRecordState,1) = "2" AND ! DELETED()
      lcTriggerType = "INSERT"
    CASE "3" $ lcRecordState OR "4" $ lcRecordState
      lcTriggerType = "INSERT"
    CASE "2" $ lcRecordState
      lcTriggerType = "UPDATE"
  ENDCASE

*** Lookup Array - RI Specifications *************************************
  lnRelations = 1
```

```
    DIMENSION laRelations[1,7]
    laRelations[1, CHILDCOL]     = 'TIME_CARDS'
    laRelations[1, PARENTCOL]    = 'EMPLOYEES'
    laRelations[1, CHILDKEYCOL]  = 'IEMPLOYEEID'
    laRelations[1, PARENTKEYCOL] = 'IEMPLOYEEID'
    laRelations[1, UPDATECOL]    = 'C'
    laRelations[1, DELETECOL]    = 'C'
    laRelations[1, INSERTCOL]    = 'R'
*** Lookup Array - RI Specifications ************************************

*!*       Find the table whose trigger is firing in the
*!*       lookup array, and if there is a rule associated
*!*       with this trigger for this table, call the
*!*       appropriate RI function
*!*       llRetVal = .T.
    DO CASE
      CASE lcTriggerType = "INSERT"
        FOR i = 1 TO lnRelations
          IF laRelations[i,CHILDCOL] = lcTable ;
             AND laRelations[i,INSERTCOL] = "R"
            lcParentKey = laRelations[i,PARENTCOL] + "." + ;
               laRelations[i,PARENTKEYCOL]
            lcChildKey = laRelations[i,CHILDCOL] + "." + ;
               laRelations[i,CHILDKEYCOL]
            llRetVal = ;
               Restrict_Insert(laRelations[i,PARENTCOL], ;
                  laRelations[i,CHILDCOL],lcParentKey,lcChildKey)
          ENDIF
          IF ! llRetVal
            EXIT
          ENDIF
        ENDFOR
      CASE lcTriggerType = "DELETE"
        FOR i = 1 TO lnRelations
          DO CASE
            CASE laRelations[i,PARENTCOL] = lcTable ;
               AND laRelations[i,DELETECOL] = "C"
              lcParentKey = laRelations[i,PARENTCOL] + "." + ;
                 laRelations[i,PARENTKEYCOL]
              lcChildKey = laRelations[i,CHILDCOL] + "." + ;
                 laRelations[i,CHILDKEYCOL]
              llRetVal = ;
                 Cascade_Delete(laRelations[i,PARENTCOL], ;
                    laRelations[i,CHILDCOL],lcParentKey,lcChildKey)
            CASE laRelations[i,PARENTCOL] = lcTable ;
               AND laRelations[i,DELETECOL] = "R"
              lcParentKey = laRelations[i,PARENTCOL] + "." + ;
                 laRelations[i,PARENTKEYCOL]
              lcChildKey = laRelations[i,CHILDCOL] + "." + ;
                 laRelations[i,CHILDKEYCOL]
              llRetVal = ;
                 Restrict_Delete(laRelations[i,PARENTCOL], ;
                    laRelations[i,CHILDCOL],lcParentKey,lcChildKey)
          ENDCASE
          IF ! llRetVal
            EXIT
          ENDIF
        ENDFOR
      CASE lcTriggerType = "UPDATE"
```

```
      FOR i = 1 TO lnRelations
        DO CASE
          CASE laRelations[i,PARENTCOL] = lcTable ;
              AND laRelations[i,UPDATECOL] = "C"
            lcParentKey = laRelations[i,PARENTCOL] + "." + ;
                laRelations[i,PARENTKEYCOL]
            lcChildKey = laRelations[i,CHILDCOL] + "." + ;
                laRelations[i,CHILDKEYCOL]
            llRetVal = ;
                Cascade_Update(laRelations[i,PARENTCOL], ;
                    laRelations[i,CHILDCOL],lcParentKey,lcChildKey)
          CASE laRelations[i,PARENTCOL] = lcTable ;
              AND laRelations[i,UPDATECOL] = "R"
            lcParentKey = laRelations[i,PARENTCOL] + "." + ;
                laRelations[i,PARENTKEYCOL]
            lcChildKey = laRelations[i,CHILDCOL] + "." + ;
                laRelations[i,CHILDKEYCOL]
            llRetVal = ;
                Restrict_Update(laRelations[i,PARENTCOL], ;
                    laRelations[i,CHILDCOL],lcParentKey,lcChildKey)
        ENDCASE
        IF ! llRetVal
          EXIT
        ENDIF
      ENDFOR
  ENDCASE
  RETURN llRetVal
ENDFUNC

* Cascading Update Function
FUNCTION Cascade_Update(tcParentTable,tcChildTable,tcParentKey,tcChildKey)
  LOCAL llRetVal, ;
    lcOldError, ;
    luKey, ;
    luNewKey
  IF _TRIGGERLEVEL = 1
    RELEASE plError
    PUBLIC plError
    lcOldError = ON("ERROR")
    ON ERROR plError = .T.
    BEGIN TRANSACTION
  ENDIF
  luKey = OLDVAL(tcParentKey)
  luNewKey = EVALUATE(tcParentKey)
  UPDATE (tcChildTable) SET &tcChildKey = luNewKey WHERE &tcChildKey = luKey
  IF _TRIGGERLEVEL = 1
    IF plError
      ROLLBACK
    ELSE
      END TRANSACTION
    ENDIF
    ON ERROR &lcOldError
  ENDIF
  llRetVal = ! plError
  RETURN llRetVal
ENDFUNC

* Cascading Delete Function
FUNCTION Cascade_Delete(tcParentTable,tcChildTable,tcParentKey,tcChildKey)
```

```
   LOCAL llRetVal, ;
     lcOldError, ;
     luKey
   IF _TRIGGERLEVEL = 1
     RELEASE plError
     PUBLIC plError
     lcOldError = ON("ERROR")
     ON ERROR plError = .T.
     BEGIN TRANSACTION
   ENDIF
   luKey = EVALUATE(tcParentKey)
   DELETE FROM (tcChildTable) WHERE &tcChildKey = luKey
   IF _TRIGGERLEVEL = 1
     IF plError
       ROLLBACK
     ELSE
       END TRANSACTION
     ENDIF
     ON ERROR &lcOldError
   ENDIF
   llRetVal = ! plError
   RETURN llRetVal
ENDFUNC

* Restricting Delete Function
FUNCTION Restrict_Delete(tcParentTable,tcChildTable,tcParentKey,tcChildKey)
   LOCAL llRetVal, ;
     luKey
   LOCAL ARRAY laCount[1]
   luKey = EVALUATE(tcParentKey)
   SELECT COUNT(*) ;
     FROM (tcChildTable) ;
     WHERE &tcChildKey == luKey ;
       AND ! DELETED(tcChildTable) ;
     INTO ARRAY laCount
   IF laCount > 0
     llRetVal = .F.
   ELSE
     llRetVal = .T.
   ENDIF
   RETURN llRetVal
ENDFUNC

* Restricting Update Function
FUNCTION Restrict_Update(tcParentTable,tcChildTable,tcParentKey,tcChildKey)
   LOCAL llRetVal, ;
     luKey
   LOCAL ARRAY laCount[1]
   luKey = OLDVAL(tcParentKey)
   SELECT COUNT(*) ;
     FROM (tcChildTable) ;
     WHERE &tcChildKey == luKey ;
       AND ! DELETED(tcChildTable) ;
     INTO ARRAY laCount
   IF laCount > 0
     llRetVal = .F.
   ELSE
     llRetVal = .T.
   ENDIF
```

```
   RETURN llRetVal
ENDFUNC

* Restricting Insert Function
FUNCTION Restrict_Insert(tcParentTable,tcChildTable,tcParentKey,tcChildKey)
   LOCAL llRetVal, ;
     luKey
   LOCAL ARRAY laCount[1]
   luKey = EVALUATE(tcChildKey)
   SELECT COUNT(*) ;
     FROM (tcParentTable) ;
     WHERE &tcParentKey == luKey ;
       AND ! DELETED(tcChildTable) ;
     INTO ARRAY laCount
   IF laCount = 0
     llRetVal = .F.
   ELSE
     llRetVal = .T.
   ENDIF
   RETURN llRetVal
ENDFUNC
```

I think that you'll find most of the foregoing code straightforward and self-documenting. I'd like to call your attention to one thing, however: the use of the OLDVAL() function in the Cascade_Update() function. This allows the field's previous value to be used in the UPDATE...FOR command to find the child records that still have the *old* foreign key value, and change them to the new one.

In case you're counting, the above listing accomplishes its task in 219 lines of code, including comments and white space. There is only one relation in the preceding listing for the specifications array, but each additional relation adds only seven lines of code (see the stored procedures for \SAS\LocalData\Time and Billing.DBC). Thus, for the 11 relations in this system, this code would require 289 lines of code. Compare this to the 2,425 lines of code that the RI builder creates to do the same job!

I don't mean to criticize the RI builder. It's very easy to use; the code it produces does the job and executes very quickly. However, if we can make this feature a little more transparent, then we're more confident of being able to understand how it works, and modify or maintain it if and when we need to. To be fair, the code created by the RI builder does something that the NewRI() function does not—it meticulously closes all tables opened in the process of execution. However, considering how many developers follow the practice of opening *all* tables at application startup, and given the reduced need to "clean up" provided by private data sessions, I felt that I could get away with this slight sloppiness.

If you're wondering whether there's an easy way to maintain the RI rules in the DBC without using the RI builder, and if there's an easy way to establish the laRelations[] array used in the NewRI() function, you'll find a form called EditRI.SCX located in \SAS\Tools\ of the download files. This form allows you to select a database, examine and modify the RI rules, and save those rules back to the database. If, before you close the form, you select the check box that reads "Rules to clipboard on close," you'll discover that the "DIMENSION laRelations" command, the "nRelations=" line and the entire block of code that assigns all of the RI rules to the laRelations lookup array has been copied to the clipboard, ready for pasting into the NewRI() function.

Functions that are still lacking from this tool (as of this writing) include the ability to stuff all RI code into the stored procedures, and to set the triggers for all tables to call the NewRI() function. These two tasks must still be performed manually.

All emptors be caveat!!

First, because this code was designed to be used on a database that uses non-compound integer surrogate keys, it won't work on a database that uses compound primary and foreign keys, nor will it work on a database that uses key expressions on other than simply the field name. Therefore, if you have a primary or foreign key based on an expression that uses a function like UPPER(), VAL(), PADR(), and so forth, this RI code won't work. To understand why, consider just the following line of code:

```
UPDATE (tcChildTable) SET &tcChildKey = luNewKey WHERE &tcChildKey = luKey
```

Note that if the child table's foreign key expression is cOrder_ID + cPart_No, the SET clause will become SET cOrder_ID + cPart_No = luNewKey, which clearly will trigger an error.

Second, please be aware that this code has been developed for a production application that (as of this writing) is in the middle of development, and has been subjected (at best) to only alpha testing. Use at your own risk. No warranties express or implied. No bailment created. Your mileage may vary. Void where prohibited. Don't take with other medications without consulting your doctor or pharmacist.

Other stuff to do with triggers

As with rules, which are primarily intended to enforce domain constraints, your own needs and creativity will determine how many other things you can do with triggers.

One of the neatest things to do with a trigger, other than enforcing RI rules, is to create an audit trail. While enforcing a referential integrity rule in response to an update is intended to deal with changes to the primary key field's value, keep in mind that *any* change to a record causes the update trigger to fire.

Also, no rule says you can't execute more than one function in response to a trigger. You could add a trigger to a table like this:

```
CREATE TRIGGER ON time_cards FOR UPDATE AS NewRI() AND Audit_Time_Cards()
CREATE TRIGGER ON time_cards FOR INSERT AS NewRI() AND Audit_Time_Cards()
```

The AS clause specifies a logical *expression*, and therefore can include a collection of user-defined functions joined by AND and OR operators.

Assuming that the audit_time_cards table has an additional primary key field, the Audit_Time_Cards() function could look something like this:

```
SCATTER MEMVAR MEMO
m.iTCAudit_ID = NewID("AUDIT_TIME_CARDS")
INSERT INTO audit_time_cards FROM MEMVAR
```

You could have timestamp and user ID fields in the time_cards table. If these fields are automatically maintained (like maybe using a row-level rule?), then the audit_time_cards table will contain a complete record of every change that has ever been made to the time_cards table, showing the date and time the change was made, and who made the change! You could get a little fancier, saving instead the name of any fields that were changed, together with their old values and current values (remember OLDVAL() always works in trigger code!). Entire articles and chapters of books have been written about how to implement audit trails. With intelligent use of the tools now available to us, we can implement a very sophisticated audit trail with just a few lines of code that works every time, no matter how many forms we add to the system, and no matter how many new developers get involved with the project. No one has to remember to implement this function—it happens automatically.

The code fired by delete triggers to enforce referential integrity determines success or failure of the trigger, depending simply on the presence or absence of child records. However, sometimes the issue isn't the *presence* of child records, but their *state,* that determines whether the trigger should succeed or fail. In the foregoing example, an update trigger calls two functions, one of which will always return .T. (the audit_time_cards() function). Thus, this function performs some action while the NewRI() function actually determines the success or failure of the trigger. We could also specify two (or more) different functions, all of which can return either a .T. or .F. As a result, if two or more functions joined by AND are specified as the trigger rule, all must "OK" the update, delete or insert, otherwise the trigger fails and the action is prohibited.

Consider a customer table whose relation with the orders table has a cascade delete rule. However, we don't want to delete any orders that are "open"—that is, not cancelled and not paid. We could specify the delete trigger as:

```
CREATE TRIGGER ON orders FOR DELETE AS Closed_Order() AND NewRI()
```

In this example, the NewRI() function would handle the cascading of the deletion to the order detail table, but only if Closed_Order returns .T. Closed_Order() might look something like this:

```
FUNCTION Closed_Order()
   LOCAL llRetVal
   IF INLIST(cStatus,"P","X") && Paid or cancelled
      llRetVal = .T.
   ELSE
      llRetVal = .F.
   ENDIF
   RETURN llRetVal
ENDFUNC
```

Summary

As with any other powerful feature in Visual FoxPro, rules, triggers and referential integrity can hose you pretty quick if you use them indiscriminately or without much forethought. However, they can, if carefully and thoughtfully employed, make the development process easier. Every process implemented at the engine level is one less thing you have to implement elsewhere in the application. Some things are quite gnarly to implement at the UI level, but become a walk in the park if implemented using a rule or trigger.

Chapter 7
Data Manipulation Classes

Visual FoxPro is a database management language, and we use it to build data-centric applications. Our applications manipulate data in many different ways. We present data for editing and/or review on screen, we produce reports on paper or on screen, we even send data or information over phone lines through fax machines and the Internet. Manipulating data is what we do. Is there any way to reduce the effort needed to manage this data? Can we create reusable data-manipulation objects so we write code only once and use it in various places? These are some of the questions that this chapter will address.

Common data manipulation requirements

There is a common set of things that we need to do with data and the tables and views that hold it. The code for these common operations can be designed into our classes. Once we design these behaviors into our classes, they'll automatically be included in the objects we use in our applications. The whole idea is to relegate these responsibilities to our classes so that we don't need to concern ourselves with them again. We can just call on the behaviors and let the class code handle them for us. In this section of the chapter we will look at the various behaviors of concern. In later sections we will construct classes that handle these behaviors for us.

So what is included in this list of behaviors? The following sections will discuss each of these behaviors in detail:

* Opening and closing tables and views
* Detecting changes to data
* Committing or canceling changes to data
* Navigating through data
* Providing data source independence

Opening and closing tables and views

In procedural applications, one central procedure usually opened and/or closed a table for us. This gave us the ability to centralize problems, such as deciding which directory of data to use and what options to include on the USE command line. Once it was written, we would call this procedure and pass it the name of the table we wanted to open.

With Visual FoxPro, we initially seem to have given up this ability. If we are using the form designer and its data environment, we find out that the path to the database for each table is hard-coded into the form's data environment. However, if we create our own classes for managing data, we can provide the functionality to alter the path to the database as well as provide any options we might want regarding the opening of a data source. The same things are true of closing a data source.

Detecting changes to data

Detecting when some aspect of the data has changed would allow us to update the sources only if they needed to be updated. This can improve the performance of our systems. It takes time to write to a file; if we can limit that writing to when changes occur, we can reduce the overhead in our applications.

Visual FoxPro gives us the ability, in the language, to check for changes to the data. It can be as easy as using a combination of GetNextModified() and GetFldState(). We could probably do this in just a few lines of code. However, if we need those few lines of code everywhere, we might update a table or view which would add up to a lot of lines of code. By using data classes, we can centralize this responsibility and forget about it.

Committing or canceling changes to data

Every form should give the user the option of accepting or rejecting edits, and leaving the data unchanged. In Visual FoxPro, the TableUpdate() and TableRevert() functions handle this for us. Although these two functions are fairly simple, we don't want to rewrite them for every table we need to manage. By using data management classes, we can centralize this code and reuse it as needed.

Navigating through data

Navigation through data can be simple or complex, depending on the data being presented. Also, there is the issue of views, both local and remote; and how we implement navigation with those is quite different from the way we would do it when using tables directly.

In our forms, we don't want to write complex code to handle all the possibilities. It is much better to use a data manager class that is programmed to do the necessary things and then selectively instantiate the correct data manager for the situation. By using good object-oriented design principles, we can make these data managers interchangeable, so that the code in our form is the same regardless of which data manager we use. If we have a data situation where navigation actions are not applicable, then those methods of our data manager would be empty and would faithfully do nothing if called.

Providing data source independence

As mentioned in the previous section, our data can take many different forms. We can use tables directly, we can use local views, or we can use remote views. We can even have systems where forms may change their data source at runtime.

We want to have consistent code for accessing data within our forms and controls, but these different data sources require that different code be executed to do various things with the data. Data manager classes can provide a consistent interface to our forms and controls, and still execute different code when those methods are called. We can have a data manager class for each type of data source we need and instantiate the appropriate one for the job at hand. For example you may have the need to deal with test data and real data in your application or you may supply tutorial data for training purposes. Using a data manager can allow you to provide for these different data sources.

Buffering Data

Before we venture into a discussion of data manipulation classes, let's take a moment to investigate the data-buffering capabilities of Visual FoxPro. To understand buffering, we can look back at our experiences with earlier versions of FoxPro. Many of us had the habit, in FoxPro 2.x, of using memory variables for editing data. This was because we wanted the ability to decide whether or not the user's changes were written to the table. The assumption, at that time, was that if we connected the data-entry screen to the fields in the table, we were directly editing the record in the table. If you ever watched the disk drive light, you'd have to conclude that this wasn't true. If the editing were truly direct to disk, then the drive light would have flashed every time the user pressed a key, but it did not. That means that FoxPro must have been working in some kind of a memory buffer.

The problem we had in FoxPro 2.x was that we weren't given any control over when and if that memory buffer would be committed to disk. We knew it would be committed sooner or later, and that was that. Visual FoxPro has given us access to control that memory buffer. We can now control when and if the memory buffer will be written to the table. This allows us the code simplicity of "direct editing" but we still have the control of selectively updating.

Visual FoxPro provides five types of buffering. The first type is *none*, which causes the data to be handled the same way it was in FoxPro 2.x. The other four provide options for buffering optimistically or pessimistically, and to buffer a single row at a time, or the entire table.

The table vs. row aspect of buffering controls the amount of pending data that will be held in the buffer for a table or view. If buffering is set to *row*, then only one record can be buffered at a time; a setting of *table* will allow multiple records to be buffered simultaneously for that table or view.

The optimistic and pessimistic options control the multi-user aspects of the data buffering. Optimistic buffering doesn't lock records while the data is being edited, and it doesn't prevent multiple users from working on the same records simultaneously. Instead, the optimistic setting locks the records when we attempt to update the table from the buffer, and it detects any logical data conflicts at that time. Pessimistic buffering works the other way. It locks the record when a user begins to edit it and won't allow any other user to begin editing until the lock is released.

By combining these two settings, table/row and optimistic/pessimistic, we get four buffering modes: Optimistic Row, Pessimistic Row, Optimistic Table, and Pessimistic Table. Add these four to the setting for no buffering at all, and we see the five buffering settings.

Which buffering mode do I use?

If we were to survey all Visual FoxPro developers, we would probably find that there is almost an even split between the optimistic and pessimistic school of thought. In fact, there is no "correct" one—if there were, Microsoft would not have given us a choice.

We need to understand clearly how the two approaches work and then use the one that is most appropriate for our requirements. **Table 1** shows a comparison of the optimistic and pessimistic options.

Table 1. *Comparison of optimistic and pessimistic buffering approaches.*

Issue	Optimistic	Pessimistic
Resource Contention	Does not hold locks at the server during editing.	Holds a lock at the server for every edited record until that record is either committed or reverted.
Conflict Detection	Potential conflicts are detected at the time of committing the record to the table.	Attempts to insure write rights by locking records before the editing is allowed to begin. There is still a possibility of a failure to update caused by other issues like network cable failure, or server crash, etc.
Programming Requirements	Update routines must sense any conflict at the time of commit and respond to them in some way.	Routines that begin an edit must sense errors generated if a record is not available and respond to that occurrence.

You can see in Table 1 that neither the optimistic nor pessimistic approach to buffering is really any better than the other. They both manage multi-user conflict issues, but they do it in different ways. Each one has its own set of requirements for our code.

The other issue related to buffering is the row vs. table setting. This one does have a "better" approach, depending on the situation. Let's first consider overall buffering. When the buffer mode is set to *row,* Visual FoxPro will allow one record to be "dirty" (meaning that the record has pending changes) at a time. To enforce this one-record limit, Visual FoxPro will attempt to update the table whenever the record pointer is moved in that work area. If you think about this, you can see that it is a potential problem. If we want buffered editing and we choose a row-buffering mode, we must ensure that no operation that ever occurs during an edit will attempt to move the record pointer in the work area of any cursor that has pending changes. If the record pointer is moved, there will be an automatic attempt to commit the changes. This automatic updating defeats the whole purpose of buffering the edit in the first place, which was for us to take control of writing or reverting the edit.

It isn't necessary to use row buffering to limit edits to one record at a time. We can limit the number of records edited in the way we program our forms. Therefore, we can use table buffering, preventing any automatic updating, and still restrict the user to editing one record at a time.

Row buffering is required in one situation: when trying to create an index on a view. If a view is table buffered and we issue an INDEX ON command, Visual FoxPro will generate an error. We cannot index a table-buffered view; therefore, it's necessary to put a view into row buffering while we create any indexes and then change it to table buffering once the indexes have been built. We can use the CursorSetProp() function to do this:

```
* Indexing a view
LOCAL lnBufferMode
SELECT TheView
```

```
lnBufferMode = CursorGetProp( "BUFFERING", "TheView" )
CursorSetProp( "BUFFERING", 3, "TheView" )
INDEX ON Name TAG Name
CursorSetProp( "BUFFERING", lnBufferMode, "TheView" )
```

Buffering is the technology in Visual FoxPro that we use to manage control of data editing for a single cursor. To coordinate updating multiple cursors, we use transactions, which are described later in this chapter.

Data manipulation classes

There are many approaches we can take to provide the functionality we are after. We can use the Visual FoxPro base classes or we can build our own classes. We can use the classes that our forms are based on and put the data-handling code in those classes. We will examine each of these approaches and see the benefits and problems associated with them.

The final decision of which approach is best will be dependent on the application we are building and its requirements. Some approaches are simpler to build but less flexible, while others are extremely flexible but require more up-front work in planning and design.

The native Visual FoxPro classes

Before we can investigate creating our own data manager classes, we need to look at the data classes that are native to Visual FoxPro. Visual FoxPro provides three base classes that directly manage data: DataEnvironment, Cursor, and Relation. Each of these classes is described in detail in the following sections.

DataEnvironment class

Visual FoxPro's DataEnvironment class is the container that manages the data for a FormSet, Form, Report, or Toolbar class. The DataEnvironment can open tables and views automatically or on command from your form code. The classes that a DataEnvironment can contain are limited to Cursor and Relation.

The following tables list the properties, events, and methods that are native to the DataEnvironment class with a description of their purpose. **Table 2** lists the properties.

Table 2. *Properties of the DataEnvironment class.*

Property Name	Purpose
AutoCloseTables	Setting this property to .T. (default) will cause the DataEnvironment to close its cursors on destruction of itself. A setting of .F. will not automatically close the cursors, and the closing must be done programmatically.
AutoOpenTables	Similar to the AutoCloseTables except that it controls the opening of the tables.
Class	Contains the name of the class that the DataEnvironment is created from.
ClassLibrary	The name of the ClassLibrary that the DataEnvironment class is contained in.
Comment	Programmer's comment text.

InitialSelectedAlias	Selects an alias associated with one of the DataEnvironment's cursors to be the initially selected work area on loading the DataEnvironment,
Name	The name of the DataEnvironment object.
OpenViews	Controls the opening of any views that may be in the DataEnvironment. Accepts one of four settings numbered from 0 to 3. 0 – Opens all views automatically, 1 – Opens only local views, 2 – Opens only remote views, and 3 – Opens no views automatically. Any views that are not opened automatically must be opened programmatically
Parent	An object reference to the parent container of the DataEnvironment. For a DataEnvironment contained within a form, the DataEnvironment's parent property would be an object reference to the form.
ParentClass	The parent class that this class inherits from.
Tag	A character property that can be used by the programmer to hold any extra data that the programmer may need.

Table 3 shows the methods of the DataEnvironment class. A few methods have been left out of this list because they are not related to the data aspects of the class: ReadExpression, ReadMethod, WriteExpression, and SaveAsClass.

***Table 3**. Methods of the DataEnvironment class.*

Method	Purpose
AddObject	Used to add an object to the DataEnvironment at runtime.
AddProperty	Used to add a property to the DataEnvironment at runtime.
CloseTables	Closes the tables and views in the data environment. Automatically called if the AutoCloseTables property is set to .T.; must be explicitly called if the AutoCloseTables property is set to .F.
NewObject	Adds an object to the DataEnvironment at runtime. The difference between this method and the AddObject method is that with AddObject the class library for the object being added must be open prior to using the AddObject. With NewObject the class library can be named in the call to NewObject thereby obviating the need to open the class library separately.
OpenTables	Opens the tables and views. Like CloseTables, it respects the setting of AutoOpenTables. If AutoOpenTables is set to .T. the OpenTables method is automatically called upon creation of the Data Environment. If AutoOpenTables is set to .F. then the OpenTables method must be called explicitly.
RemoveObject	Removes a cursor or relation object from the DataEnvironment object.

Table 4 lists the DataEnvironment's event methods.

Table 4. *Event methods of the DataEnvironment class.*

Event Method	Purpose
AfterCloseTables	Fires after the tables and/or views of the DataEnvironment have been closed. Fires after the CloseTables method finishes and before the Destroy event for the DataEnvironment. For a Form or FormSet, this event fires after the Unload of the Form or FormSet.
BeforeOpenTables	Fires just before the tables and/or views of the DataEnvironment are opened. In a Form or FormSet this event fires before the Form's or FormSet's Load event.
Destroy	Fires during the destruction of the DataEnvironment. The Destroy for the DataEnvironment fires before the Destroy of its contained objects, thereby allowing the code in the Destroy event to refer to the contained objects.
Error	Fires whenever an error occurs in the code of any of the methods or events for this object.
Init	Executes once on creation of the DataEnvironment.

The OpenTables and CloseTables methods can act like event methods when the respective Auto properties are set to .T. That is, they will run automatically during creation and destruction of the DataEnvironment object.

It is important to understand the firing order of events during the creation and destruction of the DataEnvironment. **Tables 5 and 6** show the creation order and the destruction order, respectively. Both of these tables assume that the AutoOpenTables and AutoCloseTables are set to .T. The event sequence is for a form named *form1*.

Table 5. *The sequence of events during form creation with a DataEnvironment.*

Event
form1.dataenvironment.opentables()
form1.dataenvironment.beforeopentables()
form1.load()
form1.dataenvironment.cursor1.Init()
form1.dataenvironment.Init()
form1.Init()

Table 6. *The sequence of events during form destruction with a DataEnvironment.*

Event
form1.Destroy()
form1.Unload()
form1.dataenvironment.CloseTables()
form1.dataenvironment.AfterCloseTables()
form1.dataenvironment.Destroy()
form1.dataenvironment.cursor1.Destroy()

An important thing to note in the creation sequence is that the OpenTables method is called before the BeforeOpenTables event fires. This is because the BeforeOpenTables event fires just before the tables and views are opened. Because the OpenTables method opens them, the BeforeOpenTables event will not be fired until after the OpenTables method has started. BeforeOpenTables fires only in response to an execution of the OpenTables method—either automatically as a result of the AutoOpenTables property being .T. or when the OpenTables method is called in code.

Data sessions

Visual FoxPro's concept of data sessions should not be confused with the DataEnvironment. A data session in Visual FoxPro is a set of work areas where tables and views can be opened and manipulated. Visual FoxPro starts in the command window with the default data session, which is numbered 1. Forms, formsets, reports, and toolbars can have what is called a *private data session*. When one of these objects requests a private data session from Visual FoxPro, a new, separate set of work areas is created and given a new data session number. The default data session (1) still exists, but the object with the private data session is manipulating its own set of work areas and does not affect the default or any other data session that might exist.

Using private data sessions can allow great flexibility in the options you give your users. Just as multiple users in an application each can access data in the app in their own way, private data sessions allow a user to open more than one copy of a form and work on different records in each copy simultaneously, without those forms interfering with each other.

One thing that is commonly misunderstood is the options we have in the forms, formsets, toolbars, and reports for choosing a data session. We have a choice of two - default or private. However, the choice of default does not necessarily mean that the object will participate in data session 1; it means it will participate in the data session of the object from which it was created.

To understand this, imagine that we have a form with a private data session. This form opens some tables and does some work to prepare data for a report. When we build the report, do we choose the default data session or a private one? If we give the report a private data session, it won't be able to see the tables in the form's data session, and we just set those up for the report. We might suspect that choosing the default data session is equally poor thinking, that it would use the command window's data session, but we would be wrong. Because the report is running from code inside the form, the form's data session is the default data session for that report. Therefore, if we build the report to use the default data session and then run that report from inside the form, the report will use the form's data session.

Cursor class

The Visual FoxPro cursor object is derived from the cursor class, and can be contained within a DataEnvironment object. This object controls access to a table or a view. We can use a number of properties and events associated with a cursor object to affect its nature and behavior. **Tables 7**, **8**, and **9** list and describe the properties, methods, and events respectively. Again, the ReadExpression, ReadMethod, WriteExpression, and SaveAsClass methods are not listed.

A little preface to the properties of cursor objects: Trying to change the value of any cursor property except for Order and Filter at runtime will cause an error. To change a property other than Order or Filter at runtime, you must first call the DataEnvironment's CloseTables method, then make your changes, and finally call the DataEnvironment's OpenTables method.

Remember, this means that all tables will be closed and reopened, which may take some management. We will present example code later in the chapter.

Table 7. *Properties of the cursor class.*

Property	Description
Alias	Contains the alias name for this cursor. Usually the alias name will default to the same name as the table or view that is the CursorSource for this cursor. This property can be modified to cause the cursor to have any alias name you like.
BaseClass	The name of the BaseClass, Cursor, for this object.
BufferModeOverride	This is the property that affects the buffer mode for the cursor. There are six possible settings:
	0 - No buffering at all
	1 - Use the BufferMode of the form
	2 - Pessimistic Row Buffering
	3 - Optimistic Row Buffering
	4 - Pessimistic Table Buffering
	5 - Optimistic Table Buffering
	These buffer mode settings were described earlier in this chapter. Setting 1 is ambiguous because the form can only have optimistic or pessimistic buffering set with no regard to table or row. It is suggested that a setting of 1 not be used for this property.
Class	The name of the class that this object was created from—usually Cursor, but it could be a subclass of Cursor, as we will see later.
ClassLibrary	The ClassLibrary where the class is defined.
Comment	Programmer's comments about this cursor.
CursorSource	The name of the table or view that this cursor is related to. In the case of a table in a database this will be the long table name; for free tables this will be the complete path and table name.
Database	The name of the database that the table or view is stored in. Includes the complete path.
Exclusive	Logical property that controls whether this cursor is opened exclusively or in shared mode. A value of .T. causes the cursor to be opened exclusively.
Filter	This property stores an expression that is used as a filter on the data in the cursor. For example, if we wanted to filter a cursor to show only those records where the field State had a value of "NY" we would put [State = "NY"] in this property without the square brackets. This is one of two properties that can be changed at runtime without causing an error.
Name	The name of this cursor object. Do not confuse this property with the Alias property. When you want to select the work area where this cursor is open, use Alias; when you want to manipulate this cursor object, such as modifying the Filter property, use Name.

NoDataOnLoad	This property applies only to cursors that have a view as the CursorSource. If this property is set to .T. then the view's structure will be open but no data will be obtained for the view. This can allow you to open a view without running the query that populates it. You would then need to use the Requery() function to fetch data at a later point in time. Setting up a view this way can be very helpful, especially with parameterized views. Using NoDataOnLoad true ??? Does this make sense? NoDataOnLoad true??? will prevent the dialogs asking for the parameter values from being shown to the user as the form is created. You can set the parameter values later and then Requery() the view. This can also speed up the creation of indexes on a view since you would be able to index a view that has no records, then fetch the data.
Order	This property contains the name of the index tag that is controlling the order of the view. This is the second property that you can freely change at runtime. Keep in mind, though, that changing the order on a cursor may break relations that are set, and will move the record pointer in that cursor to the first logical record.
Parent	This is an object reference to the DataEnvironment that contains this cursor object.
ParentClass	If this cursor object is derived from a subclass, this property contains the name of the parent class.
ReadOnly	This logical property controls the read-only vs. read/write status of the cursor. Setting this property to .T. will disallow any data from being written to the cursor. If you set ReadOnly to .T. for a view, either local or remote, you will not be able to use the Requery() function on that view. Your only recourse to repopulating the view will be to close it and then reopen it.
Tag	A character property that can be used by the programmer to hold any extra data that the programmer may need.

Table 8 describes the methods for a cursor object.

Table 8. Methods for the cursor object.

Method	Description
AddProperty	Allows the addition of new properties to the object at runtime.

Table 9 lists the events for the cursor object.

Table 9. Events for the cursor object.

Event Method	Description
Destroy	Fires during the destruction of the Cursor object and before the cursor is completely gone from memory.
Error	Fires whenever an error occurs in the code of the object's methods or events.
Init	Executes once on creation of the Cursor object.

So far we have cursors that are associated with tables or views and a DataEnvironment that can contain those cursors. What more do we need? Well, we need a way to establish relations between the cursors—and that is the purpose of the Relation class.

Relation class

As we examine the properties of this class, we'll see that it maps very easily to what we already know about the SET RELATION command in Visual FoxPro.

Table 10 lists the properties of the Relation class. For the sake of clarity, we have omitted describing again those properties already listed for the DataEnvironment and Cursor classes.

Table 10. Properties of the Relation class.

Property	Description
ChildAlias	The alias name for the cursor that is the target of the relation.
ChildOrder	The name of the index tag for the target of the relation.
OneToMany	Logical where a value of .T. is equivalent to the SET SKIP TO command.
ParentAlias	The alias name of the source of the relation.
RelationalExpr	The expression that the relation is based on.

As an example of using the properties of the Relation object, assume we have two cursors with the alias names of *Customer* and *Invoice*. The primary key for the Customer cursor is CustID, and the index tag name for the Invoice table that is keyed on CustID is InvCust. The following code shows the values of the Relation object's properties:

```
Relation.ChildAlias = "Invoice"
Relation.ChildOrder = "InvCust"
Relation.ParentAlias = "Customer"
Relation.RelationalExpr = "CustID"
```

Of course, if we wanted this relationship to be a one-to-many relation, we would set the OneToMany property to .T.

Subclassing the native Visual FoxPro data management classes

As with any base class in Visual FoxPro, we can subclass the data classes. The limitation is that we cannot do it visually with the class designer—it must be done in code with a program file. This isn't really a limitation on what we can do with our subclasses; it is only a limitation on how we can build them. In a subclass of these data classes, we can add new properties and methods, we can provide default code for the existing events and methods or for our new methods, and we can provide default values for the properties—both the native ones and any new ones we may have added. **Listing 7-1** shows an example of subclassing the DataEnvironment class.

Listing 7-1. An example of subclassing a DataEnvironment.

```
DEFINE CLASS deBase AS DataEnvironment
   * Set automatic opening of tables to false
   AutoOpenTables = .F.

   * Modify the Init to accept a path to the databases
   PROCEDURE Init
      LPARAMETERS pcDbcPath
      LOCAL lnCursors, laCursors(1), loObjName, kursor
      IF EMPTY( pcDbcPath )
         * Problem, the path is no good, so leave things alone
         RETURN
      ENDIF
      IF TYPE( "pcDbcPath" ) <> "C"
         * Problem, the path is the wrong data type, so leave things alone
         RETURN
      ENDIF
      * Remove all leading and trailing spaces
      pcDbcPath = ALLTRIM( pcDbcPath )
      * Make sure the path ends with a \
      * You can use VFP 6.0's new ADDBS() function here...
      pcDbcPath = ADDBS(pcDbcPath)

      * Get a list of the cursors
      lnCursors = AMEMBERS( laCursors, THIS, 2 )
      * If there aren't any, get out
      IF lnCursors = 0
         RETURN
      ENDIF
      * Now work through the cursors
      FOR EACH kursor IN laCursors
         loObjName = EVALUATE( "THIS." + kursor )
         IF loObjName.BaseClass <> "Cursor"
            LOOP
         ENDIF
         WITH loObjName
            IF NOT EMPTY( .Database)
                  * If this cursor has a database assigned
                  .Database = pcDbcPath + SUBSTR( .Database;
                     RAT( "\", .Database ) + 1 )
            ENDIF
         ENDWITH
      ENDFOR
      * Now open the cursors
      THIS.OpenTables()
   ENDPROC
ENDDEFINE
```

This example isn't really usable because there is no way to add the cursors to this DataEnvironment. Its purpose is simply to act as a base from which we will further subclass and add other things. In object-oriented design, this type of class is referred to as *abstract*—that is, a class that will never be used to create an object.

There are a few things to notice in this class definition. First, note the spelling of the variable used to refer to the cursors in our list. We used the spelling *kursor* (with a "k") to avoid using the Visual FoxPro keyword *cursor*, because it's always a good idea to avoid using keywords for variable, field, table, and file names. This prevents some bugs from showing up that can be very difficult to nail down later.

Also, we used the AMEMBERS() function to get the list of cursors. We need to do this because the DataEnvironment class has no collection of its contained members like other containers. Once the list is obtained, we use the FOR EACH construct to work through the list. The line `loObjName = EVALUATE( "THIS." + kursor )` is creating an object reference out of the name of the cursor object. We need to do this because, for any row in our list of cursors, the value is the object name and we need a reference to the object. We must prepend the cursor's name with its container's name to get that object reference. We use the indirect reference of THIS to refer to the DataEnvironment without knowing what its name might be. When this line is executed, the variable `loObjName` will be an object reference to the cursor we are working with, and it allows us to continue with setting the Database property.

We now have a DataEnvironment class that will set the database path for our cursors at runtime. Now let's create a subclass of this class and try to get some data into the DataEnvironment. **Listing 7-2** shows a class definition for a subclass of our deBase class.

Listing 7-2. *A subclass of our deBase DataEnvironment class.*

```
* Define ClientProject DE
DEFINE CLASS deClntProj AS deBase

    * Modify the Init to accept a path to the databases
    PROCEDURE Init
        LPARAMETERS pcDbcPath
        * Add cursors and relation
        WITH THIS
            * Add the Clients cursor
            .AddObject("Cursor1","Cursor")
            WITH .Cursor1
                .CursorSource = "Clients"
                .Database = ".\Data\time and billing.dbc"
                .Alias = "Clients"
                .Order = "LastName"
            ENDWITH
            * Add the projects cursor
            .AddObject("Cursor2","Cursor")
            WITH .Cursor2
                .CursorSource = "Projects"
                .Database = ".\Data\time and billing.dbc"
                .Alias = "Projects"
                .Order = "ClientID"
            ENDWITH
            * Add the one-to-many relation
            .AddObject("Relation1","Relation")
            WITH .Relation1
                .ParentAlias = "Clients"
                .ChildAlias = "Projects"
                .ChildOrder = "ClientID"
                .RelationalExpr = "iClientId"
                .OneToMany = .T.
            ENDWITH
        ENDWITH
        DoDefault( pcDbcPath )
```

```
        ENDPROC
ENDDEFINE
```

This DataEnvironment (DE) class uses the tables in the Time and Billing database that are on the CD for this book. In the Init method of the object, we add the cursors and relation to the DE and set the properties for them. At the end of the Init method for this class, we call the Init method of the deBase class with the DoDefault() function. We know that the deBase Init method will take the passed parameter and adjust the path to the databases for each cursor and then call the OpenTables() method to open the cursors for use.

Regardless of how we might get this DE into a form, we can already see some problems with this approach. The first problem is that we will need a subclass for every conceivable DE that a form may need, and these DE's must be programmed in code. That completely precludes getting any benefit from the visual designer that Visual FoxPro's form designer gives for building DE's.

Let's see if there is a way to reap the benefits of having our own data-management class while still retaining the ability to visually design our DE's.

Creating our own data-manipulation classes

We have seen in the previous section that we can, in fact, subclass the Visual FoxPro data-management base classes. We can add useful behavior to them through this subclassing. However, we found a few problems with that approach, including the requirement to create DataEnvironment classes for every data configuration a form might need. Another problem was the preclusion of ever using the form designer's DataEnvironment designer.

This second problem is more far-reaching than we might think at first. If we don't use the form designer's DE designer, we give up the value of field mapping, which allows us to connect a data type with a specific control class and have that class instantiated whenever we drag and drop a field of that data type onto our form. If we are not using the visual DE designer, then we aren't dragging and dropping our fields onto the form, so this feature is lost.

Is there a way we can get the benefits of a smart data-manager class and still retain the benefits of using the visual tools and their features? The answer is yes.

In order to accomplish our goal, we will design a data-management approach that spreads the responsibility of the data over a number of classes. Because we want to use the features of the form designer, we'll start our data system with a form class named frmData.

Data form class

The data form class will be responsible for the behaviors listed in **Table 11**.

Table 11. Responsibilities of our data-aware form class.

Data Behavior
Provide the data behaviors
Read and save the contents of the DataEnvironment
Clear out the DataEnvironment
Reconstruct the DataEnvironment using our Cursor and Relation classes

To accomplish these goals, we need to enter into the process at a point during form creation where the DE exists and the controls are not yet bound to their data. This is because, in the process of meeting these responsibilities, we will be destroying the DE. This could cause problems if the controls are already data bound. The form's Load event will fire at the point in time that we need it.

Setting the path

We will support the dynamic setting of data paths by giving our form class a property to be used to point to the path for the data. To handle the directory for our data, we will add a property named DataDirectory to the data-aware form class.

Listing 7-3 shows the code we put in our data-aware form class's Load event.

Listing 7-3. The frmData class's Load event.

```
* This is our data aware form class
* Close the tables in the DE
THISFORM.DataEnvironment.CloseTables()

* Now we read the current DE into an array structure
LOCAL laDEStuff(1), laCursors(1,12), laRelations(1,8), loObject, lnRow, lo-
Parms, lnCnt
WITH THISFORM
* Check to see if there is a data environment
    IF TYPE("THISFORM.Dataenvironment.Name") = "C"
        * Get a list of all objects using two arrays, one for cursors and one
          for relations
        AMEMBERS( laDEStuff, .Dataenvironment, 2 )
        FOR lnCnt = 1 to alen(laDEStuff,1)
            loObject = EVALUATE( "THISFORM.Dataenvironment." + laDEStuff(lnCnt))
            IF loObject.BaseClass = "Cursor"
                * Populate the columns with the cursor properties
                IF NOT EMPTY( laCursors(ALEN(laCursors,1),1) )
                    * If the last row is full add a new one
                    DIMENSION laCursors( ALEN(laCursors,1)+1, ALEN(
                      laCursors, 2 ) )
                ENDIF
                * Get the row number
                lnRow = ALEN( laCursors,1)
                laCursors(lnRow,1)  = loObject.Name
                laCursors(lnRow,2)  = loObject.Alias
                laCursors(lnRow,3)  = loObject.BufferModeOverride
                laCursors(lnRow,4)  = loObject.Comment
                laCursors(lnRow,5)  = loObject.CursorSource
                laCursors(lnRow,6)  = loObject.Database
                laCursors(lnRow,7)  = loObject.Exclusive
                laCursors(lnRow,8)  = loObject.Filter
                laCursors(lnRow,9)  = loObject.NoDataOnLoad
                laCursors(lnRow,10) = loObject.Order
                laCursors(lnRow,11) = loObject.ReadOnly
                laCursors(lnRow,12) = loObject.Tag
            ENDIF
            IF loObject.BaseClass = "Relation"
                * Populate the columns with the relation properties
                IF NOT EMPTY( laRelations(ALEN(laRelations,1),1) )
                    * If the last row is full add a new one
```

```
            DIMENSION laRelations( ALEN(laRelations,1)+1, 
               ALEN( laRelations, 2 ) )
         ENDIF
         * Get the row number
         lnRow = ALEN( laRelations,1)
         laRelations(lnRow,1)   = loObject.Name
         laRelations(lnRow,2)   = loObject.ChildAlias
         laRelations(lnRow,3)   = loObject.ChildOrder
         laRelations(lnRow,4)   = loObject.Comment
         laRelations(lnRow,5)   = loObject.OneToMany
         laRelations(lnRow,6)   = loObject.ParentAlias
         laRelations(lnRow,7)   = loObject.RelationalExpr
         laRelations(lnRow,8)   = loObject.Tag
      ENDIF
   ENDFOR
ENDIF

* Ok now we have read the members of the DE let's replace them with
* our own classes
WITH .DataEnvironment
   * For each object in the DE call the RemoveObject
   FOR lnCnt = 1 TO ALEN( laDEStuff )
      .RemoveObject( laDEStuff( lnCnt ) )
   ENDFOR
   * Now let's add our classes
   * First we create an object for parameter passing.
   loParms = CreateObject("Cursor")
   FOR lnCnt = 1 TO ALEN( laCursors,1 )
      loParms.Alias             = laCursors(lnCnt,2)
      loParms.BufferModeOverride = laCursors(lnCnt,3)
      loParms.Comment           = laCursors(lnCnt,4)
      loParms.CursorSource      = laCursors(lnCnt,5)
      IF NOT EMPTY(THISFORM.DataDirectory)
         THISFORM.DataDirectory = ADDBS(THISFORM.DataDirectory)
         loParms.Database = THISFORM.DataDirectory + ;
            SUBSTR(laCursors(lnCnt,6),RAT("\",laCursors(lnCnt,6))+1)
      ELSE
         loParms.Database = laCursors(lnCnt,6)
      ENDIF
      loParms.Exclusive         = laCursors(lnCnt,7)
      loParms.Filter            = laCursors(lnCnt,8)
      loParms.NoDataOnLoad      = laCursors(lnCnt,9)
      loParms.Order             = laCursors(lnCnt,10)
      loParms.ReadOnly          = laCursors(lnCnt,11)
      loParms.Tag               = laCursors(lnCnt,12)

      .NewObject( laCursors(lnCnt,1), THISFORM.CursorClassName, ;
                THISFORM.CursorClassLibrary,, loParms )
   ENDFOR
   loParms = CreateObject("Relation")
   FOR lnCnt = 1 TO ALEN( laRelations,1 )
      loParms.ChildAlias        = laRelations(lnCnt,2)
      loParms.ChildOrder        = laRelations(lnCnt,3)
      loParms.Comment           = laRelations(lnCnt,4)
      loParms.OneToMany         = laRelations(lnCnt,5)
      loParms.ParentAlias       = laRelations(lnCnt,6)
      loParms.RelationalExpr    = laRelations(lnCnt,7)
      loParms.Tag               = laRelations(lnCnt,8)
      .NewObject( laRelations(lnCnt,1), THISFORM.RelationClassName, ;
```

```
                      THISFORM.RelationClassLibrary,, loParms )
      ENDFOR
      * Now open the tables
      IF .AutoOpenTables
         .OpenTables()
      ENDIF
   ENDWITH
ENDWITH
```

Let's look at this code in some detail to see exactly what it's doing. The first thing we do is to close all tables in the existing DataEnvironment of the form. Then we build an array of all member objects, the cursors and relations, which are in the DataEnvironment. We work through that array and build two separate arrays—one for the cursors and one for the relations. In each of these arrays we are storing the value for all pertinent properties for each object.

Once we have the objects stored into the arrays, we remove each object from the DataEnvironment and replace it with an object based on our own class definitions. We are using a parameter object to pass the property settings to each object as we create it.

Notice that we are using the new VFP 6.0 method named NewObject() to accomplish this. This new method allows us to create objects from classes without using a SET PROCEDURE or SET CLASSLIB command to first open the class definitions. With NewObject, we simply pass the name of the library as an argument to the function. Notice, also, that we are using properties of the form to hold the class names and the library names. This allows us the flexibility to use different classes in different forms by simply changing the value of those form properties. In frmData these properties are set to default values of cursor class csrBase in library prgs\dataclasses.prg, and relation class of relBase in the same library.

Finally, we check the AutoOpenTables property of the DataEnvironment; if it is True, we call OpenTables to open all tables for the form.

Cursor and Relation classes

Because our code in the form class is using certain cursor and relation classes, we should look at those class definitions. **Listing 7-4** shows the code for the csrBase class.

Listing 7-4. The csrBase class definition.

```
DEFINE CLASS csrBase AS Cursor
   PROCEDURE Init
      LPARAMETERS poParms
      WITH THIS
         .Alias               = poParms.Alias
         .BufferModeOverride  = poParms.BufferModeOverride
         .Comment             = poParms.Comment
         .CursorSource        = poParms.CursorSource
         .Database            = poParms.Database
         .Exclusive           = poParms.Exclusive
         .Filter              = poParms.Filter
         .NoDataOnLoad        = poParms.NoDataOnLoad
         .Order               = poParms.Order
         .ReadOnly            = poParms.ReadOnly
         .Tag                 = poParms.Tag
```

```
      ENDWITH
   ENDPROC
ENDDEFINE
```

The csrBase class simply accepts the parameter object and then sets its own properties to the values in the parameter object. Later in this chapter, we'll examine how we might enhance this class to provide more functionality.

Listing 7-5 shows the class definition of the relBase class used in our frmData class.

***Listing 7-5**. The relBase class definition.*

```
* Our base relation class
DEFINE CLASS relBase AS Relation
   PROCEDURE Init
      LPARAMETERS poParms
      WITH THIS
         .ChildAlias     = poParms.ChildAlias
         .ChildOrder     = poParms.ChildOrder
         .Comment        = poParms.Comment
         .OneToMany      = poParms.OneToMany
         .ParentAlias    = poParms.ParentAlias
         .RelationalExpr = poParms.RelationalExpr
         .Tag            = poParms.Tag
      ENDWITH
   ENDPROC
ENDDEFINE
```

This relation class is essentially the same as the csrBase class, except that it's a relation rather than a cursor. It accepts a parameter object and sets its properties according to those of the parameter object.

Enhancing the cursor class

To really appreciate the power and flexibility of this approach to handling data, we need to investigate enhancing our cursor classes. We will add two methods to our cursor classes, named CursorUpdate and CursorRevert. **Listing 7-6** shows the new cursor class definition.

***Listing 7-6**. Our enhanced cursor class.*

```
* Now for an enhanced cursor class
DEFINE CLASS csrUpdate AS csrBase

   PROCEDURE CursorUpdate
      LOCAL llRet
      IF CURSORGETPROP("BUFFERING",THIS.Alias) > 1
         llRet = TableUpdate( 0,.F., THIS.Alias )
      ELSE
         llRet = .T.
      ENDIF
      RETURN llRet
   ENDPROC
   PROCEDURE CursorRevert
      LOCAL llRet
      IF CURSORGETPROP("BUFFERING",THIS.Alias) > 1
```

```
           llRet = TableRevert( .T., THIS.Alias )
      ELSE
           llRet = .T.
      ENDIF
      RETURN llRet
  ENDPROC

ENDDEFINE
```

The enhancement here is minor, but it does show the available possibilities. Our enhancement simply provides one method for updating and another for reverting the cursor's
buffer. The code in each method first checks to see whether the cursor is buffered and then
either calls the appropriate function and returns the result, or returns True, indicating a successful completion of the operation.

Adding these methods to the class is only one example of what can be done. Making other
enhancements to these classes is left as an exercise to the reader. (We've always wanted to say
that!)

Data behavior class

In the classes we've already designed, we have dealt with a number of the data behaviors presented at the beginning of this chapter: opening and closing tables and views, updating or reverting data edits, and providing data source independence. There are two behaviors left unan-
swered: navigating through the data and detecting changes to the data. We will address these
behaviors in the data behavior class as well as expand on the "saving of changes" behavior.

Why not implement these behaviors in the classes we've already defined? We could use
the frmData class and add methods to it for these behaviors. It would also reduce the number
of objects that exist at runtime. As a matter of fact, we are going to implement these behaviors
in our frmData class.

The issue of whether we use the frmData class or define another class is an implementation detail and not a design issue. The design issue is that we *have* a class that handles these
behaviors—not *which* class that is.

Dividing the behaviors

We have two behaviors left to handle; let's address navigation first. Navigation involves
moving through the data forward or backward, and it may involve searching for a particular
value or criteria. It may involve a multi-table situation, a single-table situation, local views, or
remote views.

We can start by designing the interface to the behaviors. What methods will exist and how
are they called? There are five basic navigation operations: move to the next record, move to
the previous record, move to the last record, move to the first record, and search for a record.
These behaviors can be presented by creating the methods shown in **Table 12**.

Table 12. *The data-manipulation methods of our frmData class.*

Method	Description
GoNext	Moves to the next record in the MasterAlias of the form or the InitialSelectedAlias of the DE and refreshes the IsAtEof property of the form. The MasterAlias is something that we will add to our frmData class later.

GoPrevious	Moves to the previous record in the MasterAlias of the form or the InitialSelectedAlias of the DE and refreshes the IsAtBof property of the form.
GoBottom	Moves to the last record in the MasterAlias of the form or the InitialSelectedAlias of the DE and refreshes the IsAtEof property of the form.
GoTop	Moves to the first record in the MasterAlias of the form or the InitialSelectedAlias of the DE and refreshes the IsAtBof property of the form.
GoSearch	Brings up a search form, allowing the user to search for a record by various criteria, and refreshes both the IsAtEof and IsAtBof properties of the form.
SetEof	Sets the IsAtEof property.
SetBof	Sets the IsAtBof property.

Note that Table 12 lists two additional methods, SetEof and SetBof. These methods will be used to set logical properties of frmData to indicate that the record pointer is at the logical last and/or first record, respectively.

In addition to the methods mentioned in Table 12, we will need some new properties to keep track of record positions and also to enable the developer to turn certain behaviors on or off for particular forms. **Table 13** lists the properties we will add to our frmData class.

Table 13. Properties used by the navigation behaviors of the frmData class.

Property	Description
IsAtEof	Logical .T. if the record pointer in the MasterAlias or the InitialSelectedAlias of the DE is on the last record in the table.
IsAtBof	Logical .T. if the record pointer in the MasterAlias or the InitialSelectedAlias of the DE is on the first record in the table.
AllowGoNext	Logical for enabling or disabling the GoNext method.
AllowGoPrevious	Logical for enabling or disabling the GoPrevious method.
AllowGoBottom	Logical for enabling or disabling the GoBottom method.
AllowGoTop	Logical for enabling or disabling the GoTop method.
AllowGoSearch	Logical for enabling or disabling the GoSearch method.
SearchFormName	The name of the form to run when GoSearch is fired.
MasterAlias	Form property to hold the name of an alias that should be used by the navigation methods. If this property is blank, the InitialSelectedAlias of the DE will be used. If both this and the InitialSelectedAlias are blank, then the current work area is used.

Using the properties in Table 13, the developer can turn any of the behaviors on or off. The Allow* properties are used to do this. An Allow* property that is set to .F. will disallow that behavior in the form. These properties will be used in the code of the Go* methods and can also be used by the developer to enable or disable any button or toolbar that might provide access to the behaviors. The IsAtEof and IsAtBof properties can also be used to enable and disable buttons controlling the navigation.

Let's look at some code that implements these behaviors. **Listing 7-7** shows the code in the GoNext method of our frmData class.

Listing 7-7. The GoNext method of our frmData class.

```
* Moves to the next record
* First check to see if this behavior is turned on
IF NOT THISFORM.AllowGoNext
   * Short circuit
   RETURN
ENDIF


* Declare local variables
LOCAL lcAlias, llCheckDE
* Save the current work area
lcAlias = ALIAS()
* Now select the work area of concern
IF NOT EMPTY(THISFORM.MasterAlias)
   * If we have a masterAlias set
   IF USED(THISFORM.MasterAlias)
      * If there is a work area of that name, select it
      SELECT (THISFORM.MasterAlias)
   ELSE
      * If there is no work area set to check the DE
      llCheckDE = .T.
   ENDIF
ELSE
   * If there is no MasterAlias set to check the DE
   llCheckDE = .T.
ENDIF
IF llCheckDE
   * If we need to check the DE
   IF NOT EMPTY(THISFORM.DataEnvironment.InitialSelectedAlias)
      * If there is an InitialSelectedAlias
      IF USED(THISFORM.DataEnvironment.InitialSelectedAlias)
         * If there is a work area of that name, select it
         SELECT (THISFORM.DataEnvironment.InitialSelectedAlias)
      ENDIF
   ENDIF
ENDIF


* Now move the pointer

IF NOT THISFORM.IsAtEOF
   SKIP
ENDIF
* Call the SetEof/Bof to set the IsAtEof/Bof property
THISFORM.SetEof()
THISFORM.SetBof()

* Now reselect the work area
IF NOT EMPTY( lcAlias )
   SELECT ( lcAlias )
```

```
ELSE
   SELECT 0
ENDIF

* Now refresh the display
THISFORM.Refresh()

* And return
RETURN
```

This seems like a lot of code, but if you take it apart you can see exactly what it's doing. First, it checks to see if the behavior is turned on; if it is not, it gets out without doing anything. Next, it checks the aliases to find out which one it should be moving in. If the form has a MasterAlias set, it uses that one. If the MasterAlias is not set, we check the InitialSelectedAlias of the data environment. If neither of those is set, it uses the currently selected work area.

Once it has the proper work area selected, it moves the record pointer forward one record. Then it calls the form's SetEof and SetBof methods (seen below), and finally it refreshes the form display. It then reselects the work area that was current when it was called.

The GoTop, GoPrevious, and GoBottom methods are all essentially the same except for the record movement. This raises the question of whether we could design this better and reduce the repeated code in these methods. By adding a method to our class for selecting the master alias, we could remove that portion of code from these methods. **Listing 7-8** shows the SelectMasterAlias method we have added.

Listing 7-8. The SelectMasterAlias method of our frmData class.

```
* Selects the master alias for this form
* Declare local variables
LOCAL llCheckDE
* Select the work area of concern
IF NOT EMPTY(THISFORM.MasterAlias)
   * If we have a masterAlias set
   IF USED(THISFORM.MasterAlias)
      * If there is a work area of that name, select it
      SELECT (THISFORM.MasterAlias)
   ELSE
      * If there is no work area set to check the DE
      llCheckDE = .T.
   ENDIF
ELSE
   * If there is no MasterAlias set to check the DE
   llCheckDE = .T.
ENDIF
IF llCheckDE
   * If we need to check the DE
   IF NOT EMPTY(THISFORM.DataEnvironment.InitialSelectedAlias)
      * If there is an InitialSelectedAlias
      IF USED(THISFORM.DataEnvironment.InitialSelectedAlias)
         * If there is a work area of that name, select it
         SELECT (THISFORM.DataEnvironment.InitialSelectedAlias)
      ENDIF
   ENDIF
```

```
ENDIF
RETURN
```

By adding this method, we reduce the amount of code in the Go* methods. **Listing 7-9** shows the revised GoNext method.

Listing 7-9. The GoNext method revised to use the SelectMasterAlias method of the frmData class.

```
* Moves to the next record
* First check to see if this behavior is turned on
IF NOT THISFORM.AllowGoNext
   * Short circuit
   RETURN
ENDIF

* Declare local variables
LOCAL lcAlias
* Save the current work area
lcAlias = ALIAS()

* Now select the work area of concern
THISFORM.SelectMasterAlias()

* Now move the pointer
IF NOT THISFORM.IsAtEof
   SKIP
ENDIF
* Call the SetEof/Bof to set the IsAtEof/Bof property
THISFORM.SetEof()
THISFORM.SetBof()

* Now reselect the work area
IF NOT EMPTY( lcAlias )
   SELECT ( lcAlias )
ELSE
   SELECT 0
ENDIF

* Now refresh the display
THISFORM.Refresh()

* And return
RETURN
```

Notice how much simpler this method has become. Besides, with all of the selecting code moved into a separate method, if we find a better or faster way to select the work area of concern, we have only one place to implement it and it will affect all of the other methods.

The only Go* method that is quite different from the others is the GoSearch method. Listing **7-10** shows the code in this method.

Listing 7-10. *The GoSearch method of our frmData class.*

```
* Calls the search form

* First check to see if this behavior is turned on
IF NOT THISFORM.AllowGoSearch
   * Short circuit
   RETURN
ENDIF

* An assertion for the developer

ASSERT THISFORM.AllowGoSearch AND NOT EMPTY( THISFORM.SearchFormName ) ;
   MESSAGE "You have Allow searching turned on and there is no search " + ;
         "form set up in the SearchFormName property."

* Now check to see if there is a search form set up
IF EMPTY( THISFORM.SearchFormName )
   * Short circuit
   RETURN
ENDIF

* The search form should have its data session set to default so it partici-
pates in this
* form's data session.  It will be passed the alias to search in and it should
leave
* the record pointers at the result of the search. The search form also must
be modal.

* Declare local variables
LOCAL lcAlias
* Save the current work area
lcAlias = ALIAS()

* Now select the work area of concern
THISFORM.SelectMasterAlias()

* Now run the search form
DO FORM (THISFORM.SearchFormName) WITH ALIAS()

IF NOT EMPTY( lcAlias )
   SELECT ( lcAlias )
ELSE
   SELECT 0
ENDIF

* Call the SetEof/Bof to set the IsAtEof/Bof property
THISFORM.SetBof()
THISFORM.SetEof()

* Now refresh the display
THISFORM.Refresh()

* and return
RETURN
```

This method checks the AllowGoSearch property first to see if the behavior is turned on. It then also checks to be sure that there is a SearchFormName set up. Notice the ASSERT line, which warns the developer that he/she has set inconsistent properties at development time. The developer should fix this problem before the system is released to users.

Once we know that the behavior is turned on and that we have a search form name to use, we run the search form. The search form is designed with its data session set to default, so it participates in the data session of the form that runs it. This way, the search form can locate the desired record and then simply return to this form. Because the search form is participating in this form's data session, any record movement will be reflected in the calling form.

It is also necessary for the search form to be modal so that the code in the GoSearch method will wait for the search form to complete its work before continuing.

The next couple of methods we need to examine are the SetEof and SetBof methods. These two are very similar, so we'll look at one of them and discuss the other one. **Listing 7-11** shows the SetEof method of our frmData class.

Listing 7-11. The SetEof method of our frmData class.

```
* This method can be used to both set the IsAtEof property
* and to return the IsAtEof property setting

* Declare local variables
LOCAL lnRecNo, llEof, lcAlias, llCheckDE
* Save the current work area
lcAlias = ALIAS()

* Now select the work area of concern
THISFORM.SelectMasterAlias()

* Check to see if there is anything open
IF NOT EMPTY( ALIAS() )
   * Check to see if we are at eof already
   IF NOT EOF()
      * If not save the record number we are on
      lnRecno = RECNO()
      SKIP
      llEof = EOF()
      GOTO lnRecno
   ELSE
      llEof = .T.
   ENDIF
ELSE
   * Nothing open so set eof to .T.
   llEof = .T.
ENDIF
* Set the form property
THISFORM.IsAtEof = llEof
* Now restore the work area
IF NOT EMPTY( lcAlias )
   SELECT ( lcAlias )
ELSE
   SELECT 0
ENDIF
```

```
* Return the property setting
RETURN llEof
```

This method begins much the same as the Go* methods, by saving the current work area's alias and then selecting the master alias for the form. It then checks to see that something is open in the selected work area. If something is open, the method saves the record number, moves one record forward, checks to see if it is at EOF, and then puts the record pointer back. It then sets the form's IsAtEof property and returns the IsAtEof value. This method can be used to set the property and check the status. Its return value tells us if we are at EOF. Although this dual personality overloads the method, it does provide for checking the return value when we're moving around in the alias and checking only the property when we don't need to execute the code. When might we just check the property without calling the method? Perhaps in a form's refresh method that is setting the enabled and disabled properties of some navigation buttons. Obviously the code in the Go* methods calls this method to set the properties, so calling the methods again in the refresh for the form would run the code twice and slow the performance accordingly. The properties are there for this purpose.

The SetBof method is much the same, except it moves backward one record rather than forward, and it sets and returns the BOF value.

What's the point of all this? The project named Chapter7 includes a form named Data-Form. If you open this form for editing and double-click it to get to the code windows, you'll find that the form has no code. Instead, it uses a container class that has buttons for the navigation behaviors. You can see those classes in the Controls class library, which is part of the project. (We'll discuss control classes in a later chapter.) **Figure 1** shows a screen shot of Da-taForm.

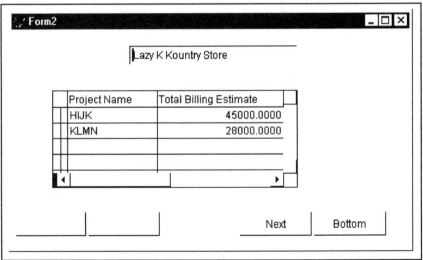

Figure 1. *The DataForm from the Chapter7 project.*

Run the DataForm form and you'll see that the navigation buttons work flawlessly. You can edit the form and change the Allow* properties and then run it to see the behavior changes. By using the frmData class for this form, we have allowed the developer to modify the behavior of the form by simply changing properties. The developer does not have to write any record-navigation code unless he or she wants something other than the default behavior our class provides.

Keep in mind that creating classes like these does not restrict developers. They always have the option of overriding our class code with their own code to get alternate behaviors.

Detecting changes to data

The last of the behaviors that we listed at the beginning of this chapter is detecting that data has changed. This detection can be useful in preventing unnecessary updates to the tables and views. If the user has not changed anything, we should not go through the process of updating the cursors.

Visual FoxPro gives us two functions that can be useful in detecting changes to data. These are the GetFldState() and the GetNextModified() functions. GetFldState() will tell us the condition of the fields and the deleted status flag for a record, while GetNextModified() will find the modified records in a table-buffered cursor. It's important to note that GetNextModified moves the record pointer in the affected alias and therefore will cause the evaluation of any field or table validation rules, as well as any uniqueness checks on primary and candidate indexes.

We'll implement the detection of changes in our frmData class in conjunction with methods for saving or reverting an edit. We will add three methods: DoSave to save our changes, DoRevert to revert an edit session, and DetectChanges to detect any changes.

Our DoSave method will call each cursor's CursorUpdate method, while DoRevert will call the cursor's CursorRevert method. Both of these methods will first call DetectChanges to find out if any updating or reverting is necessary.

Listing 7-12 shows the code in the DetectChanges method.

Listing 7-12. The DetectChanges method of our frmData class.

```
* Checks all cursors for any changes and returns .T. if there are any
* updates pending and .F. if all buffers are clean

* Declare local variables
LOCAL laMembers(1), lnRecno, lcAlias, llRet, cName
* Save current alias
lcAlias = ALIAS()

* Get an array of all the member objects in the DE
AMEMBERS( laMembers, THISFORM.DataEnvironment, 2 )

* Work through the array
FOR EACH cName IN laMembers
   IF THISFORM.DataEnvironment.&cName..BaseClass <> "Cursor"
      * If this item is not a cursor loop
      LOOP
   ENDIF
   * Select the work area for this cursor
   SELECT ( THISFORM.DataEnvironment.&cName..Alias )
   * Save the current record number
   lnRecno = RECNO()
   IF GetNextModified(0) <> 0
```

```
      * If there is a modified record
      * Return to the original record
      GOTO lnRecno
      * Set the return variable to indicate changes
      llRet = .T.
      * Get out of here
      EXIT
   ENDIF
ENDFOR
* Restore the work area
IF NOT EMPTY( lcAlias )
   SELECT ( lcAlias )
ELSE
   SELECT 0
ENDIF
* Return the status
RETURN llRet
```

The above code starts by getting an array of the member objects in the form's DataEnvironment. It then works through that array and checks each cursor for any changes. If it finds any change to any cursor it returns .T.—otherwise it returns .F. This method can be called from our DoSave and DoRevert methods early on, and its return value can be used to determine whether or not we continue with the process.

> ### Macro Note
> *A macro expansion using the ampersand (&) uses a period (.) as the symbol to mark the end of the variable name that is to be expanded. When you want the expanded variable to be followed by a period, you must use two periods, as in this line:*

```
THISFORM.DataEnvironment.&cName..BaseClass
```

Managing multi-table updating—transactions

Before we venture into our DoSave method, we need to consider another issue: How do we handle the problem of multi-table updates? On initial examination it may not seem like much of a problem; we could just update each table in sequence. But if we examine a real-world situation, we'll see the problem with this simple approach.

Consider a form for entering an invoice. The user enters the customer identification, the invoice information, the invoice details, and so on. When the user saves his or her work, we need to update the invoice table, the invoice details table, the inventory table (to reduce the amount on hand), and the accounts receivable table. What happens if the save routine updates the invoice and invoice detail tables and then fails on the inventory table? This would leave our database in an unbalanced state: Inventory would indicate items available that had been sold, and accounts receivable would not reflect an invoice properly.

In situations like this, it's much better to tell the user that we were unable to save the invoice and leave the tables in a known state—that is, not including the new invoice. The user can re-enter the invoice at a later time. This is much better than having the invoice half-entered into the system.

Visual FoxPro gives us the ability to handle this with transactions. A transaction groups a number of updates so they are treated as an all-or-none operation. We used three commands to create transactions, which are described in **Table 14**.

***Table 14**. Commands used for processing transactions.*

Command	Description
BEGIN TRANSACTION	Marks the beginning of a transaction. All cursor operations between this and the ending command will be cached and not committed until the ending command is encountered.
END TRANSACTION	Marks the end of a successful transaction. Commits the cursor operations.
ROLLBACK	Marks the end of an unsuccessful transaction. All cached cursor operations are discarded.

Transactions can be nested inside one another to a level of five deep. This allows us to use transactions in our code while other transactions are being used in the trigger or validation operations of the database. The function TxnLevel() can be used to determine at what level of nesting a transaction resides.

Transactions in Visual FoxPro work by caching each operation in order. As each operation in the transaction completes, the necessary locks are obtained and held for the duration of the transaction. This ensures that at the END TRANSACTION there will not be any locking problems in committing the transaction. Nothing is written to the cursors during the transaction. Upon encountering the END TRANSACTION command, Visual FoxPro writes all updates to the cursors and releases the locks it obtained. A ROLLBACK discards all updates and also releases the locks.

It is evident that if a transaction were holding locks, it would be wise to locate the BEGIN TRANSACTION and END TRANSACTION or ROLLBACK commands as physically close to each other as is possible in our code. This will cause the locks to be held for as short a time as possible. Any calculations or processing required to complete the updates should be done before the transaction is begun.

We are now ready to examine the DoSave method of our form class. In our frmData class, we will keep the entire transaction in the DoSave method. **Listing 7-13** shows the code for the DoSave method.

***Listing 7-13**. The DoSave method of our frmData class.*

```
* Saves all changes to the cursors

* First find out if we have any changes to handle
IF NOT THISFORM.DetectChanges()
   * There are no changes so get out
   RETURN .T.
ENDIF

* Declare local variables
LOCAL llRet, cName, laMembers(1)
llRet = .T.
```

```
* Get a list of the DE members
AMEMBERS( laMembers, THISFORM.DataEnvironment, 2 )

* Now work through the members and call the ValidateAlias method of this form
FOR EACH cName IN laMembers
    IF THISFORM.DataEnvironment.&cName..BaseClass <> "Cursor"
        * If it is not a cursor
        LOOP
    ENDIF
    * Call the ValidateAlias and pass this alias name to it
    IF NOT THISFORM.ValidateAlias( THISFORM.DataEnvironment.&cName..Alias )
        * If validate failed
        llRet = .F.
        EXIT
    ENDIF
ENDFOR
* If validate alias failed get out
IF NOT llRet
    RETURN llRet
ENDIF

* Now begin the transaction
BEGIN TRANSACTION
* Work through the cursors and update them
FOR EACH cName IN laMembers
    IF THISFORM.DataEnvironment.&cName..BaseClass <> "Cursor"
        * If it is not a cursor loop
        LOOP
    ENDIF
    IF PEMSTATUS(THISFORM.DataEnvironment.&cName , "CURSORUPDATE", 5 )
        * If the cursor has a CursorUpdate method call it
        llRet = THISFORM.DataEnvironment.&cName..CursorUpdate()
    ELSE
        * Otherwise do a table update
        IF CURSORGETPROP("BUFFERING",THISFORM.DataEnvironment.&cName..Alias) > 1
            llRet = TableUpdate( 0,.F., THISFORM.DataEnvironment.&cName..Alias )
            * If you choose to allow multiple records to be edited the above
            * command line would be
            *llRet = TableUpdate( 1,.F., THISFORM.DataEnvironment.&cName..Alias )
        ELSE
            llRet = .T.
        ENDIF
    ENDIF
    IF NOT llRet
        * If the update failed get out
        EXIT
    ENDIF
ENDFOR
IF llRet
    * If all updates were successful commit
    END TRANSACTION
ELSE
    * If any update failed rollback and revert the buffers
    ROLLBACK
    THISFORM.DoRevert()
ENDIF
RETURN llRet
```

The DoSave code starts by checking the DetectChanges method to see if there is anything to save. It then creates an array of all member objects of the form's DataEnvironment. The first FOR EACH loop works through the array and for each cursor it calls a method of the form, named ValidateAlias. The ValidateAlias method in our form class is empty except for an LPARAMETERS statement. This method allows developers to write any code they want to use to validate each alias for the form. The developer can return .F. from the ValidateAlias to stop the saving operation. If the developer doesn't write any code in ValidateAlias, then the loop will progress to completion and continue with the saving.

Before the second FOR EACH loop, a BEGIN TRANSACTION is issued. The second FOR EACH loop works through the cursors again. It checks each cursor to see if it has a CursorUpdate method; if it has one, the code calls that method and checks the return value. If a cursor does not have a CursorUpdate method, a TableUpdate is issued and the return value is checked. The variable llRet stores the return from these calls. If any cursor fails to update, the loop is exited.

The IF statement after the loop is used to decide whether to issue an END TRANSACTION and commit the changes, or issue a ROLLBACK and discard the changes. If a ROLLBACK is issued, the form's DoRevert method is called to revert the buffers to their original state. This is necessary because the ROLLBACK will discard the cached updates, but it does not change the buffered edits. You may ask why we throw away the user's work when the problem may be a simple violation of a field rule; the answer is that we are calling the ValidateAlias for the developer to check the rules and validate the record before we do any saving. These fixable errors on the part of the user should be handled there—if the developer decided not to handle them, that is his or her decision. Using only a ROLLBACK would leave the buffers "dirty" and could cause problems when trying to close the form. Also, issuing the DoRevert will ensure that the user sees the data as it appears on disk after the failed update.

Listing 7-14 shows the DoRevert method code for our form class.

Listing 7-14. The DoRevert method of our frmData class.

```
* Reverts all changes to the cursors

* First find out if we have any changes to handle
IF NOT THISFORM.DetectChanges()
   * There are no changes so get out
   RETURN .T.
ENDIF

* Declare local variables
LOCAL cName, laMembers(1)

* Get a list of the DE members
AMEMBERS( laMembers, THISFORM.DataEnvironment, 2 )

* Work through the cursors and update them
FOR EACH cName IN laMembers
   IF THISFORM.DataEnvironment.&cName..BaseClass <> "Cursor"
      * If it is not a cursor loop
      LOOP
   ENDIF
   IF PEMSTATUS(THISFORM.DataEnvironment.&cName , "CURSORREVERT", 5 )
```

```
      * If the cursor has a CursorRevert method call it
      THISFORM.DataEnvironment.&cName..CursorRevert()
   ELSE
      * Otherwise do a table revert
      IF CURSORGETPROP("BUFFERING",THISFORM.DataEnvironment.&cName..Alias) > 1
         TableRevert( .T., THISFORM.DataEnvironment.&cName..Alias )
      ENDIF
   ENDIF
ENDFOR
THISFORM.Refresh()
RETURN
```

The DoRevert method is very similar to the DoSave method. There is no call to ValidateAlias because it isn't needed. The reverts are not wrapped in a transaction because it isn't necessary when reverting.

Data management and views

As mentioned in Chapter 5, Data - Views, working with views in most cases is no different from working with tables. One area in which some differences are encountered is in data management. With views (whether local views populated with data from Visual FoxPro tables, or remote views populated with data from SQL/Server or some other database server), there is no natural concept of "previous", "next", "first", and "last". Likewise, there is no concept of EOF() or BOF(), therefore no need to keep track of one's position within a table.

This is not to say that we can't implement a mechanism for accessing records in a sequential manner, but it will be done via a much different technique than SKIP, SKIP –1, GOTO TOP and GOTO BOTTOM.

With that caveat, all other concepts presented in this chapter apply equally well when working with views or directly with Visual FoxPro tables. The important thing to remember is that some applications may need to implement a mechanism to turn sequential navigation features on and off automatically, depending on the type of data a particular cursor is working with. This is easily determined in the runtime environment by using CURSORGETPROP("SourceType"). This function returns 1 for a local SQL view, 2 for a remote SQL view, and 3 when the data source is a table.

Remember also that views, whether local or remote, can have more than one record and they may need GoNext and GoPrevious. Also, the design of our frmData class allows subclassing for a frmDataView, which would have different code in the Go* methods.

Summary of data management

At the start of this chapter, we listed the behaviors we were concerned with and described them. We then investigated the base data-management classes in Visual FoxPro and found them to be insufficient for implementing our solution.

In reviewing the possible approaches to the problems, we decided that a form class was a good candidate for handling our data-management operations, so we built the frmData class. We coded the methods in this form class to provide the behaviors we wanted. In doing this we were careful to provide properties for the developer to control the details of the behaviors, thus eliminating the requirement to subclass this form class to alter behavior in minor ways.

Our form class uses subclasses of the Cursor and Relation base classes to re-create the DataEnvironment at runtime. This was done this way to allow the developer to use the visual data environment designer in Visual FoxPro's form designer to build the data for the form and yet provide all of the additional functionality that our classes provide at runtime.

In Chapter 8 we will see another approach to handling data access that will evolve this approach to a higher level.

Chapter 8
Managing Business Logic -
N-Tier System Design

One of the new buzzwords of the day is *n-tier design*. What does this mean and how does it affect your system development work? How many tiers are *n*? What are those tiers? In this chapter we'll examine the n-tier design model and understand the advantages it can provide. We'll investigate the concept of business logic and see how it differs from data validation. The use of classes dedicated to providing business logic enforcement will be described and you will see how to incorporate these objects into your applications. Finally, we'll examine the use of ActiveX servers for the business logic objects and see how this can contribute to future evolution of your applications into new technologies.

What is n-tier system design?

The buzzwords of the past can help us to understand n-tier design. Client-server system design is based on the principle of dividing a data management system into a front end that provides the user interface and a back end that provides the data storage and retrieval. Client-server design could be called 2-Tier design because there are two tiers—the user interface tier and the database tier.

N-tier design simply indicates that there will be more than two tiers. For a while the buzzword was 3-tier design, but the "3" was replaced by "N" to address designs that had more than three levels. In the 3-tier system design model, the tiers are user interface, business logic, and database. Additional levels considered in n-tier designs can be hardware interface, communications, operating system interface, and others. With a high-level language like Visual FoxPro, you aren't often concerned with hardware and operating system interfaces because those responsibilities are handled for you.

In this chapter I will focus on the 3-tier model and especially on the middle tier—the business logic tier. **Figure 1** shows the 3-tier design model.

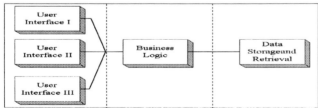

Figure 1.*The 3-tier system design model.*

Figure 1 shows three blocks for the user interface. This means there can be more than one interface for getting at the data. These interfaces might be your application's forms, a spreadsheet application, and an ad hoc report generator. There could be more than three interfaces. The data storage and retrieval might constitute more than one database, although the diagram shows only one.

The business-logic block in **Figure 1** is the focus of this chapter. It can represent a single object or many objects. I'll examine the business-logic layer in more depth for the rest of this chapter.

What is business logic?

Business logic, which is sometimes referred to as business rules, comprises the set of rules that describes the storage and retrieval of data within the context of a specific business. Business logic cannot be defined in a vacuum; it requires heavy input from the experts within the business itself. You, as a developer, can implement business-logic enforcement, but your discipline cannot define the rules. You need the consultation of experts in the business, for whom the system is being built, in order to successfully define the business logic. These people are called *business domain experts*.

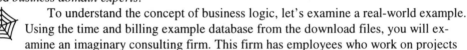 To understand the concept of business logic, let's examine a real-world example. Using the time and billing example database from the download files, you will examine an imaginary consulting firm. This firm has employees who work on projects for clients. In talking with the management of the company, you are told that employees are restricted to seeing data only regarding the projects that they are assigned to. This issue of restricting the display of data to only those projects for a particular employee is an example of a business logic rule. You would never know this from studying the database design. Even reviewing the validation rules for the data wouldn't reveal this simple but important rule.

In further discussions with management, you find out that the business considers a project to be an assignment of an employee to a client for a particular short-range or long-range task. Management tells you that the people in the office always want to see projects this way, with the client and the employee identified. Project information is meaningless to them unless they can see the client and employee information as well. This is another issue that can be enforced through the business logic rules.

How is business logic different from data validation?

You can see from the issues above that business logic encompasses a set of rules about how the business sees its data. Wouldn't some of these issues be dealt with in the data-validation rules related to the data-domain definitions? To see how these business-logic rules are different from data-domain definitions, let's look again at the two examples.

If the first example, where employees can see only their projects, were to be mapped to database design, it would likely cause you to design multiple tables for projects—one table for each employee. Although this might help to enforce of the business rule, it would certainly complicate the process of reassigning a project. It would also introduce a level of serious complexity in dealing with an employee leaving the company and being replaced by a new one. It makes much more sense to manage this issue dynamically at the time that data is displayed.

You could handle the second situation through your form design and put the burden on the user interface. Although this might seem like a good solution, it has its problems in long-term maintenance of the system. It also limits the tools that the users can leverage in managing their data. The form approach to managing data does not allow the data to be accessed from other applications like Excel or a VB application without duplicating the data-management code.

Businesses are dynamic, changing over time. Your design should allow for relatively easy adaptation to changes in the business. By moving the business logic out of the user interface and the database, you allow for adapting to changes in the business logic without requiring major overhauls of the entire system.

Another area where business logic is different from data validation can be found in the very rules you apply to the field-domain definitions. In the example database, the Clients table has a field named cPostalCode, which is a character field with a width of 20 characters. In your meetings with the management of the company, they explained that they only service clients in three states: Washington, Oregon, and Northern California. Due to international labor regulations they do not handle any clients in Canada. Okay, so what do you do with this information? Do you put a validation rule on the cPostalCode field in the database that limits the values in that field to only those three states?

If you put this constraint on the field in the database, you create an inconsistency in the data definitions. The field is defined as storing the postal code for the location of a client. Postal codes cover the entire world. Your validation rule would restrict the postal codes to only part of the world. Any future change in the company's business practices would require a redefinition of the field's domain and changes to the database itself.

It would be much better in the long run if you define the field's domain based on the entity without regard to the business practices of the company, and implement the business rule through the business-logic layer of the system. This would mean implementing a field-validation rule that would allow any postal code to be entered in the table, and using a business-logic rule that restricted the postal codes to those three states. With this design, if the company ever dealt with the international work regulations and wanted to start marketing its services in Canada, your system could handle it by making a change in the business logic. No changes to the database design would be required.

Building business logic enforcement classes

In the earlier sections of this chapter you learned about the nature of business logic. In this section you will begin the design of your business-logic class hierarchy.

Abstraction of business logic into a class design

Abstraction is the process of describing a complex problem in simple terms. The abstraction of business logic as a requirement in your systems starts with designing a top-level class for all business-logic classes. You need to list the general requirements for a business-logic class. **Table 1** is a partial list of those requirements.

Table 1. *The essential design requirements for your business-logic base class.*

Requirement	Description
Present data	The programmer's interface of a business class must be capable of presenting data to the user-interface objects in a fashion that enforces the business-logic rules and eliminates the need for the user-interface layer to store any knowledge of those business-logic rules.
Process data	The business-logic class must present programmer's interface components that allow for the processing of data to enforce the business-logic rules during data update, insert, and delete operations.
Allow for specialization on subclasses	The base business-logic class must allow for easy subclassing for specializing to implement specific business logic rule sets.

Let's design a business-logic class for the project entity as it was described above. This business class will begin with an abstract class definition as the base business class. You'll use a form as the base class so you can take advantage of a private data session to isolate the business object's data from any other data that may be in use.

The purpose of the business class is to manage access to the data and enforce business-logic rules in the process. Therefore, you'll find that using business-logic objects in your applications will preclude the use of other data-management approaches. You might successfully build an application that mixes business-logic objects with other data-management approaches, but it would be quite difficult to maintain. The maintenance problems would be related to the fact that there are multiple methods in use for managing access to the data. A much better design would be to decide which way to manage data and stick with that approach throughout the application.

Let's get on to describing the base business class. In the project named *Chapter8*, you'll find a class library named *Business*. This class library holds two class definitions, busBase and busProject. Your base business class is busBase. This class is a subclass of the form with the properties and methods added to it. The properties and methods are listed in **Table 2** and **Table 3**, respectively.

Table 2. *The properties of your busBase class.*

Custom Property	Description
CurrentView	Contains a value that represents the current view of the business data. A business object may present data that can be seen in different "views," such as the Project business object, which can be seen as client projects or as employee projects. This property will track the current "view" of the data in the business object.
DataPath	The path for finding the database and tables.

Table 3. *The custom methods of the busBase class.*

Custom Method	Description
SetUpDataView	Moves the business object's data to a requested "record." Not coded in the base class due to the fact that the code is totally dependent on the detailed nature of the business object.

GetFields	Returns a string of field names (including the cursor alias) delimited with commas for the business data. Not coded in the base class.
GetFldData	Returns the current value for a specific field. Not coded in the base class.
GetNext	Moves to the next or previous record in the business data. Not coded in the base class.
OpenData	Opens the data for the business object. Not coded in the base class because it is coded differently for each subclass.
PutFldData	Puts a value into a field in the business data. Accepts two parameters: the alias.fieldname and the value to be put into the field. Returns a numeric value of 1 (successful), -1 (bad field name), -2 (data type mismatch), -3 (business rule violated), and -4 (bad alias name).
RevertData	Issues TableRevert for each cursor open in the business object.
SaveData	Issues TableUpdate for each cursor in the business object. The updates are wrapped in a transaction so it will be an all-or-none proposition. The ValidateRecord method is called for each alias. Returns .T. if successful and .F. if unsuccessful.
ValidateField	Called for each PutFldData operation. Accepts two parameters the alias.fieldname and the value to be tested. Can return logical, .T. for OK and .F. for bad data value. Not coded in the base class.
ValidateRecord	Similar to ValidateField except it is a record-level validation. One parameter is passed—the alias name to be validated. Not coded in the base class.

The three methods that contain code in the busBase class are PutFldData, RevertData, and SaveData. **Listing 8-1** shows the code for PutFldData.

Listing 8-1. The code for PutFldData.

```
LPARAMETERS pcField, pxValue
* Puts data into a field
* pcField is the alias qualified field name
* pxValue is the expression to be put into the field
*
* Calls ValidateField to check the validity of the field's value
* Returns 1 for success
*        -1 for invalid field name
*        -2 for data type mismatch
*        -3 for rule violation
*        -4 Invalid alias in the field name
*
LOCAL lcAlias, lcUpdateAlias
IF TYPE(pcField) = "U" OR NOT "." $ pcField
   * Invalid field name
   RETURN -1
ENDIF
IF TYPE("pxValue") <> TYPE(pcField)
   * Data type mismatch
   RETURN -2
```

```
ENDIF
IF NOT THISFORM.ValidateField( pcField, pxValue )
  * Invalid data
  RETURN -3
ENDIF
* Save the currently select alias
lcAlias = ALIAS()
* get the alias portion of the field name
lcUpdateAlias = LEFT( pcField, AT(".",pcField) -1 )
* Check to see that the alias of the field is valid
IF NOT USED( lcUpdateAlias )
  RETURN -4
ENDIF
* If we have a valid alias select it
SELECT ( lcUpdateAlias )
* Update the field in the buffer
REPLACE (pcField) WITH pxValue

* Reselect the alias we had at the start of this method
IF NOT EMPTY( lcAlias )
  SELECT ( lcAlias )
ELSE
  SELECT 0
ENDIF
* Return success
RETURN 1
```

This code shows the RevertData method.

```
* Tablereverts all alias'
lnHowMany = AUSED( laAlias )
IF lnHowmany = 0
  RETURN
ENDIF
FOR lnCnt = 1 TO lnHowmany
  IF CursorGetProp("BUFFERING",laAlais(lnCnt,1)) > 1
    TableRevert( .T., laAlias( lnCnt, 1 ) )
  ENDIF
ENDFOR
RETURN
```

Finally, the SaveData method code for the busBase class:

```
* Tableupdates the alias's in a transaction
* Returns .T. for success and .F. for failure and reversion
LOCAL laAlias(1,2), llRollback, lnHowmany, lnCnt
* Get the number of alias' open
lnHowMany = AUSED( laAlias )
IF lnHowmany = 0
  * If there are no alias' open get out
  RETURN
ENDIF
* Work the alias'
FOR lnCnt = 1 TO lnHowmany
  * Call the ValidateRecord for this alias
  IF NOT THISFORM.ValidateRecord( laAlias( lnCnt, 1 ) )
    * Failed validation
```

```
   * Revert the data
   THISFORM.RevertData()
   * Get out
   RETURN .F.
 ENDIF
ENDFOR

* Start a transaction
BEGIN TRANSACTION
* Work the alias'
FOR lnCnt = 1 TO lnHowmany
  * TableUpdate this alias
  IF NOT TableUpdate( 1, .F., laAlias( lnCnt, 1 ) )
    * Failed update
    * Set rollback variable
    llRollBack = .T.
    * End the loop
    EXIT
  ENDIF
ENDFOR
IF llRollBack
  * If the rollback variable is set
  ROLLBACK
  * Revert the buffers
  THISFORM.RevertData()
ELSE
  * No rollback then commit the transaction
  END TRANSACTION
ENDIF
* Return the result
RETURN NOT llRollBack
```

The code in these methods is simplified to demonstrate the ideas involved. Any one of the methods could be expanded to handle additional behavior. For example, the SaveData method could be expanded to detect the reason why a table update failed and recover from those situations where recovery is possible. Expanding these methods for additional functionality is left as an exercise for the reader. Here, the purpose is to understand the nature of business classes and how you can build them.

Building a subclass

To demonstrate how to customize a business class, try building a project business class that enforces the following rules: Projects are only seen as related to either clients or employees, and the project size limit in your application is $100,000. For this example you'll use the Time and Billing data supplied on the book's CD.

The methods and events that have code added to them in your busProject class are Init, OpenData, Load, SetUpDataView, GetFldData, GetNext, and ValidateField. The code below shows the Init event for your busProject class.

```
SET MULTILOCKS ON
```

The following code shows the OpenData method:

```
* Open the tables and set the buffering mode for the project data
USE Data\Employees ORDER PrimaryKey ALIAS Employees IN 0
SELECT Employees
CursorSetProp("BUFFERING",5)
USE Data\Clients ORDER PrimaryKey ALIAS Clients IN 0
SELECT Clients
CursorSetProp("BUFFERING",5)
USE Data\Projects ALIAS Projects IN 0
SELECT Projects
CursorSetProp("BUFFERING",5)
```

The Init and OpenData methods simply open the tables required and set their buffering mode to optimistic table buffering. Following is the code in the Load event for your class:

```
SET DELETED ON
SET TALK OFF
```

This code sets a few environment options for the class. **Listing 8-2** shows the SetUpDataView code.

Listing 8-2 . The SetUpDataView method code.

```
LPARAMETERS pcView, piId
* pcView = "CLIENTS" or "EMPLOYEES"
* piId = The PK for the client or employee to get projects for

IF EMPTY(pcView)
  * No view supplied
  RETURN .F.
ENDIF
IF pcView = "CLIENTS"
  * We want the client view
  IF THISFORM.CurrentView <> "CLIENTS"
   * If we are not already seeing the Client
   * view of the data set it up
   SELECT Employees
   SET RELATION TO
   SELECT Projects
   SET ORDER TO ClientId
   SET RELATION TO iEmployeeID INTO Employees
   SELECT Clients
   IF EMPTY( piId )
     SET KEY TO iClientID
   ELSE
     SET KEY TO piId
   ENDIF
   SET RELATION TO iClientID INTO Projects
   LOCATE
  ENDIF
ELSE
  * We want the employee view
  IF THISFORM.CurrentView <> "EMPLOYEES"
   * If we are not already seeing the Employee
   * view of the data set it up
   SELECT Clients
   SET RELATION TO
```

```
   SELECT Projects
   SET ORDER TO EmployeeId
   SET RELATION TO iClientID INTO Clients
   SELECT Employees
   IF EMPTY( piID )
     SET KEY TO iEmployeeID
   ELSE
     SET KEY TO piId
   ENDIF
   SET RELATION TO iEmployeeID INTO Projects
   LOCATE
  ENDIF
ENDIF
* Set the current view property
THISFORM.CurrentView = pcView

RETURN .T.
```

The SetUpDataView method simply sets up the data relations and cursor orders to provide the requested "view" of the data. This code uses tables from the database directly. The
code could just as easily use local views or even remote views for its data (see Chapter 5 for
more on views). Also notice that the code above uses the SET KEY command on the master
table to restrict the child table to only the records for a given key. You might think of using a
SET FILTER, but SET KEY is much faster, even if the filter condition is fully optimizable.

Here is the GetFldData method for the busProject class:

```
LPARAMETERS pcField
IF EMPTY(pcField)
   * No field supplied
   RETURN .NULL.
ENDIF

RETURN EVALUATE(pcField)
```

The code listed above is very simple, returning the contents of a field passed as a parameter to the method. This code could be much more complex, depending on the business
object you are creating. Perhaps you'd need to make calculations or requery views before returning the field value.

Listing 8-3 is the code that moves the record pointer.

Listing 8-3. *The GetNext method code*
```
LPARAMETERS pcWhat, pnHowMany
* pcWhat = "PROJECT" or empty indicating next master record
IF EMPTY( pcWhat )
   * Force pcWhat to character
   pcWhat = ""
ENDIF
IF EMPTY( pnHowMany )
   * Default to 1
   pnHowMany = 1
ENDIF
LOCAL lnRecno, llRet, lcAlias
IF EMPTY(THISFORM.CurrentView)
   * If SetUpDataView has never been successful
```

```
    RETURN llRet
ENDIF
* Save current alias
lcAlias = ALIAS()
IF THISFORM.CurrentView = "CLIENTS"
  * If we are in client view
  IF UPPER(pcWhat) = "PROJECT"
   * If the request is for the next project
   SELECT Projects
   IF NOT EOF() AND NOT BOF()
     * If we are not at eof or bof
     lnRecno = RECNO()
     * move in the direction requested
     SKIP pnHowMany
     IF EOF() OR BOF() OR iClientID <> Clients.iClientID
      * If hit eof or bof or the project is not for the current client
      GOTO lnRecno
     ELSE
      * We've got one
      llRet = .T.
     ENDIF
   ENDIF
  ELSE
   * If the request was the next client
   SELECT Clients
   * Shut off the set key
   SET KEY TO
   IF NOT EOF() AND NOT BOF()
     * If we are not at eof or bof
     lnRecno = RECNO()
     * move in the direction requested
     SKIP pnHowMany
     IF EOF() OR BOF()
      * if we hit eof or bof
      GOTO lnRecno
     ELSE
      * We've got one
      llRet = .T.
     ENDIF
   ENDIF
   * Reset the set key
   SET KEY TO iClientID
  ENDIF
ELSE
  IF UPPER(pcWhat) = "PROJECT"
   SELECT Projects
   IF NOT EOF() AND NOT BOF()
     lnRecno = RECNO()
     SKIP pnHowMany
     IF EOF() OR BOF() OR iEmployeeID <> Employees.iEmployeeID
      GOTO lnRecno
     ELSE
      llRet = .T.
     ENDIF
   ENDIF
  ELSE
   SELECT Employees
   SET KEY TO
   IF NOT EOF() AND NOT BOF()
```

```
    lnRecno = RECNO()
    SKIP pnHowMany
    IF EOF() OR BOF()
     GOTO lnRecno
    ELSE
     llRet = .T.
    ENDIF
   ENDIF
   SET KEY TO iEmployeeID
  ENDIF
ENDIF
* Reselect the alias
IF NOT EMPTY( lcAlias )
  SELECT ( lcAlias )
ELSE
  SELECT 0
ENDIF
* Return the result
RETURN llRet
```

The GetNext method allows the developer to request a movement in either the master or child cursor. The master is either the Clients or the Employees cursor, depending on the current view, and the child is the Projects cursor. The movement can be any number of records either forward or backward. This functionality is provided through the two accepted parameters: pcWhat and pnHowMany.

The first parameter, pcWhat, is either blank or "PROJECTS." If it's blank, the master alias for the view is used. If pcWhat is "PROJECTS," then the movement will be in the Projects alias. The second parameter, pnHowMany, is a number indicating the number of records to move. A positive number moves forward and a negative number moves backward.

The code for the client view movement is commented to describe each part of the operation. The employee view is essentially the same except it uses the employee alias instead of the client alias. The method returns either .T. or .F., indicating success or failure, respectively.

The following code shows the ValidateField method for the busProject class, and it implements the limitation on the billing estimate for the project to $100,000:

```
LPARAMETERS pcField, pxValue
* Validates field values according to the business logic rules
LOCAL llRet
llRet = .T.
DO CASE
  CASE pcField = "Projects.yProjectTotalBillingEstimate"
    * Now allowed to exceed 100,000
    IF pxValue > 100000 OR pxValue < 0
      llRet = .F.
    ENDIF
ENDCASE
RETURN llRet
```

Again, this code is greatly simplified from what you might see in a real business-class definition, but it does demonstrate the idea of validating on a field-by-field basis. In any real situation, the DO CASE construct would probably be much larger to handle the many fields requiring validation. If the validation code for any one field is complex enough, it might be implemented in a custom method of its own that is called from this method.

Implementing business-logic classes into an application

To demonstrate how you might put these business logic classes to use, I built a form named *ClProj* in the *Chapter8* project. This form is based on your frmData class from Chapter 7 and uses the busProject business class as its data source. The data environment for ClProj is empty because the business class provides all data. In Chapter 7 you built a form class that managed the data. In that situation you used the form's data environment. Here you are building an n-tier system, one requirement of which is that the tiers you build be independent of each other. If you were to use and depend on the form's data environment in any way, you'd preclude the design from being used when the user interface is not Visual FoxPro. So here you don't use the form's data environment.

There is code in a number of methods and events of the form. The code listed below shows the code in the form's Load event.

```
THISFORM.BusObj = NewObject("busProject","VCX\Business.vcx")
THISFORM.BusObj.SetUpDataView("CLIENTS")
```

This code first creates an instance of the busProject class. It then calls the busProject object's SetUpDataView method, requesting the Client view of the data. Notice that you are storing the reference to the business object in a form property named BusObj. Using the BusObj property to hold the reference to the business object allows you to easily refer to the business object form with any code in any method of the form, or any objects in the form.

This line of code shows the Init of the form:

```
THISFORM.RefreshData()
```

The Init is calling a form method named RefreshData, which is a custom method that you have added to this form. The following code shows the code in the RefreshData method:

```
WITH THISFORM
   .txtBase1.Value = .BusObj.GetFldData("Clients.cCompanyName")
   .txtBase2.Value = .BusObj.GetFldData("Projects.cProjectName")
   .txtBase3.Value = .BusObj.GetFldData("Employees.cLastName")
   .txtBase4.Value = BusObj.GetFldData("Projects.yProjectTotalBillingEstimate")
ENDWITH
```

This method sets the value properties of various textboxes in the form to the value returned from calls to the business object's GetFldData method. The next methods you will examine are two of the frmData class's methods and two new ones you have added to this form. These are the GoNext, GoPrevious, GoNextProj, and GoPrevProj methods, respectively. Here is the GoNext method:

```
IF THISFORM.busObj.GetNext()
   THISFORM.RefreshData()
ELSE
```

```
  MessageBox( "This is the last client record", MB_OK+MB_ICONINFORMATION,
"Last Record")
ENDIF
```

Here is the GoPrevious method:

```
IF THISFORM.busObj.GetNext("", -1)
  THISFORM.RefreshData()
ELSE
  MessageBox( "This is the first client record", MB_OK+MB_ICONINFORMATION,
"First Record")
ENDIF
```

Notice the simplicity of the code in these two methods. They call the business object's GetNext method, passing the numeric argument for the proper movement. If GetNext fails, the form's code displays a message box to the user. An important thing to note here is that none of the code in the business class definitions ever displays any messages to the user.

This is because the business classes are data managers and therefore they have no responsibility to interact with the user. It is the responsibility of the form, which is the user interface object, to provide the interaction with the user.

Here is the GoNextProj method:

```
IF THISFORM.busObj.GetNext("PROJECT")
  THISFORM.RefreshData()
ELSE
  MessageBox( "This is the last project record for this client", ;
   MB_OK+MB_ICONINFORMATION, "Last Record")
ENDIF
```

And here is the GoPrevProj method:

```
IF THISFORM.busObj.GetNext("PROJECT", -1)
  THISFORM.RefreshData()
ELSE
  MessageBox( "This is the first project record for this client", ;
   MB_OK+MB_ICONINFORMATION, "First Record")
ENDIF
```

These last two methods are similar to the previous two, except for the first argument to the GetNext method and the text of the messages.

The click methods of the command buttons call the respective form methods listed above. **Listing 8-4** shows the valid event for the textbox, which displays the estimated dollars.

Listing 8-4. *The Valid for the textbox showing estimated dollars.*

```
LOCAL lnReturn, llRet, lcMessage
IF THISFORM.ReleaseType > 0
  * If the user is exiting the form discard the edit
  RETURN
ENDIF
lcMessage = ""
lnReturn = ;
```

```
THISFORM.BusObj.PutFldData("Projects.yProjectTotalBillingEstimate",
THIS.Value)
DO CASE
  CASE lnReturn = 1
    * Success
    llRet = .T.
  CASE lnReturn = -1
    * Bad field name error
    lcMessage = "PROGRAM ERROR - Projects.yProjectTotalBillingEstimate " + ;
        "is not a valid field name"
  CASE lnReturn = -2
    * Data type mismatch
    lcMessage = "PROGRAM ERROR - Data type mismatch for field update"
  CASE lnReturn = -3
    * Rule violation
    lcMessage = "Estimated $ has an invalid value"
  CASE lnReturn = -4
    * Invalid alias
    lcMessage = "PROGRAM ERROR - The alias name for the field is invalid"
  OTHERWISE
    * Unknown error
    lcMessage = "PROGRAM ERROR - error nature is unknown"
ENDCASE
IF NOT llRet
  Messagebox( lcMessage, MB_OK+MB_ICONEXCLAMATION, "Data error")
  THISFORM.BusObj.RevertData()
  THISFORM.RefreshData()
ELSE
  THISFORM.BusObj.SaveData()
ENDIF
RETURN IIF(llRet, llRet, 0)
```

Figure 2 shows the form as it's running.

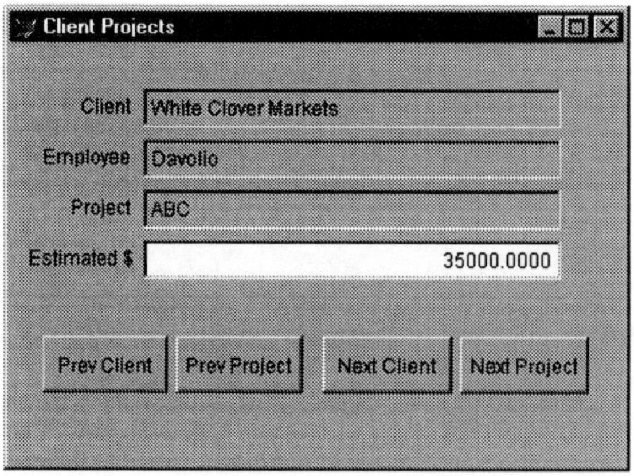

Figure 2. The ClProjX form.

What's the point?

This chapter has discussed the design and programming of business-logic classes. The objects created from these classes provide data-management and rule-enforcement functionality. If

Visual FoxPro's database can enforce rules and the form's data environment can provide data access, why do you need these business-logic objects?

The accurate answer to the question is that you *don't* need them. Data access and rule enforcement can be accomplished without business-logic objects. However, using business-logic objects encapsulates the data access and rules enforcement in a layer that is separate from the database or the user interface. This separation provides the ability to modify an application to use a different interface application without affecting the database, and to change the database without affecting the interface.

In object-oriented design terminology, you have to provide a consistent interface between the database and the user interface through the business-logic object. You can change the interface or the database being used by simply making changes to the business-logic object's code.

Given this "feature" of business-logic objects, there is a flaw in what you've done in these exercises so far. That flaw is that the user-interface layer of this design is restricted to Visual FoxPro. Although the business objects do make the coding of your forms consistent, they do not allow you to use a different application for the interface layer.

The next section will address this weakness and provide business classes that can be used even when Visual FoxPro is not the user-interface application.

Using ActiveX servers for business-logic objects

Visual FoxPro can build ActiveX servers that contain your classes. These servers will expose your classes so they can be created using applications other than Visual FoxPro. A complete discussion of ActiveX servers is beyond the scope of this book, so this discussion will address only those issues that have a direct effect on your goal.

The first thing to do is create a new project named *Chap8x* to hold the classes for your server DLL. A copy of this project is in the download files. Your project contains the business class library. You need to edit each of the two classes and set them to be OLEPublic classes (using the **Class Info** dialog on the **Project** menu). **Figure 3** shows this dialog for the busBase class.

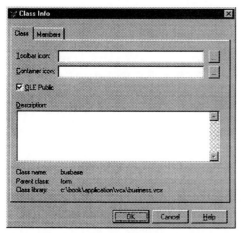

*Figure 3. The **Class Info** dialog for the busBase class.*

Once the classes have been made OLEPublic, you have to build the DLL. In the project, click the Build button and select the **Build OLE DLL** option button. **Figure 4** shows the build dialog set up in the proper way.

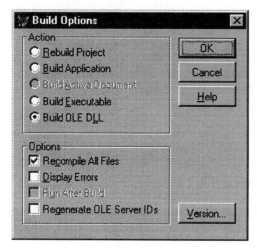

Figure 4. The ClProj form.

The process of building the DLL builds a DLL file and all of the required associated files, and then registers the DLL on the machine. If you distribute this DLL to other machines, you'll need to register it on those machines before it can be used.

Let's use your server

In the project *Chapter8* there is a second form named ClProjX. If you open this form for editing and look at the Load event, you'll see the following code:

```
THISFORM.BusObj = CreateObject("Chap8X.busProject")
THISFORM.BusObj.SetUpDataView("CLIENTS")
```

The difference between this form and the ClProj form is the code used to create the busProject object. Here, the class used is *chap8x.busproject,* which refers to your ActiveX server. All of the remaining code in this form is exactly the same as in the ClProj form. The code doesn't need to be changed because the methods of the business object have the same names. The only difference is that one is a native VFP object and the other is an ActiveX server object.

Where's the beef?

You now have your busProject class built as an ActiveX server. The major advantage of creating the business class in an ActiveX server is that you can now use this object in applications other than Visual FoxPro. To demonstrate this, try creating an Excel macro that uses your busProject class to create an object and then fills the cells in the Excel worksheet with data from your Visual FoxPro tables.

Listing 8-5 shows the Excel Visual Basic for Applications macro code.

Listing 8-5
```
Dim oProject As New chap8x.busproject
Sub project()
  With ActiveSheet
    .Cells(1, 1).Value = oProject.SETUPDATAVIEW("CLIENTS", "")
    .Cells(1, 1).Value = "Client"
    .Cells(1, 2).Value = RTrim(oProject.GETFLDDATA("Clients.cCompanyName"))
    .Cells(2, 1).Value = "Employee"
    .Cells(2, 2).Value = RTrim(oProject.GETFLDDATA("Employees.cLastName")) + ",
       " +RTrim(oProject.GETFLDDATA("Employees.cFirstName"))
    .Cells(3, 1).Value = "Project"
    .Cells(3, 2).Value = RTrim(oProject.GETFLDDATA("Projects.cProjectName"))
    .Cells(4, 1).Value = "Estimate"
    .Cells(4, 2).Value = oProject.GETFLDDATA("Projects.
       yProjectTotalBillingEstimate")
  End With
End Sub
```

Note that the line getting the employee's name should be one line of code—not two as formatted above. The two-line formatting was used here to fit the listing in the available space. The code in this macro first declares a new object from your busProject class in the chap8x.dll that you created earlier. Then a subprocedure is created that first sets up the view of the data and then calls the GetFldData method of your object to read data and write it to certain cells of the currently active Excel worksheet.

This Excel file is named Chapter8.xls in the download files. **Figure 5** shows the Excel worksheet after you have chosen **Tools – Macros,** highlighted your macro, and clicked **Run.**

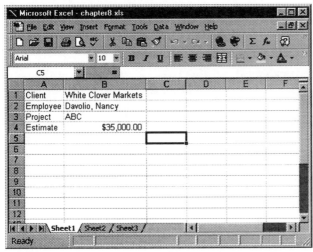

***Figure 5.** The Excel worksheet after using your busProject class to get data.*

Summary

In Chapter 7, you built data-management classes for use exclusively within Visual FoxPro. These classes represented one way to approach accessing data. In this chapter you were introduced to a new way to handle data by using business-logic objects. These objects added some new dimensions to the data-management process. Among the new features was enforcement of logical rules, in addition to the database-integrity rules and presenting data in accordance with the natural way that a business sees its information.

The business classes you built were, admittedly, only demonstrations of the ideas. They were not complete business-logic classes; however, they did show you some ways of accomplishing the goals involved.

With these classes, you saw a mechanism of separating the user interface from the business logic and the business logic from the data. Using a form, you could easily change the data source to Microsoft SQL Server or Oracle by making changes only to the business logic classes—and not to the form itself.

Then you took it all one step further by producing your business classes as an ActiveX server. This allowed you to use the same business logic in both Visual FoxPro and Excel. Microsoft Visual Basic, Microsoft Access, Borland Delphi, or any other application or development language that supports ActiveX servers could use this same busProject ActiveX server.

If you think about the last two chapters for a while, you'll begin to notice that there are advantages and disadvantages to either approach. The approach in Chapter 7 suffers from being limited to Visual FoxPro, only because there is a dependence on FoxPro's data environment and its data-binding capabilities. However, the Chapter 7 approach has the advantage of letting you work with the visual designers within Visual FoxPro, and that can reduce your development time considerably.

The Chapter 8 approach has the advantage of providing a degree of independence between the user interface and the data storage. The N-Tier design model allows you to use the same data with different front ends. One disadvantage of the N-Tier model is that the use of the Visual FoxPro developer's interface is somewhat restricted when it comes to dealing with the data.

So, what do you do? Which approach should you use? The answers to those questions lie in a pragmatic review of the requirements of the application you are building. You should know how to build both models and choose the one that is best suited to the application at hand. It doesn't make sense to build an N-Tier model, with all of its inherent flexibility, if the application will never use any other interface than Visual FoxPro forms and never access data stored in any other database. It's equally nonsensical to build a model that only supports Visual FoxPro tiers, if that information will need to be accessed by Microsoft Excel or some other application.

The conclusion: Build the model that solves the problem at hand.

Chapter 9
Forms

In many ways, the forms for an application are what it's all about—everything else is just along to hand 'em the saw! Forms allow the user to interact with the data, so from the user's standpoint, forms can arguably be considered the "heart" of the application. This chapter begins to look at forms as containers for the form controls that are discussed in chapters 10 and 11, and discusses issues that relate to forms without regard to what you put on them and what data they manipulate.

Loose coupling and forms

Without getting too esoteric, let me simply offer the advice that all forms *should* be capable of running independently from an application or from other forms. This accomplishes a couple of things. First, it greatly facilitates development, testing and debugging. I'm much more inclined to create a form incrementally (adding a little piece of functionality at a time and testing) if I don't have to fire up the entire application in order to test it.

Secondly, it encourages a good design principle known as *loose coupling* (more on this a little later). Clearly, it isn't possible to follow this stricture in all cases. At a minimum, some forms are designed to accept an optional parameter, and it will be necessary to test another form's ability to pass the argument and for the form being tested to receive and act on the parameter. Then, too, there are cases in which two forms operate cooperatively in some way. In general, if your app has a form that you can't simply run using DO FORM <form name> from the command window, the design of that form deserves a second look. The dependencies of such a form may indeed be unavoidable; however, forms that display this level of dependence should be the exception rather than the rule.

Steve McConnell, in his landmark book *Code Complete* (Microsoft Press, 1993), presents the concept of Loose Coupling. While much of his book does not address object-oriented or object-based systems specifically, the principles he sets forth are often just as applicable (with some conceptual adaptation) to an object-oriented development tool like Visual FoxPro. "Loose Coupling" in a procedural language simply means "black-boxing" your code. A loosely coupled routine can be called from anywhere in a system and it will do its job, without regard to where it is called or the state of the system when it is called. The knowledge that the rest of the system requires of the routine's inner workings is minimized to (at most) a parameter list.

If Steve McConnell's book Code Complete *(Microsoft Press, 1993, ISBN 1-55615-484-4) isn't on your bookshelf (or maybe even on your nightstand), it should be. In my opinion, any programmer or application developer absolutely* must *read this book if they consider themselves a professional. Other books are important, too (see Appendix 4), but this is the one you absolutely cannot ignore. If you can't spare the time or expense to find, buy and read this book, you might want to consider taking up something else for a living. I keep it on my desk (alongside the* Hacker's Guide to Visual FoxPro*) and read* *from it randomly on a regular basis for inspiration, just as others will consult the* Book of Changes, *or* The Prophet *or* Thoughts of Chairman Mao.

Extending this idea to Visual FoxPro forms, loose coupling means that our forms should ideally be able to run in any context. Clearly, a form is usually pretty dependent on the availability of data structured in a specific way, with certain expectations as to the names of tables, fields, indexes and so on. However, given that minimal requirement, the form should be able to function, at least in some manner, without dependence on other parts of the system.

In Chapter 3, I discussed "system-level services," and it is perfectly reasonable to have our forms make use of these services *when available*, but be able to function properly even if the system-level services in question are unavailable. As an example, consider an application with the following features:

- The application employs a form manager object. This object is responsible for actually launching all forms, keeping track of which forms are in use, and allowing us to programmatically manipulate our running forms—to cascade them, close them, tile them, and so on.
- The application is one in which one form frequently launches another related (modeless) form; thus it will make calls to the DoForm() method of the form manager object.
- The form manager object always passes a self-reference to any form it launches so that the form can easily communicate with the form manager.

As you might imagine, to support these features requires a method of the foundation form class called DoForm(). This method passes the name (and any optional parameters) to the form manager object, telling it what form it needs to launch, and has code in its Init() method to accept the reference to the form manager object. While at first it sounds like it will be difficult to test these forms without having the form manager object hanging about, the solution is to just bracket the necessary code as shown in **Listing 9-1**.

Listing 9-1. Bracketing form method code to reduce dependence on system-level services.

```
* Init() Method
LPARAMETERS toFormManager
ThisForm.oFormManger = toFormManager

* DoForm() Method
LPARAMETERS tcFormName, tuParm1, tuParm2
IF VARTYPE(ThisForm.oFormManager) = ""O"" ;
     AND NOT ISNULL(ThisForm.oFormManager)
   ThisForm.oFormManger.DoForm(tcFormName,tuParm1,tuParm2)
ELSE
   DO CASE
   CASE PCOUNT() = 1
      DO FORM (tcFormName) WITH .NULL.
   CASE PCOUNT() = 2
      DO FORM (tcFormName) WITH .NULL., tuParm1
   CASE PCOUNT() = 3
      DO FORM (tcFormName) WITH .NULL., tuParm1, tuParm2
```

```
    ENDCASE
ENDIF
```

The point here is that the form can make use of the system-level service if it's available, but can function just fine without it when necessary. There are several ways this can be accomplished.

First, as shown in Listing 9-1, the form (or any other object) can simply provide the required service itself, in the absence of another object that normally provides the service. The form is only interested in getting another form launched. The other services of the form manager object are not really of much interest to the form, although they are very important to the application as a whole. It's like a worker who needs to have a bunch of photocopies run off, but finds that the clerical person who normally handles this is out to lunch. The worker simply does the job himself. Unlike the clerical person, however, they ignore the "toner low" message, and don't log the information as to how many copies were run and for which department!

Second, in the absence of an object to provide certain services, the form can instantiate the object that normally provides the services, or a substitute object that can provide the services. For example, an application object might provide a service to read information from and write information to the system registry. In the context of the application, the form, when run, normally asks the application object what 'its position and WindowState was the last time the user opened this form, so it can restore those settings. If the form is running from the command window (without the application object present), it could simply instantiate an object that provides those services (like the registry object that is included in the VFP 6 REGISTRY.VCX sample class library).

Finally, the form can simply exhibit certain default behaviors or settings in the absence of a system-level service. As in the example above, if the application object doesn't exist, the form simply centers itself on the screen at a default size.

You may feel that providing application-level support for a certain function, and then providing the means for a form to provide this service directly, is redundant. It is, and should lead you to think about how you want to provide this functionality. I prefer to provide this kind of functionality globally to the application. You may prefer to simply have the form provide the service in all cases. With my approach, the ability of the form to provide the service is useful only during testing an action of a form that relies on the application-level service. Using the registry example above, my code checks for the existence of a registry interface object, and if it doesn't exist, simply establishes default values that it would have retrieved from the registry had the registry object been available. Does this mean that I can only test the code that depends on values obtained from the registry object by running the entire application? No. My registry classes "register" themselves as the registry object if they find that their parent object is a form. The following code is the Init() code from my registry class:

```
DODEFAULT()
IF VARTYPE(This.Parent) = "O" ;
        AND UPPER(This.Parent.BaseClass) = "FORM"
  llHasRegObjectProp = PEMSTATUS(This.Parent,"oregistry",5)
  IF llHasRegObjectProp
        ThisForm.oRegistry = This
  ENDIF
ENDIF
```

Thus, when I need to test the form's ability to read and write to the registry, rather than firing up the entire application, I can simply drop an instance of the registry object onto the form, run and test the form, then remove the registry object from the form.

If I were to find that I was testing this functionality on every form, I'd be inclined to include the registry object in my form foundation class, and abandon the approach of providing these services only through the an application-level registry object

However application independence is achieved for our forms, it makes our lives as developers much easier, and in the long run makes our forms and the applications in which they're used a little more flexible, and much better designed.

Private data sessions

Right on the heels of the transition from procedurally generated "screens" to object-based forms and the ability to create modeless forms without any special coding, the introduction of the *private data session* is one of the most significant advances in user-interface creation gained with Visual FoxPro. Only those of you who used FoxPro and other Xbase languages prior to Visual FoxPro 3.0 can appreciate this feature. Literally millions of lines of code have probably been written to allow different FoxPro 2.x screens to operate simultaneously on their own set of data without hosing the other screen's data environment. The private data session "scopes" the tables, views, index files, relations, filters, record pointers, controlling indexes and many of the environmental settings that affect how data-related elements behave to the *form*. Without a private data session, forms would all be playing in the same sandbox. Form "B" could open a table, and if it wasn't careful to select an empty work area, could inadvertently close a table that was currently in use by Form "A". Form "B" or a procedure could change an environmental setting, say SET NEAR from "OFF" to "ON", significantly changing the behavior of Form "A".

Provided that your intention is to create a modeless, event-driven application, "2 - Private Data Session" should be just about the only setting that you use for the DataSession property. There may be situations in which you might have system-level tables open in the default data session and need to have a form to interact with them; however, this should be the exception.

Sharing data sessions

One issue that developers often have to face is the concept of a "child" form, that is, a form (usually modal) that is launched from and intended to interact with the data displayed on another form. One technique is to create a parent form with a private data session, and from that form launch a modal child form that uses a default data session. This will, indeed, allow the child form to interact with the parent form's data, and will, in effect, "share" the parent form's data session. However, there is a piece of anomalous behavior that has not (in my experience) caused any difficulty, but certainly causes many of us to think twice about using this method.

When a form with a private data session is run, its data session is identified by number and the name of the form that created it in the Data Session window (for example, frmTest1(2)). When this form launches a modal form that uses the default data session, the Data Session will show the new form name along with the data session (that is, frmTest2(2)). So far, so good. Now, however, when the second modal form is closed, the Data Session window shows Unknown(2). VFP knows what data session is in use, but for some reason no longer recognizes the form participating in this data session. If you want to use this method of sharing data sessions, be aware of this behavior, so that if something does get a little squirrelly at some point, you won't be too surprised. On the other hand, Microsoft has assured me that this behavior is indeed "by design," and that no unexpected or undesired effects of this anomalous reference to an "unknown" data session are to be expected.

Another issue with sharing a data session in this way is that if the child form is *not* modal, the parent form can be destroyed, taking the data session with it and closing all tables that the child table is using. Some steps must be taken to ensure that the parent form cannot be closed, leaving the child form hanging around. The easiest way to do this with a non-modal child form is to link the child form to the parent form via a property of the parent form, so that destruction of the parent form destroys the child form. Create a new property of the parent form, something like oChildForm, and then launch the child form with a line of code like this:

```
DO FORM <childForm> NAME ThisForm.oChildForm LINKED
```

Running the child form in this way, using the NAME...LINKED keywords, allows the parent form to call the methods and set the properties of the child form if necessary. It also allows the child form to be closed programmatically, and causes the child form to be destroyed automatically when closing the parent form.

I prefer to have all of my forms use a private data session, but have successfully used the "private parent, default child" technique described above. If I have two forms that must share a data session, another technique I use is to pass the parent form's DataSessionID to the child form as an argument, and the Init() code of the child form then sets its DataSessionID to match that of the parent. Just as with the technique of setting the child form's DataSession to "1- Default", the tables are opened and closed by the parent table, and thus can leave the child table without any tables to work with if the child table isn't modal. In addition to the technique illustrated above, setting the DataEnvironment.AutoCloseTables property to .F. in the parent form also prevents this problem. If the child form isn't running, the tables are closed anyway when the parent form's destruction also destroys the data session.

In general, I haven't found too many uses for FormSets, given the availability of PageFrames, and now with the inclusion of scrollbars in VFP 6 forms, FormSets in my opinion have even less utility. However, they are very well suited to sharing data sessions between different forms. The problem is that it isn't possible to get any form in a FormSet to behave as a modal child form—even if the FormSet is modal, all forms within the set are active, and the user can switch freely between the forms within the set.

Making the modal/modeless decision at runtime

While most of our forms are modeless, a modal form in the right place at the right time can really do the trick. For instance, if you have a "Search" or "Filter" form, it doesn't make much sense to allow the user to return focus to whatever form called the Search or Filter form until they've either made their choices or canceled the operation.

However, not all forms fall easily into either the modal or modeless category. If I have a search form that allows me to search and narrow down the list of all customers by name, sales volume, territory, zip code or last activity, and I call this form from the form that allows me to edit customer information, I want it to be modal. This forces the user to either select a customer, who'se ID is passed back to the calling form, or to cancel the search, in which case the user is returned to the calling form in its previous state. On the other hand, If I launch this search form from a menu pad that says "Customers", allowing the user to select a customer and then launching one of several customer-oriented forms based on that selection, I want the search form to be modeless. How can I make the form modal in one situation but modeless in another?

The WindowType property is indeed read/write at runtime, but take care when changing this property. When a modeless (WindowType = 0) form is run, any lines of code following the DO FORM command are executed after the form is instantiated. By contrast, when a modal form (WindowType = 1) is launched, the instantiation of that form introduces a *wait state*. This means that the execution of the code following the DO FORM command does *not* execute until the form is closed. If a modeless form is instantiated, and its WindowType property is changed from 0 to 1 by calling the Show() method (by passing an argument of "1"), the wait state commences with the execution of the Show() method. Thus you can instantiate a form, and then immediately call the form's Show method to both make the form visible and change its WindowType property:

```
DO FORM <FormName> NAME oForm NOSHOW
oForm.Show(1)
```

Doing this will introduce a wait state with the call to the Show() method. So far, so good.

However, sometimes it's necessary to have the form return a value using DO FORM <FormName> TO <memvar>. In this case, an error will occur as soon as the calling routine tries to make the form visible. Visual FoxPro expects the form to be modal when run with the TO <memvar> clause, and in this case the calling routine executes another line of code immediately after the form is instantiated.

The solution is to toggle the WindowType within the Init() or other method of the form (called by the Init()), but to do so by changing the property directly and *not* by calling the Show() method. Remember, Show(1) introduces a wait state that is terminated only with the destruction of the form. This puts us in a catch-22 situation: The form can't be terminated because one of its methods is executing. You've probably observed this when you suspended execution of a form method and then tried to release the form before canceling or resuming the method. The form will usually become invisible, but you can't edit the form in the form designer because the form hasn't been destroyed. Trying to force destruction of the form with CLEAR ALL will trigger a "Can't clear the object in use" error. The object is "in use" because code in one of its methods is still in the process of being executed (though it is currently suspended).

Thus, depending on the circumstance, the proper method of making an otherwise modeless form modal at runtime is to either use the Form.Show(1) method from the calling routine, or toggle the WindowType property in the form's Init() method.

Continuing with the example of the search form mentioned above, the calling form passes a self-reference to the search form, so that the search form knows that it should be run modally. If its Init() method does not see a form reference passed, it doesn't change the WindowType property, and it runs as a modeless form. This also has the advantage of allowing such a form, made modeless at runtime, to return a value to the calling procedure. This can't be done when setting the WindowType property to "1 - Modal" from the calling procedure—an error is triggered as soon as VFP detects (by recognizing that the next line in the calling pro-n error is triggered as soon as VFP detects (by recognizing that the next line in the calling procedure is executing) that you've executed a DO FORM...TO on a modeless form.

Passing data between forms

As with procedures and functions, values can be passed to a form by launching it with arguments that are received as parameters by the form's Init() method. As with procedures and functions, a form (provided it's modal) can return a value to the calling routine. However, some limitations to this process can present problems, particularly when multiple values need to be transferred to or retrieved from a form:

- Entire arrays can be passed to forms by reference, but go "out of scope" as soon as the Init() method code completes, necessitating transfer of the array data to a form array property.
- Object (including form) array properties cannot be passed as arguments, nor can they be returned as return values from the Unload() event of the form.

The solution to these problems is to stop thinking in the usual terms of "passing data." In procedural programming, data is passed from one routine to another as arguments/parameters, (dare I say it?) public or global memory variables, or as a value returned from a function call. A common practice in Visual FoxPro is to call a method of an object, or instantiate an object and pass data to it via an argument: DO FORM <whatever> WITH <some value>. If it's necessary for the form or the function to handle a set of data, an array is passed by reference, which has the added benefit (for a function, anyway) of allowing the function to return multiple values in the array.

Why be limited to this way of passing data when working with *objects*? After all, an object can contain a virtually unlimited amount of data (of any type) in its properties. Some folks have suggested creating a "wrapper" procedure that establishes a private array that is scoped to the procedure, and therefore to any form the procedure calls. Others have suggested passing an object containing an array property to a form instead of an array. The form can then store a reference to the passed object to a property and manipulate the array property; and the calling routine (which passed the reference to the object) can then retrieve the values from the array after the form runs. When working with forms, however, the "middle man" can be eliminated by simply passing a reference to the calling form, and allowing the called form to manipulate the calling form's properties directly.

Going back to the search form mentioned previously, one might execute a line like this in a customer editing form launching the search form:

```
DO FORM CustSearch TO ThisForm.cCust_ID
```

This is okay, as long as the desired result is a single value. However, if you need a series of customer ID's that can be navigated through using VCR-style buttons, it would be possible to do this:

```
DO FORM CustSearch WITH ThisForm
```

And the CustSearch form can store a reference to the customer form to one of its properties.

Now, the user can use the CustSearch form to filter the list of all customers to only those in Cleveland, and select the customer that showed the largest volume of purchases for last year. When the user is finished, the CustSearch form can manipulate several properties of the Customer form. In this way, the information that the CustSearch can "return" is not limited to just the cCust_ID of the best customer in Cleveland. The CustSearch form can set a property of the calling form that indicates the number of customers in the subset the user selected (those in Cleveland), set another property of the calling form to indicate the Customer ID of a single customer in the subset, and populate an array property of the calling form with the customer ID's of all the customers in the subset. The calling form can then use this information in navigation methods and related objects to allow the user to "browse" or examine in sequence the customers in the subset.

How about the situation where I'm actually launching Form "B" from Form "A," and I want to pass some god-awful complex set of information to Form "B"? Yes, I could pass a whole bunch of parameters, or even some kind of specialized object. On the other hand, my launching code could look something like this: (Note that this contradicts some of what I've said previously, but read on.)

```
DO FORM <FormName> NAME ThisForm.oFormLaunched
ThisForm.oFormLaunched.cCust_ID = ThisForm.cCust_ID
DIMENSION ThisForm.oFormLaunched.aCustList[ThisForm.nCustomers]
ACOPY(ThisForm.aCustList, ThisForm.oFormLaunched.aCustList)
```

As I'm sure you noticed, this code represents a couple of pretty tightly coupled forms. Manipulating a form's properties requires a lot of knowledge about that form. However, this is the kind of thing that could be built into the foundation classes or application framework, so that the properties being manipulated, or the methods being called, are not unique to a single form, but part of every form of a particular type in the system.

Our technical editor expressed interest in an example of building inter-form communications techniques into a framework. Rather than bore you with a bunch of code, I thought I'd explain one approach I've used for an application.

The situation was the need (as in the text) to allow the user to select a subset of patients, or patient families, or services, or any other large set of records in a health-care facility application, and then navigate through the resulting list using VCR-type navigation buttons. Because this application would be installed as a client/server application at some sites, all data manipulation had to be done using views. In a C/S app, pulling up a list of all 10,000 patients in a picklist is something to be discouraged; however, navigation through a reasonable subset was part of the application's spec.

All data-aware forms in the framework have two properties to support this functionality: oNavList and a property to hold the key value for the current record, uKeyValue. The framework also includes a composite object, cntNavButtons, which includes the four VCR buttons, a label that indicates the number of items in the subset, and an array property to hold the ID's of the items in the subset. The cntNavButtons object also has the four navigation methods GoNext(), GoPrev(), GoFirst() and GoLast(), and a couple of numeric properties, nCurrentInList, to act as a "pointer" to the currently selected item, and nLastInList to indicate the total number of items in the list. The navigation methods manipulate the nCurrentInList property, enable and disable the VCR buttons depending on the position within the list, transfer the record ID from the array to the form's uKeyValue property, and call the form's Requery() method to requery the current views.

The Init() method of cntNavButtons "registers" the VCR-button object with the form by storing a self-reference to the form's oNavList property. When the user wants to launch the (modal) search form, the foundation data-aware form class's Search() method executes the search form:

DO FORM PatSearch WITH This TO ThisForm.uKeyValue

The search can simply return a single value through 'its Unload() method. It checks the passed calling form to see if it has a non-null object oNavList property. If not, it simply passes the user's selection back to the calling form's Search() method via the search form's Unload() method. If the calling form does have a non-null object oNavList property, the search form also stores the ID's of the sub-set to the array property of the calling form's oNavList object, sets the oNavList object's nLastInList and nCurrentInList properties, and sets returning the ID of the currently selected item in the list via the Unload() method.

As pointed out in the text, these forms are very tightly linked. However, this is tolerable because the knowledge that each form requires of the other is not unique to each form instance but to the form classes, which are common throughout the application. Thus, while the forms are tightly coupled, they are loosely coupled within the context of the application framework.

Other issues with private data sessions

One somewhat bothersome thing about private data sessions is that a bunch of environmental settings are scoped to the data session. This means that any settings you have established globally, such as SET TALK, SET DELETED, SET NEAR, and so on, immediately revert to their default values as soon as a form with a private data session is instantiated. As a result, the desired settings must be re-established for each form instance. (See the VFP help file entry for SET DATASESSION for a complete list of all data session-scoped settings.)

The brute-force approach is to simply SET TALK OFF, SET DELETED ON, and so forth, in the Init() or the Load() of each form. This requires you to remember to include all settings that are needed for each form, and place the needed code in each form. A better, and more object-oriented way, is to establish all preferred settings in a form foundation class (say, in the LOAD() event method, then simply issue a DODEFAULT() in each form and override any of these new "default" settings as needed.

A very popular approach (which I use) is to create an object class that handles this chore, and to drop an instance of this object onto the data-aware form foundation class. This approach relies on the automatic execution of the Init() and Destroy() event methods. The Init()

event method calls a Set() method, which stores the current values, and by reading its own object properties, sets each environmental setting to the desired value. The Destroy() code can optionally call a Reset() method to restore all settings to their original values. This is useful when the object is used to set environmental settings in the default data session. The object classes I use for manipulating environmental settings are slightly adapted from the ones presented in the *Visual FoxPro 3.0 Codebook* by Y. Alan Griver. Just to give you a taste of how these work, **Listing 9-2** shows a few lines of code that the cSessionEnvironment object executes in its Set() method.

Listing 9-2. A piece of the cSessionEnvironment.Set() method.

```
IF EMPTY(this.cCentury)
    SET CENTURY OFF
ELSE
    luTemp = this.cCentury
    SET CENTURY &luTemp
ENDIF

IF This.nCenturyTo = 0
    SET CENTURY TO
ELSE
    IF This.nCenturyToRollover = 0
        luTemp = LTRIM(STR(This.nCenturyTo))
        SET CENTURY TO &luTemp
    ELSE
        luTemp1 = LTRIM(STR(This.nCenturyTo))
        luTemp2 = LTRIM(STR(This.nCenturyToRollover))
        SET CENTURY TO &luTemp1 ROLLOVER &luTemp2
    ENDIF
ENDIF
```

If you create applications for many different clients, you might want to subclass this type of object class, setting your preferences in the subclass. On the other hand, if you are a corporate developer, you might prefer to include your preferred settings in the foundation class. Either way, overriding these settings for a particular form is no problem. Since the object in the form is an instance of the cSessionEnvironment class, you can simply change the settings by adjusting the properties in the object instance on the form that needs something set differently.

Because this object is always the first object on the form (since it's added in the form foundation class), its Init() and Set() methods always execute before any other control is instantiated, so the new settings are in effect when the rest of the controls show up for work. However, realize that a *lot* of stuff happens before the environment-setting object instantiates, some of which is affected by the settings that are manipulated via the environment-setting object.

Here is the sequence of events that occur when a form that uses the DataEnvironment is launched:

1. DataEnvironment.OpenTables()
2. DataEnvironment.BeforeOpenTables()
3. Form.Load()
4. Cursor.Init()

5. DataEnvironmnent.Init()
6. FirstObject.Init()
7. Form.Activate()
8. Form.Paint()

Note that at the time the cSessionEnvironment object instantiates, all objects associated with the data tables and their setup are up and running. The cSessionEnvironment is instantiated at event 6 in the list above. To show the effects this can have, consider two settings: TALK and DELETED. TALK defaults to "ON" and DELETED defaults to "OFF". If you have a view that is being opened in the data environment, these default values are in effect. This means that the query will not ignore deleted records, and the message "Selected x records in .028 seconds" will appear either on the status bar if STATUS BAR is set ON, or on the VFP desktop if STATUS BAR is set OFF.

In the case of the views and deleted records, the solution is to make sure you always set the NoDataOnLoad property to .T. and REQUERY() the view from the form's Init(), or, alternatively, set AutoOpenTables to .F. and call the OpenTables() method from the Form.Init().

The problem with the TALK setting is not as simple. Actually, with the status bar set ON, it might not be an issue (the user might not even notice the message), but if your application doesn't use the status bar and it's turned off, then the only work-around is to issue a SET TALK OFF in the BeforeOpenTables() method. Unfortunately, this must be done in each form. It still isn't possible to subclass the data environment where you could employ the SET TALK OFF command and have your forms use this user-defined DataEnvironment class rather than the standard VFP DataEnvironment class. You might be tempted to instead add the environment setting object via the form's Load() event method, which works fine and does indeed get the environmental settings in effect a little sooner, but not soon enough for these two issues—the tables are already open when the Load() fires.

To form or not to form—running forms as object instances

There is a school of thought that says forms should be instantiated from a class, using CREATEOBJECT() rather than using DO FORM. The arguments in favor of this line of thought make some sense. For those of us who tend to be a bit purist in our thinking when it comes to object-oriented programming, it just seems to be the "right" thing to do. Everything should be stored as an object class and instantiated at runtime. It encourages us to design our forms in a manner that allows more opportunities to subclass the forms and to specialize their functions.

This last argument becomes greatly compelling when you've just completed the last of three or four complex forms that have almost identical features and functionality. Running forms as forms rather than as object instances certainly doesn't preclude creating a form class that provides certain common features that are then specialized either in a subclass or in the form instance. However, if you get into the habit of basing all forms directly on foundation classes rather than specialized form classes, you can miss opportunities to really take advantage of the power of object-oriented programming.

Despite the "purity" and "rightness" of doing so, many believe that the disadvantages of designing forms as classes rather than form instances outweigh the advantages.

The greatest disadvantage of running forms as object instances is the fact that form classes do not have a DataEnvironment object. Because you still can't work with the DataEnvironment object class the way you can most other baseclass objects, and can't add a DataEnvironment object to form classes in the Form or Class Designers, it becomes necessary to programmatically add a DataEnvironment object, or to programmatically open all necessary tables and supporting files at runtime. While this isn't really that big a deal, it does mean that you give up the ability to create drag-and-drop form controls from the form's data environment, and the property sheet picklists for each control's ControlSource property are empty.

Some would argue that the necessity of programmatically adding a DataEnvironment object or its equivalent is a strength of running forms as class instances rather than as forms, because it rewards developing a subclassed version of the DataEnvironment that can provide far greater functionality than the native DataEnvironment object. However, this is not precluded by running forms, as you can see from the ideas presented in Chapter 7.

In the final analysis, making a decision to run forms or objects instantiated from form classes is influenced by a number of things. There is no "right" or "wrong" answer to this question, but here are some factors that are likely to influence your decision:

- The experience and skill level of the programmers working on the project. Forms are a little easier to learn to use because they include the data environment, and they're a little easier to run, test and debug. Instantiating forms from form classes is a bit more complex, often aided by builders for creating data environments or adding data manipulation classes, and may have a "deeper" class hierarchy, making it more difficult for the novice VFP developer to understand and adopt.
- The need to access more than one type of data source. Instantiating forms from object classes is sometimes done as a consequence of the need for more flexibility in the type of data environment and data manipulation classes that must be defined at runtime. Some developers, once they've decided to chuck the Visual FoxPro DataEnvironment, decide that there is little reason to recommend forms over form classes (although Chapter 7 shows that you can have your cake and eat it, too!).
- The scope of the foundation classes. Foundation classes can be developed for use in a single application or a uniform corporate development environment, or might be intended to eventually form the basis of a more robust and broadly applied application framework. Again the considerations involve ease-of-use, flexibility and adaptability, as well as the difficulty a new user might experience in learning to use the foundation classes.
- The personal preferences and inclinations of the developers working on the project. Some of us think instantiating from form classes just "feels right" and enjoy the challenge of pushing the envelope, while others prefer to use the tools as Microsoft has provided them.

Forms and delegation

As I've learned to create applications in Visual FoxPro, I've gradually learned the importance of delegating functionality to the appropriate object. This usually means delegating responsibility to form methods rather than performing complex tasks in control methods.

You should see many "red flags" when a certain pattern appears in your programming. Here are some that are commonly cited:

- A segment of code indented five to seven levels deep, indicating numerous nested IF…ENDIF and DO CASE…ENDCASE control structures—an indication that the code's logic is overly complex, and could possibly be simplified by moving some of the logic into smaller, more concise methods.
- Overriding a class method without issuing a DoDefault()—an indication that perhaps some functionality in the superclass really belongs in a subclass.
- A long list of 10 or 12 arguments to a method or function—an indication of a tightly coupled routine.
- A routine (function, procedure or method) structured as a single DO CASE, each CASE testing the value of a single parameter and then executing a large block of code depending on the value of that parameter—evidence of a routine that is possibly logically cohesive and should be broken into several appropriately named methods or routines, one for each CASE condition.

Similarly, in an object-oriented language like Visual FoxPro (and other object-based tools like Access and Visual Basic), a red flag should go up any time you see more than three to seven lines of code in a control method. I'm not referring here to method code in a control class. The method code in a reusable control class can often be quite complex. However, the programmer should recognize the limited role of a form control.

A form control performs two functions. The first is to present a single piece of information, or a set of related pieces of information. The second is to act as a locus of interaction between the user and the form.

Consider a knob on a radio. You can tell from the position of the red line engraved on the knob the approximate frequency to which the radio is tuned. You can also grasp the knob, and by turning it, change the station you're listening to. Does the knob actually change the frequency that the circuitry is tuned to? No, it's just a beige plastic thingy that is attached to a metal shaft that is in turn attached to a variable capacitor that actually does the tuning. The knob gives us a discrete piece of information and allows us to indicate our wishes. The knob is not responsible for carrying out our wishes, only for conveying our desire to the component in the radio that is designed to act on our desire to listen to the news instead of some R & B. The garage door opener on my sun visor is not responsible for actually opening the garage door. It's a control that is only responsible for conveying my desire to open or close the door to the device designed to receive that request. Neither is the receiver responsible for moving the garage door. It delegates that responsibility to the opener itself, simply sending a signal to the opener to say "HEY! Open the Door!"

Similarly, in our forms, the Save button shouldn't have 50 lines of code in 'its Click() event method that loops through all of the work areas and executes a TableUpdate() on each one. It should, instead, simply have a single line that says:

```
ThisForm.Save()
```

As another example, a text box that is used to enter an order number should not have a bunch of code in its LostFocus() method for establishing a view parameter and executing a REQUERY(), or selecting a work area and performing a SEEK(). The LostFocus() method might contain some check to see if the user has keyed in a new order number, and if so, it calls a Requery() or LookUp() method belonging to the form.

There are several reasons that the amount of control method code should be kept to a minimum. First, while initially it may seem that a certain block of code should only be executed in response to this *one* event, it quite often turns out that there are several events that need to trigger execution of this block of code. There's no law that says these other events can't call the method of the control, but remember that method names should bear some resemblance to the functions they perform. If the Save function is being performed by a Click() event method, and a LookUp function is performed by a LostFocus() event method, it can be a little difficult to find the code that performs a particular task.

This leads to another argument in favor of delegating important operations to form methods. When an application is in need of modification, it becomes a simple matter to open a form in the form designer, go to the methods page of the property sheet, and have in front of you all methods that do the "real work" of the form. This is especially true if you opt to display non-default properties only. You might need to do a search to determine which events are triggering which methods, but at least you have a list of all methods that accomplish the work of the form.

Another delegation issue argues against a lot of chit-chat back and forth between controls. A control might enable or disable another control based on its own value. However, if you see a long list of controls being enabled or disabled, it's likely that this function would be better delegated to a form method. If you have a control method that is enabling or disabling a whole set of controls, depending on the value of several controls, I can almost guarantee that you'll make your life much easier by moving this functionality to a form method. The form method can then be called from any event that indicates that some state has changed.

The issue of enabling and disabling controls is an opportunity to look at another mistake that I have often made. While it might be logical to have a form method that determines the "state" of the form and manipulates the appearance of specific controls in response to the current state, this kind of thing becomes difficult to maintain as controls are added or removed from a form during development. Why not make each control responsible for its own state? (I'll discuss this further in Chapter 11.)

Again, this is a matter of delegating responsibility to the proper object. While this chapter is about forms, not about controls, it's just as important not to overload our forms with tasks that are more easily and properly performed by the controls. The principle here is to look around and ask, "Who can I make responsible for this job?" In a way it's like being the ultimate dictatorial boss or supervisor, with perfect mindless little employees working for you. You can delegate responsibility to anyone you designate, knowing that they can't file a grievance or complain to *your* boss. They'll do whatever job you decide it's best that they do. If you decide that one employee (object) is doing too much, and needs too much of your attention to make sure that they do their job properly as conditions change, you can distribute their responsibilities among other objects that can better adapt to changing conditions, and keep the "factory" turning out widgets.

Forms as business objects
If you ever do any reading on the subject of object-oriented analysis and design, you'll be confronted with a great deal of discussion about *business objects*.

In an object-oriented software system, real-world things are modeled in the software. The things being modeled are the objects that are part of the business and what it does. These things can be employees, orders, products, customers, invoices, credit memos, purchase orders, pick tickets, time cards, patients, physicians, vendors, production lines, and on and on. In many object-oriented systems, an attempt is made to define all of these various objects and the ways in which they interact in the context of the business or enterprise. In order for the software system to function properly, it must accurately model the enterprise it is used to manage.

Each object in the system must have behaviors that accurately mimic those real-world objects they model. The various objects must interact with each other in the same manner as those in the enterprise being modeled. In modeling real-world things as business objects, the desire is to encapsulate all behaviors of the real-world thing in the software object. Keep in mind that there is often a tangible, visible aspect to the real-world objects, just as there can be for the software objects that model them. However, there are other intangible and invisible aspects to both the real-world and software objects.

Let's consider, as an example, a specific company's invoice. The tangible, visible aspect of an invoice is a piece of paper (a *document*) on which is listed all information pertinent to the invoice: the customer, the terms, the date, the purchase order number, the total, and an itemized list of the items the invoice covers.

However, an invoice could be only one aspect of another, more abstract concept. For a business in which there is a one-to-one relationship between orders and invoices, there are (at least) *two* documents, or real-world objects, that represent a different aspect of what could be viewed as the same thing, that could be referred to perhaps as a *transaction*. The order form represents a transaction from the time it is received by the company to the time that the goods have been shipped or the services delivered. The invoice represents the same abstract idea, but reflects the information needed by the company to inform its customer of the amount due for the goods or services, and the information the customer needs to process the invoice for payment. There might be other documents that reflect a different aspect of this transaction. For instance, a job ticket or pick-list might provide information that the folks on the shop floor need to properly fill the order.

Each document mentioned thus far could have a different set of information that is of interest to the various departments in the company and to the customer. This is illustrated in **Table 1**.

Table 1. A hypothetical industrial products company and various documents related to a "transaction", and who might have an interest in each.

Document	Company Departments	Customer Departments
Order Form	Sales, Customer Service	None
Job Ticket	Production, Shipping, Quality Control	Engineering
Shipper	Shipping	Receiving, Production
Invoice	Accounts Receivable, Sales	Accounts Payable

As shown in **Table 1**, an order form contains very little information of interest to the customer, but is of significant interest to sales and customer service. You could add an additional document called an "acknowledgement" that would be of interest to the customer's purchasing department. Similarly, an invoice is of no interest to the production department, but life revolves around the invoice for the accounting departments of both the company and its customers.

So what you have are a bunch of documents that you might be tempted to implement as separate forms in your application. However, they are really only different views of the same thing—the transaction from buyer to seller. If you can create an object that encapsulates all behaviors of this transaction-thing, you've done much of the work required by the five (or more) documents listed above. Such an object, when modeled in software, is referred to as a *business object*.

It is possible that a particular business needs only one user interface for this type of business object—one that allows order entry and displays the status of the order, from receipt to fulfillment and shipping, to invoicing, to payment.

There has been considerable discussion of creating reusable business objects with Visual FoxPro. Some frameworks have even incorporated the concept of the business object into their design. However, in most object-oriented systems, the business object is a non-visual entity that abstracts the behaviors and relationships but delegates user interaction with the object to another component in the system. The reasoning is that (to continue with the example above) a "transaction-thing" object does not have, as part of its properties or behavior, a text box to display the name of the customer. The customer placing the order is, indeed, a property of the object, but it is incorrect to assume that all instances of the transaction object will require user interaction, and therefore require a text box to display this information on-screen.

To implement this type of business object in Visual FoxPro, you would create an object class based on the Custom baseclass, and add properties and methods as appropriate to model the behavior of a transaction for this company. However, you'd like to drop the resulting object onto an "Order" form, or a "Job Ticket" form, or an "Invoice" form, add the necessary interface elements and be done with it. However, we're talking about database applications here, and an integral part of such an application is the data that allows us to refer to a *specific* invoice, or order, or job ticket. The elements provided by Visual FoxPro to abstract this part of a business object—DataEnvironment and Cursor objects, and the private data session—can't be contained by any object other than a form.

Ideally, you would have DataEnvironment objects that could be added to objects based on baseclasses other than forms, and you would be able to create objects that could declare a private data session, just as you can with forms. You could then create abstract, non-visual business objects as described above, and leave the interface to forms to which you add these business objects. However, you don't have those capabilities. Do you give up on the business object idea? Not on your life.

To do some really slick things with business objects in Visual FoxPro, you just need to change your perspective slightly and use some of VFP's tools.

What follows is a description of a business object I created for an application. It demonstrates how you can use a form as a business object without being constrained by the fact that a form is usually a visible application component intended to interact with a user. As in the example above, this object is a transaction object, and needed to perform the following tasks:

- Display an order-entry and credit-entry interface.
- Display an order-fulfillment interface (for the warehouse and shipping department).

- Print a shipper.
- Post the order.
- Un-post the order.
- Print an invoice.
- Update inventory.
- Update sales history.

I decided to "go with the flow" and just make this transaction object a form. I added methods to allow this transaction object to perform each task and interact with all required data. I then created two different interfaces for the form, each on a different page of a border-less, tabless PageFrame. By passing an argument, I could select either of the two interfaces when the form was instantiated. In addition to these two "modes" of operation, I allowed a third mode. This third mode caused me to begin thinking about using a form as a business object in the first place.

Normally, transactions are called up using one of two methods. One is to pass the trans-action number (an order number, an invoice number or a credit memo number) as an argument from another form that displays a list of open/completed/invoiced transactions. Another is to run the form and key the transaction number into a text box. In either case, the identifying transaction number is stored to a form property, and a form Requery() method is called, which requeries the necessary views so the transaction can be displayed or edited. If the Requery() method is unable to find any records matching the transaction number, it raises a dialog box to inform the user. After adding a new order or saving edits to an existing transaction, a WAIT "Saved..." WINDOW NOWAIT confirms to the user that the save was successful. As always, a failed save results in a message box informing the user of the failure and explaining the problem.

One function of this transaction object is the ability to post (or "un-post") an individual order, which is sometimes necessary. The process of posting changes the transaction from a pending transaction into an invoice or credit memo, and updates the product inventory to re-flect the transaction. However, this company usually posts its orders in "batch" mode, once per week. Rather than writing a separate procedural program to perform this task, I used the Post() method that is part of the transaction form/object.

To implement this, I created a *third* mode of operation, which I call a "silent" mode. If the form is called with *no* arguments, the Init() sets the lSilentMode property of the form, and essentially does nothing further. I also added a RetrieveTxn() method, which does what is normally accomplished by entering a transaction ID into the text box, or passing it as an ar-gument: It accepts this ID as an argument, stores it to the appropriate form property, and calls the form's Requery() method. I refer to this as a "silent" mode because the Requery() method does not raise any error dialogs if the transaction ID can't be found, but simply returns a logi-cal value indicating success or failure back to the RetrieveTxn() method, which in turn returns this value to the process that called RetrieveTxn().

Now, here's all you need to do:

1. Compile a list of transactions that are ready for posting.
2. Instantiate the transaction form object *without making it visible.*
3. Pass each transaction ID in turn to the non-visible transaction form object.

4. If the transaction form object successfully retrieves the transaction, call the Post() method of the transaction form object.

The transaction form object is instantiated as a non-visible object using the following syntax:

```
DO FORM frmTxn NAME loTxn LINKED NOSHOW
```

The NAME...LINKED keywords cause the form to be instantiated to a specified memory variable. The NOSHOW keyword allows the form to be instantiated without being made visible.

The Post() method automatically calls the Save() method. If the Save() is successful, Post() returns .T. If the Save() is unsuccessful, the Cancel() method is called (to clear the buffers of changes made by the Post() method), and Post() returns .F.

Thus it's possible to create another form or procedure that compiles the necessary list, instantiates the transaction object, asks the transaction object to retrieve each transaction in the list and then post each one, keeping a tally of successful and unsuccessful posts. Because the Save() method of the form already wraps any changes in a TRANSACTION...END TRANSACTION/ROLLBACK, the half-dozen or so tables that are modified by the Post() method are committed in an all-or-nothing manner.

Listing 9-3 shows (in pseudo-code) a summary of this entire technique.

Listing 9-3. Pseudo-code illustrating the use of a form as a business object.

```
* Init() Method
LPARAMETERS tcTxnNo, tcInterface
IF PCOUNT() = 0
   Store .T. to ThisForm.lSilentMode
ELSE
   Store tcTxnNo to ThisForm.cTxnNo
   Store tcInterface to ThisForm.cInterface
   If Requery() retrieves a record
      Check ThisForm.cInterface -
         (Activate Page1 of page frame if it's "ENTRY", ;)
         Or Page2 of the page frame if it's "FULFILL"
ENDIF

* RetrieveTxn() Method
LPARAMETERS tcTxnNo
Store tcTxnNo to ThisForm.cTxnNo
Call ThisForm.Requery()
If Requery() retrieves a record
   RETURN .T.
Else
   RETURN .F.
ENDIF

* Post() Method
Determine if the transaction is a credit and if the business
   rules permit issuance of the credit at this time
Change status of transaction from pending to posted
Calculate due-date based on terms and posting date
Update the customer's sales history to reflect the sale or credit
```

```
Update the inventory records to reflect the items being sold/returned
Save() the changes
If Save() is successful RETURN .T.
If Save() is unsuccessful call Cancel() and RETURN .F.

PROCEDURE BatchPost
DO FORM frmTxn NAME loTxn LINKED NOSHOW
SELECT cTxnNo FROM TxnHeaders WHERE complete INTO ARRAY laTxnList
LOOP through the array
    IF loTxn.RetrieveTxn(laTxnList[i]) ;
           AND LoTxn.Post()
       Record the success of the posting
    ELSE
       Record the failure of the posting
    ENDIF
```

To begin thinking about forms as business objects, think in terms of the following ideas:

- Encapsulation of all business object behaviors into a single object.
- Separation of interface from the business object and the business logic it enforces.
- Utilization of the business object by other procedures and processes that need to rely on the business object's knowledge of business logic and rules, but have no need of any of the business object's user interfaces.

I've included a very simple example of these business object ideas. The code for this example can be found in the Chap9.PJX project.

To quickly demonstrate the form-as-business-object idea, change to the directory where you installed the sample code containing the projects for chapters 5, 9 and 11, run the LOCALPATH.PRG that sets the paths to all of the demo file folders, and execute the following in the command window:

```
DO FORM bizobject WITH .NULL.,"order"
```

This will launch the bizobject form which should appear as shown in **Figure 1**.

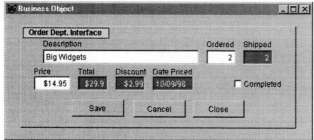

Figure 1. *A business-object form with an interface for the order dept.*

Close this form, and run it again, but this time pass a different set of arguments:

```
DO FORM bizobject WITH .NULL.,"shipping"
```

This command launches the same form, but presents a different interface as shown in **Figure 2**. Note that the interface object has a 3D border which is included here to call attention to the object producing the interface. You could just as easily implement this idea with an invisible border on the object containing the form controls.

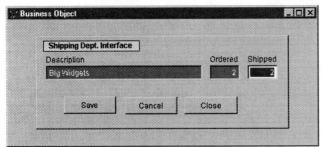

Figure 9-2 *A business-object form with an interface for the shipping department*

The Init() code (**Listing 9-4**) for this form shows how the different interfaces are applied.

Listing 9-4 *The Init() code for a business-object form*
```
LPARAMETERS toappobject, tcMode
DODEFAULT(toAppObject)
SET CLASSLIB TO Chap9 ADDITIVE
IF VARTYPE(tcMode) = "C" && We've passed some kind of non-logical argument
   DO CASE
   CASE UPPER(tcMode) = "SHIPPING"
      * Add the shipping dept interface
      ThisForm.AddObject("cntInterface","cntInterfaceShipping")
      ThisForm.cntInterface.Visible = .T.
   CASE UPPER(tcMode) = "ORDER"
      * Add the order dept interface
      ThisForm.AddObject("cntInterface","cntInterfaceOrder")
      ThisForm.cntInterface.Visible = .T.
   OTHERWISE
      * we're running as a non-visible
      * business object
      * Even if we run the form with the NOSHOW
      * clause, the Visible property is still .T.
      ThisForm.Visible = .F.
   ENDCASE
ELSE
   * we're running as a non-visible
   * business object
   * Even if we run the form with the NOSHOW
   * clause, the Visible property is still .T.
   ThisForm.Visible = .F.
ENDIF
```

You might guess from looking at Listing 4 that if we were to run this form with no arguments, it would instantiate, but would not be visible. Unfortunately, this is not the case. To instantiate a form without the form becoming visible, it's necessary to use the NOSHOW clause. As noted in the code above, using the NOSHOW clause does indeed make the form invisible, but counter-intuitively, the Visible property is still .T. It's handy to rely on this property to determine at runtime whether the form is being run with or without an interface, so I've set the Visible property .T. in those circumstances in which I have not requested an interface, and will be using the NOSHOW clause. Also, if you're wondering about the .NULL., remember that the foundation form class I use is prepared to accept a reference to the application object – the .NULL. is simply a place-holder in the argument list.

BizObject is a form that can be run using more than one interface. Note that the order department can set item descriptions, order quantities, and prices and can set the order's "completed" flag. However, the order department can't set the shipped quantity. On the other hand, the shipping department *can* set the shipped quantity, but has no interest in price, discount, order total, and is prohibited from changing the order quantity and item description.

While we have two different interfaces, the code that implements the business logic are part of the form and are therefore available to any interface used. **Table 2** lists all the non-default methods of this form.

Table 2. *Non-default methods of the form*

Method	Purpose	Business Logic
Init()	Provides interface when needed	
QueryUn-load()	Prevents closure of the form unless the Close() method allows it	
Refresh()	Refreshes controls only if the form is visible	
Cancel()	Discards changes to the cursor	
Close()	Checks for changes to the cursor and closes the form if no edits are pending. Returns a logical value indicating success or failure. If the form is visible, informs the user via a dialog box that they have changes pending	
Complete()	Changes the lComplete flag on the cursor record for use when an interface is not being used	
Discount()	Applies a 10% discount during pricing if the order is priced prior to the 15th of the month	●
Price()	Extends the pricing of the item if the lComplete flag is .T., and updates the yTotal and dPriced fields. Since discounting is dependent on the pricing date, the Price() method calls the Discount() method	●
Save()	Saves changes to the cursor, but first checks for valid input via the Validate() method. Returns a logical value indicating success or failure.	
SetShipped()	Allows manipulation of the shipped quantity when an interface is not being used	

Validate()	Checks to make sure the shipped quantity does not exceed the order quantity. Returns a logical value and sets a form property to indicate whether or not the entries are valid. The form property is used when a save() fails, to differentiate between invalid data and something like an update conflict.	●

You'll note that some of the methods such as SetShipped() and Complete() exist to allow data to be manipulated when the form has no interface. To see this in action, enter the following code in the command window. The comments describe what is happening in response to each command. Before trying these commands, open the BizObject table and make sure that there are entries only in the cDescript, yPrice and iOrdered fields.

```
DO FORM bizobject WITH .NULL. NAME oBizObj LINKED NOSHOW
* Run the form, but don't make it visible. Assign a reference to the
* memvar "oBizObj" and link the reference so we can destroy the form
* by destroying the oBizObj reference
oBizObj.SetShipped(3) && Set the shipped quantity to a value higher than or-
dered
? oBizObj.Validate() && Returns .F. as we've violated a business rule
oBizObj.SetShipped(2) && Fix the rule violation
? oBizObj.Close() && Returns .F. as we have uncommitted changes
? oBizObj.Price() && Returns .F. as the order is not yet flagged as complete
oBizObj.Complete() && Sets the lComplete flag
? oBizObj.Price() && Returns .T. - Successfully priced
? oBizObj.Save()      && Returns .T. - Successfully saved
? oBizObj.Close() && Returns .T. - Closed ok
DO FORM bizobject WITH .NULL.,"ORDER"
```

The last line above will open the form with the order department's interface, so you can verify that the manipulations of the business object have been successfully stored in the BizObject table.

What this demonstrates is a single software object that encapsulates all of the business logic of a real-world entity, like an order, or a job ticket, or a customer or an employee or anything else we may be modeling in a software system. As long as we use this object to act as an intermediary between the user and the data, we only have one place within our code to maintain the business logic for this entity. The logic can either be hard-coded as in this simple example, or data-driven. Instead of applying the before-the-15th rule for discounts, the form could instead consult a lookup table that could fine-tune this type of rule for individual customers, products, seasons or terms of sale.

When necessary to allow a user to interact directly with this business object, we can make it visible and slap an appropriate interface on it. If other objects (such as another form) have need of information that can be provided by this business object, it can be instantiated in code within that other object, and exposed methods of the business object can provide whatever information is required.

The business object can also be manipulated by batch processes similar to those demonstrated above. Assume that the vast majority of orders ship 100%, and the job of the shipping department is only to record exceptions. It's then possible to add a "shipped" flag to the orders table, have the shipping department flag each order as shipped, and then write procedural code that instantiates the business object, calls a method of the business object to locate each "shipped" record, flag each as "complete", then price each and make it ready for invoicing.

> *One thing you must be careful of with a business object like the BizObject form, is that there is no way to prevent destruction of the form by releasing it's object reference. If, in the code above you RELEASE oBizObj, it'll release just fine, discarding any unsaved changes made. The reason for this limitation is that the QueryUnload event does not fire when the object is released. However, this is a minor limitation. Being able to prevent destruction of the object would require code which checks to see if the object is still hanging around after the RELEASE command, and the need to address concerns about the form reference memvar going out of scope, and the possibility of the reference persisting and preventing the release of an object that instantiated it. It's much better to release the oBizObj form by calling the Close() method, which will not close if there are unsaved edits, and return a value of .F. if it's unable to close.*

Once you begin thinking about business objects in this way, it's a short step to realize that you can instantiate business objects like this as a COM object, accessible via internet information server and active server pages that would allow the sales force to enter orders via the internet using a browser interface, but interacting with the same business object that the in-house order department uses! Such a COM object could also be designed to work against a SQL/Server database, and interact with a VB user interface. N-tier architecture anyone?

Passing parameters in form methods

You might have noticed early in the previous section how data (e.g. the transaction number) is stored to a form property, and then another method is called. This called method then uses the data stored in the form property to perform its assigned task. It would be possible to pass this piece of data from one method to another as an argument, and for the called method to receive the data as a parameter. However, I've found it to be *much* better and *much* more flexible to rely on form properties to pass data from one method of the form to another.

Keep in mind that you are trying to encapsulate a set of methods and related data. If you pass data as method arguments, the data is not visible to all methods of the form—it is scoped to only the calling and called methods. The very fact that this data is of interest to more than one method is an indication that this piece of information should be stored in a form property. If two methods have an interest in this piece of data, there is a very good chance that a third method will eventually have an interest in this data. If you find yourself adding an LPARAMETERS command to a form method, you should immediately stop and ask yourself, "Is this method exposed to, or will it be called from, objects outside this form?" If the answer is "No," you should probably create a new form property to share the data between the calling method and the called method. In this context, look at passing an argument as an *optional* technique that might be suitable for some unusual circumstance, not the *default* technique that you use out of habit.

In procedural programming, we've long been used to using parameters to achieve loose coupling ("black boxing") of a function or a procedure. However, in an object-based or object-oriented language, you're "black-boxing" the *object*, not the object's *methods*. Because the methods and properties are inseparable from the object (that's part of what object *encapsulation* is), it's not that much different, conceptually, from establishing a memory variable at the beginning of a function that is referenced in several different control structures within the function.

I'm going to embarrass myself by telling you just how long this simple Truth has taken me to embrace. I'll frequently look at code I've written as recently as a few weeks ago in which I'm slavishly passing arguments from one form method to another. If you've been doing procedural programming as long as I have, it is indeed hard to break old habits and old ways of thinking. However, you will paint yourself into far fewer corners if you start employing simple practices such as this.

This chapter has taken a look at the form itself, rather than the controls that you place on the form. The next two chapters will dig down and talk about the form controls.

Chapter 10
Form Controls

Every form needs interface controls. Selecting the right control for the job is not always an obvious decision. In this chapter you will examine the various controls you have for your forms, and see what they each do well and what they do poorly. You'll see some of the nuances associated with various controls and learn how to take advantage of them. Through designing your own control classes, you'll find out that there is very little that you cannot accomplish in user-interface design.

The general use of form controls

First let's examine each control in the Visual FoxPro toolbox in terms of its purpose and use. **Table 1** is a list of the available controls.

Table 1. *The basic form controls available in Visual FoxPro.*

Control	Description
CheckBox	Used to indicate one of two states: on/off, yes/no, and so on.
ComboBox	A drop-down list. There are two styles: a list that limits the user to selecting items that are part of the available list, and a combo box that allows selection from the list or entry of values not in the list.
Command-Button	An action button. Usually used to initiate an action of some kind when the button is pressed.
Command-Group	A group of CommandButton controls.
Container	A control that is able to contain other controls.
EditBox	Used for editing character values. Allows for scrolling vertically for editing amounts of text that do not easily fit within the space allotted in the form.
Grid	Multi-record editing control that presents data from many records in a row (record) and column (field) display. The grid is a compound control that is comprised of columns, which in turn contain headers and controls. The grid will be discussed in more detail later in this chapter and in Chapter 11.
HyperLink	A HyperLink object can request that an ActiveX hyperlink-aware container, such as Microsoft Internet Explorer, jump to a particular URL.
Image	Displays a bitmap image.
Label	Displays text that cannot be changed interactively by the user.
Line	Displays a horizontal, vertical, or diagonal line.
ListBox	Displays a list of items from which one or more may be selected.
OLEControl	Hosts OLE or ActiveX objects in a Visual FoxPro form.
OLEBound-Control	Displays the contents of a general field in a DBF file.
OptionButton	Can only be added to an OptionGroup.
OptionGroup	A container for OptionButtons. Allows the user to select one from a

	set of mutually exclusive choices.
PageFrame	A container for holding Pages. A PageFrame is sometimes referred to as a tabbed dialog.
Page	A single tab within a PageFrame.
Shape	A graphical object that can display a box, circle, or ellipse.
Spinner	Allows the setting of a numeric value by "spinning" through a range of acceptable values. Number can also be typed into the spinner.
Timer	An invisible control that allows for the execution of code at a certain time interval.
TextBox	A control that allows the editing of data.

The following sections will examine many of the **Table 1** controls in more detail, focusing on the uses of these controls for user-interface design. I'll discuss when to use which control and how to make the controls exhibit the behavior you want.

Label

The label is one of the simplest controls at your disposal. It is most often used for displaying prompt information alongside other controls. Because it is "fixed" text, it's quite well adapted for the prompt job.

The label is often underestimated, though. It can do quite a bit more than prompt the user. Even though it isn't editable by the user, you can change its Caption property at will in your code. You could use a label for displaying non-editable data by simply setting its caption property whenever a new record is encountered.

For example, assume you have a customer table with a field named *balance*. This balance field can't be edited because it is a calculated value from other tables. You could put a label in the form, make its name lblBalance, and enter the following in the form's refresh method:

```
THISFORM.lblBalance.Caption = TRANSFORM(Customer.Balance,
"$999,999,999.99")
```

You need the TRANSFORM() in the above code because label captions can only accept character values.

Another strength of the label control is that it's a very lightweight object, meaning that it doesn't take a lot of memory to create. This makes it a candidate for being the base class for many non-visible classes. Add to its light weight the fact that it can have a descriptive caption that is seen in the form designer, and the label becomes an even better candidate for non-visible objects. You make the label non-visible by setting its visible property to .F.

In designing a label class, you can add to it any methods or properties that you need, so the fact that it is a label does not limit its functionality.

TextBox

The TextBox is the workhorse control for data entry. It is universal in the types of data it can handle and its user interface is simple. Users naturally seem to know how to use a TextBox—they type in it.

You could say that the TextBox is also an underestimated control. Its flexibility for data entry is often not fully appreciated. You have virtually unlimited control over the look of a TextBox. The *Chapter10* project in the download files contains a form named *Textbox*. **Figure 1** shows the *Textbox* form.

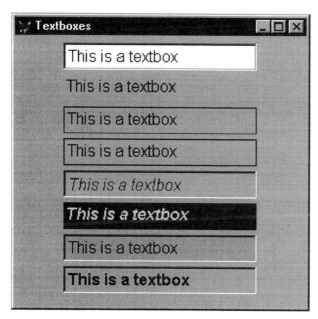

Figure 1. *The Textbox form.*

Figure 1 is an example of the variety of ways that a TextBox can look. It can have a border or not, the border can be 3-D or plain, and the color schemes and fonts can be modified. All of these features of the TextBox make it a versatile control for your forms. But I haven't even scratched the surface of it yet.

The TextBox will inherently process the user's keystrokes. In most situations this is exactly what you want, and you don't have to do anything special to handle the user's typing. But there are circumstances where creating a TextBox class and overriding the inherent key processing can be beneficial.

How often have you used a TextBox for entering numeric values? You want the value formatted with commas and a decimal point, so you set the InputMask property to "999,999,999.99" and hope for the best. The problem is that when users starts typing into the TextBox, the formatting gets messed up until they finish. See **Figure 2** for an example.

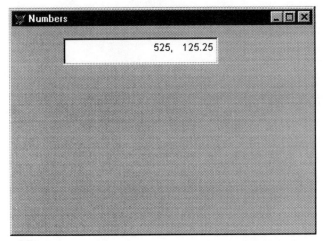

Figure 2. *Messed-up numbers in a TextBox.*

Notice the "525" in the TextBox in **Figure 2** - it looks weird. The TextBox started with the value 125.25 in it and I typed *525* at the beginning of the TextBox to get the result shown in Figure 2. Users are easily confused by this formatting problem. There is no native property setting of the TextBox that will correct the problem, either.

In this chapter you'll build a TextBox class that will provide for number entry similar to a calculator, where the digits enter the TextBox from the right to the left and are correctly formatted as they are entered. The *Chapter10* project has a TextBox class named txtNumber in the Controls class library. This class was built to intercept the user's keystrokes and process them in a special fashion. **Listing 10-1** shows the Keypress code for this class.

Listing 10-1. *The Keypress event code for the numeric textbox.*

```
LPARAMETERS nKeyCode, nShiftAltCtrl
DO CASE
  CASE nKeyCode >= 48 AND nKeyCode <= 57
    * Digits 0 to 9
    NODEFAULT
    THIS.cSoFar = THIS.cSoFar + CHR(nKeyCode)
    THIS.SetValue()
  CASE nKeyCode = 43
    * + key
    NODEFAULT
    IF LEFT(THIS.cSoFar,1) = "-"
      THIS.cSoFar = SUBSTR(THIS.cSoFar,2)
      THIS.SetValue()
    ENDIF
  CASE nKeyCode = 45
    * - key
    NODEFAULT
    IF LEFT(THIS.cSoFar,1) <> "-"
      THIS.cSoFar = "-" + THIS.cSoFar
```

```
      THIS.SetValue()
   ENDIF
 CASE nKeyCode = 9 OR nKeyCode = 15
   * Tab and Backtab
 CASE nKeyCode = 7
   * Del
   NODEFAULT
   THIS.cSoFar = "0"
   THIS.SetValue()
 OTHERWISE
   * Ignore all other keys
   NODEFAULT
ENDCASE
```

Notice the use of NODEFAULT in the code above. This command prevents Visual FoxPro from executing its default behavior for the KeyPress event. You use the NODEFAULT so you can process these keystrokes yourself.

The txtNumber class has two added properties named cSoFar and nDecimal. The cSoFar property is used to store a character representation of what the user has typed so far, and the nDecimal property is used to store a divisor used to position the decimal point. The cSoFar is set to "0" in the GotFocus so that users always replace the entire current value when they type in the control. nDecimal is set in the Init for the control by finding the decimal point in the InputMask property doing a calculation. A SetDecimal method has been added to the class; it contains the following code:

```
LOCAL lnDec
lnDec = LEN(ALLTRIM(THIS.InputMask)) - RAT(".",ALLTRIM(THIS.InputMask))
THIS.nDecimal = MAX(1,10 ^ lnDec)
```

The Init event has one line that calls THIS.SetDecimal(). The InputMask property has been given an assign method so that any time the value of the InputMask property is changed, the assign method will run. The code for the assign method is listed below.

> *Visual FoxPro 6.0 gives us two new types of methods: assign and access. These methods allow you to trap activities involving properties and write code to manage them. An assign method is executed whenever there is an attempt to assign a value to a property and it is passed the value that is being assigned. The access method is executed whenever there is an attempt to read the value of a property and the RETURN value of that method is the value that the code accessing the property will see.*
>
> *These methods are named <PropertyName>_access and <Property-Name>_assign. In the numeric TextBox, I used a method named Input-Mask_assign so it could react to any changes made to the InputMask of the TextBox control at runtime.*

```
LPARAMETERS vNewVal
THIS.InputMask = m.vNewVal
```

```
THIS.SetDecimal()
THIS.SetValue()
```

Figure 3 shows a form using the txtNumber class. In this form, I typed the same *525* that I typed earlier.

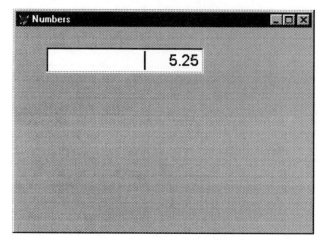

Figure 3. The txtNumber class in use.

Notice that the display is now 5.25. This is because the InputMask of 999,999.99 is setting the decimal point. To get 525.00, I would type *52500* in the TextBox.

The key point of this class is to demonstrate the fact that you are not limited in the usage of any control in Visual FoxPro. You can override the default behavior and provide your own behavior, thereby creating a new control. When you feel frustrated by the way things are happening, stop and ask yourself, "How can I make it happen the way I want it to happen?"

EditBox

Similar to the TextBox, the EditBox is a fairly simple editing control: It can be used to present and edit character data. The EditBox has the added functionality of being able to present data that is too large to fit neatly inside the control. With vertical scrollbars on the right side, this control allows the user to scroll through large amounts of character data.

When you need to present free-form character data, such as the contents of a memo field, the EditBox really shines. **Figure 4** shows a form with an EditBox being used to edit the mNotes field of the Clients table in the Time and Billing sample data.

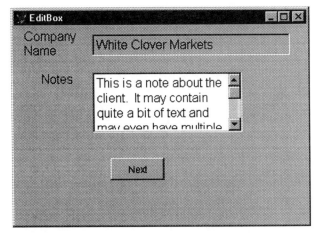

Figure 4. *An EditBox used for a memo field.*

The scroll bars on the right are enabled, indicating that more data follows what you can see. Note the way the last visible line is cut in half. This occurs because of the height of the EditBox and the FontSize used. The spacing of the lines causes a partial display of the last line.

You can fix this partial display by making the height of the EditBox neatly fit the line height for the font and FontSize being used. You may see that as a painful process, calculating the height of the font and then figuring out the correct control height. But lucky for us, Microsoft gave us a property that handles this specific problem: the IntegralHeight property.

When IntegralHeight is set to .F. (the default), the results are similar to **Figure 4**. However, setting IntegralHeight to .T. will resize the control to fit an exact number of lines. **Figure 5** shows the same form, only this time the IntegralHeight for the EditBox is set to .T.

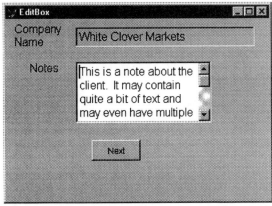

Figure 5. *Using IntegralHeight on an EditBox control.*

The EditBox allows you to control just about every detail of its appearance. You can make the scrollbar go away by setting the ScrollBars property to 0–None. You can affect the appearance of the border around the EditBox using the BorderStyle, BorderColor, and SpecialEffect properties. A full complement of event methods are available in the EditBox for controlling the behavior of the control.

To view the EditBox as a tool only for editing memo fields would greatly limit the utility of this control. A little imagination will reveal some uses for this control that go well beyond its obvious utility for editing memos. **Figure 6** shows an EditBox being used in quite a different way.

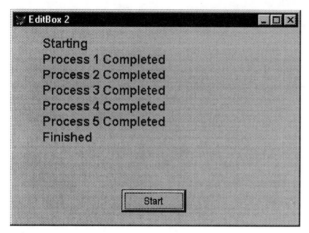

Figure 6. *Using an EditBox for a unique purpose.*

 The red text in **Figure 6** is in an EditBox. The form is in the *Chapter10* project in the download files and is named *EditBox2.scx*. The code in the Start button's click method is a very simple simulation of some processing. That code is listed here:

```
THISFORM.Edit1.Value = "Starting"
LOCAL lnCnt
FOR lnCnt = 1 TO 5
   INKEY(1.0)
   THISFORM.Edit1.Value = THISFORM.Edit1.Value + CHR(13) + ;
            "Process " + LTRIM(STR(lnCnt)) + " Completed"
ENDFOR
THISFORM.Edit1.Value = THISFORM.Edit1.Value + CHR(13) + "Finished"
```

Table 2 shows the non-default property setting for the EditBox in **Figure 6**.

Table 2. *The property settings for the EditBox in the EditBox2 form.*

Property	Setting
BackStyle	0 – Transparent
BorderStyle	0 – None

FontBold	.T.
FontSize	12
ForeColor	255,0,0
IntegralHeight	.T.
ReadOnly	.T.
ScrollBars	0 – None

The EditBox control, like all of the other controls, has an obvious use and also some not-so-obvious uses. "Thinking outside the box" will allow you to exploit the unique qualities of any control to suit your requirements, and the EditBox is no different in this respect.

Spinner

The Spinner is designed for numeric data types. It allows the user to input or change its value in two ways — by typing directly into the control or by using the up and down-arrow buttons at the right side of the control. **Figure 7** shows a form with a Spinner control.

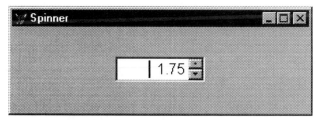

Figure 7. The Spinner control.

The Spinner in **Figure 7** has some property settings that are worth mentioning. **Table 3** lists the non-default properties and their settings.

Table 3. Property settings for the Spinner seen in Figure 7.

Property	Setting
Increment	0.25
InputMask	999.99
KeyboardHighValue	100
KeyboardLowValue	0
SpinnerHighValue	100
SpinnerLowValue	0

Some other properties are set to values other than their defaults — like Top, Height, Name, and so on — however, those properties are not important to the behavior of the control. Table 3 lists the important properties.

The Increment property controls how much the value of the control will be increased or decreased when the spin buttons are used. The up- and down-arrow keys have the same effect as the respective spin buttons when the Spinner has the focus.

InputMask has the same effect on a Spinner as it does on any other control: It defines the display mask for the data. In the Spinner above, the InputMask defines a display of three digits, a decimal point, and two digits.

The next four properties seem to be two sets of two properties, and in fact they are. Why two sets? Users can alter the value of the Spinner in two distinctly different ways. They can use the keyboard to type into the control, or they can use the Spinner buttons. The Keyboard properties control the range of values that can be typed in, and the Spinner properties affect the range of values for the spin buttons.

Hmm, now wait one minute … why would these two sets of properties be set differently from one another? It does seem unlikely that you would want them to be different, but "unlikely" is not the same as "never."

Here's one example situation where you might want these properties to have different ranges. Suppose you are using a Spinner to present the data for a bowling alley's number of strings for a league game. The business rules say that the range for the number of strings is always between 1 and 3. An additional rule says that in rare situations the number of strings may be more or less than that range. Your analysis finds that 97 percent of the leagues have a number of strings within the range. So you decide to use a Spinner and set the SpinnerHighValue to 3, the SpinnerLowValue to 1, the KeyboardHighValue to 15 and the KeyboardLowValue to 1. This allows the user to spin within the common range but prevents an unusually high number from being entered without the user expressly typing that number into the control.

CheckBox

This is an easy one. The CheckBox is either checked or not checked. It is a two-state control that can be used for such data entry tasks as true/false, on/off, or yes/no. Seems simple enough.

The CheckBox supports two data types: logical and numeric. When using a logical data type, true is represented by a checked state of the control, and false is unchecked. For numeric data types, 0 represents unchecked and non-zero (any value other than 0) represents the checked state. **Figure 8** shows the form in the *Chapter10* project named *Check.scx*.

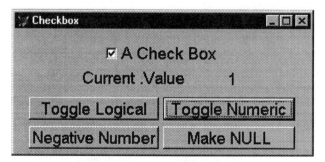

Figure 8. *A CheckBox in the Check form.*

The form in **Figure 8** was built to demonstrate the possible values for a CheckBox control. The Toggle Logical and Toggle Numeric buttons alter the values between .T./.F. and 0/1, respectively. By running the form and clicking the buttons, you can see the checked state of the CheckBox change. The Current Value line in the form shows you the current value for the CheckBox. Clicking on the CheckBox will toggle the value just like the buttons do. However, note that clicking the CheckBox toggles the value within the current data type for the value property of the CheckBox, while using the buttons will change the data type.

The Negative Number button assigns a value of –1 to the CheckBox. When you click that button, the CheckBox's state becomes checked. But you'll see that the CheckBox takes on the disabled colors. Clicking the CheckBox will show you that the control is not disabled. You can only assume that the disabled colors are used to visually show negative numbers differently than positive numbers. Setting the value to a negative number reinforces the fact that a value of 0 will be unchecked and any value other than 0 will be checked.

Clicking the Make NULL button assigns a value of NULL to the CheckBox. The value of NULL displays the same as a negative number—checked with disabled colors. The NULL-valued CheckBox isn't really disabled, though. Clicking the NULL valued CheckBox toggles it to the unchecked value for the data type—a logical .F. or numeric 0.

Graphical CheckBox
A graphical CheckBox is not another control—it is just a CheckBox with the Style property set to 1–Graphical instead of 0–Standard. So what is a graphical CheckBox? **Figure 9** shows a pair of graphical CheckBoxes, with the left one unchecked and the right one checked.

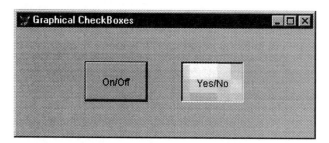

Figure 9. Graphical CheckBoxes in the CheckG form.

The **Figure 9** form is the CheckG form in the *Chapter10* project of the download files. Graphical CheckBoxes are those buttons that "stay pushed" when you click them. Other than their appearance, they are no different from the standard CheckBoxes.

One issue that relates to both the CheckBox just discussed and the OptionGroup discussed later in this chapter is that they act differently when the user presses the Enter key to move to the next control. Both the CheckBox and the OptionButton change the selection status of the control before moving on when the Enter key is pressed. This often causes a user to grab the mouse to navigate through these controls and can therefore slow down data entry. It is wise to avoid both of these controls in a "heads-down" data-entry form.

ComboBox

The ComboBox is the first of the *complex controls*—those that have more than one part to their interfaces. The ComboBox has the data-entry box and the drop-down list as its two parts.

The ComboBox is a very flexible and useful control with two distinct personalities that are controlled by its Style property. One of these personalities is the *drop-down combo* and the other is the *drop-down list*. Both styles provide a list of values in the ComboBox from which the user can make a selection. The drop-down combo style also allows the user to type a value into the control that is not included in the list. The drop-down list restricts the user's selection to only those items in the list. In Chapter 11 there is a detailed discussion of the ComboBox, along with other complex controls. Here I will focus on the general aspects of the control and the "when and where" of using it.

Drop-down combo

The "drop-down combo" style ComboBox allows the user the ease of selecting an entry from a list of possible values but doesn't limit him to selections from that list. That is the party line on the drop-down combo, but in truth things won't work that way without some coding on your part.

Both combo styles have two properties that hold values. The Value property is connected to the ControlSource for the combo and the DisplayValue (the value that is visible when the combo's list is not dropped down). The DisplayValue and the Value will only be the same when the DisplayValue is found in the list. If the DisplayValue is not found in the list, then the Value will be blank.

If you choose the drop-down combo style, thinking that the user can type in any value and that value will be saved to the ControlSource, you are mistaken. Unless you have written some code to add the DisplayValue to the combo's list when it isn't found in the list, the typed value won't be stored in the ControlSource.

 In the *Chapter10* project, the form named *DDCombo.scx* was built to demonstrate the effects just described. **Figure 10** illustrates this form.

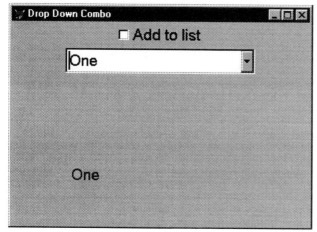

Figure 10. Drop-down combo demonstration form.

The form has three controls in it: a CheckBox that is used to turn on and off the ability to add a value to the combo's list, the combo itself, and a TextBox at the bottom that shows the value of the ControlSource for the combo. The combo has its ControlSource set to a property (cValue) that has been added to the form, so that changing the value of the combo will change the value of the form's cValue property. The TextBox has its ControlSource set to the same form property as the combo.

Here is the code in the combo's Init that populates the list with values:

```
THIS.AddListItem("One",this.NewItemId+1)
THIS.AddListItem("Two",this.NewItemId+1)
THIS.AddListItem("Three",this.NewItemId+1)
```

This combo has its RowSourceType set to *none* (there will be more discussion of RowSourceType later) and uses the AddListItem method to add items to the list. The When event of the combo contains the following code:

```
THISFORM.txtcValue.Refresh()
```

This line simply refreshes the display of the TextBox each time the selected item in the combo is changed. Finally, there is the code in the Valid event:

```
IF THISFORM.chkAdd.Value
  * If the checkbox is checked
  IF NOT ALLTRIM(THIS.DisplayValue) == ALLTRIM(THIS.Value)
    * Declare variable to temporarily hold the DisplayValue
    LOCAL lcValue
    * Save the DisplayValue
    lcValue = THIS.DisplayValue
    * Add the DisplayValue to the list
    THIS.AddListItem(THIS.DisplayValue,THIS.NewItemId + 1)
    * Requery the combo's list
    THIS.Requery()
```

```
   * Set the combo's Value to be the same as the DisplayValue was
   THIS.Value = lcValue
   * Now refresh the textbox
   THISFORM.txtcValue.Refresh()
   ENDIF
ENDIF
```

This code first checks to see if the CheckBox on the form is checked; if not, the code does nothing. If the CheckBox is checked, the code then looks to see if the DisplayValue and the Value properties have different values. If these two properties have the same value, then you don't need to do anything. The DisplayValue is different from the Value when the user types a string that isn't in the list. In that situation, you execute the code inside the IF statement in order to add the item to the combo's list, requery the combo's list, and then set the Value property to the same value that the DisplayValue property had. Finally, the TextBox is refreshed.

If you run this form and try using the ComboBox to enter the value of "Four" with and without checking the CheckBox, you'll see for yourself the difference in behavior. If the CheckBox is checked, the ComboBox will put the value of "Four" into the form's cValue property. When the CheckBox is not checked, the value of "Four" appears when you type it in, but that value is lost once you try to leave the Combo-Box. Both the ComboBox and the TextBox show a value that is blank.

In the next section, you'll see the various types of row sources that a combo can have. The code in the above example works well when the ComboBox has a RowSourceType of None, meaning that the combo manages its own list internally. In the example, you used the AddListItem method to populate the list. If you had used one of the other RowSourceTypes available, you would have then needed to add the typed value to the RowSource for the combo, rather than using the AddListItem.

Drop-down list

The other style for ComboBoxes is "drop-down list." The drop-down list does not allow the user to type values that are not in the list, but forces the user to make a selection from the list. This style is useful in situations where you know the available options ahead of time, so that only the possible choices can be included in the list.

You can obtain the available choices from a number of different places. They might be in a table, or obtained through a SQL SELECT command. The RowSource property controls the source for the list items. The RowSourceType setting dictates the acceptable values for the RowSource property. The possible values for the Row-SourceType property are shown in **Table 4**.

Table 4. RowSourceType settings for Lists and ComboBoxes.

RowSourceType	RowSource
0 – None	There is no RowSource; the list is filled using the AddItem and/or the AddListItem methods.
1 – Value	The RowSource will be a comma-delimited list of values, such as "Apples, Oranges, Bananas."

2 – Alias	RowSource will be an alias name for an open table or cursor. The ColumnCount and ColumnWidth properties can be used to control the fields that are displayed.
3 – SQL Select	The RowSource will contain an SQL SELECT command that produces a table or cursor—perhaps something like "SELECT Name FROM Customer WHERE State = 'NY' INTO CURSOR MyList."
4 – Query (QPR)	RowSource will contain the name of a .QPR file. QPR files are produced from the Query wizard and contain an SQL SELECT command.
5 – Array	RowSource will contain the name of a memory variable array (or an array property of an object). The ColumnCount and ColumnWidth properties can be used to control the display of multiple columns from the array.
6 – Fields	RowSource will contain a comma-delimited list of field names, which may or may not include the alias and period. Example: "Name, Address, State" or "Customer.Name, Address, State". Notice that when using the alias name, only the first field in the list gets it. Repeating the alias name on the other field names will cause an error at runtime. The list will be populated from the values of the fields in the list.
7 – Files	The ComboBox will be populated with a list of files in the current directory. The RowSource property can contain a filename mask such as "*.DBF" or "*.TXT" to limit the filenames shown in the list.
8 – Structure	The list will contain the field names for the table whose alias name is in the RowSource. If the RowSource is left blank, then the currently selected alias will be used to obtain the field names for the list.
9 – Popup	The items in the list will be obtained from a popup menu's bars as defined with the DEFINE POPUP and DEFINE BAR commands. **This option for RowSourceType is present in the product for backward compatibility and should be avoided.**

With all these choices, how do you decide what to use? The most common four choices by far are None, Alias, SQL Select, and Array. The others may be useful in certain situations; when you're faced with one of those situations, you'll know it.

The Alias, SQL Select, and Array settings are self-explanatory, but where does the setting of None come in? To be truthful, the None setting is probably the most flexible of all the settings. It requires that the AddListItem or AddItem methods be used to populate the list of the control. This may initially seem to be a hindrance, but although it requires you to populate the list, it also gives you complete control over what gets into the list.

For example, what if a certain alias has all of the possible choices in it? It might be easier to just use the Alias RowSourceType and be done with it. But what if not all of the values in the alias are valid in all situations? This would require using the Valid method of the control to disallow making certain choices from the list. The problem with this technique is that a list control shouldn't include items that the user cannot choose. By using the None setting, you could write code in the Requery method of the control that would scan the alias and call the list's AddListItem method to add only those values that were valid choices. That way, the user could never choose an invalid value from the list.

There are a few other benefits to the None RowSourceType. Along with the Value RowSourceType, None can have its Sorted property set to .T. to provide a sorting of the items in the list. In a List control, the MoverBars can be used to rearrange the order of the items in the control if the RowSourceType is set to None or Value.

ListBox

The ListBox control is similar to the ComboBox in that it presents a list of values from which the user can choose. The difference is that with the ListBox, more than one item from the list is visible all the time, and the selected item is highlighted. The ComboBox only shows the list when the list has been "dropped down;" otherwise it shows only the currently selected value. This means the ListBox will take up more real estate in the form. Besides the space requirement, the ListBox may be inappropriate because it can cause confusion for the user by showing multiple items.

These are considerations for choosing a ListBox over a ComboBox in your interface. Keep in mind, though, that what is a problem in one situation may be exactly what is needed in another situation. One feature of a ListBox is the ability to allow multi-selection—that is, to allow the user to select more than one item in the list. In this situation, it's important to make it clear to the user what items are currently selected. The ListBox can do this by highlighting multiple items in the list. Later in this chapter I'll show you a better method of multi-selection than the ListBox alone.

The ListBox and ComboBox controls are both valuable when you need to present a list of possible choices to the user. Their limitation is that they must keep their entire list in memory; therefore, they aren't very good candidate controls when the possible list of choices is greater than between 100 and 500. Of course, if you think about it from the user's perspective, a ListBox or ComboBox is not an easy way to make a choice from a large number of possibilities. I try to limit my lists to fewer than 100 items, believing that any more than 100 choices would be better presented to the user in a different way.

 The ListBox has the same choices for RowSourceType as the ComboBox: Alias, Array, SQL SELECT Statement, and None. The download files contain a list form named *MoverJB.scx*. **Figure 11** shows this form with both lists populated.

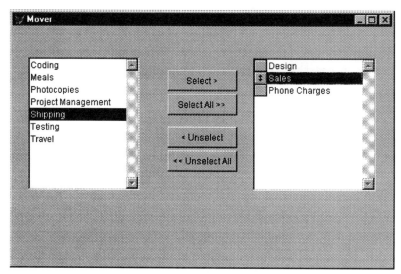

Figure 11. *A mover dialog using two ListBoxes.*

The interesting thing about this mover dialog is that both of the ListBoxes have None as their RowSourceType. The population of the lists is done through program code. Selecting and unselecting are handled in methods of the form. Here is the code that originally populates the ListBox on the left:

```
LOCAL lcAlias, lnNextItem
lcAlias = ALIAS()
SELECT SystemCodes
WITH THISFORM
  WITH .lstSource
    .Sorted = .F.
    .Clear()
    SCAN
      lnNextItem = .NewItemId + 1
      .AddListItem( cDescription, lnNextItem,1)
      .AddListItem( cType, lnNextItem,2)
      .AddListItem( STR(icode_id,4,0), lnNextItem,3)
    ENDSCAN
    .Sorted = .T.
  ENDWITH
  .ResetButtons()
ENDWITH
```

Notice the use of the NewItemId property of the ListBox to get an ItemId for adding an item. Using AddListItem rather than AddItem allows you to add multiple columns of information. Also note the use of the Sorted property to sort the items in the list.

The code in **Listing 10-2** will select one item from the list on the left and move it to the list on the right. This method of the form is named SelectOne; it is called from the Select One button as well as the DblClick event of the left list.

Listing 10-2. *The SelectOne method of the form.*

```
LOCAL lcCol1, lcCol2, lcCol3, lnSourceItem
WITH THIS
  * Shut off sorting to speed things up
  .lstSource.Sorted = .F.
  WITH .lstSource
    * Pick up values from source list
    lcCol1 = .ListItem( .ListItemId, 1 )
    lcCol2 = .ListItem( .ListItemId, 2 )
    lcCol3 = .ListItem( .ListItemId, 3 )
    .RemoveListItem( .ListItemId )
  ENDWITH
  WITH .lstTarget
    * Add the item to the target list
    lnItemId = .NewItemId + 1
    .AddListItem( lcCol1, lnItemId, 1 )
    .AddListItem( lcCol2, lnItemId, 2 )
    .AddListItem( lcCol3, lnItemId, 3 )
  ENDWITH
  * Set focus to the target list
  .lstTarget.SetFocus()
  * Sort the source list
  .lstSource.Sorted = .T.
  * Process all events
  DOEVENTS
  * Now reset the buttons
  .ResetButtons()
ENDWITH
```

This code first saves the three columns of information from the source list to variables. Then it removes the item from the source list. Next it adds an item to the target list with the variables as the data.

Notice that the source list's sorted property is first set to .F. and then reset to .T. after all is done. This is because if the list is sorted while you manipulate its contents, everything slows down while Visual FoxPro tries to keep the list items sorted.

The SelectAll method of this form is essentially the same as the SelectOne method, except that it moves all items in the source list to the target list. The Unselect methods are also similar, except they move the data the other way.

Next, there is the DoEvents command, which tells Visual FoxPro to process all pending events in the event queue. This command is needed here to deal with a timing problem related to the ResetButtons method that is called next. As you'll see in the ResetButtons code, you will refer to the items in the two lists to determine which buttons should be enabled and disabled. Calling the DoEvents command will ensure that the proper settings have affected the lists before you run the ResetButtons method.

The ResetButtons method is used to enable and disable the buttons for selecting and unselecting items from the lists. Here is the code for this method:

```
WITH THIS
  * Enable the Unselect buttons only if there is at least one item
    selected
```

```
.cmdUnselectOne.Enabled = (.lstTarget.ListItemId <> 0)
.cmdUnselectAll.Enabled = (.lstTarget.ListCount > 0)

* Enable the Select buttons if there is at least one item in the
    source list
.cmdSelectOne.Enabled = (.lstSource.ListItemId <> 0)
.cmdSelectAll.Enabled = (.lstSource.ListCount > 0)

ENDWITH
```

One last note about the mover dialog: Notice the button-like objects to the left of each item in the selected list on the right. These are MoverBars, which allow the user to rearrange the order of the list items. You could use code to read the items in the selected list from top to bottom and do something with the data. These MoverBars allow the user to determine in which order those things will be done. MoverBars are available only when the RowSourceType for the list is either None or Value. Any other choice of RowSourceType will force the list's MoverBars property to be .F..

OptionGroup

The OptionGroup used to be called a set of radio buttons, which were so named after the '50s and '60s car radios that had a front panel of buttons with which to select stations. The OptionGroup is used when there is a short list of options that are mutually exclusive. The OptionGroup can contain any number of OptionButtons. Each OptionButton represents a single choice. Only one OptionButton can be "selected" at any one time; selecting a different OptionButton will deselect the previously selected one.

Where do these OptionGroups fit into user-interface design? Not very many places, because they tend to slow down the data-entry person rather than speed him up. The OptionGroup has to be manipulated differently from the other controls, and that alone will slow down a user. I find myself using OptionGroups in some of the forms I design for report criteria setup, because in those forms there are often opportunities to use the OptionGroup effectively. However, a TextBox or short list is more effective in common data-entry situations, such as *marital status,* which could have Single, Married, Widowed, or Divorced as choices.

Okay, so how do they work? The OptionGroup is a specialized container that is limited to containing only OptionButtons. By default the OptionGroup has two buttons in it, and you can vary the number of buttons by adjusting the OptionGroup's ButtonCount property. The OptionGroup has a Value property that contains the number of the currently selected button.

Another useful property of the OptionGroup is Autosize. Setting this property to .T. will size the OptionGroup box to surround the contained buttons perfectly. If you change the ButtonCount, the OptionGroup will resize itself.

The buttons inside the OptionGroup do not need to be placed vertically in a column, although that is their default positioning. **Figure 12** shows a number of different arrangements of the OptionButtons in an OptionGroup.

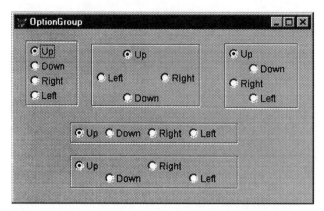

Figure 12. *Various configurations of OptionGroups.*

CommandButton and CommandGroup

I'm going to address the CommandButton and CommandGroup controls at the same time because they relate so closely to each other. The CommandButton is used for starting an action like saving the user's work or closing a form. The CommandGroup is a special container that, similarly to an OptionGroup, can only contain Command-Buttons, which allows you to group buttons into inseparable units.

Whether it's a good or bad idea to combine CommandButtons into Command-Groups is a matter of opinion. I can say that when CommandButtons are combined into CommandGroups, the buttons should be fully defined before they are added to the group. This is the issue of "early vs. late" composition. The later the composition—that is, building the whole from its parts—the better the design.

Consider a set of four buttons that navigate in a table: forward, backward, to the first record and to the last record. You could design this CommandGroup in two different ways. You could create a CommandGroup class, add four buttons to it, and write the necessary code in each button's click event.

The second choice would be to define a command button class named cmdNavigate. Then define each of the navigation command buttons as a subclass of cmdNavigate with all of the code that provides each button with its behavior. You would then have four command button classes, one for each button. Then you could define a container class and place one of each of the command button classes into the container.

Which way is "better"? The latter method is preferred. But why? Because the latter method - defining each button as part of a class of buttons and then combining them into the group—provides the most flexibility in evolving the construct in the future. You can change the behavior of any one button by altering its class code, but you can also affect the entire group by altering the cmdNavigate class. You don't need to find the CommandGroup that contains those buttons to make the changes.

On an even more important level, what if your design required you to have a set of all four navigation buttons in some forms, but only two buttons (next and previous) in other forms? Then you would have two CommandGroups—one with four buttons and one with two buttons. If you followed the first methodology of constructing the CommandGroups, there would be no cmdNext class because you defined the button inside its container. If you wanted to improve the functionality of cmdNext, you'd have to edit two class definitions—the CommandGroup with four buttons and the one with two buttons. If you followed the concept of late composition, you'd have a class for cmdNext that was used in both CommandGroups, and therefore you'd have only one place to alter your code.

This discussion of CommandGroups and CommandButtons is equally true for all composition situations. Build the pieces completely before you try to assemble the whole.

Timer

The timer is at once the simplest and most complex control in Visual FoxPro. It's simple in its elegant design and ease of use. It's complex in the types of problems it can solve.

The timer has three properties and methods of concern. The Enabled property turns the timer on and off, the Interval property determines how often the timer will "fire," and the Timer method holds the code that runs when the timer "fires."

The Enabled property can be set to .T. to turn the timer on, and .F. to turn it off. The Interval property sets the time between firings of the timer event when the timer is turned on. The Interval is set in milliseconds, so a one-second interval has a value of 1000.

> The interval of a timer is set in milliseconds. It's easy to bring an application to its knees by setting the interval thinking it is in seconds rather than milliseconds.

Finally, the code written in the timer event will be executed every time the interval expires. One caution: Be sure that the code runs in less time than the interval for the timer.

It is also important to note that the timer event will *not* fire if other Visual FoxPro code is running. In this case the timer will wait until the other code finishes and then it will run its timer event code.

So what can a timer be used for? The answer to that question is in your own imagination. You could use a timer to check for a condition after each interval, or to cause a delayed action to occur. The possibilities are limited only by your own imagination.

PageFrames and Pages

A tabbed dialog is a control with tabs across the top; when clicked, each tab presents a different set of controls. To produce a tabbed dialog in Visual FoxPro, use a PageFrame, which is a special container that can contain only Pages. Pages are containers that can contain any object except a form or formset. Pages can actually contain other PageFrames, although the interface design might become confusing to the user.

One of the properties available on the PageFrame is the Tabs property. When set to .T. (the default) each page has a tab at the top of the PageFrame that can be clicked to select that page. When the Tabs property is set to .F., there are no tabs at the top and the only way to change pages is programmatically. Imagining a PageFrame without tabs may seem silly at first, but consider a simple data-entry form. You might want to provide a searching capability for this form where the user can specify a number of different values to assist in the search.

Your first thought might be to bring up another form when the user clicks the Search button. But what if your PageFrame in the data-entry form had all data-entry controls on page 1 and the searching controls on page 2? If that PageFrame had no tabs and it filled the form, the user would have no idea the PageFrame was even there.

When the user clicked the Search button, you'd simply set the ActivePage property of the PageFrame to 2, which would display the search controls. When the user finished the search, your code would reset the ActivePage of the PageFrame to 1, again showing the edit controls. This provides search functionality without throwing another form in the user's face. **Figure 13** shows such a form.

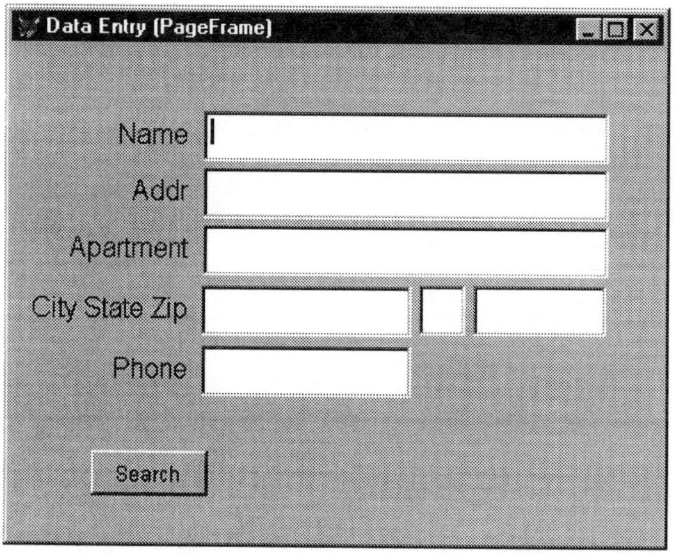

Figure 13. An edit form with a PageFrame that has no tabs.

Figure 14 shows the same form after the user has clicked the Search button.

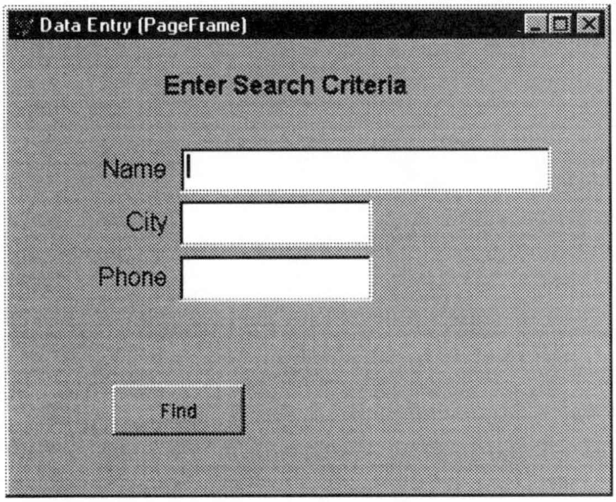

Figure 14. *The same form as Figure 13 after the user has clicked the Search button.*

 The form in Figures 13 and 14 is included in the download files in the *Chapter10* project and is named *PgfSrch.scx*.

Another use for PageFrames is to simplify the design of a data-entry form. Often, the amount of data required to describe a certain entity can easily make any data-entry form appear crowded and cluttered. A PageFrame can reduce the clutter and confusion. *PageFram.scx*, also included in the *Chapter10* project, demonstrates the use of a PageFrame to accomplish this goal of simplifying the interface for the user. **Figure 15** shows the first page of the form.

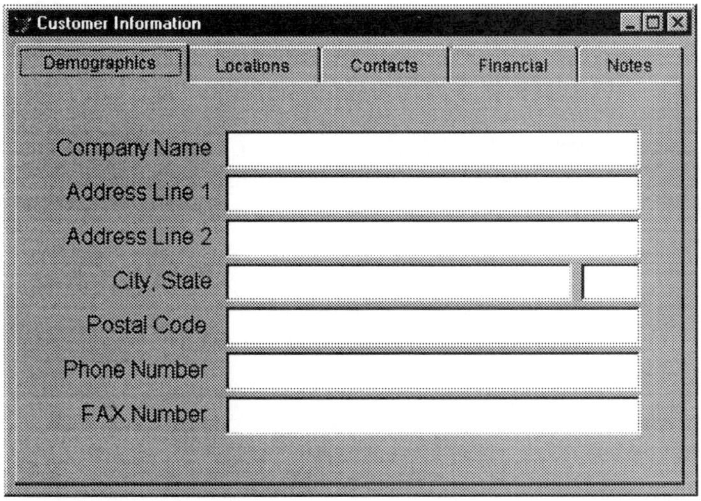

Figure 15. *The demographic page of a customer edit form.*

Figure 16 shows the financial page of the same form.

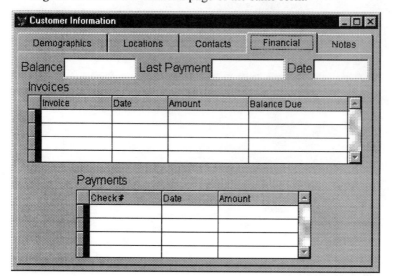

Figure 16. The financial page of the customer edit form in Figure 15.

Without viewing every one of the five pages here, you can imagine that if a PageFrame were not used, the amount of information required for one entity would crowd and clutter a single form. The user would have to work harder to find what he was looking for. With the PageFrame tool you can separate the information into groups of related data and thus make the user's job easier.

What about speed?

From the previous example, you can readily see that by using PageFrames a form could become quite complex with a large number of controls in it. This could have an impact on the amount of time it takes for that form to be created in memory. Is there a way to have the best of both worlds—that is, the quick response of a simple, single-page form and the simplicity of the interface of a multi-page form? Yes, and it's called *delayed instantiation*. With delayed instantiation you only put the controls on the page of the form that the user can see. The other pages have a single control on them called a proxy—a stand-in for the real controls. The real controls for the page are defined in a container-class definition and are instantiated when the user brings that page to the front.

Try using *PageFram.scx* to create a delayed-instantiation situation. **Figure 17** shows page 4, the financial page, of the form.

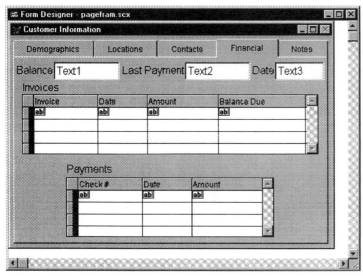

Figure 17. *The financial page of the customer edit form.*

In order to use delayed instantiation, first save the controls in question as a class, and then instantiate that class at runtime. You can select all controls on the page (use Shift-Click to select each control), then choose **Save As Class** from the **File** menu as shown in **Figure 18**.

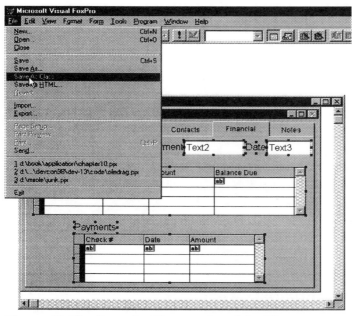

Figure 18. *The* **Save As Class** *option of the* **File** *menu.*

Once you click **Save As Class**, you can fill in the dialog as shown in **Figure 19**.

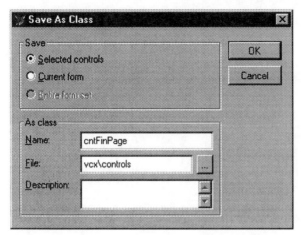

*Figure 19. The **Save As Class** dialog completed for your class.*

The controls you selected will appear in a container class, so you can delete those controls from the page in the form designer.

Next, in the Project Manager, select the **Classes** tab as shown in **Figure 20**.

Figure 20. The Classes tab of the Project Manager.

Notice that your cntFinPage class is already in the Controls.vcx class library. Edit the cntFinPage class and make one minor change—change the BorderWidth property to 0 so the container has no border. Highlight the cntFinPage class and then click the Modify button. This will open that class in the Visual Class Designer. Right-click the class and choose **Properties**, find the BorderWidth property and change its value to 0. Then click the Close button in the class designer and click Yes to save the changes.

Finally, create the proxy class. Highlight any class in the controls library and then click the New button. **Figure 21** shows the resulting **New Class** dialog, filled in the way you want it to be.

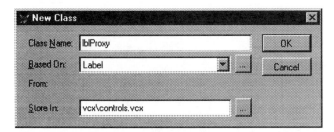

Figure 21. The **New Class** dialog filled in for your proxy class.

Figure 22 shows the lblProxy class after a few properties have been changed. Set the BackColor to red, the ForeColor to yellow, the Caption to "Proxy for actual controls", and the Visible property to .F.

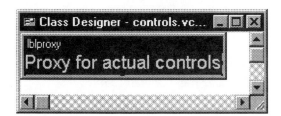

Figure 22. The lblProxy class with your property settings.

From the **Class** menu select **New Property** and add two properties named ProxyClassLib and ProxyClass. You'll notice that these properties are added to the end of the property list in the property sheet. Go to each of these properties and give them each a value of a single space to set their data type to *character*. Now add some code to the UIEnable event of your class. The UIEnable event is fired for all objects in a page whenever that page is activated or deactivated. Because you want your proxy object to do its thing when the page is activated, the UIEnable event is the correct one to choose. Put this code in the UIEnable event:

```
LOCAL lcVisible
IF TYPE("THIS.Parent."+THIS.ProxyClass+".Name") <> "C"
```

```
SET CLASSLIB TO (THIS.ProxyClassLib) ADDITIVE
THIS.Parent.AddObject(THIS.ProxyClass,THIS.ProxyClass)
lcVisible = "THIS.Parent." + THIS.ProxyClass + ".Visible"
&lcVisible = .T.
ENDIF
```

This code first checks to see if the container is there already; if it is, it does nothing. If the container isn't there, the code opens the class library and then adds that container object to the page.

Now return to your *PageFram.scx* form, open the financial page, and put an lblProxy object on that page. **Figure 23** shows this form designer for your Page-Frame form.

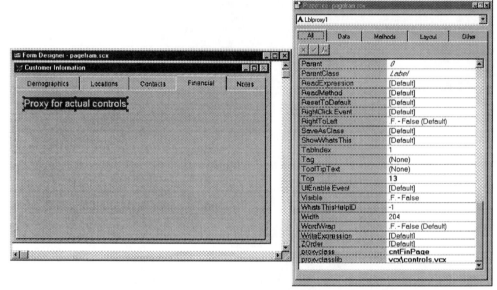

Figure 23. *The lblProxy class added to the financial page of your form.*

Notice in the properties sheet that you've set the ProxyClass property to cntFinPage, the name of your controls container for this page; and the ProxyClassLib property to VCX\Controls.vcx, the class library that holds your container class. The *label* base class was used so you could give it a caption that is visible in the form designer — reminding you of its purpose.

At runtime the label can't be seen because its Visible property is set to .F., but once that page is brought to the front the controls are present as shown in **Figure 24**.

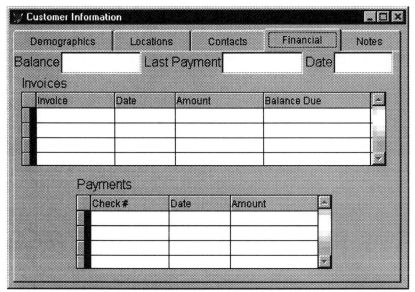

Figure 24. *The PageFrame form at runtime after the lblProxy class has added the container to the page.*

By using this proxy technique for every page in the PageFrame, except for page 1, you can greatly reduce the amount of time it takes the form to initially be created by reducing the number of controls that need to be instantiated.

The actual gain in performance achieved depends on how many pages are involved and how many controls are on each of those pages. The downside of this proxy approach is that you must edit the controls in the class designer instead of in the form designer.

Grid

The next control is the one most often requested by FoxPro 2.x developers. The Grid is not unlike the FoxPro 2.x Browse control because it displays multiple records in a row-and-column orientation, and allows the user to navigate in both row (record) and column (field) directions. The major weakness of Browse in earlier versions of FoxPro was that it wouldn't coordinate well with a data-entry screen or form.

The Grid control in Visual FoxPro is, in fact, a control that can be placed inside a form, and it acts just like any other control in the form. **Figure 25** shows a Visual FoxPro form with a Grid as the only control.

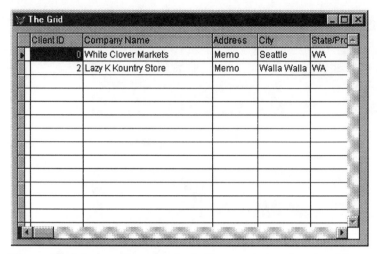

Figure 25. A form with a simple Grid control showing the Clients table in the Time and Billing database.

Figure 26 shows this form in the form designer.

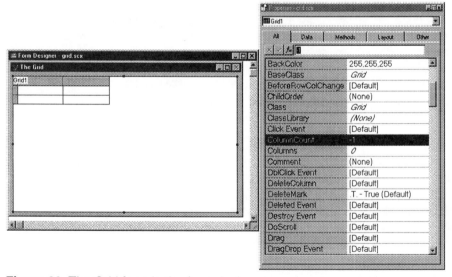

Figure 26. The Grid form in the form designer.

Notice that the ColumnCount property for the grid is set to –1—this is a special ColumnCount that indicates that the Grid should have one column for each field in its record source. The actual count of columns will be determined at runtime.

This format for a Grid can be used to get the simplest Grid into a form. Of course you can set the ColumnCount property to any number you choose, and fully control the number of columns the Grid will have. Let's step back a moment before you dig into this, and take a more general look at the Grid itself and its construction.

The Grid is a container that can contain only one object class: a column. A column, also a container, can contain one header object and one or more controls. The default control in a column is a TextBox. **Figure 27** shows this containership relationship.

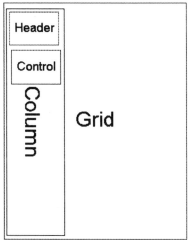

Figure 27. *The Visual FoxPro Grid containership structure.*

In Figure 27 the outer box is the Grid, which can contain only columns. The columns in turn can contain one header and one or more controls.

As stated earlier, the default control for a column is a TextBox. However, you can actually put any control you like into the column of a Grid. Right-clicking the Grid and choosing the **Edit** option will allow you to add a different control to a column. When you choose **Edit** from the right-click menu, the Grid will get a colored box around it, indicating that you are now editing the Grid and its contents.

Once the Grid is in edit mode, you can choose a control from the form controls toolbar and simply drop it on one of the columns in the Grid. Note that this can only be done on Grids with a ColumnCount other than -1. **Figure 28** shows your Grid form after you have changed the ColumnCount to 4 and you are about to select **Edit**.

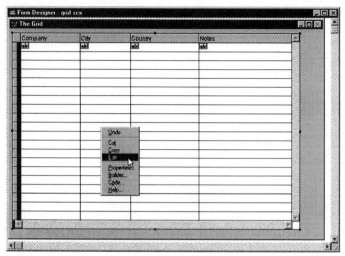

Figure 28. *The shortcut menu for your Grid, ready to select the **Edit** option.*

Next, click the EditBox control in the form controls toolbar and drop that control over the fourth column of the Grid. See **Figure 29**.

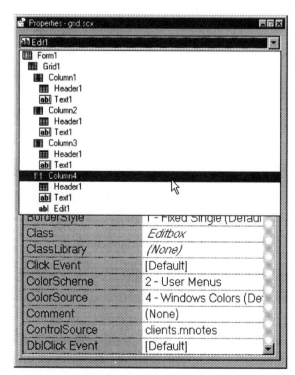

Figure 29. *Dropping the EditBox control in column 4 of the Grid.*

To confirm that the EditBox has actually been added to column 4, you can use the ComboBox at the top of the property sheet as shown in **Figure 30**.

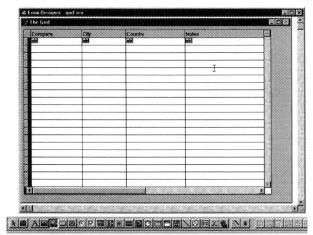

Figure 30. *The Grid form in the form designer.*

The listing under column 4 contains a Header, a TextBox, and an EditBox. Consider that any column can contain more than one control, but at any time only one of those controls is the current control — the one that the user will see. You can change the CurrentControl property for column 4 to be the Edit1 EditBox.

While you're editing the Grid, you can also increase its row height by dragging the line between rows. Make your Grid look like the one in **Figure 31**.

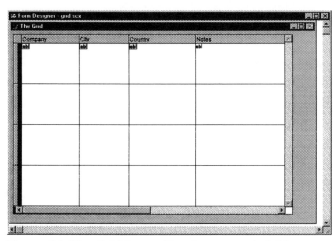

Figure 31. *The Grid form with a larger row height.*

You can also change the RowHeight of the Grid by typing a new height in the property sheet for the RowHeight property.

Now run the form and see what it looks like. **Figure 32** shows the Grid form running.

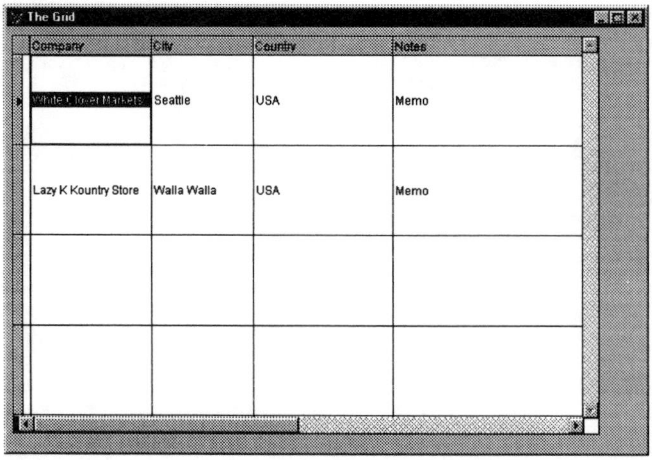

Figure 32. *The Grid form as it's running.*

Notice that column 4 contains the word "Memo" rather than the contents of the memo field. This is because of one column property that is very important to understand: Sparse. This property tells the column whether to show the control in the column, or just the data, when a cell doesn't have focus. By default the Sparse property is .T., which only shows the data and does not draw the CurrentControl in all cells of the column except the cell that has focus. That is why you see the word "Memo" — the data when an EditBox is not used for a memo field. If you simply change the Sparse property of column 4 to .F. and then run the form, you'll see something similar to **Figure 33**.

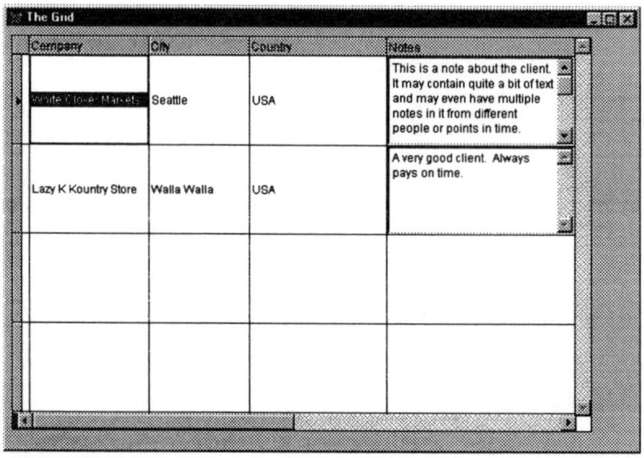

Figure 33. *Column 4 with the Sparse property set to .F.*

I'll discuss more about the Grid control in Chapter 11, "Advanced Form Control Topics."

Container

The Container control is simply a holder for other controls. In the PageFrame section of this chapter, which presented the idea of delayed instantiation, you saved all controls on a page into a class library. Visual FoxPro automatically placed these controls inside a container for you.

You can use containers in your class designs as well. Whenever you need more than one control to perform a function, there is a possibility that a container might make the job easier.

You'll still have to deal with the issue of "early vs. late" composition when using containers. It's always a good idea to fully define each control as a class of its own before adding it to the container. Chapter 11, "Advanced Form Control Topics," will discuss the use of containers in more depth.

Misusing and abusing the controls

Ah, the misuse and abuse of controls. You see it everywhere. One issue that comes up quite often is the question of how long it takes a ListBox to load a list of 20,000 items. Think about it. Would *you* want to scroll through a ListBox of 20,000 items looking for the one you wanted? ListBox and ComboBox are powerful controls for presenting a relatively small number of choices to the user. When the number of options grows too large, then it's time to find another way to present the choices.

How about the form with nothing in it but a Grid that has ComboBoxes in some columns, EditBoxes in others, and even a Grid in one of the columns? Wouldn't this interface be better presented to the user by diverging and using more than one control?

Take a look at **Figure 34**. Can you see anything wrong with this interface design?

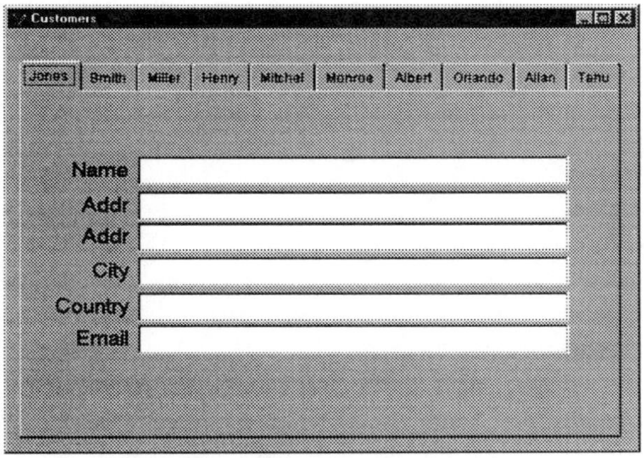

Figure 34. A PageFrame gone wild.

This is obviously a poor use of a PageFrame. What do you do when you have more customers than you can fit into pages?

Another abuse of PageFrames is using one when the interface should actually use multiple forms. Another is where the PageFrame is unnecessary, (all of the controls could fit in one form without a PageFrame).

An OptionGroup should never have more than four or five options in it. More choices than that should use a ComboBox or ListBox control. Using an Option-Group for more than four or five choices is another example of abuse of a control.

I can go on and on listing the abuses of various controls, the point is that each control has its strengths and weaknesses. The design of an interface should take advantage of the strengths of a control and avoid its weaknesses.

As a developer, you need to understand the purpose for the form and then build its contents to meet that purpose. You need to know the strengths and weaknesses for each of the controls available and choose the control that best meets the requirements at hand.

The misuse of containers isn't uncommon. You should use a container only when it adds to the functionality or reusability of the controls it contains. Do not use containers simply to "Lasso" a bunch of controls together.

Summary

The control is the object closest to the user. Although the user sees and interacts with forms, the controls provide a message path between the user and the application. The selection of controls is not always a simple process. Many times you will need to change your initial choices to better meet the user's needs.

Visual FoxPro 6.0 not only provides a variety of base controls for you to choose from, but it provides you the ability to create your own controls. Using the class designer you can modify the behavior of the Visual FoxPro base classes and create new controls that are specialized for whatever purpose you have.

You can combine multiple controls, using containers, into more complex interface objects that meet the needs of the user. These containers can also be used reduce your own development time. By using containers to combine the controls that are "always" found together, you reduce the time it takes to build the forms. For example, building an address block container as a class would allow you to place that address block in the customer form, the employee form, the vendor form, etc.

Choosing the right control is critically important to building a good user interface. While is possible to misuse any control discussed in this chapter, each one deserves a place in your toolbox.

The next chapter, "Using Complex Controls," will introduce you to more advanced controls. Chapter 12, "User Interface Design - or- Selecting the Best Way to Present Information to the User," will examine the problems inherent in user-interface design and offer some ideas on how to approach them.

Chapter 11
Advanced Form Control Topics

Chapter 10 gave a quick overview of form controls and discussed some of the basic issues. This chapter discusses some of the subtleties of using form controls. In particular, I'll address some effective techniques of using the more complex form controls, the ComboBox, ListBox and Grid, as well as using combinations of controls to get the job done.

Delegating to form controls

In Chapter 9, I suggested that a control method with more than a handful of lines of code should be a "red flag," indicating that the method code should be transferred to a form method. What I didn't discuss was when you should nod and say, "Yup—all this code belongs in this control's method."

Recall the OOP principal of encapsulation. Putting this idea together with Steve McConnell's discussion of cohesion (particularly what Steve describes as *functional* cohesion and *communicational* cohesion), it makes sense that if a control's method manipulates nothing outside the control to which it belongs, then a lengthy chunk of code is often appropriate.

> *If you don't have Steve's book handy (and again, you should), functional cohesion is the idea that a routine (or an object) does one thing and one thing only. Communicational cohesion is the idea that while a routine may perform more than one operation, the routine is cohesive in that the two operations share a common data set. In the context of this discussion, I'm making the point that a form control should encapsulate certain operations that relate only to that control, or that share data belonging to that control object, which we refer to as the object's properties.*

While it describes a foundation class method, rather than an instance method, the Key-Press() event code in Chapter 10 is a good example of complex method code that does not represent a problem. In fact, a good rule-of-thumb question to ask about control methods is, "Can this code be successfully placed into a reusable object class rather than this instance?" If the answer is "yes," indicating that the code isn't manipulating controls or properties, or calling methods unique to the form instance that you're currently working with, then you're probably okay.

A second consideration is whether the code is in an event that is responding to user input, or if the code performs a "setup" or "maintenance" function. In general, events and methods like Init(), Refresh() and Requery() are more likely to have lengthy code segments, whereas LostFocus(), Valid(), Click(), InteractiveChange(), GotFocus(), and so on, all of which are triggered by user actions, are more likely to delegate the actual "work" to a form method.

Hopefully it's understood that I'm laying out *principles* and not hard-and-fast rules. Look at each control method with a critical eye and question whether you delegated that particular operation to the proper object.

Enabling/disabling controls

There is one operation whose proper delegation has taken me some time to finally understand. For years I've placed code in various control and form methods that was responsible for enabling and disabling various other controls. This has often been a frustrating exercise, sometimes requiring the creation of large result tables to figure out all the various conditions, and under which conditions a particular control should be enabled. Not a trivial exercise with a dozen controls and four or five different conditions all requiring a different combination of enabled and disabled controls.

The solution has been delegation—make each control responsible for enabling or disabling itself, depending only on those conditions that affect that particular control. The logical place to do this evaluation is in the control's Refresh() method.

Once a decision has been made to use this approach, the trick becomes figuring out how to determine the form state. Triggering such an evaluation is the easy part. Any change in form state is almost always accompanied by a call to the Refresh() method of the form. Likewise, any activation of a page in a PageFrame is often used to trigger a call to the Refresh() method of the page. The result is a call to the Refresh() method of all controls contained on the form, or the refreshed page. You can take advantage of this to allow each control to evaluate the current state of the form, and set its own properties accordingly.

For example, consider a form that has an "edit mode." The developer, after consulting with the end users, decides that this form will initially only display data. To actually make any modifications, the user must first put the form into an "edit mode" by clicking the Edit command button. It's reasonable that when the user clicks the Add command button, the form should also go into edit mode.

When in edit mode, certain changes need to take place. First, all data-bound controls are toggled from disabled to enabled. Second, the Edit and Add buttons are disabled, and the Save and Cancel buttons are enabled. You could put a bunch of code in the Edit() method that would step through a long list of controls and enable them, enable the Save and Cancel buttons, and then disable the Edit and Add buttons. However, if this kind of behavior is common throughout the application, you could establish a new property for your forms, add a new property to your foundation control classes, and add a bit of code in the Refresh() event-methods. For example, establish a new form property called lEditMode to indicate whether the form is in edit mode. Add a new property to your foundation control classes, lEditWatch, to indicate whether this control needs to keep an eye on the form's lEditMode property. Then in the foundation control class Refresh() methods, add:

```
IF This.lEditWatch ;
    AND TYPE("ThisForm.lEditMode") = "L"
  IF ThisForm.lEditMode
    This.Enabled = .T.
  ELSE
    This.Enabled = .F.
  ENDIF
ENDIF
```

Or more succinctly:

```
IF This.lEditWatch ;
     AND TYPE("ThisForm.lEditMode") = "L"
   This.Enabled = ThisForm.lEditMode
ENDIF
```

Once this is accomplished, set the lEditWatch property to .T. on all the controls, and have the form's Edit() and Add() methods simply set the form's lEditMode property to .T. and refresh the form. Each control then enables or disables itself. Occasionally you'll want a control to exhibit *inverse* behavior; that is, disabled when in edit mode but enabled when not in edit mode, as in the Add and Edit buttons. In this case, add the following code to the control's Refresh() methods in the form instance:

```
DoDefault()
This.Enabled = NOT This.Enabled
```

With this technique, if you have a control that is *always* enabled or disabled, simply set this property and leave the lEditWatch property set to .F.

For further discussion of delegating responsibility to form controls, see the next section.

List objects

Of all the controls introduced with Visual FoxPro, none have been so frustrating to so many as the list objects. I have heard the phrase "spawn of the devil" in a discussion of list objects. Even when compared to the grid, they are the most complex single controls in the Visual FoxPro toolbox, and for some reason seem to give folks more problems than any other control.

A significant factor in their apparent difficulty is the plethora of ways that one can populate a list object. In Chapter 10, I discussed the family of list objects (the ListBox, and the ComboBox in both of its flavors, the Drop-Down Combo and the Drop-Down List). In that discussion, I pointed out that while these controls can be populated using any one of nine different settings for the list object's RowSource type, the most common options used in an application are 0 – None, 2 – Alias, 3 – SQL Statement and 5 – Array. Another commonly used setting is 1 – Value, but this is used only for hard-coded static lists. Most list objects are data-driven in some way, which is their greatest strength. Instead of having to modify any code if the user needs another option, it's much simpler to add a new item to a table that is used, in turn, to populate the list object. Chapter 10 also suggests that you can cut this list further to only *one* option. How's that for cutting a complex control down to size?

The key to simplifying list objects, while at the same time gaining great consistency and flexibility, is to understand that the information used to populate a list object is always converted to a character value and stored in the control's List property. This property is an "array-like" property in that it can be referenced by rows and columns, just as you can reference an array. In fact, you can manipulate the List "array" directly if you wish. However, though it can be described as "array-like," it isn't an array. You don't need to dimension it, and you can't execute any array functions or commands on it (such as ALEN() or ASORT()).

The important point here is that no matter how you populate the list object, the object ends up with the list items in the same property. This being the case, why not standardize the method used to populate data-driven list objects?

When using a RowSourceType other than "0 – None" or "1 – Value", the list object is driven by an outside source. When the data in the RowSource changes, the List property of the list object is not automatically updated with those changes. To repopulate the list to reflect these changes, the list object's Requery() method must be called.

> *Few methods are so misunderstood and overused as Refresh(). The Refresh() method performs one very simple function: If a control is bound to some external value (the ControlSource specifies a table field, memory variable or object property), and that external value changes, the value property of the control does not change automatically; the control must be refreshed. This is completely different from the situation where a change is made to a list object's RowSource, hence the need for a separate method, and the Requery() to re-populate the List property with the new values. Thus, with the exception of any code added to the Refresh() method, keeping a control's Value property "in sync" with its ControlSource is the method's sole function.*

The Requery() method looks at the entity specified in the RowSource property and re-stuffs the values into the List property.

If the goal is to simplify the list objects by limiting the RowSourceType to one of the four available, it's possible (as was suggested in Chapter 10) to settle on "0 – None", and programmatically populate the List property using the AddListItem() method. It's also possible to create an array property (named something creative like "aList") in your foundation class list objects, and use a RowSourceType of "5 – Array", and a RowSource of This.aList, again programmatically populating the array. Either approach has certain advantages, but before we discuss them, let's consider where to place the code to populate our lists.

If you've worked much with list objects, you're probably used to calling their Requery() method to repopulate them when their RowSource values have changed. As a result, this is an ideal place to put code to populate the list. In the case of using an array property, view or cursor as the RowSource, it's necessary to call Requery() after populating the array or changing the contents of the view or cursor. Since this is going to be a required step, it makes sense to put the code to populate the cursor, view, array, or whatever our RowSource is going to be, in the Requery() method.

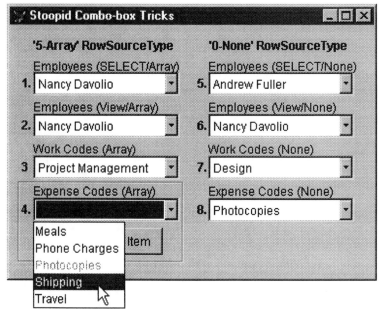

Figure 1. *The COMBOS.SCX example form. Note the disabled third item in combo box 4.*

If you examine the project for this chapter (Chap11.PJX from the download files), you'll see the form COMBOS.SCX, shown in Figure 1. In contrast with the fairly straightforward combo boxes used back in Chapter 5, COMBOS.SCX shows a collection of combo boxes that demonstrate how to use a single RowSourceType for most of your data-driven combo and list boxes, and gain some valuable capabilities in the bargain.

The combo boxes in the left column (numbered 1 through 4) use "5 – Array" as their RowSourceType, while the combo boxes in the right column (numbered 5 through 8) use "0 – None". The simplest example is shown in the Requery() method of combo number 1, shown in **Listing 11-1**:

Listing 11-1. *Data-driving a combo or list box through an array property.*

```
*cboEmployeeList1.Requery()
SELECT employees.cfirstname-(" "+employees.clastname) AS cfullname,;
     Employees.cemployeenumber, ;
     Employees.iemployeeid, ;
     Employees.clastname ;
  FROM "time and billing!employees";
  ORDER BY Employees.cLastName ;
  INTO ARRAY This.aList
```

With this first example, some advantages of employing one of these techniques become apparent. First, using a RowSourceType of "5 – Array" (or "0 – None") provides (in my experience) the most stable and predictable behavior in all environments. Second, by specifying a RowSource that is a part of the class (the aList property), and placing the code to populate that array in one of the classes' methods, you can encapsulate the data that drives the control. This opens the way to the creation of an independent, reusable, data-driven object class.

Listing 11-2 shows how you can accomplish the same thing using a pre-established view rather than executing a SELECT in the Requery() method. Note the extra code that is necessary here. COPY TO ARRAY will automatically create the target array if it doesn't already exist, and dimension it appropriately. However, it will not automatically re-dimension the array when the array already exists. As a result, it's necessary to re-dimension the array before executing the COPY TO ARRAY command.

Listing 11-2. Data-driving a combo or list box using a view through an array property.

```
IF NOT USED("v_EmployeeListRO")
  USE "time and billing!v_EmployeeListRO" IN 0
ENDIF
SELECT v_EmployeeListRO
DIMENSION This.aList[RECCOUNT("v_EmployeeListRO"),FCOUNT("v_EmployeeListRO")]
COPY TO ARRAY This.aList
```

The combo boxes numbered 5 and 6 demonstrate doing essentially the same thing as 1 and 2. However, instead of using the aList property, these combo boxes use the AddListItem() method to manually "stuff" the table values into the List property. As with the technique using the custom aList property, this very neatly encapsulates the population of the control within the control, and makes the control independent of the form and its properties and methods.

> *If the list that you're building in your combo box is only a single column of values, you can substitute the AddItem() method for the AddListItem() method. However, remember that the effect of AddItem() is to insert the specified item into the list, while the AddListItem() method replaces the specified item. This means that each time you execute AddItem(), it adds an additional row to the list, when you might really want to add an additional value for a column in the current row. As a result, the only way to create a multi-column list object using AddItem() is to use AddItem() to create a new row and specify the value for the first column, then use AddListItem() to replace the (initially) empty values in columns 2 and above. Given the necessity of using AddListItem() any time you have multiple columns, and the ability of AddListItem() to create single-column lists, it makes no sense to use AddItem() except in those circumstances in which a row must be inserted.*

Listing 11-3 shows that, when adding the values in the third column of the list (from the Employees.iEmployeeID), which are *integer* values, you must convert them to character values (using the LTRIM(STR()) expression), because the AddListItem() method supports inserting only character values into the List property. This is not surprising, considering that the list objects store the values internally as character strings.

Listing 11-3. *Using AddListItem() to populate a data-driven list object from a query.*

```
SELECT employees.cfirstname-(" "+employees.clastname) AS cfullname,;
       Employees.cemployeenumber, ;
       Employees.iemployeeid, ;
       Employees.clastname ;
  FROM "time and billing!employees";
  ORDER BY Employees.cLastName ;
  INTO CURSOR cTemp
lnItem = 0
SCAN
  lnItem = lnItem + 1
  This.AddListItem[cTemp.cFullName,lnItem,1]
  This.AddListItem[cTemp.cEmployeeNumber,lnItem,2]
  This.AddListItem[LTRIM(STR(cTemp.iEmployeeID)),lnItem,3]
ENDSCAN
USE IN cTemp
```

Similarly, you can use a view, as shown in **Listing 11-4**.

Listing 11-4. *Using a view to data-drive a list object using AddListItem().*

```
IF NOT USED("v_EmployeeListRO")
  USE "time and billing!v_EmployeeListRO" IN 0
ENDIF
SELECT v_EmployeeListRO
lnItem = 0
SCAN
  lnItem = lnItem + 1
  This.AddListItem[v_EmployeeListRO.cFullName,lnItem,1]
  This.AddListItem[v_EmployeeListRO.cEmployeeNumber,lnItem,2]
  This.AddListItem[LTRIM(STR(v_EmployeeListRO.iEmployeeID)),lnItem,3]
ENDSCAN
```

Things get even more interesting when using a parameterized view for a list object. The combo boxes numbered 3, 4, 7 and 8 all demonstrate using a parameterized view to populate a combo box with either work codes or expense codes using the same view by simply using a different parameter. If you run the form and open the Data Session window, the v_SystemCodes view is opened only once, but is used to populate four different combo boxes, with two different subsets of the SystemCodes table.

Listing 11-5 shows sample Requery() code for this type of list object, using the array technique.

Listing 11-5. *Populating a list object array from a parameterized view.*

```
IF NOT USED("v_SystemCodesRO")
   USE "time and billing!v_SystemCodesRO" IN 0 NODATA
ENDIF
vp_cType = "WORK"
REQUERY("v_SystemCodesRO")
DIMENSION This.aList[RECCOUNT("v_SystemCodesRO"),FCOUNT("v_SystemCodesRO")]
SELECT v_SystemCodesRO
COPY TO ARRAY This.aList
```

```
FOR i = 1 TO ALEN(This.aList,1)
This.aList[i,1] = ALLTRIM(This.aList[i,1])
ENDFOR
```

Notice the three lines of code immediately following the COPY TO ARRAY command. The other sample list objects have a ColumnCount of more than 1. As a result, the width of the columns can be adjusted using the ColumnWidths property. However, when there is only a single column displayed, the column sizes itself to the width of the data, hence the need to "trim" excess spaces from the contents of the array to avoid an unsightly oversized list when the list is opened.

So tell me, which technique should I standardize on?

While both techniques outlined here work very well and very consistently, each technique has its advantages. While you or your company may standardize on "A" over "B," you will find circumstances in which "B" works better than "A."

Using an array has a couple of advantages. First, it's easy to manipulate and "read" the array property from outside the control. Second, it makes it possible to disable controls when desired. Combo box number 4 illustrates these advantages. Clicking the command button just below Combo 4 toggles the enabled status of the third item in the list. Note that this is done by placing a "\" character at the beginning of the item in the first column of the list. This is not possible when using a RowSourceType of "0 – None" and the AddListItem() method. Note the code in the Requery() of combo box 8—cboExpenseCodes4. The third item in the list is hard-coded with a "\" character to disable it. Note that this has no effect. Visual FoxPro also has a bunch of useful functions that operate on arrays, like ASCAN(), which can be used when the RowSource of the list object is an array.

As shown in **Listing 11-6**, when you plan on manipulating the list from outside the control (perhaps in a composite control) it's necessary to have a way to tell the Requery() method *not* to repopulate the array, but to simply execute the default Requery() method to repopulate the List property from the array. Otherwise, if you put a "\" on some items to disable them, the Requery() method will overwrite these changes.

An advantage of building the list object using AddListItem() is that two features of list objects are available only when the RowSourceType is "0 – None" or "1 – Value"—the MoverBars and Sorted properties. This would normally preclude these features from being used when creating a data-driven list object, but as I've shown here, you can data-drive a list object and still use a RowSourceType of "0 – None". Even though the Sorted property is not available when using a RowSourceType of "5 – Array", you can still use the ASORT() function to sort the array, then call the Requery() of the list object (without, of course, repopulating the array). In the case of a reusable class, you could create an lSorted property, which would apply the ASORT() function on the aList array property as the last step in the Requery() code.

Listing 11-6. *Conditional Requery() code, allowing outside manipulation of the aList array property.*

```
LPARAMETERS tlRequeryOnly
IF NOT tlRequeryOnly
   IF NOT USED("v_SystemCodesRO")
      USE "time and billing!v_SystemCodesRO" IN 0 NODATA
```

```
    ENDIF
    vp_cType = "EXPENSE"
    REQUERY("v_SystemCodesRO")
    DIMENSION This.aList[RECCOUNT("v_SystemCodesRO"),FCOUNT("v_SystemCodesRO")]
    SELECT v_SystemCodesRO
    COPY TO ARRAY This.aList
    * And so on...
ENDIF
```

If this control were to be designed as a reusable class, I'd eliminate the parameter, relying on a control property instead. I would also place the code to enable or disable individual items into a new method that would accept, as a parameter, the number of the item to enable or disable.

> When using integer surrogate keys, it is often necessary for the list object's value property to reflect a numeric value in one of the list's columns. As mentioned in the text, the list objects store their list data internally as character strings. The normal behavior of a list object bound to a property or field with a numeric value is for the list object's value property to reflect the ListIndex, or the selected item's position in the list, rather than the value of the entry in the BoundColumn. This was a major limitation in Visual FoxPro 3.0, which was thankfully corrected in Visual FoxPro 5.0, but unfortunately it uses one of the worst-named properties I've ever encountered. The BoundTo property, if .T., indicates that the value in the BoundColumn is converted to a numeric value and stored to the list object's Value property. If BoundTo is .F. and the control is bound to a numeric value, the default behavior is obtained, and the Value property reflects the ListIndex of the control, which is the ordinal position of the currently selected item. I can think of several property names preferable to "BoundTo", but BoundTo it is. All of the example list objects set BoundTo to .T.

List objects—example of a reusable class

Again, encapsulating the ability to self-populate lets you create reusable object classes based on a list object. Consider a situation in which you have an overloaded Codes table (see the SYSTEMCODES table in the sample Time and Billing database), with a couple hundred code types instead of only two. Given a single parameterized view, you can add a property to hold the code category and use a single control class to display any of the hundreds of code types. The combo box used in the COMBOCLASS.SCX form (see Figure 2) is an example of such a control. The class (cboSystemCodes) is in the Chap11.VCX class library.

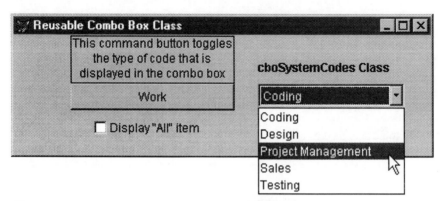

Figure 2. *A reusable, data-driven ComboBox class.*

Implementing the cboSystemCodes class is very similar to that of the cboWorkCodes1 and cboExpenseCodes2 controls in COMBOS.SCX, with the following changes:

- The vp_cType view parameter in the Requery() code is assigned from a control property (cCodeType).
- The call to the Requery() method from the Init() is now conditional, based on a logical property, lRequeryOnInit. This allows the control to be instantiated in a situation in which the cCodeType property is set by some other control, or programmatically based on some condition.
- The Requery() method inserts an "All" item as the first item in the list if the new property lIncludeAll is set .T. When an "All" item is included, it is often preferred that the "All" item be initially selected; thus the first (or any other) item can be specified as initially selected by setting the nInitialItem property. This is implemented in the Init() method.

Listings 11-7 and **11-8** show the cboSystemCodes' Init() and Requery() methods, respectively.

Listing 11-7. *cboSystemCodes.Init() showing conditional Requery() execution and setting of the initially selected list item.*

```
* cboSystemCodes.Init()
IF THIS.lRequeryOnInit
   THIS.REQUERY()
   THIS.LISTINDEX = THIS.nInitialItem
ELSE
   STORE "" TO THIS.aList
   THIS.LISTINDEX = THIS.nInitialItem
ENDIF
```

Listing 11-8. cboSystemCodes.Requery() using a property (cCodeType) to establish the view parameter and another property (lIncludeAll) to include an "All" item in the list.

```
* cboSystemCodes.Requery()
IF NOT USED("v_SystemCodesRO")
    USE "time and billing!v_SystemCodesRO" IN 0 NODATA
ENDIF
vp_cType = THIS.cCodeType
REQUERY("v_SystemCodesRO")
IF THIS.lShowAll
    DIMENSION
THIS.aList[RECCOUNT("v_SystemCodesRO")+1,FCOUNT("v_SystemCodesRO")]
ELSE
    DIMENSION THIS.aList[RECCOUNT("v_SystemCodesRO"),FCOUNT("v_SystemCodesRO")]
ENDIF
SELECT v_SystemCodesRO
COPY TO ARRAY THIS.aList
IF THIS.lShowAll
    AINS(THIS.aList,1)
    THIS.aList[1,1] = "All"
    THIS.aList[1,2] = 0
ENDIF
* Because this combo has a ColumnCount
* of 1, you can't use ColumnWidths to
* adjust the column size
lnMaxLen = 0
FOR i = 1 TO ALEN(THIS.aList,1)
THIS.aList[i,1] = ALLTRIM(THIS.aList[i,1])
ENDFOR
```

The feature allowing inclusion of an "All" item is useful when you're using a drop-down list to create a filter, rather than manipulating a field value. For example, in a contact management application, you might have a list box that displays contacts filtered by customer. The form might include a drop-down list to filter by type of contact (phone, face-to-face meeting, telex, letter, e-mail) and another to filter the list by purpose of contact (PR call, sales call, sales follow-up, problem resolution, and so on). The user can then use these lists to filter by one or the other factor, or both. This technique could be modified to insert a "None" item as the first in the list, or a "New" item at the end. In fact, the "special" prompt (None, New, All, etc.) could be stored in a control property, and you could add another logical property to determine whether the special prompt should appear at the beginning or end of the list.

In the example in the COMBOCLASS.SCX form, I've included a command button that manipulates the cCodeType property of the drop-down list, allowing you to toggle between the two code types. The form also includes a check box that toggles the lIncludeAll property. If you want to see the full demonstration of this property, set lIncludeAll to .T. in the form designer, set the nInitialItem to 1, and run the form. Since this property is used only when the control instantiates, it isn't possible to properly demonstrate it via an interactive control at runtime.

Once you start creating reusable list-object classes, you'll discover all kinds of handy functionality to add to them, such as the ability to programmatically select an item by passing the prompt, or including a logical property that indicates whether a "special" list item has been selected.

List objects—Alias and Fields RowSourceTypes

Thus far, I've been making a case for standardizing on a single method of populating data-driven list objects, by relying on either "5 – Array" or "0 – None" as the RowSourceType. As pointed out, this isn't entirely practical, because there are certain advantages to each. You'll end up using one approach 90 percent of the time, and the other perhaps 10 percent of the time.

However, there is a particularly valuable behavior of list objects with a RowSourceType of "2 – Alias" or "6 – Fields": They move the record pointer in the cursor specified as the RowSource! This makes a list object with one of these RowSourceTypes particularly valuable for navigation through a set of records. It's a matter of personal preference which to use, but given the need to rely on the structure of the cursor to properly populate the list when using "2 – Alias", I prefer to use "Fields" exclusively. Thus, what you or your shop will end up with is a standard that specifies "5 – Array" for 90 percent of the situations, "0 – None" for perhaps 5 percent and "Fields" for another 5 percent. The extent to which you use "Fields" will be determined by how much row-by-row table navigation an application requires. As I'll discuss later in this chapter, this type of list object could become quite prevalent if you are editing multiple record data sets and want to avoid using grids.

Setting visual properties example—ColumnWidths

This may be old hat to you, so if you're using these techniques, skip ahead. However, if you've ever wished that the property sheet was available at runtime so that you could manipulate visual properties, then let me tell you that it is (well, kinda sorta).

Properly setting the ColumnWidths property of a combo or list box can be a real pain. However, if you set them while the form is running, you can adjust them precisely to your liking. Although the property sheet isn't available, the Watch and Locals windows are, and you can set an object's properties directly in these windows.

You can pop open the Locals window and examine the running form to find the control, but it is much easier to get a reference to the object you need to fiddle with using the SYS(1270) function, and display this object reference in the Locals window. This avoids having to drill down into the form and find the control. The SYS(1270) function returns a reference to the object under the mouse pointer, so entering `ox=SYS(1270)` in the command window with the mouse pointer hovering over a combo box will do the trick.

Once you have a reference to the control and place "OX" in the Watch window, or open the Locals window, you can examine the ColumnWidths property and edit them until the control is laid out as desired. Make a note of the values or copy the values from the Locals or Watch window and paste them into the ColumnWidths property in the property sheet for the list object.

This technique is also useful in adjusting the width of combos, list boxes, and grid columns.

Disappearing objects, multiple objects and composite objects

It's often overlooked that not all controls need to be visible all the time. Sometimes I try to accomplish the most complex things using a single control. I'll spend several frustrating hours (or days) fiddling with it, succeeding with a bunch of code that is such a house of cards that the slightest bump or breeze brings it tumbling down. When faced with this type of situation, I ask myself whether the task can be accomplished with two or more controls, making only one visible at any moment depending on the situation. Since this entire process can be entirely transparent to the user (when the various controls are all of the same type), it adds no visual complexity to the form, and can greatly simplify the implementation.

An example of this is a simple text box that must handle two tasks. The first is to allow the user to enter a value (such as case number, invoice number, or employee ID) to retrieve a record. The second function is to *display* the identifying field for the currently displayed record. In the first case, the text box is most likely not bound to a field, and the LostFocus() or Valid() events initiate the lookup or record-retrieval process. In the second case, the text box may be bound to the appropriate field in the retrieved record.

Another example is using a drop-down combo box both to select an entity (customer, vendor, employee, client, etc.) from a list and to enter a new entity. Sometimes this can work out okay, but you have to write code to prevent a user from clicking the Add button and then selecting an existing entity, rather than typing in the name of the new entity, which would result in adding another record for that entity. Using two controls may be simpler—a text box that is visible in "add" mode, and a combo that is visible in "edit" mode.

The Time Card form, introduced in Chapter 5 and contained in CHAP5.PJX, illustrates the manipulation of the Visible property of controls.

One other "disappearing object" technique can make your life a bit easier with combo boxes. Rather than trying to dynamically manipulate the list of items in a combo box, either by removing or disabling them, consider using one separate combo control for each pattern of items that you want to display. Obviously, this is useful only if you have a finite (and hopefully small) set of different lists to display. However, manipulating the Visible property of a half-dozen different controls might be much more attractive than writing a huge glob of code to manipulate the list.

Sometimes a problem takes a lot of time and clever coding when using a single control, but gets real easy when you use more than one control. The trick is to make it appear to the user as though there is only one control. As an extreme example, look at the grid on the 2GRID.SCX form in the Chap11 project. This grid doesn't really do anything, but note how it appears to be a single control as a result of careful arrangement of the grid elements and setting the grid properties. Synchronizing the record pointer and providing automatic shifting of focus between the two grids would be an interesting challenge, but probably do-able if this was really necessary.

For a smaller and more practical demonstration, look at the TIMECTL.SCX file, also in the Chap11 project. The first text box uses what might be a first-cut attempt to get a properly formatted HH:MM entry, setting the InputMask property to "99:99". However, there is nothing that requires entry of a valid value for either the hours or minutes portion of the text box, nor is there anything that insures ensures that a value of less than 10 for either hours or minutes is padded with a leading 0. Enter "311" and you get "31:1", which does not represent a valid time value. You can enter "03:88", which represents a valid hour, but an invalid minute value, or "63:04" which is ok for the minutes, but the hours is invalid.

However, the second text box on the form is actually four text boxes. The first text box creates the familiar 3-D border. Its TabStop property is set to .F., and the WHEN method returns .F., ensuring that this text box never receives focus—its purpose is decorative only. The "real" text boxes are placed in front of the "dummy" text box, and are sized and placed to fit within its 3-D borders. The leftmost text box accepts the user's input for the hours value, the second (read-only—the WHEN returns .F.) simply displays the colon (:), and the third accepts user input for the minutes value. By splitting the entry of the hours and minutes into two separate controls, the code in the control's Init() and LostFocus() event methods becomes much less complex than it would if you tried to use a single text box.

Later in this chapter, in the section on grids, you'll see a more complex example of using this technique (which actually yields a DateTime value).

Timer-mediated program delays

It is sometimes necessary to launch a process but still give some events or program code a chance to finish executing before that process begins. The timer object is tailor-made for handling this task.

To help understand this situation, consider some type of operation that wants all forms closed before proceeding. If this process is launched from a form method, any attempt to close all the forms will fail, leaving the form that launched the process in a state most of us have seen: The form is still visible but can't be closed.

You cannot release a form while one of its methods is executing. Trying to force the release of the form by issuing a CLEAR ALL will trigger error 1951—"Cannot clear the object in use." If a form has a KickOff() method that calls (either directly or indirectly via a function or procedure) a system object's CloseAllForms() method, this method will try to close the form that called CloseAllForms(). However, the KickOff() method of the form is waiting for CloseAllForms() to complete before it finishes executing, so CloseAllForms() is unable to release the form that called it. Even if the very next line of code in the KickOff() method is ThisForm.Release(), it will not execute (along with all of the Deactivate() and Destroy() code that may be in the form) until *after* CloseAllForms() has finished.

To solve this problem, you can create an object based on the timer class. In its Timer() event, the object should kick off the desired process by calling CloseAllForms() and then instantiating the form or other object, or calling the procedure that performs the process. However, the Interval property of the timer is set to 500 milliseconds or so, giving the form that instantiates this object a chance to close down before the process is kicked off.

The code in **Listing 11-9** shows a reusable object class that is designed to handle this whole process. This object could be instantiated as a child object of a system-level object such as an application or forms manager object. You can also modify it to launch a form rather than calling an object method or .PRG as shown here.

Listing 11-9. *A timer-based object designed to briefly delay execution of a program or method.*

```
*****************************************************
*-- Class:         tmrlauncher
*-- ParentClass:   ctimer
*-- BaseClass:     timer
*
DEFINE CLASS tmrlauncher AS ctimer

  INTERVAL = 500
  *-- If .T. the launcher object will release
  *-- itself via its timer event.
  lReleaseWhenFinished = .T.
  NAME = "tmrlauncher"

  *-- The program the object is to launch
  cProgramToRun = ""

  PROCEDURE INIT
    LPARAMETERS tcProgramToRun, tlReleaseWhenFinished
    IF PCOUNT() = 2
      THIS.lReleaseWhenFinished = tlReleaseWhenFinished
    ENDIF
    THIS.cProgramToRun = tcProgramToRun
  ENDPROC

  PROCEDURE TIMER
    THIS.INTERVAL = 0
    IF "." $ THIS.cProgramToRun
    * The "program" is an object method
      lcProgramToRun = THIS.cProgramToRun
      &lcProgramToRun
    ELSE
    * the "program" is indeed a .PRG file
      DO (THIS.cProgramToRun)
    ENDIF
    IF THIS.lReleaseWhenFinished
      THIS.RELEASE()
    ENDIF
  ENDPROC

ENDDEFINE
*
*-- EndDefine: tmrlauncher
*****************************************************
```

Grids

In approaching this section, I was concerned with what you, the reader, expected to see. Many developers get excited with clever tricks that can be accomplished with grids—stuff that you see in all the whiz-bang demos that folks do when showing off Visual FoxPro: Combo Boxes, Edit Boxes and List Boxes in grids, grids in grids, rows and columns in contrasting colors, pictures, and on and on.

 I've incorporated a lot of these tricks in my applications, and most of what I've learned I learned from a fellow named Drew Speedie. Drew has learned how to do some really slick things with grids, and was kind enough to give us permission to include his demonstration code with our download files. You will find two files, MTVFPEX.ZIP and MTVFPEX5.ZIP, which include a number of interesting techniques that you can try.

However, the most important thing I've learned about grids over the last three and a half years is when to use them and when not to use them. In general, I've adopted the following "rules" in my application development:

1. Do not use grids for data entry. Never.
2. When it's necessary to display information in a rows-and-columns format, use a list box unless you need a capability unique to grids.

Well, okay, "never" is a big word. Don't take that literally. My hope here is to get you to think long and hard before you ever include grids in your design. Grids should be considered an exception to the rule in your interface design. I'd rather see you throw a grid onto a form occasionally as a last resort, than to use grids all over the place and then regret going down that road.

The trouble with grids

I arrived at Rule 1 above with much regret, after years of wishing that I'd learned it sooner. And yes, I sometimes break my own rules. (Note the sample forms used in Chapter 5!) The problem is not with the grid, but with the developers implementing it and the clients and users who interact with it.

To be more explicit, the grid is an extremely intuitive interface for developers in all circumstances. A developer usually thinks of data in a row-and-columns format, so a control that presents and accepts data in this format makes perfect sense to a developer. Grids are also extremely intuitive to the user when a form is displaying line-item details on work orders, purchase orders, shippers, invoices and the like.

To make matters worse, grids are very easy to implement, particularly in prototype forms used as "proof of concept" forms. The developer just drops them onto a form and without a lot of tweaking, displays the data in a quick-and-dirty, row-and-column layout. However, herein lies the seed of our downfall. Once a user has seen a grid and understands how it works, you're almost locked into using grids throughout the remainder of the development process.

The next thing that happens is when a form using a grid for data entry is shown to the user for testing, inevitable modifications begin to crawl out of the woodwork. The user says, "I'd like focus to shift to column 4 when column 1 is thus-and-such, and column 2 is thus-and-so, but focus should shift to column 3 otherwise." Okay. Easy enough, you say. Back to your office, a few lines of code here and there (and maybe some field- or row-level rules as shown in Chapter 5) and the user gets another crack at it.

Next, it's "Well, focus should shift to the next line under condition A when column 4 is greater than column 3 and column 5 is losing focus, but focus should shift to column 1 on the current line if column 3 is greater than or equal to column 4, and it's a Tuesday or Thursday, and why do I have to do Ctrl+Tab to exit the grid—can't it read my mind and *know* that I want to exit the grid when I press <Enter> when A and B and C but not D..." etc., etc., etc. If you haven't already been in this grid situation with a client or user, you will be.

From a business standpoint, the real danger is that these modifications don't represent "feature creep," which you may have so carefully guarded against in your client contract. It starts out innocently enough. Before you know it, each form using a grid for data entry has code stuffed into the When, BeforeRowColChange, AfterRowColChange, MouseMove, Scrolled, MouseDown, MouseUp and Deleted events of the grid, and in every GotFocus, LostFocus, Valid, KeyPress and Click event of every control in the grid, and half of them are calling form methods and setting form properties to figure out what is going on.

COWABUNGA Buffalo Bob!

So much for reusable code and object classes, huh? Even if you have unlimited time and endless patience to give users exactly what they want, chances are good that you'll encounter some screwy interaction between controls, or find some events that occur in an order other than what is expected or desired. The immediate result is writing even more code to work around the work-arounds, until you create an edifice of fussy complexity. The final result is a form in which any maintenance is likely to bring the entire structure down with a crash.

In addition, tables often contain more fields than can be displayed in a single row in a grid. As a result, you need to add horizontal scrollbars to allow access to all fields, which has the potential of bringing in another set of problems. Users will disagree over what fields should be initially visible, the order in which the fields are displayed, and the size of the fields, and you're faced with more code to allow each user to customize the grid to their liking—without breaking the complex code you've already added to accommodate those doing heads-down data entry using the grid.

You might be thinking that users make similar demands with controls on a form, particularly for heads-down data entry work. That's true, but if you use a form to display a *single record*, you're moving in a single dimension. Display (and edit) multiple records via a grid, and you're now moving in *two* dimensions, which doubles (or triples) the complexity.

So, yes, grids are cool and easy to use, but sometimes when users get through with you you'll wish you'd never heard of a grid. If you limit the functionality of grids to only simple textual data, you might be okay, but try explaining to your users why you can use grids on form "A" and not on form "B".

So whatcha gonna do now?

Life without grids (well, almost)

So how do I get along without grids? To answer this, let's examine why I would want to use a grid…what is the situation?

In many cases the user is interacting with a single record—a customer record, or an inventory record, or a raw material record. In this case I provide a mechanism for the user to select the desired record (or add a new one) and then display a form, using appropriate form controls, for editing and saving. I *could* use a grid for a picklist, but I manipulate the data using conventional form controls on a form, not via a grid.

In another situation there might be some relationship or interaction between records in a table, requiring edits of more than one record. A hypothetical example is a set of records that bear some kind of user-determined sequential numbering. If you had 10 records and forced the user to interact with only one record at a time, she could change the numbering on a record from "3" to "2." Until she changed record "2" to change its numbering to "3," there would be a violation of the sequential numbering requirement, and indeed the user could simply leave the data in this state. If you enforce a uniqueness rule like this by creating an candidate key, the user would have to change the numbering of record "2" to a unique value, save it, then change record "3" to "2," save it, then edit the original record, changing its value to "3." What a pain. The user would shoot you.

It's much more preferable to let the user freely renumber the records, and commit the changes to the entire set of records simultaneously. You can still enforce the rule—either at the interface level by examining the records prior to executing the Save() code, or at the database level by creating candidate keys.

If you're scratching your head at this point wondering what I'm talking about, I'm going to give you a more obvious example in a moment. However, the *principle* at work here is one of an interrelationship between records in a single table that requires you to look at a *set* of records as a single entity rather than individual records.

The more obvious example of this principle is that of two tables in a parent-and-child relationship. In many of these relationships, changes to the (multiple) child records cause changes in the (single) parent record, thus requiring that you consider as a single entity not only the set of child records, but the parent record as well. The classic example of this situation is any kind of header/detail or document/line items relationship such as invoices, work orders, purchase orders, pick tickets, and so forth. If the header record accumulates totals from the detail records, modifies/creates records, and then commits changes to the individual child records—without updating and also committing changes to the header record—the situation is open to corruption if the Save() of the header record fails. As a result, the set of child records must be treated as a single entity, and the user must be able to commit or abandon any changes to them as a group.

> *Strict adherence to data normalization principles, in particular third normal form, can break the dependency between the child records. For instance, if you don't store totals in the parent "Invoice" record, each "invoice detail" record then becomes independent of its siblings. With the introduction of SQL, particularly views, it became more acceptable to be this strict in our database designs. Why store totals in the header record when you can simply include virtual fields as needed in your queries that sum the appropriate fields in the child records? My database designs in the past have not been this strict in their adherence to third normal form, but I'm beginning to appreciate the greater simplicity of a user interface where maintenance of parent record data is no longer required to edit or add child records. If I successfully migrate to this way of thinking, the "multiple record edit" might become the exception rather than the rule in my applications.*

So, in this situation you have several "live," updateable records. You need to communicate to the user what these records are, allowing the user to navigate to a particular record and edit it. In some cases the records need to be edited in a rapid-fire, keyboard-centric, heads-down data-entry scenario. For the quick 'n' dirty solution, the grid does the trick. For a permanent, workable, maintainable solution, what are the alternatives? Consider the following points:

- Some of the "slick tricks" I mentioned at the beginning of this section involve tweaking a grid to behave like a list box—that is, highlighting the entire current row. Unfortunately (as of this writing and based on my limited creativity and cleverness), this is impossible. The current cell will always be displayed in a color scheme different from the current row, no matter how much you fiddle with the DynamicForColor and DynamicBackColor properties.

- One of the problems with grids is changing their RecordSource on the fly at runtime. This causes all properties of all columns to "reset" to default values, which must be rebuilt programmatically. List boxes are immune to a change in their RowSource property, provided the structure remains consistent.

Sounds like maybe you should think about using a ListBox, huh?

Also, recall from the earlier part of this chapter the fortuitous behavior of list objects that causes them to move the record pointer when the RowSourceType is "2 – Alias" or "6 – Fields".

So, a list box is used to present users with information representing the multiple records that they can edit, and allows them to select a record. The list box moves the record pointer so the selected record can be displayed in bound controls for editing. Sounds pretty simple, right?

Actually it is, but I'll be honest here and tell you that creating a gridless control for editing multiple records is more difficult (initially, anyway) than slapping a grid on a form. A couple of user-interface issues need to be addressed, and depending on how you address those issues, you might need to do some control synchronization as well.

The remainder of this discussion will use as an example the NoGrid form found in the CHAP11.PJX project. This form is a gridless version of the form used in Chapter 5. Both forms are shown in Figure 3. It provides the same functionality, and in some cases improves on the Chapter 5 form.

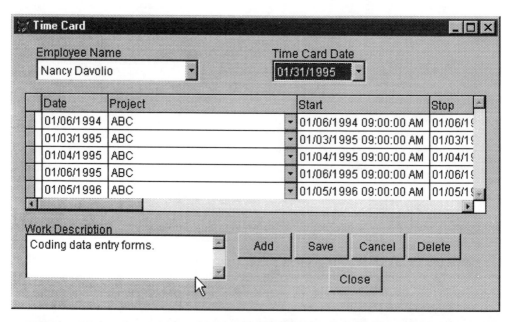

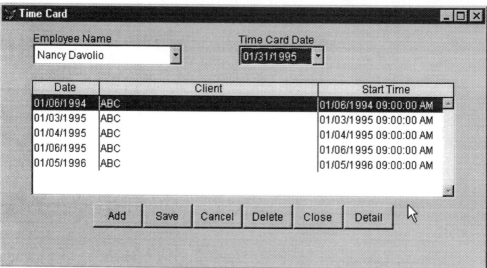

Figure 3. The Chapter 5 Time Card form, and the "gridless" Chapter 11 Time Card form. The controls and code used to select a particular time card are the same for each form, but the manipulation of the details of each time card differs.

The Time Card form used in Chapter 5 and again here represents one of the most common "multi-record" scenarios, the parent/child form. One of the first complexities encountered in deciding to forego grids is "Where do I want to display and edit the data for the child records?" You have three choices.

The first (which was actually demonstrated in the Chapter 5 Time Card form) is to display the data on the form right along with the list box (or grid, if necessary) that allows the user to navigate from one record to another. In the Chapter 5 Time Card form, the edit box for the description of the work done for each line item of the time card was not placed in the grid, but on the form itself. A line of code in the AfterRowColChange event of the grid refreshes this edit box.

The second option for displaying and editing the child records is to launch a child form in response to the user's selection of a line item. This can be accomplished by creating a modal child form using a default data session (to share the parent form's data session), or by using a FormSet.

The third option is almost a hybrid of the first two, and is the technique used for the Time Card form example for this chapter. This option uses a PageFrame to separate the list from the editable controls for the currently selected line item. If desired, the pages of the PageFrame can be un-tabbed, and the SpecialEffect property can be set to "2 – Flat" with a BorderWidth of 0. This makes it appear to the user that he is interacting with two forms rather than one. (See Chapter 12 for more discussion of this interface concept.)

Deciding which of the three methods to use depends on several factors. The first, of course, is the amount of real estate needed to display all controls needed to edit a child record. Once a list box has been placed on a form, there often isn't a lot of room available for additional controls, particularly if the list box itself displays a large amount of data. In this example, it might be possible to crowd all of the controls onto a single form without using a PageFrame, but it might also require that the user employ a screen resolution higher than 640x480.

In a gridless form it's also important to consider the concept of the "separation" of the parent record and its associated list of child records from the controls that edit a single child record. When using a grid, setting the AllowAddNew property on the grid to .T. allows the user to add a new child record simply by pressing the down arrow when on the last record. This is easily accomplished in code as well. However, when not using a grid, a single Add button on a form or a toolbar or an Add bar on a menu becomes ambiguous. Will clicking the Add control add a new parent record or a new child record? If we display the child record on a child form, or on a separate page of a PageFrame, this ambiguity can be resolved. "Add" on the page or child form displaying a child record adds a new child record. "Add" on the page displaying the parent record adds a new parent record.

You also need to address navigation from one child record to the next. If you display all the controls for editing the child records along with the list box representing the entire set of child records, you can use the list box for navigation. When separating the child record controls from the list box, by means of either a PageFrame or a child form, you must make a design decision. Can the user navigate from one child record to another without returning to the parent form or the page displaying the list? The user's requirements will determine this issue. If the user will frequently be accessing the child records sequentially, then you must include a provision for navigation without returning to the list.

If you'll examine the NOGRID.SCX form included in CHAP11.PJX, you'll see that the controls and code used to select a specific time card are identical to those for the Time Card form discussed in Chapter 5. In fact, most of the methods remain unchanged. Most of the new code in this form relates to permitting navigation through child records while on page 2 of the PageFrame.

The list box on page 1 uses "6 – Fields" as the RowSourceType, and the RowSource is selected fields from the child view, v_Time_Card_Hours. The second page of the PageFrame is activated either by clicking on the "detail" button on page 1, or by double-clicking on an item in the list box. The DblClick() method of the list box is also called if the user presses <Enter> after selecting an item. The InteractiveChange() event of the list box stores the record number of the current item to a form property, for use by the navigation buttons that appear on page 2. The bound column of the list box is the field that holds the primary key value for the Time_Card_Hours table—iTimeCardDetailID. This allows the synchronization of the list box with any navigation done on page 2. In the Activate() event of page 1 the following code ensures that the list box indicates the currently selected record:

```
WITH THIS.lstDetail
   IF .VALUE # v_Time_Card_Hours.iTimeCardDetailID
      .VALUE = v_Time_Card_Hours.iTimeCardDetailID
   ENDIF
ENDWITH
```

One of the nice features of grids is the header object that identifies each column. There is no need to do without. You can use some combination of command buttons, shapes, or, as I have in this form, labels to identify each column.

You'll note that page 2 of the PageFrame (see **Figure 4**) contains a specialized set of command buttons.

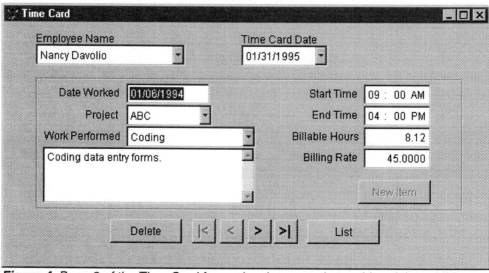

Figure 4. *Page 2 of the Time Card form, showing controls to add or delete child records and to navigate through child records.*

In addition to the VCR-style navigation buttons, there is a List button to activate page 1 of the PageFrame, a Delete button to remove child records, and a New Item button to add new child records. The New Item button is disabled unless the record pointer is positioned on the last record, which is handled via the Refresh method of the New Item button:

```
IF THISFORM.nCurrentRec # THISFORM.nLastRec ;
     AND THISFORM.nLastRec > 0
   THIS.ENABLED = .F.
ELSE
   THIS.ENABLED = .T.
ENDIF
```

This button, placed as it is in the tab order of the controls for this page (while the Delete, List and navigation buttons are not) allows this form to be used for heads-down data entry. After entering values for all controls for a new record, the user ends up with focus on the New Item button. A hit on the <Enter> key appends a new record, and shifts focus to the first control, ready to enter the next item. While the Add button on page 1 calls the form's Add() method, which creates a new time card record, the New Item button's Click() event calls the form's AddItem() method, which creates a new child record.

The decision to enable the Next Item command button only when on the last record was arbitrary. There was no technical reason to do so; it was employed to address a hypothetical user or client requirement. This particular control could be taken a step further, navigating to the next record or appending a new record depending on whether the record pointer is currently positioned on the last record. I whipped up a quick demonstration of this idea, which you'll find in NEXTBUTTON.SCX included in the CHAP11.PJX project. (See Figure 5) Rather than using a record pointer, it simply mimics record-pointer movement by manipulating two form properties, nItem (representing the current record pointer position) and nItems (representing the last record). As long as nItem is somewhere between 1 and nItems – 1, the prompt on the command button is "Next Item", and the Click() event method increments the nItem property by 1. If nItem is equal to nItems, the prompt on the command button changes to "New Item", and its behavior changes. The Click() event method increments nItems by 1 and shifts focus to the spinner. If the spinner is used to "navigate" to another "record" other than the last, the command button's Refresh() takes care of changing its prompt (and its behavior) back to "Next Item."

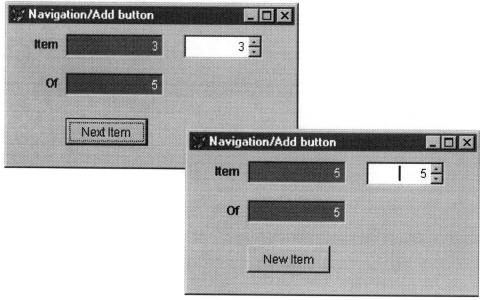

Figure 5. *A dynamic navigation/add button for navigating through and adding new child records.*

To support the navigation through child records from page 2, nFirstRec, nLastRec and nCurrentRec properties are employed, along with Last(), Next(), Prev() and First() methods. The VCR buttons enable and disable themselves via their Refresh() methods.

In general, the implementation of this form is quite straightforward. However, as you can see, using gridless forms for child-record manipulation requires more thought up-front. It also requires a higher degree of cooperation between you, the developer, and your users, to ensure that each design decision supports the way the form will actually be used. However, after years of trying to meet users' demands and requirements for data-entry forms using grids, I've found that I can do a better job and create a more flexible and maintainable product if I look on grids as a very rarely used control.

In the earlier section discussing composite controls, I showed how to use multiple controls to facilitate entry of time-related information. DateTime fields are tailor-made to store this kind of information, because they allow calculation of elapsed times, detection of the passage of midnight, the end of a month, and so on. However, the standard DateTime data format is a nightmare for data entry. (Try to quickly enter the start and stop times in the Chapter 5 Time Card form!) The example in the earlier section on composite controls stores the time information as textual data, and would require some manipulation of the information to be able to store it into a DateTime field.

In the Chapter 11 Time Card form, I've employed a custom control that started out in a manner very similar to the example shown earlier, but takes it a step further.

Instead of the rearmost text box being a passive "decoration" for the other con-
trols, the text box in the txtTime control found in the CHAP11.VCX library is used
as a mediator between the text boxes, and a control source that accepts
DateTime data.

A container, when refreshed, should call the Refresh() method of all of its con-
tained controls. This holds true for pages and forms, but I seem to have trouble
when I rely on this behavior when dealing with Container controls. As a result, the
Refresh() method of the txtTime container explicitly calls the Refresh() method of
the txtBound text box. The txtBound text box is bound at runtime to the property
or field whose name is specified in the ControlSource property of the txtTime
container. The Refresh() method of the txtBound control is used to update the
value of the txtHours and txtMinutes controls.

The Valid() events of the txtHours and txtMinutes controls are used to manipulate
the values entered, and to then trigger the Valid() event of the txtBound control.
The txtBound.Valid() then performs the necessary calculations based on the val-
ues of txtHours and txtMinutes, and stores the result as a DateTime value to the
Value property of the txtBound control.

Again, the principle here is that some up-front work has made life easier for the
user, and has done so in a manner that requires us to get it working right only
once in a reusable class.

Are grids still useful?

Yes, grids still have their place. There are times when you can use grids with ease to handle maintenance of simple textual and numeric data. However, as soon as you use the grid to add records, things start to get complicated. The mindset of the user is also important in making a grid/no-grid decision. Heads-down data entry users can be extremely demanding. Anything that forces them to take their eyes off the data they're entering, or to take their hands off the keyboard (or even off the numeric keypad) will lead to demands to "fix" the form. This is much easier to do using conventional controls on a form than it is in a grid. Even for read-only information, a list box is limited because it can display only so much data horizontally—a grid has the advantage of being able to scroll to show as many columns as necessary, and can allow users to reorder the grids to their liking. Sophisticated search functions often work very well with a grid, allowing the user to see a lot of data, and search on or order the data in a variety of ways. While I'm on the subject, don't assume that you need a grid with columns and headers to display data in different sort orders. Labels respond very nicely to click events, and option buttons and check boxes work very well for presenting options to the user that do not require use of a grid.

Is that all there is?

There are a whole gaggle of controls available to the developer in Visual FoxPro, and I've touched on only a handful here. However, these are the controls that, in my experience, eat up most of my time one way or another. Following the guidelines I've shared with you in this chapter has saved me countless hours of development and debugging time, and made my applications more solid and maintainable. For more detailed information about form controls, the section on the Form Designer in *The Pros Talk Visual FoxPro 3* from Microsoft Press is still relevant, and many have said that it helped them become much more effective when creating Visual FoxPro forms. In addition, the volumes in this series that provide more information are Whil Hentzen's *The Fundamentals: Building Visual Studio Applications on a Visual FoxPro 6.0 Foundation*, and Tamar Granor and Ted Roche's *Hacker's Guide to Visual FoxPro 6*.

Chapter 12
User Interface Design - or -
Selecting the "Best" Way to Present
Information to the User

In his book *About Face: The Essentials of User Interface Design* (ISBN: 1-56884-322-4), Alan Cooper discusses extensively the art and science of user interface design. I will be drawing a lot on Mr. Cooper's work because he has given us some great terminology for discussing user interface design. Being able to use his vocabulary makes examining a complex subject much easier. If you have read Mr. Cooper's book, you will find that I don't always agree 100 percent with his perspective on things, but his work certainly does force me to give the issues some serious thought. In this chapter, I hope to introduce the problem of user interface design and to present some ideas on how to approach solving that problem. One goal I have is to prod your mind into thinking creatively about presenting data to users. In this chapter, I will pay a lot of attention to users and how they do their job. This is because the quality of a user interface is measured not by the artful flair of the design or the creativity of the presentation, but rather the functionality of the interface in helping users to get a job done.

The three interface styles

Alan Cooper presents three major interface styles in his book: Process, Data, and Goal-centric.

Process centric

The process-centric interface has a specific system process at the center of the interface. This approach is by far the worst from users' perspective, because it provides them no control other than choosing which process to begin.

Many of the older interfaces displayed the process-centric style. Those systems were fondly referred to as "menu-driven" systems. In these menu-driven interfaces, the user was usually presented with a full-screen menu from which he could choose from a list of possibilities.

Once the user had made a choice from this menu, he was presented with another menu, and then another, and so on until the menu choice initiated a system process such as creating a new invoice. Once the process was begun, there was no way to do anything else in the system without completing or aborting the creation of the invoice.

Because the system process defines the style of the user interface, it is a process-centric interface. Most developers today have left this interface style in the dust because it gives the user very little control over what the system will do and when it will do it.

Data centric

The data-centric design is probably the most commonly used interface in database systems. That is not because it is necessarily the best design, but rather it is the design that seems most natural to the developer.

The data-centric design has all of the system's features built around the nature of the underlying data structures. This is most comfortable to database system developers because these developers are always thinking in terms of data and its structure.

Figure 1 shows a common menu structure of a data-centric design.

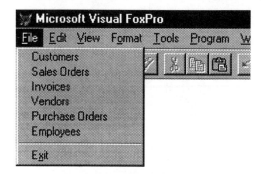

Figure 1. A data-centric menu system.

Notice that each of the choices on the file menu gives direct access to a specific entity in the underlying data structure. Data-centric interfaces also typically have a large number of grids to show the row and column orientation of the data. For example, **Figure 2** shows a data-centric interface to customer information.

Notice that page one of the PageFrame is a grid of customers, which presents the customer information in a one-row-per-customer and one-column-per-field orientation. This is a very common way to present data, and the most common argument in favor of it is "That's the way the users like it." Hogwash! The only group of folks I know of who see customer information in a row-and-column orientation is database developers.

Secretaries see customer information as a set of folders in a file cabinet. Salespeople see customer information as a set of entries in a day-timer. Collections people see customers as a name on the screen to be cajoled out of money. Marketers see customers as a line or bar on a market analysis chart.

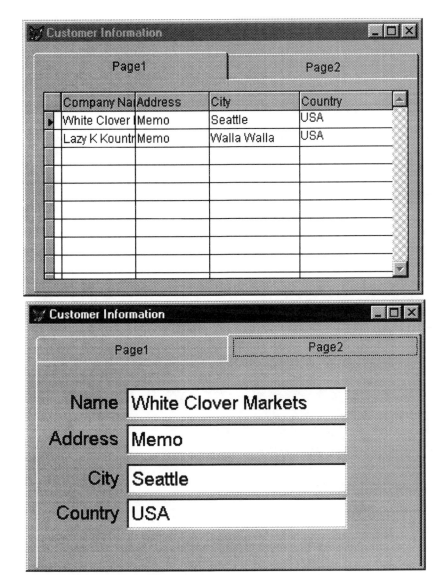

Figure 2. *A data-centric editing form.*

As you can see, each user sees the same information in a different way. Each user uses that information for different purposes. Each user has a different set of goals in his job. Which leads to the third interface style.

Goal centric

The goal-centric user interface requires that we know something about the user's job. We need to know the user's goals and then design the application interface around those goals.

Alan Cooper, on page 12 of his book *About Face,* says the goals of most users are:

- Not looking stupid
- Not making any big mistakes
- Getting an adequate amount of work done
- Having fun (or at least not being too bored)

These goals are not very surprising; I think most people would include these among their own sets of goals at work. However, Mr. Cooper goes on to list the things that most commercial software is quite adept at doing:

- Making the user look stupid
- Causing the user to make big mistakes
- Slowing the user down so he doesn't get an adequate amount of work done
- Preventing fun and boring the user

The only way we can design interfaces that work well for the user is to learn to see the user's job from the user's perspective. Let's take a moment to look at the four items in Mr. Cooper's second list.

Making the user look stupid
How often have you seen a dialog box that looks like the one in **Figure 3**?

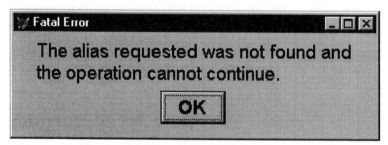

Figure 3. A dialog box from some application.

The first thing I notice is the title of the dialog box: "Fatal Error." Most people I know think a fatal error is holding a 44-magnum gun to your head and pulling the trigger, having forgotten that the gun was loaded. Secondly, the word *alias* has many meanings; the least common meaning is the name for a work area. To the average user, the text of this dialog box seems to say that the "also known as name" for the patient was not located, so the surgeon stopped the surgery. With words like "fatal" and "the operation cannot be continued," does it make sense to ask the user to click a button that says "OK"?

Perhaps this dialog box could be presented as in **Figure 4**.

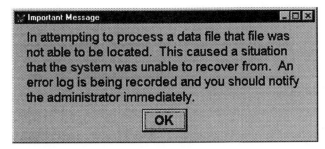

Figure 4*. A slightly better dialog box.*

I present Figure 4 as slightly better because, first, it does not use the Fatal Error caption to scare the wits out of the user. Secondly, it takes the time to explain in simple English what exactly is happening. It does not accuse the user of anything. It suggests the next action for the user to take (notify the administrator). Finally, it does not ask the user to OK the problem, but rather to acknowledge the receipt of the message.

Let me take this moment to let you know that Steve and I have checked with the powers above and have found that, in fact, there is no prize waiting for the developer who used the least number of words in their dialog boxes and prompts.

Causing the user to make big mistakes

Again, it isn't difficult to find user interfaces that easily allow a user to make a very costly mistake. Although there are times when confirmation dialogs can be a hindrance to the user's efficiency, when the action that is about to commence is irreversible and drastic, a simple confirmation dialog is in order.

Keep in mind that the days of computer phobia are gone. Most users today are comfortable with their machines, and because of that their human nature takes over. People are curious by nature, so if there is a button or menu option that they are unsure of, they will click it or choose it to find out what it does.

If you have menu options or buttons that perform irreversible and drastic changes to the data or application environment, provide a confirmation dialog box between the menu or button and the actual action. **Figure 5** shows a potentially problematic menu option.

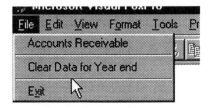

Figure 5*. A potentially problematic menu option.*

The **Clear Data for Year end** menu option could be a big mistake if all of the year-end reports and operations had not yet been completed. This is a good place for a confirmation dialog to assist the user in preventing a big mistake. **Figure 6** shows just such a dialog.

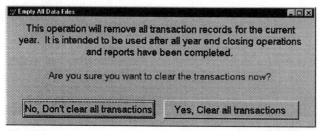

Figure 6. *A confirmation dialog box for a potentially destructive menu option.*

In this dialog box, the operation is explained in simple English so the user can understand clearly what it will do. The text also suggests which other operations should be completed before this one is executed. Also, note that the prompts on the buttons don't say OK and Cancel, but rather are descriptive of their actions. Most importantly, though, is the fact that the non-destructive button is the default. This allows for the user who clicks or presses Enter without reading anything.

Keep in mind which actions in the application are potentially destructive and protect the user from making any BIG mistakes. I emphasize the word "big" because you won't assist the user by including confirmation dialogs for every button and menu option. Rather you'll slow the user down, as you'll see in the next section.

Slowing the user down so he doesn't get an adequate amount of work done

One common problem with user interfaces is that they get in the user's way. Consider the confirmation dialog box I discussed in the previous section. If those dialogs are used everywhere, all they do is require the user do more to get less done.

I use one software product daily in my consulting practice to track my billing. One option in this software is to make a backup of the data every time I exit the program. I have set this option on because the data is critical to my business and I want it backed up every time I exit. **Figures 7, 8, 9, 10** and **11** illustrate the dialogs I see when I exit the program.

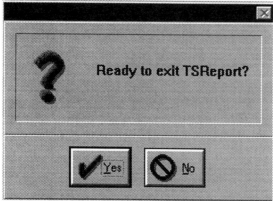

Figure 7. *Confirm exit.*

The Confirm Exit dialog box in Figure 7 comes up immediately after I click the Exit button. Is exiting the program such a terribly destructive operation that I couldn't just rerun it if I was mistaken?

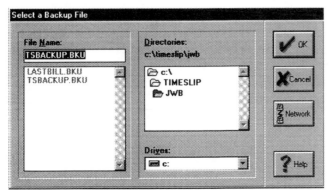

Figure 8. *A dialog box to select the name of the backup file I want to create.*

The next dialog I can understand—it gives me the opportunity to select which file I would like to create as my backup. This can be very useful if I keep sequential backups by a naming convention, but wait until you see the next screen.

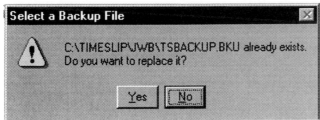

Figure 9. *Confirm the name of the file I chose in the previous dialog.*

Come on now! I just selected the file I want, and now the program is treating me as if I am some kind of idiot who doesn't know what I want. Please, Mr. or Ms. Program, just do what I said. However, it's not over yet.

Figure 10. *Confirm the backup again.*

This is a very intelligent dialog box. It tells me that I have 867,934,702 bytes of space free on my disk and that the backup will take up 564,711 bytes of that space, then asks me to confirm that operation. If the program is so smart that it knows how much space I have and how much space the backup will take, could it not see that the backup will occupy less than 0.06 percent of my available space? Shouldn't it be able to decide for itself that it doesn't need to ask me for confirmation? There's still one more, though.

Figure 11. The backup was successful.

Now, this is critically important to tell me. Come on now, if the backup failed I would want to be told. However, making me click one more OK button to get out of this program is simply getting in my way.

I am not trying to drag down this specific application; in fact, I find it to be one of the best programs for tracking time-based billing available on the market. But this exit process sure does show how the user interface can get in the user's way and slow him down. Later in this chapter, you'll see some other things that can both slow down and speed up the user in handling her data.

Preventing fun and boring the user
The most common violation of this principle is dull and uninteresting screen designs. You've all seen the data-entry screens that look like **Figure 12**.

Name	
Address	
City	
Postal Code	
Country	
Phone	
FAX	
Credit Limit	
Tax Rate	

Figure 12. A boring data-entry form.

This form could be dressed up and made much more interesting with a little rearrangement of the controls and some other minor enhancements. See **Figure 13**.

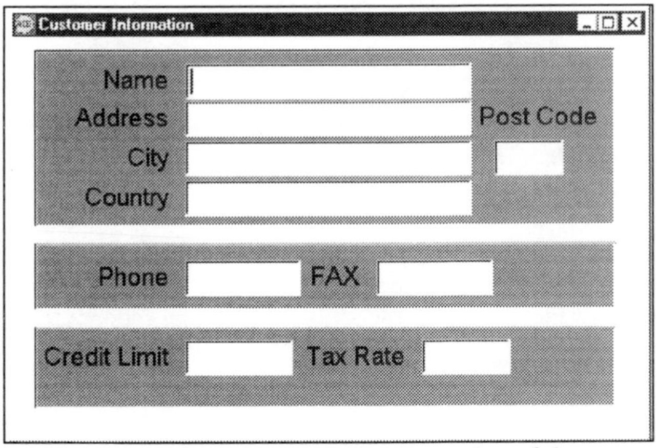

Figure 13. *A more interesting presentation of the customer information.*

Essentially, there is a container behind the data-entry controls with a sunken special effect. The horizontal bars between the sections are comprised of a white two-pixel line, a box that is light gray with a light gray border, and a two-pixel dark gray line. Also, notice that the icon in the title bar of the form has been replaced with the client's logo.

The essential point here is not the artistry, but rather the acknowledgement that the average user will stare at these forms for hours on end. If you can provide some embellishment that makes the form more interesting to look at or easier on the eyes, then do it.

Also, don't leave the aesthetics for later. Later never comes! Make the forms aesthetically pleasing on the first prototype you mock up for approval. Remember that aesthetics is not an afterthought. It is an integral part of design.

Contrary to popular belief, making a data-entry form aesthetically pleasing does not mean that it cannot also be an efficient way to get the job done. The functionality of the controls need not be dictated by their appearance.

Two major application categories

Alan Cooper presents a very important concept in his book for classifying applications that can and should have a great influence in the user interface design. Mr. Cooper speaks of *Sovereign* and *Transient* applications. Sovereign applications are those that generally take the user's full attention when they are in use. Transient applications are those "tools" that we use along with our sovereign applications.

Classifying any application into one of these two categories is instrumentally important in defining the most efficient style of user interface. The database applications that you build with Visual FoxPro may fall into either of these categories, and may even be comprised of parts that cover both categories.

Sovereign applications

Certain applications require a user's full attention while in use. These applications are sovereign because they take control of the machine. A sovereign application should occupy most of the visible display area and demand most of the user's attention.

Some examples of sovereign applications are word processors, where the user is fully involved in the typing and formatting of the document and isn't multitasking a dozen other processes simultaneously. Spreadsheet applications are also sovereign, in that when the user is working on a spreadsheet his undivided attention is given to that task. Other examples would be accounting applications, business decision support applications, and travel reservation systems.

Many applications that we database system developers build will be sovereign.

Sovereign applications are allowed to do things like occupy the entire display area of the screen and cover other applications when they have the user's focus. These applications are allowed to use a larger slice of the computer's resources because of their sovereign nature. The user won't care that her e-mail pop-up is suspended or hidden while she closes the accounting books for the month.

Transient applications

Transient applications are the antithesis of sovereign applications. These are the little "applets" that assist with other tasks. One example is the Calculator program that users can open on top of the accounting application to do some quick math. Another example is the Character Map applet that lets you look up the ASCII code for a special character you need to put on a label. These transient applications should not overtake the system when used. They need to be designed to coexist with the sovereign applications that may or may not be in use when the transient application is called on for a service.

The transient application should not occupy any more of the display area than is necessary for it to perform its task. As database developers, we don't find ourselves building quite as many transient applications as we do the sovereign ones, but we do build some. Many times, there are parts within one of our sovereign applications that need to behave like a transient application, such as small utility forms or lookup forms. Perhaps the sales management system has a form for managing a salesperson's Rolodex data. This Rolodex form would certainly qualify as a transient module within the sales management system.

Why bother to classify applications?

Give careful consideration to this important question. You should classify your systems, and forms within those systems, into sovereign and transient categories so you have guidelines on how to design the interface for the user of those systems and forms.

If the previously mentioned Rolodex form in the sales-management application were modal, it would be much less useful to the system user. That Rolodex form would be more valuable to the user if it could be opened and left open while other tasks were performed within the system.

Being able to call up the Rolodex at any time to look up a person's phone number, and perhaps even dial the phone, would be very helpful throughout the course of a user's day. Recognizing the Rolodex form as a transient application within the larger system would predict the required behaviors.

However, closing the accounting books for a period is such an important and complex task that it most certainly would be classified as a sovereign application within the system. This might even cause you to design the period-closing operation so that it was modal, except for certain controlled points in the process, in order to protect the integrity of the data.

You can see from this discussion that different user interfaces are "correct" for different parts of a system. I would go so far as to say that there probably isn't a user interface approach that can be classified as the best or the worst without first knowing the sovereignty or transience of the task at hand.

Modeless vs. Modes and Modal vs. Non-Modal

I'd like to clear up a frequently misunderstood issue before I go any further into interface design. We've all heard the cry for the modeless application. We've also heard about modal and non-modal forms. We've even heard the comparison of modal vs. modeless discussed, which is equivalent to comparing automobiles to televisions. Modality has nothing to do with modes.

Modality refers to the availability of switching to other tasks while one task has been set in motion. A modal task, or form, prevents switching to anything else until the modal task or form is dispensed with. A non-modal task or form allows other tasks or forms to be launched while the first task or form is still in process.

Modeless vs. modes is a completely different issue. In a modeless form, there is no concept of editing mode, adding mode, or viewing mode. The form is able to accomplish all tasks without visibly changing modes. A moded form is in some mode or another at all times. When the form is in edit mode, data can be edited, but when the form is in view mode the data can't be edited.

You have certainly seen forms that have Edit, Add, Save, and Revert buttons. These buttons change the form from one mode to another. The user clicks the Edit button and the form changes from view-only mode into edit mode. Just because a form is in edit mode does not necessarily mean that that form must be modal. We can certainly build systems that allow multiple forms to be open and in edit mode simultaneously.

Controlling edit/add/view functionality

Now that you understand the difference between modes and modality, let's examine some issues related to managing modes on our user interface. Contrary to the popular notion, there is no such thing as a modeless application, at least not in the database management arena. The application always has to be aware of whether or not there are pending data changes. When data changes are pending, the form is in edit mode (you might differentiate between edit and add mode, but in fact both are states of pending data changes). When a form has no pending data changes, it is not in edit mode; it is in viewing mode.

Developers frequently confuse the situation of whether the user is required to take any specific action to place a form into edit mode or not as defining the form's modality. That is, must the user click an Edit button before she can cause pending data changes? Or does the form automatically switch itself to edit mode when the user begins to change a piece of data in the form? In truth, regardless of whether the user clicks a button or starts to overwrite a value, the form is always in one mode or another.

User-initiated edit/view modes

The arguments between the two schools of thought regarding using edit buttons or not using edit buttons will never be resolved. There is no one right answer. The correct approach is dependent on the details of the application and its requirements.

The argument in favor of using buttons to start the edit mode is primarily to protect the user from unintentionally changing something. The idea is that nothing can be changed until the user has intentionally clicked the edit button.

This interface style can be very good in those situations where changes to the data have critical effects on the business, and if those changes are difficult to revert.

The major argument against the edit button style is that it requires the user to take an additional action in order to change data. The very aspect of this approach's strength is also its weakness.

When should you use the edit button approach? Use it when, in your judgement, the additional action required of the user is of less importance than the result of an inadvertent change in data.

Automatic edit/view modes

With Visual FoxPro's strong object model and its array of events on each of the data editing controls, it is easy to create an automatic mode switching system. It is easy to sense when the user changes the value of a control and then switch the mode of the form to edit mode.

The best argument in favor of the automatic approach is that it takes less effort on the part of the user to initiate an edit. He has only to begin typing and the form shifts to edit mode.

The best argument against the automatic edit mode shift is that it's easy for the user to unintentionally change data. Again, the very issue that makes this approach desirable is the same issue that can make it undesirable.

When should you implement automatic mode switching? Use it when, in your judgement, the result of an unintentional change to data is of less importance than the extra action that would be required of the user with the edit button approach.

So what's the answer here?

The truthful answer is that, regardless of whether the user clicks a button first or switches to edit mode by typing in a control, there is always an edit mode. The form must always deal with resolving the edit mode before closing. By using data buffering, the user always has the option of saving the changes or reverting them to the pre-edited state. That means that there are very few situations where the use of an edit button would be an interface requirement.

This means the decision will be one of preference, and when an interface decision is one of preference you should let the *user's* preference win. Remember, you may work with the system for a few months or longer, but the user will live with the result eight hours a day, five days a week, for a number of years.

Heads-down data entry

Ah, yes—the old room with desks all lined up in rows, and at each desk sits a data-entry person being paid by the number of records he adds per day. This situation, although somewhat exaggerated, can still be found in many medium to large business environments. Unfortunately, the graphical environment does not lend itself well to this type of interface requirement.

Pretty buttons and ComboBoxes do not assist the heads-down data entry person in entering data faster. A keyboard-controlled data entry interface that anticipates the user's next action is needed here. For example, this interface should immediately append a new record and put focus in the first control upon the user completing a record's entry. The user's eyes should never need to stray from the worksheets from which she is entering data.

Although this interface needs to give the user rapid-fire, keyboard-controlled data entry, it can and should provide some method of reviewing the work entered so far. Controls that are not part of the natural tab order should allow the user to see what she has entered, perhaps in a grid. The user should be able to select a record already entered and correct any errors. However, these capabilities and controls should not get in the user's way from doing the primary function of entering data.

Luckily for us, most data entry operations in today's business world are not of this heads-down nature. They are more relaxed in terms of speed on entry and generally require more thinking on the part of the user. With this type of data entry interface, if you master the controls you can assist the user in getting her job done faster and give her less opportunity for mistakes.

Keyboard vs. mouse, and buttons vs. toolbars vs. menus

My response to this issue is, "Why not have them all?" A menu option that saves data changes does not interfere with a toolbar button of the same functionality. Giving the menu option a shortcut key does not interfere with a command button in the form with the same purpose. The key to reusability is having all of those mechanisms call the same piece of code to do the work.

I know folks who are touch-typists who absolutely hate interfaces that require them to remove their fingers from the home row. I also know folks who hate to let go of the mouse to type something that could have been handled by using the mouse creatively (I am one of these people).

To design a successful user interface, you must make the user comfortable with the way things work. Different users are comfortable with different ways of doing things. Therefore, why not design the interface with the maximum methods available for accomplishing a certain task? This type of design pleases the highest number of users. Only a few "stick in the mud" folks will cringe at the "inefficiency" of having more than one way to do something. Most people will only notice that their favorite way works, and not even see that there are other ways to accomplish the same task.

Limiting the number of dialog boxes

Dialog boxes ask the user a question. When necessary, you certainly do need to request information from the user. However, with good planning you can design a single dialog, displayed at the beginning of a process, that asks the user everything you need to know throughout the process.

Other things to watch out for with dialogs are asking stupid questions that don't need to be asked. Earlier in this chapter I presented a dialog that asked me to confirm that a good backup was OK. That is as unnecessary a question as I have ever seen.

You walk a tight line here, though, because a form or dialog that is too crowded is almost as disturbing as too many smaller dialogs. The line is also tight because it isn't a good idea to allow the user to execute a drastic action that is either not reversible or not easily reversible without confirming the decision beforehand. Therefore, you might find yourself in a bind, which is common in this application development business. The answer lies in using common sense.

Don't bring up a dialog box to confirm the change of a phone number on a customer edit form. Do bring up a confirming dialog on erasing the entire customer file. The change of a phone number is easily reversed and does not require user confirmation before the change is made. However, erasing he entire customer file will require a large and expensive effort to reverse, so confirm the issue before the deletion.

Using the tabless PageFrame to provide multiple "views" of the data

To handle those crowded forms that you are often tempted to break into multiple forms and present them in some order or sequence, Visual FoxPro offers the PageFrame. You can put all of those forms into one and allow users to navigate them in any fashion they choose. The screen won't be cluttered with a bunch of windows. The user has only one window to close when she is finished.

As a developer, you don't have to write all the code to coordinate the separate windows. You only need to design and code one window. So for complex data entry problems, the PageFrame is an ideal tool.

In Chapter 10, I gave an example of the PageFrame being used without tabs. This approach allowed the developer to provide additional functionality to a process without requiring the user to navigate to or deal with another form or dialog box. This is helpful to the user in simplifying the interface, but for the developer it is even more helpful because all of the functionality related to that form is contained within that one form.

Here's another example of using a PageFrame to create what might otherwise be a crowded form. **Figures 14, 15,** and **16** show the sequential pages of a tabless PageFrame in an Invoice Wizard form. The form is not functional because there is no data connected to it, but it does demonstrate the use of the PageFrame.

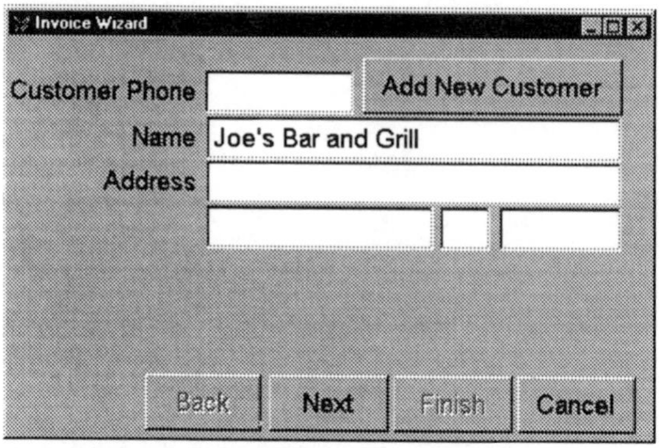

Figure 14. Page 1 of the wizard form.

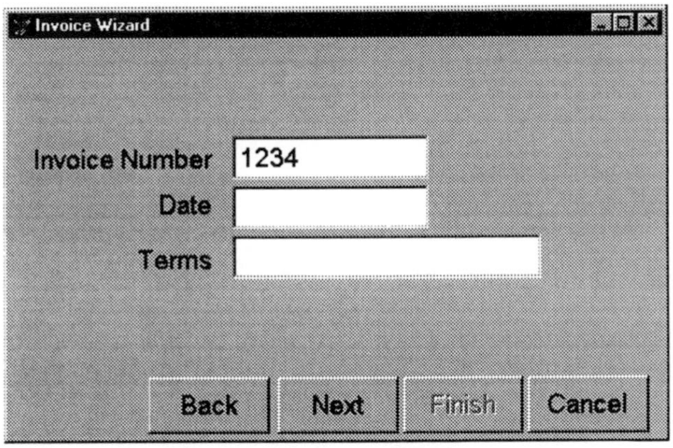

Figure 15. *Page 2 of the wizard form.*

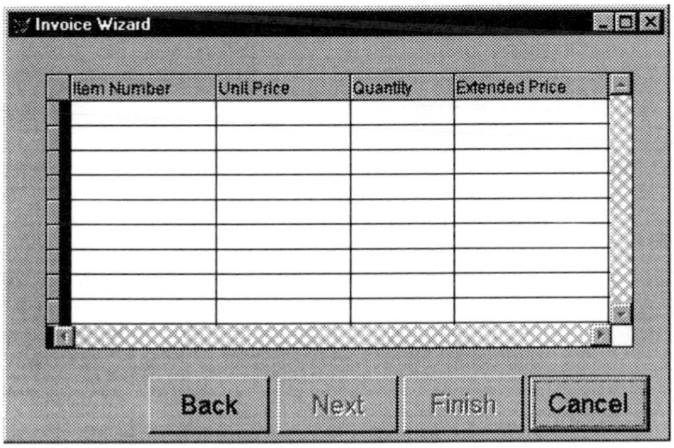

Figure 16. *Page 3 of the wizard form.*

Notice that the buttons at the lower right of the form become enabled and disabled in a context-sensitive fashion. They are also positioned in exactly the same place on each page. In truth, they aren't actually on any of the pages; they're in the form placed on top of the Page-Frame. The ResetButtons method of the form enables and disables these buttons. Here is the code for the ResetButtons method:

```
WITH THISFORM.PageFrame1
  THISFORM.cmdBack.Enabled = THISFORM.PageFrame1.ActivePage > 1
  DO CASE
    CASE .ActivePage = 1
      THISFORM.cmdNext.Enabled = NOT EMPTY(.Page1.txtCustomer.Value)
    CASE .ActivePage = 2
      THISFORM.cmdNext.Enabled = NOT EMPTY(.Page2.txtInvNum.Value)
    CASE .ActivePage = 3
      THISFORM.cmdNext.Enabled = .F.
      THISFORM.cmdFinish.Enabled = NOT EMPTY(.Page3.Grid1.Column3.Text1.Value )
  ENDCASE
ENDWITH
```

I simplified this code to demonstrate the idea. In an actual form, you would be testing for more information before turning on the Next button or the Finish button.

The code in the click event of the Next button simply adds one to the ActivePage of the PageFrame, and the Back button subtracts one from the ActivePage.

Selecting items

Users often need to select from among a group of choices. With the exception of the heads-down data entry operation, Lists and ComboBoxes are very good controls for assisting the user in making these types of choices. When the possible choices are known ahead of time, OptionGroups and even CheckBoxes can be useful.

Let's leave the CheckBoxes and OptionGroups alone for now and investigate the use of ComboBoxes and Lists. These two controls, when used properly, should render it impossible for the user to make a wrong selection. Take the form in **Figure 17** for example.

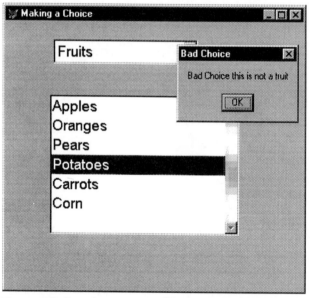

Figure 17. One form using a combo and a list for selecting values.

This form lets the user first choose from the combo whether he wants fruits or vegetables. Then he selects the particular item from the list below. In this form, the list contains both fruits and vegetables. If the user makes an incorrect choice, he gets a message box telling him that he made an error.

What's wrong with this scenario? First, why does the list have vegetables in it if the combo says *fruits*? Visual FoxPro certainly gives the developer the ability to change the contents of a control based on the value of another. The second, and more important, problem is that the message box makes users feel dumb. That message clearly points out to them that they don't know the difference between a fruit and a vegetable.

Figures 18 and **19** show the same interface style but with a slight change.

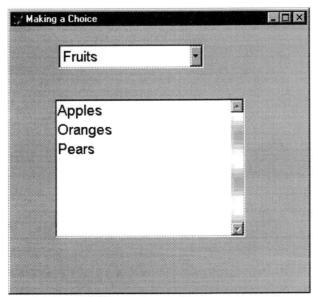

Figure 18. The fruits and vegetables form with Fruits selected in the combo.

Figure 19. The fruits and vegetables form with Vegetables selected in the combo.

Notice that the list adjusts its contents according to the value in the combo. This is accomplished by calling the list's Requery method from the combo's InteractiveChange event and coding the Requery of the list to populate itself with values according to the value of the combo. In this form, the user cannot make an invalid choice. She will never see a message box telling her that she is stupid.

The critical point here is that it is the job of the developer to prevent the user from making errors. You have to detect errors and handle them when they occur, but you should first prevent the errors as much as is humanly possible.

Multi-select

There are times when we must allow the user to select multiple items at once. One option is to use a multi-select list. **Figure 20** shows a multi-select listing in which multiple items are selected. How many items are selected and what are they?

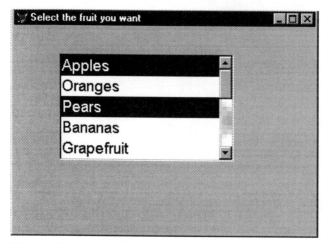

Figure 20. A multi-select list form.

If you answered two—apples and pears—you are incorrect. There are actually nine items selected, but most of them are out of view. Now compare that presentation of multi-selection to the one in **Figure 21**.

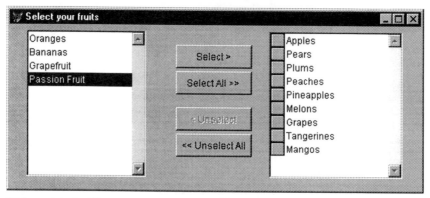

Figure 21. A different type of multi-select list form.

In this form, there is no question as to how many or what items have been selected. This "mover" type of list takes up more space, but it also leaves no question for the user about what has been selected and what has not. It is also clear to the user what is left for selection. You can use this type of mover list to allow multiple selections of the same item when appropriate.

You may also notice the gray buttons to the left of each item in the selected list. These mover buttons allow the user to rearrange the order of the items in the selected list. You may need this ability if the processing that follows is order-dependent. With a single multi-select list, this reordering is impossible.

Direct manipulation

A user performs direct manipulation when she directly modifies objects on the screen by drawing with a pencil tool, connecting items by drawing lines between them, dragging and dropping, or any other method. Direct manipulation within the interfaces you build is almost exclusively confined to drag and drop. Visual FoxPro 6.0 has two types: native Visual FoxPro drag and drop and the new OLE drag and drop.

> *Be aware that the native and the OLE drag-and-drop methodologies cannot be used together. These two options are mutually exclusive.*

Connecting things

The form in the example that follows has been simplified to demonstrate a technique. Imagine you are creating an interface for scheduling a product through various steps in the manufacturing process and that those products may not require every step. **Figure 22** shows a possible form for doing this.

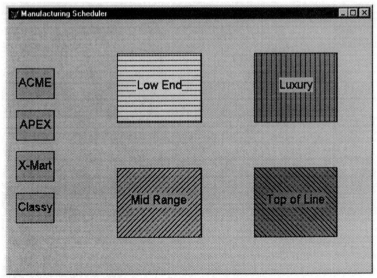

***Figure 22**. A form for selecting a manufacturing process for customers.*

The idea in this example application is that your company makes products to four levels of quality. Different customers want to purchase different quality levels. Customers are listed down the left side with their names in the boxes. This form is an example of the direct manipulation methodology of user interface design; in a real application the customer display would be managed differently. The larger boxes to the right represent the quality ranges. To assign a quality range to a customer, the user drags that customer and drops it on the chosen quality range. The user gets feedback when the customer's background color becomes that of the quality range. **Figure 23** shows some customers with their quality ranges set.

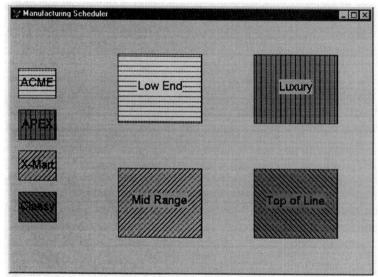

Figure 23. *Certain customers with their quality ranges set.*

This process of dragging the customer to the quality range is not readily obvious when the form is first seen, but once the user has been shown how to do this she will never forget.

Drag and drop

The terms *source object* and *target object* will be used to explain how drag and drop works. It is important to realize that the drag-and-drop operation is divided into three stages.

The first stage is the start of the drag. This stage occurs at the source object when the user presses the mouse button while the mouse is over the object.

The second stage, called capture, occurs during the dragging. This is the reaction of the various objects as the source is dragged over them. Perhaps the mouse icon changes to indicate whether or not a drop is allowed.

The final stage is the end drop. The end drop occurs at the target object when the user releases the mouse button, thus completing the drag-and-drop operation.

Native drag and drop

Let's look behind the scenes of the previous form to see how the drag-and-drop operation was accomplished. First of all, both the products and the processes are classes defined in a class.

Here is the code in the MouseDown event of the Product:

```
THIS.Drag(1)
```

The Drag method will start or end a drag operation. The parameter of 1 tells the Drag method to start a drag operation. The mouse cursor seen when dragging the object is controlled by the source object's DragIcon property. In this case, the cursor file is named DragCopy.cur. In the MouseUp event method of the Product class, the drag is stopped by making the same call as in the MouseDown event method, except it passes the number 2 as the argument.

In the DragOver event method of the Product class, the mouse icon is changed to reflect that the user cannot drop there. Here is the code:

```
THIS.DragIcon = "NoDrop.CUR"
```

The DragOver event is fired whenever something is being dragged over the object. The mouse cursor is changed in the DragOver because dropping the product on itself would do nothing at all. The change in cursor is visual feedback to the user. This same code is in the DragOver event method of the form itself, since dropping on the form will do nothing.

In the DragOver event method of the Process class, however, the code assigns the Drag-Copy.cur cursor to the DragIcon property of the source object being dragged. The code does this because this process object is where the drop has a purpose.

The major work is done in the DragDrop event method of the Process class:

```
oSource.Shape.FillType = THIS.Shape.FillType
oSource.BackColor = THIS.BackColor
```

oSource is one of the parameters passed to the DragDrop and DragOver event methods. It is an object reference to the object that is being dragged. The code above simply sets the back-color of the object being dragged to the same as the backcolor of the object it was dropped on as well has the fill pattern of the shapes.

In studying this code, notice that both the Product and Process classes are complex controls. That is, they have many parts to them. The Product class is comprised of a container (the actual product object), a shape inside that container, and a label on top of the shape. One problem the code needs to deal with is that the events fire for the object that is directly under the mouse pointer. Therefore, if you check the shape and the label objects in the Product class, you will see that events like DragOver are being passed up to the container with code like this:

```
THIS.Parent.DragOver(oSource, nXCoord, nYCoord, nState)
```

The parameters being passed are the same parameters that Visual FoxPro passed to the event in the first place. Why do this? Why not handle the drag-over action right in the label or shape? The reason is a simple one: All of the code that performs the action is written in one place only, and the long-term maintenance of this code will be much easier if it is in only one place. As Steve McConnell says in his book *Code Complete*, "Code written twice has been written once too often."

Let's look at another example of using the native drag and drop of Visual FoxPro. This time I've modified the mover list form above to include drag and drop to move items from one list to the other. Following is the code needed to add drag and drop from either list. (Each code listing identifies the object.method at the beginning with a comment, then the code follows.)

```
* lstSource.MouseMove
IF nButton = 1
  THIS.DragIcon = "NoDrop.cur"
  THIS.Drag(1)
ENDIF


* lstSource.DragOver
oSource.DragIcon = "DragList.cur"


* lstSource.DragDrop
IF oSource.Name = THIS.Name
  RETURN
ENDIF
THISFORM.UnselectOne()
```

The next section of code is from lstTarget. Notice the similarity. In actual development, you would have probably created a list class that had this functionality built into it already.

```
* lstTarget.MouseMove
IF nButton = 1
  THIS.DragIcon = "NoDrop.cur"
  THIS.Drag(1)
ENDIF


* lstTarget.DragOver
oSource.DragIcon = "DragList.cur"


* lstTarget.DragDrop
IF oSource.Name = THIS.Name
  RETURN
ENDIF
THISFORM.SelectOne()
```

The reason for the IF statement in each list's DragDrop event method is to prevent the list from being dropped on itself. Notice that the DragDrop event method of each list is calling the form's methods to do the work. Again, why have the code in more than one place?

The only other code in the form was added to the DragOver event method of the form and the buttons, and it is the same in all places:

```
* The DragOver of the Form and the Buttons
oSource.DragIcon = "NoDrop.cur"
```

You can see that adding drag and drop is not "rocket science." It does take some planning and often requires passing messages from one object to another in order to coordinate the activity. Also, drag and drop is a very natural method for users to interact with the objects in your applications.

Direct manipulation is intuitive and easily learned; once learned, it is seldom forgotten. What better method of working with your data controls could there be?

OLE drag and drop vs. native drag and drop

Now let's investigate this new beast, OLE drag and drop. OLE drag and drop provides the same functionality as the native drag and drop, except it isn't limited to Visual FoxPro objects. Visual FoxPro's OLE drag and drop can function with any other application that is OLE drag and drop-capable. The ability to function with other applications is not the only advantage of OLE drag and drop over the Visual FoxPro native drag and drop.

OLE itself

OLE has been around for a while now, and we have used it in Visual FoxPro for automating processes in other applications as well as in building ActiveX servers for other applications to automate. The overriding issue with OLE is the fact that it always involves communication between two or more objects. These objects might be within the same application, like using a Visual FoxPro ActiveX server from a Visual FoxPro application. Or they might be in different applications, as in automating a mail-merge operation in Microsoft Word from Visual FoxPro. No matter what the details may be, there is always two-way communication. A message is sent and a reply is received. OLE drag and drop is no different in this aspect, although starting a drag might involve only one object. What goes on during that drag, and what happens in the subsequent drop, is the result of communication between the *source object* (the object being dragged) and those objects it gets dragged over and ultimately the *target object* (that object where it is finally dropped).

The key issue from the user interface perspective in this process is to provide clear visual feedback to the user about the process. Give the user clear indications of where the source can and cannot be dropped.

The objects involved

In OLE drag and drop, three objects are always involved in the operation. They are the source, the object where the drag began; the target, the object where the drop occurred; and the data object, the object carrying the data from one to the other. Let's start by examining the data object.

The OLE data object

The data object is created when the drag begins. The oDataObject does not directly belong to the drag source or to the drag target; it belongs to OLE (which is a separate service under Windows). Different drag sources have different types of data they will place in the data object automatically. A data type or format identifies all data in the data object. See **Table 1** for the usual formats found in the data object.

Table 1. Common data formats found in the OLE data object.

CF_TEXT	1	Text.
CF_OEMTEXT	7	Text format containing characters from the OEM character set.

CF_UNICODETEXT	13	Text containing Unicode.
CF_FILES	15	A handle to a list of files.
CF_HDROP	15	Same as above CF_FILES.
CFSTR_OLEVARIANTARRAY	"OLE Variant Array"	An array of OLE variant values.
CFSTR_OLEVARIANT	"OLE Variant"	A variant. All data types in Visual FoxPro are represented as variants.
CFSTR_VFPSOURCEOBJECT	"VFP Source Ob-ject"	An object reference to a Visual FoxPro object.

The drag operation

The drag operation starts at the source object. As the data object is dragged over a drop-enabled object, communication between the potential target and the data object occurs. This communication may cause the data object to communicate with the drag source object. **Figure 24** shows this communication chain.

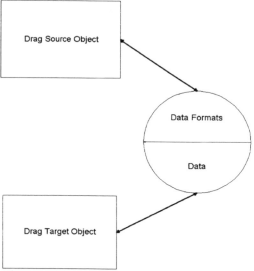

Figure 24. *Communication flow during an OLE drag and drop operation.*

Let's examine an actual example of this to understand the process better. **Figure 25** shows a form with three OLE drag-enabled and/or drop-enabled objects in it.

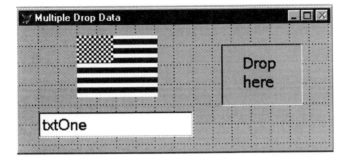

Figure 25. A form with OLE drag-enabled and drop-enabled objects.

First, look at the properties for the textbox. **Figure 26** shows the non-default properties for that object.

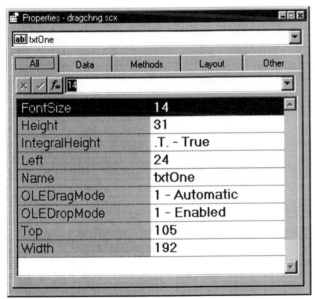

Figure 26. The non-default properties of the textbox.

The only two properties of this textbox that have been changed from their defaults that relate to OLE drag and drop are OLEDragMode and OLEDropMode, which have been set to automatic and enabled, respectively. Setting the properties this way makes this object OLE-draggable and allows OLE drops to occur. Because it's a textbox, the only data format it will understand is Text. An OLE data object carrying non-text data will show as a non-drop icon when dragged over this textbox.

Action and reaction

Let's examine the properties of the container with the label "Drop here." **Figure 27** shows the property sheet for this object.

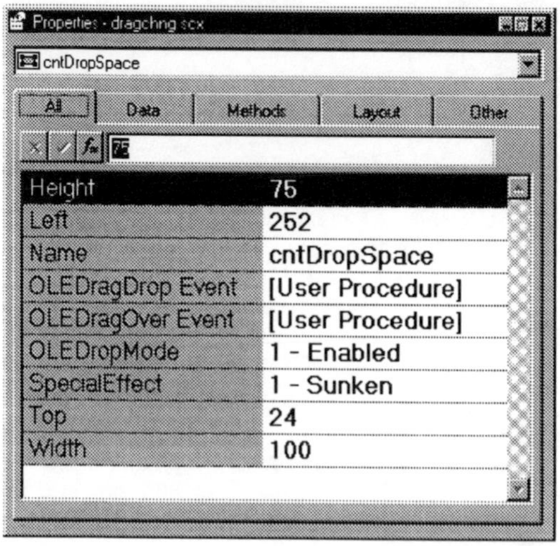

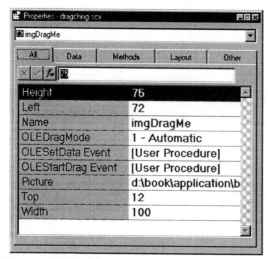

Figure 27. The non-default properties of the container.

Notice that OLEDropMode is enabled, but also notice that there is some user code in two of the OLE drag and drop events—namely OLEDragOver and OLEDragDrop. In here we will begin to see the communication chain that occurs during OLE drag-and-drop operations. Before we delve into this code, let's look at the image of the American flag. **Figure 28** shows the non-default properties and events of the American flag image.

Figure 28. The American flag image properties.

Notice that the OLEDragMode property is set to Automatic. This will allow the image to be dragged automatically without any intervention from your code. Note, however, that there is code in the OLEStartDrag event for this image. Let's examine this code:

```
LPARAMETERS oDataObject, nEffect

*  Clear out all data from the data object
oDataObject.ClearData

*-- Specify that data can only be copied
nEffect = 1

*-- Register the text (1) format
oDataObject.SetFormat( 1 )

*-- Register my private format in the data object
oDataObject.SetFormat( "Private Format" )
```

There are a few things going on in this code. First, the line `oDataObject.ClearData` removes any data that may have been automatically placed into the data object of the drag. Next, this method registers two formats in the data object with the two lines `oDataObject. SetFormat( 1 )`, which registers the text format, and `oDataObject.SetFormat( "Private Format" )`, which registers a format named "Private Format." This shows that not only can you clear the data object and place your own formats into it, but that the formats you place there do not need to come from the list shown previously.

Now let's put it to use

Listed below is the code in the Drop Here container's OLEDragOver method, which will fire whenever the data object is dragged over that object.

```
LPARAMETERS oDataObject, nEffect, nButton, nShift, nXCoord, nYCoord, nState

IF nState == 0 && Drag Enter
  *-- We only need to check out the data format once upon enter
  IF oDataObject.GetFormat( "Private Format" )
    * I can handle drops of "Private Format"
    * Tell OLEDragDrop that I know how to handle this
    This.OLEDropHasData = 1
    * Tell OLEDragDrop that I want to copy this
    This.OLEDropEffects = 1
  ENDIF
ENDIF
```

This code starts out by checking the data object to see if it has a registered format named "Private Format." This checking does two things: It returns true or false as to whether that format is registered in the data object, and it also fires the OLESetData event of the drag source object and passes it the format being requested (you'll see this code in a moment). Here, if the data object returns true, it does have this Private Format registered, and two properties of the target object are set. OLEDropHasData is set to 1, meaning that the data object does have data that this object understands. OLEDropEffects is also set to 1, meaning that this object only knows how to copy the data. Other settings for the OLEDropEffects would be 2, meaning Move, or 3, meaning copy and/or move.

Now let's look at the OLESetData method of the drag source object. Keep in mind that the data format requested is "Private Format."

```
LPARAMETERS oDataObject, eFormat

DO CASE
CASE trans( eFormat ) == '1' && Text format
  * If Text data is requested by the drop target
  * Put "American Flag" in the data object
  oDataObject.SetData( "American Flag", 1 )

CASE trans( eFormat ) == "Private Format" && Private format
  * If "My Own Private Format" is requested
  * put the picture file name into the data object
  * as "My Own Private Format"
  oDataObject.SetData( This.Picture, "Private Format" )

ENDCASE
```

In this code, the eFormat parameter received is the format that has been requested by the drop target. In the DO CASE for the "Private Format" the line `oDataObject.SetData( This.Picture, "Private Format" )` sets the data of that format to the contents of the Picture property of the image control. You know the picture property of the image control is a path and file for the American Flag bmp file.

Finally, the OLEDragDrop event of the container has the following code:

```
LPARAMETERS oDataObject, nEffect, nButton, nShift, nXCoord, nYCoord

IF oDataObject.GetFormat( "Private Format" )  && Private format
  * I can handle "Private Format" data
  * Hide the label
  This.lblDropSpace.Visible = .F.
  * Set the picture property
  This.Picture = oDataObject.GetData( "Private Format" )
  * Set the copy attribute
  nEffect = 1
  * Draw the container
  THIS.Draw
  * Stop the default action of the drag and drop event
  NODEFAULT
ENDIF
```

This code simply makes the label that says Drop Here invisible and sets the picture property of this container to the picture passed in the data object. The line `nEffect = 1` causes this to be a copy operation, and the call to the draw method redraws the container to show the new flag image. The NODEFAULT command at the end of this code is important; it prevents the OLEDragDrop event method from doing any of the things it might automatically do for you. You want to stop this because you have already fully handled the drop operation

When is drag and drop a good idea?

Drag and drop is a good idea whenever it makes sense to the user to move items from one place to another. Let's go back and revisit the mover dialog with the two lists, which we saw in Figure 21.

How much work would it take to enable OLEDragandDrop into this dialog?

To provide basic drag and drop operations between those two lists, you only need to set the OLEDragMode of each list to Automatic and the OLEDropMode of each list to Enabled. **Figures 29** and **30** show that form running after those properties have been changed.

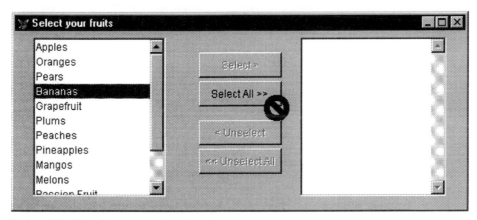

Figure 29. The drag operation in process.

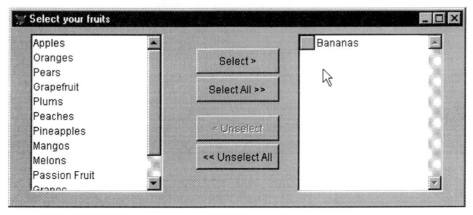

Figure 30. The drop operation is completed.

Whenever it makes sense to allow the user to manipulate the objects in your forms, do so. Direct manipulation is the most intuitive methodology for users to manipulate data in a system.

Summary

This chapter has covered a vast amount of information about user interface design. A lot of the information has been presented in abstract concepts and guidelines. There are few cold hard facts in this area of application design. An interface that works well in one place may fail horribly in another.

Many different issues influence user interface design. The project's budget might have an impact on how you build the interface. The nature of the application and its functional requirements will certainly influence the interface design. The philosophy of the management of the client will have its effect on the user interface. Don't underestimate the impact of interface on an application's success or failure.

In certain areas, this chapter contradicts itself—for example, the area of modeless vs. modes in interface design. The contradiction is part of the real world. Often the decisions made relating to the user interface are subjective. The intuition and experience of the developer plays a major role in making these decisions. One point of this chapter is to provide a set of guidelines to help make interface design decisions.

This chapter has presented and explained many design styles and pointed out their strengths and weaknesses. You need to choose the right way to build your application's interface within the context of that application and its users.

Some information presented in this chapter resulted from looking at poor interface designs and evaluating what was wrong with them. The benefit of this is that you can now try to avoid making those same mistakes in your work.

The area of drag and drop was examined in some detail, partially because it isn't covered very well in other places, but also because directly manipulating objects on screen is a fairly easy thing to teach users. Barring other constraints, direct manipulation can be a good interface. If you keep your mind on users and their goals in any given application, you will likely design an acceptable interface.

The bottom line of all of this is that user interface design is a science and an art. Here we discuss the science, but the art is just as important to the final result. Mastering the art takes experience and intuition.

Chapter 13
Manager Objects,
the Non-Visible
Application Objects

The user sees the forms, the menus, and the reports contained in a system as the entire application. If you don't know there's an entire "sub-application" built underneath these things that holds the whole show together, you soon will. This chapter investigates the ideas behind these invisible objects and the jobs that they do. It will delve into the architecture of that "sub-application" and the components that comprise it. In this examination you will discover the powerful tools that are included right in the box with Visual FoxPro 6.0, as well as learn how to enhance these tools for your own development style.

What are these non-visible objects?

These non-visible objects comprise the beginnings of an *application framework*. An application framework is the superstructure on which you build your application. It is similar to the frame and foundation of a house. You can put many different faces on a single house frame by using different materials, but the frame and its strength will dictate how well that house will stand.

So it is with applications. The more sturdy the underlying framework, the easier it is to build the application.

Managing the activities of an application

You will examine *manager classes* in this chapter. These classes manage the activity of some aspect of the overall application.

Initially you will review each of these areas of focus in a very general fashion. From this discussion you will gain an overview of what these special classes are all about and what is expected of them.

After the general discussion, you will take a tour of the Visual FoxPro 6.0 application wizard and builder. The wizard creates an application framework that includes objects of the class types you will be examining. Once the wizard-based application is complete, you will examine specific classes in detail. This examination will advance your understanding of the necessity and usefulness of these manager classes.

The next series of sections will discuss some of the areas of concern that you need to address with manager classes.

Form manager

Almost all applications you will build with Visual FoxPro will involve one or more forms for user interface. These forms are often launched by a command in the menu program that issues a DO FORM <Whatever> to run the form. Problems don't arise until you need to manage the forms that are open, either by setting focus to a certain form or cascading all open forms, or some other management requirement. Suddenly you find out that all of these forms are running and your application has no idea what they are or where they came from.

Using a form manager to manage the forms, you can keep track of the forms that are running and manage information about those forms. You can also keep the Windows menu up to date with the name or title of each form, manage toolbars that the forms may need, and perform other services that the forms require.

Menu manager

In the previous section, you saw that menus often call forms, but a menu can be called upon to handle much more. Menus can launch forms, call sub-menus, shut down the application, or any of a number of other actions. This means that a menu action might not be a DO FORM command. Because of the variety of possible actions a menu can request, it is a very good idea to provide a central processing point for all menu "hits."

The menu manager is really a communications switchboard that ensures that the request for an action gets to the correct component for processing.

Security manager

Security is one of the least understood aspects of a database application. The word *security* means everything from a user login and recognition system to Internet firewalls and client/server database access. I have seen security built into systems that provided field-level access restrictions for each user.

The responsibility of a security manager is to provide the level of security required by that application. By encapsulating the implementation of security, you make it easy to change the nature of that security without rewriting the entire application. Simply changing the code inside the security manager changes the security provided.

Error manager

Errors happen! Application development includes testing the code to remove "bugs"—programmer mistakes—but unanticipated situations do occur. A network cable might break, the server could go down, the user might reboot the computer, and so on. The error manager is the object that senses the problem and deals with it.

Some error handlers try to recover from every identifiable error condition; others simply record the error and shut the system down. Having an error manager object in an application simply means that the code for dealing with errors is encapsulated in the error handler. That code may or may not send messages to other application objects in an effort to recover from the condition, depending on the nature of the error.

Developer's interface

The key to everything discussed so far is that each of these managers has a developer's interface (a set of methods and properties). Communication with those objects occurs through that interface. All other objects in the system call on those managers to provide services.

The behavior for any one of those managers is in the code inside the methods. That implementation can change over time; however, the names of the methods and properties and the arguments for the methods should always remain the same. Following this practice allows evolution of the underlying framework without requiring changes to the other objects in the application.

Remember always: *"Program to the interface and not the implementation."* This statement is true for both application developers who are using a framework, and framework developers who are building a framework. The power of programming to the interface is that it allows the implementation of a behavior to change without requiring any changes in the code that uses that behavior.

The antithesis of programming to interface is programming to implementation. Programming to implementation means that the calling method is directly dependent on *how* the called method does something rather than on *what* it does. The only knowledge that a calling method should have of a called method is the parameters required and the value returned. There should be no dependence on how the result is derived.

The Visual FoxPro 6.0 Application Wizard

This section will walk through the process of the Visual FoxPro 6.0 application wizard and builder. The wizard creates an application framework with the manager classes defined. Once the framework project file is in place, the application wizard launches the application builder that allows you to add data, forms, reports, and more to the application.

At this point you might be wondering why, after the previous chapters that gave you class design examples, we have shifted to the application wizard and its output here. The reason is that the application wizard creates a full-featured framework with all of the "bells and whistles." By studying this framework and its features, you will gain a better insight to the wholeness of a framework. The previous chapters focused on specific functionality and did not make a serious effort to integrate that functionality into a complete picture. The goal of this chapter is to give you the big picture. Here you will see a complete framework with its components explained.

Some of you might actually use the application wizard to build your projects; others may find the framework interesting to study while developing your own. Still others may choose to use a third-party framework. Regardless, the framework supplied with Visual FoxPro 6.0 is a good tool to use to study and learn about the manager classes and other things that create an application framework. Okay, let's get started with the wizard and builder.

Choose the Application Wizard from the Tools - Wizards menu as shown in **Figure 1**.

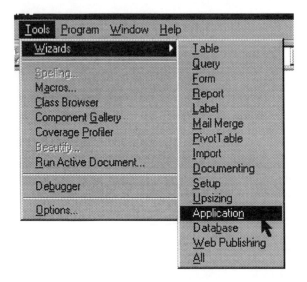

Figure 1. Choosing the Application Wizard from the Tools - Wizards menu.

Once chosen, the wizard presents the dialog shown in **Figure 2**.

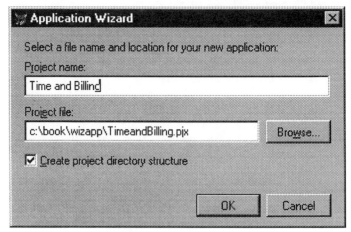

Figure 2. The Application Wizard dialog.

We have already filled in the project name as *Time and Billing* and changed the current directory in Visual FoxPro 6.0 to the WizApp subdirectory of our Book directory. The only other choice in this dialog is the check box labeled "Create project directory structure." This check box is checked by default and we left it that way. The project directory structure created by the application wizard has a number of subdirectories under the project's home directory. In the example, the home directory is Book\WizApp and the directories that the wizard created are Data (for the data files), Forms (for form files), Graphics (for icons, bitmaps and other graphics), Help (for the help system), Include (for the .H header files), Libs (for the class libraries), Menus (for the menus), Progs (for the program .PRG files), and Reports (for the report files).

After clicking OK, you get the wait window in **Figure 3**.

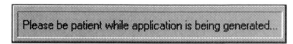

Figure 3. A wait window.

We present this figure here because on our Pentium 166 MHz machine it stayed there for quite awhile, while on our P300 it flashed by so fast we couldn't read it. While the wait window is open, the application wizard creates the directory structure for our new application and the project file for the framework.

General tab

Once the wait window disappears, the Application Wizard is finished. The wizard then opens the project file and launches the Application Builder, which displays the dialog in **Figure 4**.

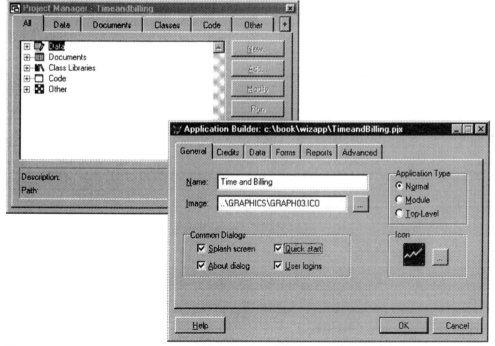

Figure 4. Our project file with the Application Builder form on top of it.

When the dialog in Figure 4 first appears, the Visual FoxPro help file also appears. We minimized the help window to get it out of our way while working with the builder. From this point on, we'll work within the Application Builder form. You might find it helpful to keep the help window minimized but open, so you can refer to it quickly to find out the details of any particular option.

Notice that the first page in this dialog contains four distinct sections. The first section, to the upper left, asks us for the Name and Image for our application. The name is obvious in its meaning, but what is the image?

In the Image textbox, specify the image you want displayed in your application's splash screen and About box. We filled ours in with an .ICO file of a graph.

The second section in the upper right asks for the application type you want to build. The three types available are Normal, Module, and Top-Level. **Table 1** explains the differences between them.

Table1. The types of applications available to the Application Wizard.

Application type	Description
Normal	Your application runs inside the main Visual FoxPro screen and your menu replaces the standard Visual FoxPro menu.
Module	An application that is intended to be called from other applications. It therefore does not alter the Visual FoxPro environment or issue a READ EVENTS command. The menu for this type of application will be a single pad added to the existing Visual FoxPro System menu.
Top-Level	Creates an application that runs on the Windows desktop and not inside the Visual FoxPro screen.

The third section, on the bottom left, titled Common Dialogs, allows you to choose which of the listed dialogs you want in your application. We chose to include them all. **Table 2** lists each dialog with a description.

Table 2. The common dialog types.

Dialog Name	Description
Splash Screen	A screen displayed at system startup that shows the system image and the credits.
Quick Start	A dialog that provides access to the forms and reports included in the application. Like a menu screen.
About Dialog	The About dialog in one option under the Help menu. This dialog displays the application title and author as well as any copyright statements.
User Logins	Including this optional dialog puts a lot more into your application than just a user login screen. It also allows the user to save preferences for the Options dialog and the Favorites menu.

The fourth and final section of this dialog asks us about our icon. Choosing an icon file here controls the icon that will appear in the main Visual FoxPro screen, or your top-level form. All forms in the application use this icon. We chose the same icon that we used for the image.

Credits tab

The Credits tab, as shown in **Figure 5**, allows you to enter author and copyright information.

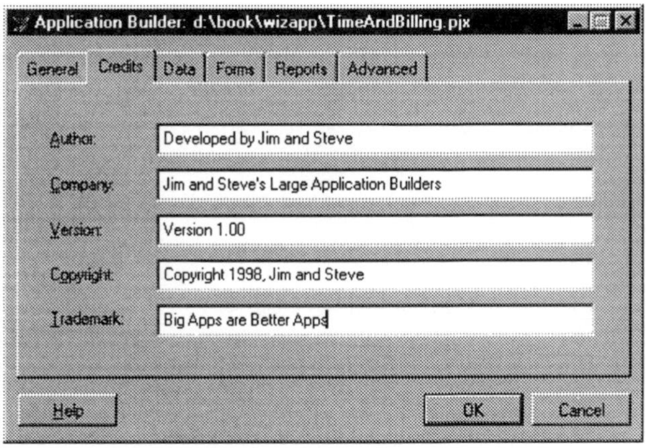

Figure 5. *The Application Builder's Credits tab.*

The information shown in Figure 5 is displayed in various dialogs exactly as it is entered, so be sure to enter it the way you want it to look.

Data tab

All applications that deal with data need to store the data somewhere. The Application Builder uses the Data tab for this purpose. **Figure 6** shows the Data tab for the Application Builder. We got the files in there by choosing our Time and Billing database with the Select button in the Builder dialog.

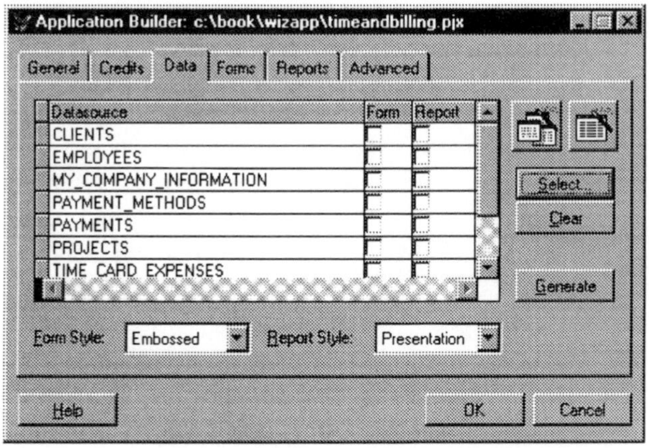

Figure 6. *The Data tab of the Application Builder.*

Notice the Form and Report columns with check boxes. If you check those boxes, the builder will create a form or report for that table. The two combo boxes below the list of tables control the form and report styles used in creating these items. Being lazy, we went ahead and checked every one of them.

Forms, Reports, and Advanced tabs

The Forms and Reports tabs allow you to add forms and reports that you've already created to the application. The Advanced tab allows you to add a help file and to decide whether to include a Favorites menu option and other issues. We stop here because our focus is not on the Application Wizard or Builder, but rather on what it builds and the classes it uses.

Visual FoxPro foundation classes

The classes you are about to examine come as part of the Visual FoxPro 6.0 package. You will be examining these classes in some detail to learn how they are constructed and to gain some insight into their design.

Framework class design will vary according to the requirements of that framework. The design of the foundation classes provides extreme flexibility. With flexibility comes complexity. Microsoft has no idea who will use these classes and how they might choose to use them; therefore, the classes must be flexible.

In examining these classes, you won't see a distinct Form Manager or Menu Manager. However, you will find classes that deal with the issues handled by those objects.

The framework provided in the foundation classes is capable of handling applications that use a READ EVENTS environment as well as those that do not. Some examples of the latter are developers' tools or add-on sub-applications (designed to run inside other applications).

The Application Wizard and the Application Builder

How is the Application Wizard different from the builder, and why is this important? The Application Wizard creates the directory structure and the project. When the wizard is finished, the project has nothing in it except the framework class libraries for an application. When the wizard finishes its work, it runs the Application Builder, which allows you to add forms, data, reports, and more to the project.

There is one major difference between a wizard and a builder in Visual FoxPro—a builder is *reentrant* and a wizard is not. The word reentrant, as used here, means that you can run the builder on an existing project and it won't make any alterations other than those you indicate. The original project will remain intact except, of course, for those changes you make in the builder.

The wizard will overwrite any existing project with a new one, and all of your previous modifications will be lost (the wizard cannot be reentered to modify an existing project).

Parts of the framework

Figure 7 shows the structure of the framework created by the wizard.

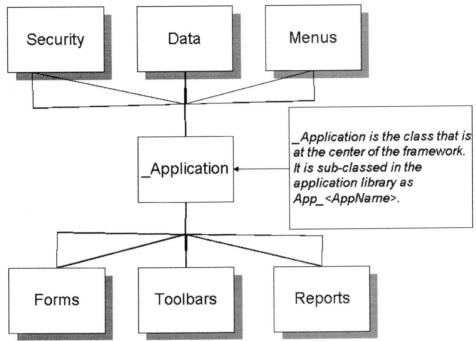

Figure 7. *The structure of the Visual FoxPro framework.*

Figure 7 does not demonstrate any kind of formal design. It is a simple block diagram depicting the way the various pieces of an application work together within the wizard's framework. The abstract class _Application, found in the class library _Framewk, is the center of the structure. This class is sub-classed in the <AppName>_app library as App_<AppName>. The startup program creates an instance of the subclass when the application runs.

In the sections that follow, we'll examine many of these classes in detail. However, before you bury yourself in code, you should have at least a general idea of how this thing works.

The _Application class is a *composite class*. A composite class contains other classes. The classes contained in the _Application class are cusError (which handles errors), cusDataSession (which handles data sessions), cusWindowHandler (which handles forms and their windows), cusTableSort (which handles table- and cursor-level activities), and cusTableNav (which handles navigation in a table or cursor). Although this seems like a complex structure, it is simplified by the interface provided by the _Application class. The developer needs to interact only with the methods of the application object. For example, if you were to create a form and place a button in the form to move to the next record, you would call a method of the application object. The variable name for that object in a running application is goApp. The code in the Click event of your next button might be this:

```
GoApp.GoNext ()
```

The GoNext method of the _Application class has the following line of code:

```
THIS.cusTableNav.GoNext()
```

This code passes the message to the cusTableNav object inside the goApp object for you. Your code is insulated from the complexity of the internals of the goApp object and can address a simple programmer's interface.

This type of structure does something else for you. It allows you to alter the behavior of the cusTableNav class in any way you want without requiring that you go and change all forms that call on that behavior. You only need to keep the _Application_ class aware of any changes you make in the interface of the cusTableNav class. If the only changes you make to cusTableNav are in the code, and you don't change the method names or parameters passed, you don't even need to alter _Application.

_Application acts as a mediator between the code in the form button and the code that causes the actual behavior. This indirection allows you to create reusable components because it doesn't require any component to have knowledge of the environment in which it exists. The framework hides the implementation of dealing with the current data environment, as in the case of cusTableNav and moving to the next record. This design allows you to have one cusTableNav class that deals with local data and another that deals with remote data. The _Application_Application object could switch the cusTableNav object at runtime according to the type of data you are using.

Keep this concept in mind as you examine the detailed descriptions that follow. The concept of hiding the implementation exists throughout the framework.

Frameworks are abstract things and are therefore somewhat difficult to understand. You will come to understand this framework by examining the classes involved and studying the code in those classes.

Startup program

The Application Wizard creates a startup program for the application. You can find that program on the Programs tab of the Project Manager. Its name, in our example wizard project, is *TimeAndBilling_app.prg*. The following listing excerpts some of this program:

```
* TIMEANDBILLING_APP.PRG

* This file is a generated, framework-enabling component
* created by APPBUILDER
* (c) Microsoft Corporation

* Framework-generated application startup program
* for D:\BOOK\WIZAPP\TIMEANDBILLING Project

#INCLUDE [..\TIMEANDBILLING_APP.H]
```

Notice the #INCLUDE line. This line of code reads an Include file that contains a number of *manifest constant* definitions. Manifest constants are like compile-time variables—that is, the compiler will replace the constant name with the constant value when it compiles the code. Unlike regular variables, these constants cannot change value while the code is running.

The next listing shows an excerpt from the *TimeandBilling.h* file that defines those manifest constants:

```
* D:\BOOK\WIZAPP\TIMEANDBILLING_APP.H

* This file is a generated, framework-enabling component
* created by APPBUILDER
* (c) Microsoft Corporation

* header file holding framework-generated project data for
* D:\BOOK\WIZAPP\TIMEANDBILLING Project


...


#DEFINE APP_SUPERCLASS      "_Application"


* developer can change this one
* to use a different global reference
* if desired -- a BUILD ALL/RECOMPILE
* is required afterwards to synch up
* references in generated menus and PRGs.
#DEFINE APP_GLOBAL          goApp

* This one indicates the member name of the object
* placed on "framework-enabled" forms:
#DEFINE APP_MEDIATOR_NAME    "app_mediator"

* developer can change these to a different subclass
* of APP_SUPERCLASS if desired:
#DEFINE APP_CLASSLIB         "LIBS\TIMEANDBILLING_APP.VCX"
#DEFINE APP_CLASSNAME        "app_Application"
```

In this header (.H) file you see the definitions of the constants used in the startup program. The **#DEFINE** compiler directive is used to define these constants.

Another part of the startup program uses other compiler directives:

```
#IFDEF APP_SPLASHCLASS

  IF NOT EMPTY(APP_SPLASHCLASS)
   loSplash = NEWOBJECT(APP_SPLASHCLASS, APP_SPLASHCLASSLIB)
   IF VARTYPE(loSplash) = "O"
     lnSeconds = SECONDS()
     loSplash.Show()
   ENDIF
  ENDIF

#ENDIF
```

In the above listing you can see the **#IFDEF/#ENDIF** compiler directive. The compiler evaluates this directive at compile time for the program and either includes or doesn't include the code inside the structure in the compiled program. The **#IFDEF** checks to see if there is a manifest constant defined, named APP_SPLASHCLASS. If so, the code inside is included in the program; if not, the code is not compiled into the program.

What benefit does this approach give the developer? It centralizes the location for making modifications to the behavior of the startup program. Instead of editing the program itself, you can edit the header file, changing the constant definitions and causing a change in how the program is compiled.

The next listing shows more of the header file for the wizard application:

```
* the splash class can be anything you want:
#DEFINE APP_SPLASHCLASS     "app_splash"
#DEFINE APP_SPLASHCLASSLIB   "LIBS\TIMEANDBILLING_APP.VCX"
* how long should the splash screen stay up if
* no key is pressed and if the app object initializes
* too quickly? (this figure is in seconds)
#DEFINE APP_SPLASHDELAY      3
```

Notice the line that defines APP_SPLASHCLASS. With this line in the header file, the #IFDEF in the previous listing would evaluate to .T. and the contained code would be compiled. Placing an asterisk at the start of the #DEFINE line for APP_SPLASHCLASS as seen in the next listing will prevent the program code in the previous #IFDEF construct from being compiled:

```
* the splash class can be anything you want:
* #DEFINE APP_SPLASHCLASS     "app_splash"
#DEFINE APP_SPLASHCLASSLIB   "LIBS\TIMEANDBILLING_APP.VCX"
* how long should the splash screen stay up if
* no key is pressed and if the app object initializes
* too quickly? (this figure is in seconds)
#DEFINE APP_SPLASHDELAY      3
```

The minor change here, commenting the #DEFINE line for APP_SPLASHCLASS, will stop the compiling of the code inside the program's #IFDEF structure because the manifest constant APP_SPLASHCLASS is not defined in the header file. Consequently, the compiler evaluates #IFDEF APP_SPLASHCLASS to .F. and doesn't compile code inside the construct.

Ultimately, the startup program reaches this code:

```
APP_GLOBAL = NEWOBJECT(APP_CLASSNAME, APP_CLASSLIB)

IF VARTYPE(APP_GLOBAL) = "O" ;
  AND ACLASS(laCheck,APP_GLOBAL) > 0 AND ;
  ASCAN(laCheck,UPPER(APP_SUPERCLASS)) > 0

  APP_GLOBAL.cReference =[APP_GLOBAL]
  APP_GLOBAL.cFormMediatorName = APP_MEDIATOR_NAME

  #IFDEF APP_CD
   APP_CD
  #ENDIF

  #IFDEF APP_PATH
   APP_PATH
  #ENDIF

  #IFDEF APP_INITIALIZE
    APP_INITIALIZE
  #ENDIF

  IF VARTYPE(loSplash) = "O"

   IF SECONDS() < lnSeconds + APP_SPLASHDELAY
```

```
       =INKEY(APP_SPLASHDELAY-(SECONDS()-lnSeconds),"MH")
   ENDIF

   loSplash.Release()
   loSplash = .NULL.

 ENDIF

 RELEASE laCheck, loSplash, lnSeconds

 IF NOT APP_GLOBAL.Show()

   IF TYPE([APP_GLOBAL.Name]) = "C"
     MESSAGEBOX(APP_CANNOT_RUN_LOC,16, ;
         APP_GLOBAL.cCaption )
     APP_GLOBAL.Release()
   ELSE
     MESSAGEBOX(APP_CANNOT_RUN_LOC,16)
   ENDIF

 ELSE
   llAppRan = .T.
 ENDIF

 IF TYPE([APP_GLOBAL.lReadEvents]) = "L"

   IF APP_GLOBAL.lReadEvents
     * the Release() method was not used
     * but we've somehow gotten out of READ EVENTS...
     APP_GLOBAL.Release()
   ENDIF
 ELSE
   RELEASE APP_GLOBAL
 ENDIF

ELSE

 MESSAGEBOX(APP_WRONG_SUPERCLASS_LOC,16)
 RELEASE APP_GLOBAL

ENDIF
```

The startup program launches the application on the first line in the above listing,
APP_GLOBAL = NEWOBJECT(APP_CLASSNAME, APP_CLASSLIB). This line creates an object
based on the manifest constants for its class name and its class library and stores the reference
to that object in the variable referred to by the APP_GLOBAL constant.

The balance of the code responds to various options selected during the app builder run.

Classes tab of the Application Builder
Figure 8 shows the Classes tab of the application's project.

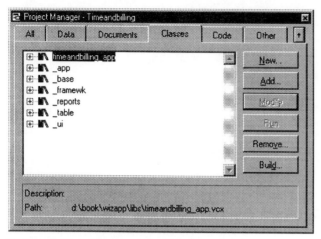

Figure 8. *The Classes tab of the application project.*

The class libraries that begin with an underscore are the Visual FoxPro foundation classes. The library named *TimeAndBilling_app* includes classes that the wizard created that are specific to this application. In the following sections you will see what each class library is and what each contains.

TimeAndBilling_app
This class library contains classes that are specific to this application. We will show you the first few classes as screen shots from the running application so you can see the value of the application framework classes provided with Visual FoxPro 6.0. **Table 3** lists the rest of the classes in this library, with brief descriptions.

App_aboutbox
This form class is used to create the About box from the Help menu. This form shows the chosen graphic, the name of the application, and the credits information entered in the builder. This is a subclass of the *_aboutbox* class in the library *_Framewk*. There is no code in this class, which means its entire behavior is inherited from its parent. **Figure 9** shows the About box for this application.

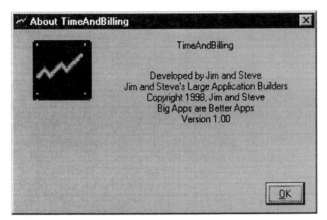

Figure 9. The About box in the wizard-generated application.

App_application
This is the main application class. The startup program uses this class to create the application object. Like all other classes in this library, there is no code in this class definition.

App_changepassword
This form class is used to change the password for the application. **Figure 10** shows this password-change form.

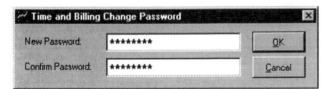

Figure 10. The change-password form generated by the Application Wizard.

App_errorlogviewer
Use this form to view the error log of the application. The wizard-generated application records errors in an error log file. The framework creates this log file when the first error occurs. Actually, the framework asks you if you want to log the error when it occurs.

To demonstrate this, create a form named Error in the Forms directory. Place a command button in this form and put the following code in the Click event of the button:

```
ERROR 101
```

This line of code causes an error (number 101). Run the TimeandBilling application and choose Favorites-Add to Favorites from the system menu. Use the browse button to select Error.scx in the Forms directory. Confirm your choices and then choose the Error form from the Favorites menu to run it.

Click the button in the error form. The dialog in **Figure 11** appears.

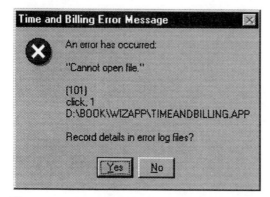

Figure 11. The first dialog in the error-handling system of the wizard-generated application.

Click Yes in this dialog to record the error in an error log file. **Figure 12** shows the next dialog that appears.

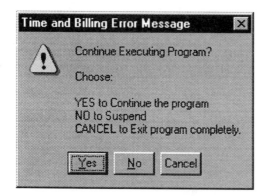

Figure 12. The second dialog in the error-handling system of the wizard application.

This dialog allows the user to decide whether to continue running the application, suspend the application, or exit the application. Click Yes to continue running the application.

Now select Tools-Error Logs-Display Error Log from the menu. **Figure 13** shows the *App_errorlogviewer* form.

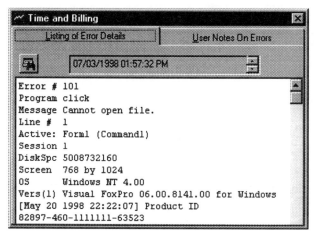

Figure 13. The error log display form.

The error log records a great amount of information about the error and the environment in which it occurred. This information will be invaluable to you, the developer, when you are trying to determine the cause of the error. On the second page of the PageFrame in this dialog, the user can add notes concerning the error, such as what they were doing at the time. See **Figure 14**.

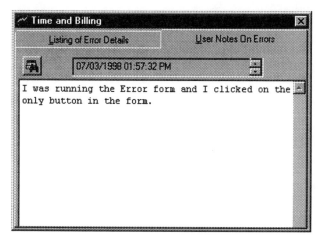

Figure 14. The User Notes page of the error log dialog.

The last thing to examine in this dialog is the button with the binoculars on it. Use this button to browse all records in the error log. See **Figure 15**.

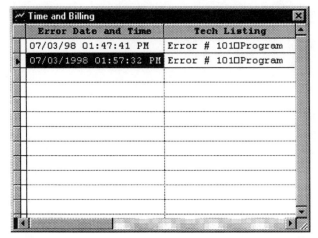

Figure 15. *Browsing the error log in the wizard-generated application.*

App_favoritepicker

This form is used to add/remove a document to/from the Favorites menu. See **Figure 16**.

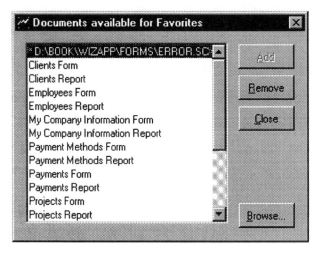

Figure 16. *The app_favoritepicker form.*

The rest of the classes TimeAndBilling_app

The rest of the classes in the *TimeAndBilling_app* class library are similar to those above. **Table 3** lists these classes with a brief description of each.

Table 3. *The rest of the classes in the TimeAndBilling_app library.*

Class	Description
App_navtoolbar	A navigation toolbar with the Top, Previous, Next, and Bottom buttons, and a spinner to select a specific record number.
App_newopen	A form that allows the user to open a form.
App_options	A form that allows the users to set system-wide options like SET CONFIRM or the 12/24-hour time display, among others.
App_reportpicker	A form used to select a report for processing.
App_splash	The splash screen at the startup of the application.
App_standardtoolbar	A toolbar with New, Open, Save, and Revert buttons, in addition to Cut, Copy, Paste, and Help.
App_topform	A form class used to provide the top-level form. This class is used when the options in the wizard indicated that the application should run outside the Visual FoxPro screen.
App_userlogin	The user login form.

_Framewk

The wizard uses classes in this library to construct other classes. This type of class, one that is never used to directly create an object at runtime, is called an *abstract class*. Most of the remaining classes you will see are abstract classes.

In the *_Framewk* library is the *_Application* parent class for the *app_application* class you saw in the *TimeAndBilling_app* library.

_Application

As you saw in the previous section titled "Parts of the framework," the *_Application* class is a composite class — a container that acts as the mediator between the "outside world" and the objects it contains. The following sections describe some methods of the *_Application* class.

Init

The Init event fires automatically when the startup program creates an instance of the class. The Init fires as the very last thing in the creation order, meaning that all of the objects contained in the application object exist and are fully addressable.

The code from the Init of the *_Application* class is as follows.

```
IF NOT DODEFAULT()
   RETURN .F.
ENDIF
```

The first IF in the code runs any code that might exist in a parent class' Init and respects the return value from that code. If the parent class' Init returns false (.F.) then this code will also return false without attempting anything else. A return of false from the Init of an object prevents the creation of that object.

```
THIS.cIcon = THIS.GetResourceFileName(THIS.cIcon, ".ico", .T.)
THIS.cImage = THIS.GetResourceFileName(THIS.cImage, ".bmp .ico .gif", .T.)
```

Once the parent class code returns .T., this code sets two properties of the application object. The cIcon and cImage properties are set to reflect the icon and image selected during the Application Builder run. These properties are set through method calls to the GetResourceFileName method of the *_Application* class. The GetResourceFileName method accepts a filename and extension and ensures that a file with that name exists.

```
IF VARTYPE(THIS.cReference) = "C" AND (NOT EMPTY(THIS.cReference))
  THIS.cReference = THIS.cReference
ENDIF
```

Next, the Init checks the cReference property for validity. The cReference property contains the name of the variable that refers to the application object. If the property has a valid value, it assigns the existing value the same property.

Why assign the property's value to the property itself? Doesn't it already have that value? Yes, it does. However, executing the code to assign that value to the property will fire the Assign method for that property. This listing shows the cReference_assign code:

```
LPARAMETERS tcReference

IF VARTYPE(tcReference) = "C"

  IF (TYPE(THIS.cReference+".Name") = "C" AND ;
    EVAL(THIS.cReference) = THIS)
    RELEASE (THIS.cReference)
  ENDIF

  THIS.cReference = tcReference

ENDIF

IF (NOT EMPTY(THIS.cReference)) AND ;
  (TYPE(THIS.cReference+".Name") # "C" OR ;
  EVAL(THIS.cReference) # THIS)

  RELEASE (THIS.cReference)
  PUBLIC (THIS.cReference)
  STORE THIS TO (THIS.cReference)

ENDIF
```

The code in the Assign method shows clearly that it is validating the value being assigned and making sure that the variable name in that property is an object reference to the application being created. The first **IF** checks to see that the variable tcReference is a character string.

If it is, the next **IF** checks to see if the cReference property of the application object is filled and that it refers to the object to which this code belongs. It checks the object references by using Visual FoxPro 6.0's new ability to compare object references with the = sign—if the two object references on either side of the equal sign are exactly the same object, they are considered equal.

If the Assign method finds that cReference contains an object reference to this object, it releases the variable and assigns the new name to the property.

The line **IF (NOT (EMPTY(THIS.cReference))** ... checks to see if the cReference property contains the name of a variable that does *not* refer to the application object. If the code finds this situation, it releases the variable named in cReference, declares the variable **PUBLIC** and assigns it an object reference to the application object.

The next occurrence in the Init is a call to the SetAppFileNames method:

```
IF NOT THIS.SetAppFileNames()
  RETURN .F.
ENDIF
```

The SetAppFileNames method gets the top-level filename and the name of the module—the .EXE or .APP—that is creating this object. This information is needed to handle the IN option of the SET CLASSLIB command. The information is stored in two properties of this object: cAppFileName, which holds the application filename, and cClassContainerFileName, which holds the name of the .EXE, .APP, or .DLL that is running.

The final action in the Init of this object checks a number of conditions. The IF statement checks for an identical class name and application name, which indicates that this application was not called from another application. The IF also checks to see if the application is running with the runtime libraries of Visual FoxPro, and if Visual FoxPro started as a distributed application.

The **VERSION(2)** = **0** is true (.T.) if the runtime library is being used. **_VFP.StartMode** = **4** will be true (.T.) if Visual FoxPro was started as a distributed application. If these conditions are all .T., the application needs a read events command regardless of whether the developer set it up that way. The following code sequence shows these tests. You can see inside the IF construct that the lReadEvents property is set to .T. if the conditions are all true.

```
IF VERSION(2) = 0 AND _VFP.StartMode = 4 AND ;
  UPPER(THIS.cClassContainerFileName) == UPPER(THIS.cAppFileName)
  * if the running EXE is this file, and this file
  * is not set up to be Read Events, make it Read Events anyway.
  THIS.lReadEvents = .T.
ENDIF

RETURN (THIS.IsErrorFree())
```

Finally, the Init returns the value from another method, IsErrorFree, which has one line of code:

```
RETURN (ISNULL(THIS.iLastError))
```

If the iLastError property has a value of NULL, this method returns true (.T.); otherwise it returns false (.F.). A return of false from this method will cause the Init to also return false and therefore stop the creation of the application object. The property iLastError is set in the Error event of the object.

Returning to the startup program for a moment, notice that the next step in that program after creating the application object is to call the Show method of that object. The following code shows an excerpt from the startup program:

```
APP_GLOBAL = NEWOBJECT(APP_CLASSNAME, APP_CLASSLIB)

IF VARTYPE(APP_GLOBAL) = "O" ;
```

```
   AND ACLASS(laCheck,APP_GLOBAL) > 0 AND ;
   ASCAN(laCheck,UPPER(APP_SUPERCLASS)) > 0

 * A bunch of code is not reprinted here
 * The code omitted sets paths and other housekeeping actions

 IF NOT APP_GLOBAL.Show()

   IF TYPE([APP_GLOBAL.Name]) = "C"
     MESSAGEBOX(APP_CANNOT_RUN_LOC,16, APP_GLOBAL.cCaption )
     APP_GLOBAL.Release()
   ELSE
     MESSAGEBOX(APP_CANNOT_RUN_LOC,16)
   ENDIF

 ELSE
   llAppRan = .T.
 ENDIF


 IF TYPE([APP_GLOBAL.lReadEvents]) = "L"

   IF APP_GLOBAL.lReadEvents
     * the Release() method was not used
     * but we've somehow gotten out of READ EVENTS...
     APP_GLOBAL.Release()
   ENDIF
 ELSE
   RELEASE APP_GLOBAL
 ENDIF

ELSE

 MESSAGEBOX(APP_WRONG_SUPERCLASS_LOC,16)
 RELEASE APP_GLOBAL

ENDIF
```

The NewObject() call actually creates the application object. The next IF statement tests to see if the application object actually succeeded in getting created. If the application did get created, this program calls the Show method for the application object.

The Show code starts out by declaring the variable llSuccess as LOCAL. This variable is used throughout the Show method to store return values from various other methods. The LOCAL declaration prevents any possible conflicts with a variable of the same name in one of the called methods.

The code in the Show method is quite simple. First it calls the SaveEnvironment method and stores the return value in llSuccess. All other actions are in an **IF llSuccess** construct. If any call returns .F., the rest of the IF clauses prevent other calls from being made and the code falls through to the Return command at the end.

```
LOCAL llSuccess

llSuccess = THIS.SaveEnvironment()

IF llSuccess
```

```
  llSuccess = THIS.ValidateMetaTable()
ENDIF

IF llSuccess
  llSuccess = THIS.CreateFrame()
ENDIF

IF llSuccess AND NOT EMPTY(APP_LOADING_LOC)

  IF VARTYPE(THIS.oFrame) = "O"
    THIS.oFrame.Show()
  ENDIF

  WAIT WINDOW NOWAIT ;
   LEFT(APP_LOADING_LOC,254)

ENDIF

IF llSuccess
  llSuccess = THIS.ResetFormsCollection()
ENDIF

IF llSuccess
  llSuccess = THIS.CreateCollaborators()
ENDIF

IF llSuccess
  llSuccess = THIS.HandleProjectWindow()
ENDIF

IF llSuccess
  llSuccess = THIS.SetEnvironment()
ENDIF

IF llSuccess
  THIS.cUserTableAlias = JUSTSTEM(THIS.cUserTableName)
  llSuccess = NOT EMPTY(THIS.cUserTableAlias)
ENDIF

IF llSuccess
  llSuccess = THIS.SetCurrentUser()
ENDIF

IF llSuccess
  llSuccess = THIS.ShowStartupElements()
ENDIF

WAIT CLEAR

IF llSuccess
  llSuccess = THIS.Activate()
ENDIF

THIS.RestoreEnvironment()

RETURN llSuccess
```

Table 4 describes the methods called from the Show method.

Table 4. *Methods called from the application's Show method.*

Method	Description
SaveEnvironment	Saves some current environment settings to properties of the application object.
ValidateMetaTable	Validates the structure and contents of the application's meta table. The meta table stores information used by the application while it is running.
CreateFrame	Creates a top-level form to contain the application if that is the way things have been set up by the developer.
ResetFormsCollection	Empties the forms collection array property of the application.
CreateCollaborators	This method is a hook for the developer's use. There is no code in it except for a return command. The developer can create collaborating objects by calling the AddCollaborator method from this method.
HandleProjectWindow	Handles the hiding of the project manager window.
SetEnvironment	Sets the environment for the application.
SetCurrentUser	Sets the current user, calls the login form if necessary, and sets up all properties for the current user.
ShowStartupElements	Creates toolbars and menus required at startup of the application.
Activate	Calls three methods of the application object. First it calls ClearLastError, which clears any error information. Then it calls BeforeReadEvents, which is an empty hook method for the developer to write any code he may want executed before the read events command. Finally, it calls the ReadEvents method, which actually issues the READ EVENTS command.
RestoreEnvironment	Resets the environment that was saved to the properties of the application object.

The following listing shows the only excerpt of code in the Show method of the application object that is not described in Table 4.

```
IF llSuccess AND NOT EMPTY(APP_LOADING_LOC)

  IF VARTYPE(THIS.oFrame) = "O"
    THIS.oFrame.Show()
  ENDIF

  WAIT WINDOW NOWAIT ;
    LEFT(APP_LOADING_LOC,254)

ENDIF
```

This code checks to see whether there is a message to be displayed during the application's load. If there is a message, the code shows the top-level form if necessary and finally issues a **WAIT WINDOW ... NOWAIT** to display the message.

At this point, after the Show method of the application object has been executed, the application is up and running.

The code you have reviewed so far has been relatively simple. You have seen a number of different methods called during the creation process.

Some questions you may be asking yourself are, "Why are there are so many different methods? Why not put all of the startup code into one method or even in the startup program?" Breaking up the code into individual methods with very specific responsibilities allows those methods to be called at times other than startup. The *specialization* of the methods provides the ability for the developer, or the framework, to execute discrete pieces of code designed to provide a specific service at any time. It removes the need to use large numbers of parameters in a single large code block in order to control what the block will and will not do when called.

In the next sections of this chapter we'll examine the Visual FoxPro 6.0 foundation classes involved in form, report, menu, security, and error management.

Form management

The _Application_ class is the center of all activity in the framework. It carries the responsibility of creating all other objects needed by the application. One method of the _Application_ class is CreateFormMediator. Its function is to create an instance of the _FormMediator_ class defined in the _Framewk_ class library.

The _Application_ class has a DoForm method that runs a form. The DoForm method of the application object creates the form and the FormMediator object for the form. The application uses an array property to keep track of all of the "comings and goings" of the forms.

The FormMediator is a "go-between" for the form and the application object. Each form has its own mediator object. **Table 5** lists the methods in the form mediator with a brief description.

Table 5*. The methods of the _FormMediator class.*

Method	Description
Destroy	Calls the application object to remove menus and /or toolbars that the form may have created.
DataChanged	Calls the QueryDataChanged method of the application object to determine if any data change has occurred.
DoSessionSets	Sets the data environment setting in the application object to match the form by calling either the application object's SetDataSessionEnvironment or ApplyUserOptsForSession methods.
GetAppRef	Returns the variable name that references the application object.
LoadApp	Creates any context menus and/or toolbars that a form may need by calling upon the application object to create them. Calls the DoContextMenu and DoToolbar methods of the application object to create the respective menu and/or toolbars. The DoForm method calls LoadApp right after the form has successfully been created.
OutPut	Manages table navigation by calling the DoTableOutput method of the application object. The FormMediator mediates table navigation so the application can derive the information it needs from the form.
OutPutOneRecord	Identical to the OutPut method except it passes the value of .T. to the DoTableOutput method of the application object. The argument of .T. causes the application object to use a scope of NEXT 1 in its efforts to move the record pointer.
QueryUnload	Calls the QueryDataSessionUnload method of the application object. The QueryDataSessionUnload method of the application object ensures that any data changes are handled before allowing the form to be released.
SetDocumentToNew	Stores the lAddingNewDocument flag of the application object to the mediator's lAdding property so the form knows which record to work on.

Except for the name of the method called, the code in all methods of the form mediator is similar. This listing shows the code for the DataChanged method:

```
LOCAL loApp, llReturn

loApp = THIS.GetAppRef()

IF ISNULL(loApp)
   RETURN
ENDIF

llReturn = loApp.QueryDataChanged(THISFORM,THIS.iChangeMode)

loApp = .NULL.

RETURN llReturn
```

After some local variables are declared, this code calls the GetAppRef method to get the variable name for the application object. The `IF ISNULL(loApp)` line causes the code to terminate if there is no application object; otherwise the method goes on to make its call to the application object for services. This approach of checking for an application object before calling methods of the application allows you to run a form for testing without running the whole application. When the form runs in the application, the method calls to the application object are called. When the form runs outside the application, the application object methods are not called.

Figure 17 shows the relationships between the form, the form mediator, and the application object.

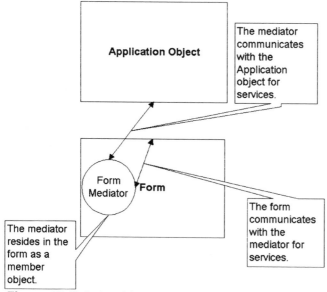

Figure 17. *Relationships between the form, form mediator, and application object.*

By having the mediator reside in the form as a member object, you ensure that every time you create an instance of the form, you also create an instance of the mediator. This causes the mediator to go through its initialization process and register the form properly with the application object.

The application object does the actual form management. The application's DoForm method creates forms and enters them into its collection of forms, the aForms array property of the application object. The ReleaseForm method of the application object releases a form and removes it from the collection of forms.

With all of this cooperation going on, where, exactly, is the form manager? The form manager is the application object with the assistance of the form mediator. As you further examine the framework, you'll find that the application object plays many roles. Using one object to play multiple roles is neither a good nor bad approach to framework design. One advantage is that all of the code for supporting those roles is located in one place, making it easy to find and manage. On the other hand, using discrete objects for each manager role allows each of those objects to be specialized to its role, which can simplify the design and the code. The important issue here is not how many objects support the manager roles, but rather how well those roles are supported.

Report management

The application object also handles report management. A number of different methods in the application object relate to report production and management. **Table 6** lists the methods that involve themselves with reports.

Table 6. Methods of the application object that handle reports.

Method	Description
DoReport	The report picker dialog calls this method. The code in this method creates an instance of the Options dialog for a report using the class _OutputDialog. The _OutputDialog class is discussed in more detail below.
DoLabel	Calls the DoReport method.
DoReportDialog	Runs the document picker dialog to allow the user to choose a report.
DoTableOutput	Checks the current alias for the current form and produces an instance of the _OutputDialog class for selecting reports.
ExportErrorLog	Prints a report of the error log by creating a cursor of the entries in the log and creating an instance of the _OutputDialog class.
RefreshFavoritePopup	Refreshes the Favorite popup menu for all favorites. Produces a DoReport method call for the bars of the popup that call reports.
DoFile	Called from the Favorites menu, this method examines the requested file to see if it is a report. If the request is for a report, the method calls the DoReport method.

Table 6 shows that the application object manages reports through a number of different mechanisms. There are a number of different mechanisms for calling reports to provide for flexibility in the ways a user may request a report.

The rest of this section assumes that you are dealing with a report created by the Application Builder. These reports follow a direct path through the application object. **Figure 18** shows the Quick Start form in the application.

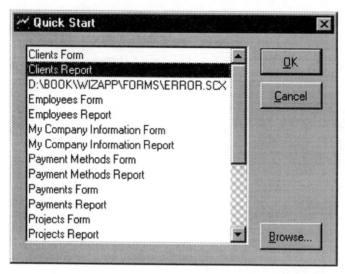

Figure 18. *The QuickStart form in the application built with the Application Builder.*

The form in Figure 18 highlights the Clients Report. The QuickStart form is an instance of the class *App_FavoritePicker* found in the application class library, in this case the *Time-AndBilling_app* class library. The class in the application library is a subclass of the *_FavoritePicker* class in the *_Application* library. The OK button in this form calls the Exec-Document method of the form.

The *_FavoritePicker* is a multi-purpose dialog. It serves for adding items to the Favorites menu as well as being the QuickStart form. In the ExecDocument method of the class, the code exists for handling both possibilities. The code of interest to us right now is near the end of the method and is excerpted in the following listing:

```
IF ALLTR(THIS.aDocuments[liRow,10]) = PJX_META_DOC_REPORT_TYPE

  THIS.oApp.DoReport(ALLTRIM(THIS.aDocuments[liRow,2]), ;
          ALLTRIM(THIS.aDocuments[liRow,1]))

ELSE

  THIS.oApp.DoForm(ALLTRIM(THIS.aDocuments[liRow,2]), ;
          ALLTRIM(THIS.aDocuments[liRow,3]), ;
          THIS.aDocuments[liRow,4], ;
          THIS.aDocuments[liRow,5], ;
          THIS.aDocuments[liRow,6], ;
          THIS.aDocuments[liRow,7])

ENDIF
```

The form has an array property named aDocuments that holds information about all items in the listbox. That array property is referenced in the IF statement above. The *_Framewk.h* header file, which is included for the *_FavoritePicker* class, sets PJX_META_DOC_REPORT_TYPE manifest constant to "R". Column 10 of the aDocuments array of the form holds the value of "R" for reports. If the ExecDocument sees an R in the 10th column for the current choice, it calls the application's DoReport method.

The DoReport method creates an instance of the _OutputDialog class by calling the Do-ModalDialogClass method of the application object. **Figure 19** shows the output dialog for the Clients Report.

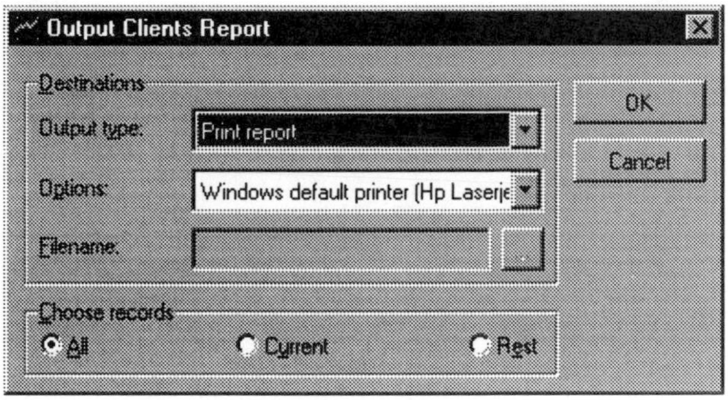

Figure 19. The output dialog for the Clients Report.

Figure 19 shows a modification of the _OutputDialog class. The parameters passed to the dialog indicate that source changes are not allowed through the dialog. The disallowance of source changes causes the Init of the form to set the lPreventSourceChanges property of the dialog to .T. Setting this property fires the lPreventSourceChanges_Assign method for the property. The Assign method for the property hides and/or shows the appropriate controls in the dialog. If you open the _OutputDialog class you see that it also contains controls at the bottom for managing the editing of the file being processed. These controls do not show up in Figure 19 because this instance of the dialog was told that changes were not allowed.

The Click event of the OK button calls the Output method of the form. The Output method of the form passes this call to the Output method of the cusOutput object contained in the form. The cusOutput object is an instance of the class _Output in the _Reports class library.

The code in the Output method of the _Output class calls the PrintReport method of the _Output class. After checking out the settings for report production, the PrintReport method uses this code to produce the report (or label set):

```
IF ".LBX" $ UPPER(THIS.cReport)
   * not that I think it makes any difference!!
   LABEL FORM (THIS.cReport) &lcClauses &lcDestination NOCONSOLE
ELSE
   REPORT FORM (THIS.cReport) &lcClauses &lcDestination NOCONSOLE
ENDIF
```

In the report management functionality, you see many different possible routes to producing a report. The _Application class of the framework has addressed all possibilities because it must be flexible enough to handle whatever we developers may throw at it. In following the production of a report that was created by the Application Builder, you see the clear path that is followed when the report is *framework aware*. Framework aware means that the dialogs involved are aware and compliant with the framework's *contracts*.

A contract, in the scope of a framework, is a set of rules that the components of an application must follow. For components that follow these rules, the framework will provide a high degree of services. The framework produced by the Application Wizard allows for components that do not strictly follow the contracts. However, these components will not get the full benefit of the services of the framework and, therefore, will require the developer to do more work within the component.

You will see the concept of contracts throughout the framework discussion. Previously, in the "Form management" section, you learned that the form must have a form mediator to be framework-aware. This requirement for the mediator is a contract between a form and the framework.

Menu management

The Application Builder created two menus for you: *TimeAndBilling_Main* and *TimeAndBilling_Go*. These two menus are framework-aware in that they comply with the contracts for menus within the framework.

The contracts for menus state that the menu does not execute anything directly, but rather calls a method of the application object for the services needed. For example, on the popup menu for the File menu in the *TimeAndBilling_Main* menu, there is a Print Reports option. The command for this option is not a direct call to the Reports Selection dialog; rather, it is a call to the DoReportDialog method of the application object. Other options are set up similarly. They call the application object for services rather than executing things directly.

The menu delegates the operation to the application object. This allows the application object to keep track of everything that the user does from the menu.

The Favorites pad of the *TimeAndBilling_Main* menu not only calls methods of the application object; its contents are managed by the RefreshFavoritePopup method of the application object. The listing below excerpts from this method:

```
* release all but top bars:
FOR liBarNo = 4 TO CNTBAR(THIS.cFavoritePopupName)
   RELEASE BAR liBarNo OF (THIS.cFavoritePopupName)
ENDFOR
```

This first bit of code clears the Favorite popup of all bars except the first three, which are Add to favorites, Clear favorites, and a separator line, respectively:

```
liBarNo = 3

* open metatable
THIS.ClearLastError()

IF NOT EMPTY(THIS.cMetaTable)
   lcAlias = "M"+SYS(2015)
   USE (THIS.cMetaTable) ALIAS (lcAlias) AGAIN SHARED IN 0
ENDIF
```

In the above code, the first line sets the bar counter to 3 so that the first three items are not overwritten by the code that follows. The next code opens the meta data table to look up the favorite menu options for the current user:

```
IF NOT (THIS.IsErrorFree())
   SET SKIP OF BAR 1 OF (THIS.cFavoritePopupName) .T.
   SET SKIP OF BAR 2 OF (THIS.cFavoritePopupName) .T.
   RETURN
ENDIF

liSelect = SELECT()
IF NOT EMPTY(lcAlias)
   SELECT (lcAlias)
ENDIF
```

The above code responds to any error that might have occurred in opening the meta data table. If no error occurred, the code selects the alias for the meta data table as the current work area. The SetCurrentUser method of the application object, which was called on loading the application, makes a call to the SetCurrentUserFavoriteIDs method of the application object. The SetCurrentUserFavoriteIDs method sets the cCurrentUserFavoriteIDs property of the application object with data from the meta data table.

The balance of the code parses each individual favorite from the cCurrentUserFavoriteIDs property and creates a **DEFINE BAR** command with a corresponding **ON SELECTION** command and executes them. If necessary, the meta data table is used to look up any required information.

The menu passes any user actions to the application object for handling, and through this approach the application object acts as a menu handler object. **Figure 20** shows the interaction of the menus with the application object.

The relationship between a menu option and the resultant behavior is indirect. The menu does not execute the behavior; rather, it sends a message to the application object requesting the behavior. The application object then processes the request and executes the appropriate behavior.

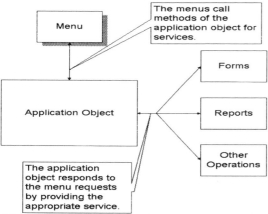

Figure 20*. Relationships between menus, the application object, and the other functionality of the application.*

Security management

The *_UserLogin* class implements the security features of the application framework included with Visual FoxPro 6.0. The application object uses the *_UserLogin* class to log a user into an application. You enable this feature by checking the User Logins check box on the General tab of the Application Builder dialog, as previously seen in Figure 4.

The security features provided by the framework are minimal. The framework provides for user login only; the developer must add any other security handling by enhancing the framework classes. The section titled "Extending the foundation classes" later in this chapter discusses the mechanisms for adding functionality to the framework classes.

Figure 21 shows the User Login form.

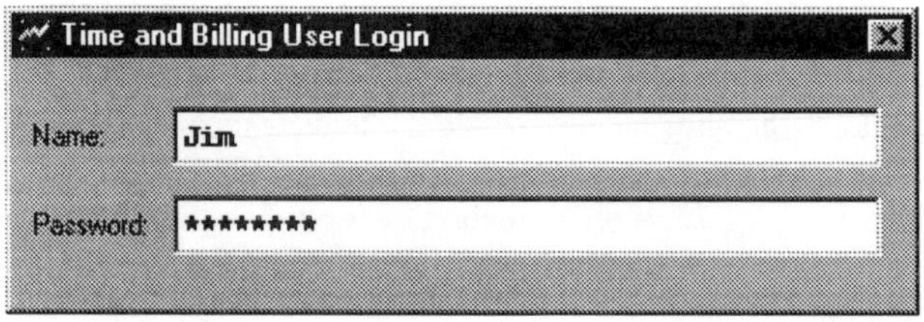

Figure 21. The User Login form of the Application Builder application.

As stated earlier, this form is an instance of the *_UserLogin* class in the *_Framewk* class library. The Show method of the application object calls the SetCurrentUser method of the same object to set up the current user in the system. The SetCurrentUser method determines by looking at the lUserPreferences property of the application object whether to turn on or off the user login option. The SetCurrentUser method calls a user login form if the lUserPreferences property value is true. The code excerpt below shows this functionality in the SetCurrentUser method of the *_Application* class:

```
IF THIS.lUserPreferences

   IF EMPTY(THIS.cCurrentUser) OR tlChangeUser
    llSuccess = THIS.DoUserLogIn()
   ELSE
    llSuccess = THIS.SeekCurrentUser()
   ENDIF
ELSE
   * we are using a global set of preferences
   * to cover all users
   THIS.SeekDefaultUser()
   llSuccess = .T.
ENDIF
```

In the *_UserLogin* class, the valid on the password textbox calls the CheckPasswordInfo method of the form. The CheckPasswordInfo method of the form class calls the CheckPasswordInfo method of the application object, which validates whether the password is correct for the user name entered. You can see where this is going — once again, the behavior is provided by the application object.

The Valid event for the password textbox will release the form if everything is okay. If the password is invalid, the attempts counter is incremented and the focus is set to the password textbox. If the number of attempts has exceeded the allowed attempts, reflected in the iTriesAllowed property of the form, the FailLogin method of the form is called. This listing shows an excerpt of the DoUserLogin method of the _Application class:

```
IF (NOT THIS.lUserPreferences)
  RETURN .F.
ENDIF
LOCAL loForm

loForm = THIS.DoModalDialogClass(THIS.cUserLogInClass,
THIS.cUserLogInClassLib, .T.)
IF VARTYPE(loForm) = "O"
  loForm.Show(1)
  RETURN (NOT EOF(THIS.cUserTableAlias))
ELSE
  RETURN .F.
ENDIF
```

The line **RETURN (NOT EOF(THIS.cUserTableAlias))** causes the login to succeed or fail. You can see that this is true by reviewing the next listing of the FailLogin method of the _UserLogin form class:

```
IF RECCOUNT(THIS.oApp.cUserTableAlias) > 0
  GO BOTTOM IN (THIS.oApp.cUserTableAlias)
  SKIP IN (THIS.oApp.cUserTableAlias)
ENDIF
```

This code moves the record pointer in the user table to end of file if the login failed. Being at EOF in the use table will cause the application object to abort running the application.

If the login process is successful, the _UserLogin form leaves the record pointer on the record for the user logging into the application. The DoUserLogin method of the _Application class will then return a value of true and the system will start.

Again, you can see the interaction between the objects in the application and the application object itself. Here the user login form calls on the application object to validate the password for the user. The user login form sets the environment for the DoUserLogin method of the application object and then releases itself. The application object then reacts to the environment set by the form. You see that the application object provides all of the actual security services.

Error handling
The application object also manages the error handling. The SetEnvironment method of the _Application class contains the following lines of code:

```
lcTemp = THIS.cReference+".Error(ERROR(),PROGRAM(),LINENO())"
ON ERROR &lcTemp
```

These two lines set the ON ERROR command that reacts to any error that occurs. The call built by these lines is a call to the Error event of the application object. If the variable referencing the application object is goApp, the macro expansion creates the command here:

```
ON ERROR goApp.Error(ERROR(),PROGRAM(),LINENO())
```

This command passes all errors to the Error event of the application object. Here is the Error event code:

```
LPARAMETERS nError, cMethod, nLine
THIS.iLastError = nError
```

The first thing the Error event does is record the error number in the application object property named iLastError. All other objects in the framework will examine the iLastError property to see if an error occurred during any particular operation.

```
IF THIS.lSkipErrorHandling
  * special cases -- right
  * now this is done when
  * trying to USE the error log EXCLUSIVEly
  * for purging
  RETURN
ENDIF
```

Next, seen in the listing above, the Error event checks to see if error handling is turned off by the lSkipErrorHandling property of the application object. An example of the error handling being shut off is when the framework tries to open the error log file exclusively. During this attempt to open the file exclusively, the framework sets the lSkipErrorHandling to true. The IF statement above causes a simple return before any of the error handling code is encountered.

```
THIS.cusError.Handle(nError,cMethod,nLine)
```

Here again, we see delegation. In the line of code above, the Error event passes the error condition to the cusError object. The cusError Handle event has no code in it and derives its entire behavior from its parent class *_error* in the *_app* library. We'll examine the *_error* class later in this section.

```
LOCAL llFatal, llUserCancelled, lcCaller, lcProg, ;
  llNoCodeExecuting, liLevel, lcTemp

llFatal = THIS.cusError.IsFatal()
llUserCancelled = THIS.cusError.UserCancelled()
```

After declaring some local variables, the Error event of the application object makes two calls to the cusError object. The first call is to the cusError.IsFatal method and the second to the cusError.UserCancelled method. Neither of these methods has code in its cusError class definition. The code is in the parent of the cusError class, *_error,* which is in the *_app* library.

```
IF NOT (llFatal OR llUserCancelled)
  liLevel = 0
  lcCaller = ""
  lcProg = PROGRAM(0)
  DO WHILE .T.
   lcCaller = PROGRAM(liLevel)
   liLevel = liLevel + 1
   lcProg = PROGRAM(liLevel)
   IF EMPTY(lcProg) OR (UPPER(lcProg) == UPPER(THIS.Name+".ERROR"))
     EXIT
   ENDIF
  ENDDO
  llNoCodeExecuting = (UPPER(lcCaller) == UPPER(THIS.Name+".READEVENTS"))
ENDIF
```

The above code examines the program calling stack to see where the error occurred. If the code encounters the program call to the Error event, it exits the processing. The llNoCode-Executing variable is set to true if the code encounters the ReadEvents method of the application object just before exiting. The llNoCodeExecuting variable is referred to later in the error processing.

```
DO CASE
CASE THIS.iLastError # nError
  * an error in the error handler!
  * this will have been taken care of
  * and we don't want to get
  * into a recursive situation
```

The above listing shows the beginning of a **DO CASE** construct in the Error event of the application object. The first **CASE** checks to see if the iLastError property is not equal to the error number passed to this event. This will be true if an error occurred in the error handler itself. Under this condition, the Error event allows the code execution to fall through to the end. It does this to prevent recursive actions.

```
CASE llFatal OR llUserCancelled

  IF THIS.lReadEvents
   lcTemp = THIS.cLastOnError
   ON ERROR &lcTemp
   * remove reference to App Object
   * in error handler *now* before
   * it can start messing about with
   * destroying itself
  ENDIF
  THIS.Release()
```

The next **CASE** checks to see if either llFatal or llUserCancelled is true. If either of those variables is true, the code inside the case statement resets the **ON ERROR** command and releases the application object.

```
CASE llNoCodeExecuting
  RETRY
```

If the prior code found that there was no code executing, the Error event issues a **RETRY** command to execute the line that caused this error call again.

```
OTHERWISE
   RETURN
ENDCASE
```

If none of the other **CASE**s were true, the **OTHERWISE** case is executed. This otherwise simply returns to wherever the error occurred on the line following the one that caused the error.

Once this code has finished, either the application has been shut down or the application is still running and the iLastError property contains the number of the error that caused the call.

The application object also has a method named IsErrorFree. You can see a call to the IsErrorFree method in the SetEnvironment method of the *_Application* class. The SetEnvironment method ends with the following line of code

```
RETURN THIS.IsErrorFree()
```

This line simply passes back the return value from the IsErrorFree method of the application object. The IsErrorFree method contains this line of code:

```
RETURN (ISNULL(THIS.iLastError))
```

This causes a return of true if the iLastError property has a value of NULL and false if the value is anything but NULL. A non-NULL value indicates that an error occurred during the running of the SetEnvironment method. How do you know the error occurred during the SetEnvironment method and not somewhere else? You know because the first line of code in the SetEnvironment method, shown here, clears the iLastError property:

```
THIS.ClearLastError()
```

The ClearLastError method of the application object has one line of code that sets the iLastError property to NULL.

The next class to examine is the *_error* class in the *_app* library. The cusError object contained in the *_Application* class is derived from the *_error* class.

The *_error* class has most of the code that deals with errors. Its Error method, listed below, handles errors occurring during the error handling routines:

```
LPARAMETERS nError, cMethod, nLine
* special case, must override
* any use of ON ERROR which
* might call this object recursively
IF "setlog" $ LOWER(cMethod)
   THIS.cLogDBF = ""
ELSE
   ERROR ERROR_IN_ERROR_METHOD_LOC+":"+CHR(13)+ ;
    "#"+ALLTR(STR(nError))+CHR(13)+ ;
    THIS.Name+" "+cMethod+", "+ALLTR(STR(nLine))+CHR(13)+ ;
```

```
THIS.cCurrentMessage
ENDIF
```

The only time this event executes is if the error occurred in the cusError object. The IF checks to see if the error occurred while trying to set up the error log file for output. If the error log was set up, the error log filename property is blanked out and the event returns to the calling code.

If the error was not in the setup of the error log, this code executes an ERROR command to cause the ON ERROR handler to be called, passing the values that this event received as parameters.

Recall that in the Error event of the _Application object, the Handle method of the cusError object was called. The code that executes in the Handle method is in the _error class. The next listing shows the Handle method of the _error class.

```
LPARAMETERS tiError, tcMethod, tiLine

THIS.cCurrentMessage = MESSAGE()
THIS.cCurrentErrorParam = SYS(2018)
THIS.iCurrentError = tiError
THIS.cCurrentMethod = tcMethod
THIS.iCurrentLine = tiLine
THIS.cCurrentClass = ""
THIS.lUserCancelled = .F. && it's possible for an outside program
                && to ignore a previous CANCEL instruction
```

This first section of code sets some properties of the _error object. This allows the object to read its properties later on to display messages to the user and record the error log entry.

```
THIS.FillArrays()

* note: FillArrays() does an early bail for memory
* errors,which will be messaged by THIS.IsFatal() below

* see FillArrays() for structure
* of aErrorClass array --
* GetErrorAttribute
* gets a particular element by looking
* up error numbers in the first array column and specifying
* what column of the array is needed. This column
* is passed as GetErrorAttribute's first parameter
* (you can also pass a second parameter containing
* a particular error number to look up -- this defaults
* to the iCurrentError contents)
THIS.cCurrentClass = THIS.GetErrorAttribute(2)
* for example,
* THIS.cCurrentLevel = THIS.GetErrorAttribute(3)
* for a property that used a third column of
* the array to store some error severity classification system
```

In the above listing, the FillArrays method of the _error object is called. The FillArrays method creates, if needed, and fills an array property named aErrorClass with two columns. The first column is a delimited list of error numbers and the second column is a name for the error group. For example, the first row of the array is set to

"/21/22/43/1012/1149/1150/1151/1201/1202/1507/1600/1809/1986/2000/" in the first column and "memory" in the second column. The error numbers listed are all memory errors of some kind.

The above code goes on to call the GetErrorAttribute method of the *_error* object. The GetErrorAttribute will return the column passed as an argument from the row of the array that has a matching error number to the iCurrentError property, which was previously set. As the comments in the code indicate, you can call the GetErrorAttribute and pass a second argument so it will return the data for a particular error.

Also note in the comments that the GetErrorAttribute has code to bail out if the error is a memory error. This is because populating the aErrorClass could make a memory problem worse.

```
IF NOT (THIS.IsFatal(.T.) OR ;
   THIS.IsTrivial(.T.))

  IF THIS.OKToReport()

  THIS.LogErrorReport()

  ENDIF

  IF THIS.OKToContinue()

  THIS.UserHandlesError()

  ENDIF


ENDIF
```

The above listing accomplishes much more than it looks like. The **IF** statement calls two methods of the *_error* object, IsFatal and IsTrivial. IsFatal checks for memory, disk, program, or resource file errors. If it finds that the current error is one of these, it returns true. The IsTrivial method checks for print or lock errors and returns true if the error is one of these. If either of these methods returns false, the code inside the **IF** is not executed. If either of these methods returns false, the error is serious and the system should be shut down.

The two **IF** statements inside this outer **IF** will check if it is okay to log the error; if so, the application can continue. The two methods called, OKToReport and OKToContinue, are abstract in the *_error* class. That means they contain no code and always return true. Developers can use these methods by adding appropriate code to the methods in a subclass of *_error*.

Inside the two **IF** statements are calls to LogErrorReport and UserHandlesError methods. The LogErrorReport method records the error in the error log file. The UserHandlesError method presents the user with a dialog to allow them to decide whether to continue running the application.

Figure 22 shows a diagram of the error object and its relation to the other objects in the application.

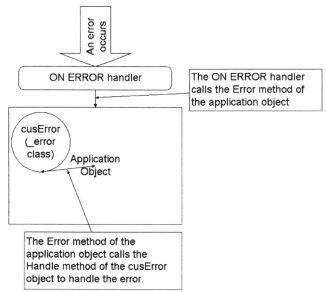

Figure 22. *Relationships during error handling.*

Extending the foundation classes

So far in this chapter, you have read about the concepts behind non-visible manager classes and application frameworks. You have examined the application framework created by the application wizard in Visual FoxPro 6.0 in some detail. You have seen forms management, reports management, menu management, security management, and error management. Regardless of whether you agree or disagree with the framework's approaches, it's good to be aware that it provides these services.

What happens if you have your own form classes that you've built over time to provide exactly what you want? Can you include forms from these classes in an application that uses the built-in framework? How about report dialogs? Can you use your own instead of the ones that are included?

The answers to these questions are the target of this section of the chapter. Here you will see a variety of ways to enhance the framework classes to make use of additional behavior and to allow the use of your own classes within the framework.

We'll examine the following mechanisms of enhancement:

- Modifying the foundation classes themselves.
- Creating your own set of subclasses that add the enhancements you want.
- Using the abstract methods (hook methods) of the foundation classes.
- Using mediator classes to facilitate interaction between your classes and the framework classes.
- Creating decorator classes to encapsulate the framework classes and provide the developer's interface you want.

In the sections that follow, you'll see some examples of modifications to the framework foundation classes using the methods in the above list. Unfortunately, space limitations preclude examining all of the possible modifications that you might want to make, so we have selected some general examples. These examples should give you a good start on making your own modifications.

Modifying the code in the class definitions

The first mechanism of modifying the framework classes is direct modification of the class code. While this mechanism is direct and easy to understand, it is the least desirable of all of the mechanisms. The downside of this approach is that when a new version of the foundation classes becomes available, you cannot simply replace the libraries and run with it. You have to redo all of your modifications before you can use any features of the newer version of the framework. Even more important, though, modifying the framework classes requires that you fully understand the implementation of each method you change. The other mechanisms for enhancing the framework require less understanding of the implementation of the behaviors.

To demonstrate this technique, we'll modify the DoForm method of the _Application_ class so it will be able to pass additional parameters to the form called. The listing below shows the code of the DoForm method, excerpted to show only the code where changes are made:

```
LPARAMETERS tcFileName,tcClass,tlNoMultipleInstances,tlNoShow, tlGoMenu,
tlNavToolbar
...

IF NOT EMPTY(lcClass)
  THIS.aForms[THIS.nFormCount] = ;
    THIS.Instantiate(lcClass, lcFileName)
ELSE
  DO FORM (lcFileName) NAME THIS.aForms[THIS.nFormCount] LINKED NOSHOW
ENDIF
...

RETURN (THIS.IsErrorFree())
```

The following listing shows the same code segments with our changes made to them:

```
LPARAMETERS tcFileName,tcClass,tlNoMultipleInstances,tlNoShow, tlGoMenu, ;
      TlNavToolbar, tcExtraParms
...

IF NOT EMPTY(lcClass)
  THIS.aForms[THIS.nFormCount] = ;
  IF EMPTY(tcExtraParms)
   THIS.Instantiate(lcClass, lcFileName)
  ELSE
   THIS.Instantiate(lcClass, lcFileName,, tcExtraParms)
  ENDIF

ELSE
  IF EMPTY(tcExtraParms)
   DO FORM (lcFileName) NAME THIS.aForms[THIS.nFormCount] LINKED NOSHOW
  ELSE
```

```
   DO FORM (lcFileName) NAME THIS.aForms[THIS.nFormCount], &tcExtraParms
LINKED NOSHOW
   ENDIF
ENDIF
...
```

```
RETURN (THIS.IsErrorFree())
```

Making this change here requires that the Instantiate method accept the parameter. How-ever, examining the Instantiate method shows that it already addresses this requirement in its fourth parameter, tcParamString. The **LPARAMETERS** line is from the Instantiate method of the _Application_ class:

```
LPARAMETERS tcClass, tcClassLib, tcClassContainerFileName, ;
    tcParamString, toParent, tcMemberName
```

The contents of tcParamString are macro-expanded to pass them on to the object being created. This is a good example of the flexibility of the framework classes. You've modified the Instantiate method without needing to modify the DoForm method because the DoForm method already had the capability you wanted.

In this particular example of modifying the framework classes directly, you did not en-counter a cascading modification—one that requires changing other methods, which in turn require changing still other methods. This is another reason that direct modification of the framework classes is a less desirable way to add features to the framework.

Subclassing the classes in the foundation class libraries

This technique, subclassing the framework classes, is better than direct modifications, though it still has it limitations. Subclassing to modify behavior requires that you have an intimate knowledge of the methods you are overriding and their functionality. You must know all of the requirements that the framework places on a particular method, or else you stand the chance of causing the framework to function incorrectly.

As an example of subclassing, we will create a subclass of the _FormMediator_ class in the _Framewk_ library. We will add this class to the _TimeAndBilling_app_ library as _My-FormMediator_.

> You might encounter a problem while editing the MyFormMediator class on your machine. This is because the VCX stores the path to the _Framewk class library. Therefore, if you installed Visual FoxPro into a different directory than we did, you'll encounter an error when you try to open the class for editing because Visual FoxPro cannot find the library. You can fix this by following these steps:
>
> 1. USE Libs\TimeAndBilling_app.vcx form the WizApp directory.
> 2. BROWSE the class library file.
> 3. Find the record with the value of _formmediator in the Class field.
> 4. Update the Classloc field to point to your Visual FoxPro installation directory.
> 5. Close the class library by issuing a USE command in the command window.

The following listing shows the code in the OutPut method of the *_FormMediator* class:

```
LOCAL loApp, llReturn

loApp = THIS.GetAppRef()

IF ISNULL(loApp)
  RETURN
ENDIF

llReturn = loApp.DoTableOutput()

loApp = .NULL.

RETURN llReturn
```

In *MyFormMediator*, you will enhance this code to check first for a custom form property to see if output is a valid option. This listing shows the code in your *MyFormMediator* class:

```
LOCAL llRet
IF VARTYPE(THISFORM.OkToOutPut) = "L"
  IF THISFORM.OkToOutPut
    llRet = DoDefault()
  ENDIF
ELSE
  llRet = DoDefault()
ENDIF
RETURN llRet
```

First, the code declares a local variable for holding the return value. It then checks to see if there is a property of the form named OkToOutPut and that it is a data type of logical. If the property exists and is logical, it calls the default code of the parent class (*_FormMediator*) if the value of the property is true. If the form property does not exist or is some other data type than logical, this method calls the default code in *_FormMediator*. In the default calls, the return value from the *_FormMediator* method is stored in the variable and eventually returned by this code to the caller.

To accomplish the modifications above, you need to know that the OutPut method of the *_FormMediator* class returns a logical value. This is not a lot of information to know about the method; however, it does show you that subclassing requires some knowledge of the parent class' implementation. Other subclassing modifications might require a great deal of knowledge of the parent class code.

Using the hook methods provided in the foundation classes

The framework class code in many places calls a "hook method" before executing the default behavior. These hook methods return a logical value. A return of false will stop the default behavior, while a return of true will allow the default to occur.

One such place is in the *_Application* class' DoForm method. A BeforeDoForm method provided in the *_Application* class has no code in it. The developer can use this BeforeDo-Form method to decide whether the DoForm operation should occur.

To prevent making modifications to the _Application_ class and therefore creating a problem if a newer version of the library becomes available, you can write the code in the Before-DoForm method of the _App_Application_ class in the _TimeAndBilling_app_ library. By writing your code in the subclass, you can then install a newer _Framewk_ library without needing to redo your code in the BeforeDoForm method.

The following listing shows some code from a possible BeforeDoForm method:

```
LPARAMETERS tcfile-
name,tcclass,tlnomultipleinstances,tlnoshow,tlgomenu,tlnavtoolbar
LOCAL llRet
llRet = .T.
IF TYPE("_screen.activeform.name") = "C"
  IF TYPE("_screen.activeform.Allownewform") = "L"
       llRet = _screen.activeform.allownewform
  ENDIF
ENDIF
IF NOT llRet
  Messagebox("The active form does not allow running other forms", ;
       0,"New form not allowed")
ENDIF

RETURN llRet
```

The first thing to notice is that, when you start to modify the BeforeDoForm method, the parameter statement is already there. This is new functionality in Visual FoxPro 6.0. If the parent class has a parameter statement, that statement automatically appears in the child class methods. You no longer need to keep looking up the parameters when working with subclasses.

The code we added to the BeforeDoForm method is simple. It checks to see if there is a currently active form; if so, it checks to see if the form has an AllowNewForm property. If it does, the code returns the value of that property. We modified our Error form from earlier in the chapter to give it the AllowNewForm property and set it to false for testing this code.

To see this behavior, you can run the application _TimeAndBilling.app_ and choose the Clients form in the QuickStart form that is displayed at startup. While the Clients form is visible, select the Error form from the Favorites menu. The Error form will run because the Clients form does not have an AllowNewForm property. If you choose the Error form on the Favorites menu again, a message box will tell you that new forms are not allowed.

Using the hook methods provided by the framework classes is a very good mechanism for altering the behavior of the framework. It is a good approach because the designer of the framework intended those methods to be used that way. As long as you are writing your code in a subclass and not making modifications to the classes in the foundation class libraries, this approach can be very useful and will not present problems for you later.

Creating decorator classes

Creating a decorator class is another good way to modify the behavior of the framework classes. As an example of this, you will see a class named _MyFormReleaseDecorator_. The purpose of this decorator is to stop the release of a form when there is an edit in progress.

To make this work, we created a subclass of the *_form* class in the *_base* library named *App_form* and placed it in the *TimeAndBilling_app* class library. To the form class, we added a property named lEditing that is logical and holds a true if an edit is in progress in the form.

Then we modified the Release method of the form class to the code in the following listing:

```
IF NOT THISFORM.MyFormReleaseDecorator.Release()
  NODEFAULT
  RETURN .F.
ENDIF
IF NOT DoDefault()
  NODEFAULT
  RETURN .F.
ENDIF
```

This code calls the MyFormReleaseDecorator before it calls the default release code of the *_form* class. If the decorator's Release method returns false, this code returns .F. after issuing a NODEFAULT to stop the release of the form. If the decorator returns true, this code goes on to call the form class' default behavior with a DoDefault(), and if the class' Release method returns false, this code issues a NODEFAULT to stop the release of the form and then returns .F.. *MyFormReleaseDecorator* is in the *TimeAndBilling_app* library as a subclass of the custom base class. To the *MyFormReleaseDecorator* class, we added a method named Release. This line of code shows the Release method of the new class:

```
RETURN NOT THISFORM.lEditing
```

This simple return statement will cause the *App_form* class' release to stop if the lEditing property is true. If the lEditing property is false, the releasing will continue in the *_form* class code.

The last thing we did was to add an instance of *MyFormReleaseDecorator* to the *App_form* class and changed its name from MyFormReleaseDecorator1 to MyFormReleaseDecorator, without the "1" on the end.

You could now create forms within the application using the *App_form* class and get the behavior of disallowing release when the lEditing property is true.

This simple example of a decorator class shows you the mechanism involved. You can create decorators for almost anything you like. Using decorators is a good way to enhance the functionality of the framework. One advantage of this method is that you aren't making any changes to the framework classes themselves, thereby leaving them easy to update with new versions.

Creating mediator classes

A decorator is different from a mediator in that the decorator does not have a two-way conversation between objects. A decorator simply alters the behavior of one class alone. In the next example, we'll use a mediator class to modify the framework behavior.

For a mediator example, let's return to the *MyFormMediator* class we created earlier. The first thing you need to do is to get the framework to use the new *MyFormMediator*. To do so, change two properties in the *app_Application* class in the *TimeAndBilling_app* class library. **Figure 23** shows the change made to the cMediatorClass and cMediatorClassLib properties.

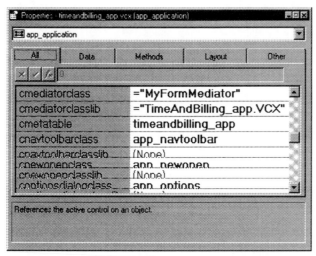

Figure 23*. The property sheet for the app_Application class showing the changes made to the cMediatorClass and the cMediatorClassLib properties.*

Let's focus on the first two properties in Figure 23. The cMediatorClass holds the name of the mediator class to use as a form mediator, and the cMediatorClassLib holds the name of the class library that contains the cMediatorClass class.

By making the above changes, the application will now use your form mediator instead of the default mediator for all forms launched. You can now modify the behavior of *MyFormMediator* as you like, and all forms in the application will gain the new behavior.

Using mediators is another effective mechanism for modifying the behavior of the framework. The real advantage of using mediators is that the mediator is already part of the framework design. You only need to subclass it and alter the behavior. In other situations, you might actually be adding a mediator in a place where the framework doesn't have one. In these situations, you only need to deal with the mediator and the class that uses it. There is no need to modify the framework, because the mediator only calls the framework methods and doesn't need to be called by those methods. The framework doesn't need to even know that the mediator is there. The object using the mediator calls the mediator, and the mediator, in turn, calls the framework. Whatever value is returned by the framework is simply returned back to the object using the mediator.

By using mediators, you can even create objects that work well in different frameworks. You can do this by writing code in the mediator that figures out which framework it is running in and makes the appropriate framework calls. The objects using the mediator don't even know which framework they are running in.

Summary

In the first section of this chapter, you saw the abstract concepts of non-visible manager objects. You examined the idea of the application framework acting like the frame of the application, upon which you hang your forms, menus, reports, and other components. The framework, through its manager objects, handles the housekeeping issues and provides services to the other components.

Programming to interface may be new to you. In this chapter, you saw that there are very powerful benefits to using this approach to system design because it allows you to use interchangeable components much more easily. Since you program to the interface, which is composed of methods, their parameters, and the properties of the various classes, you can swap components at will as long as each component expects and honors the same interface. Because the framework provides a standard interface for all components, creating interchangeable classes is easy.

By following the program-to-interface principle, you also allow the evolution of both the framework and the components without negative effects on the other. If you enhance the behavior of the framework, but maintain the same interface to components, the existing components will get the enhanced behavior without you altering their code. The same is true for modifying the components, as long as you maintain the interface design. *Programming to interface is the most important lesson in this chapter.*

You took a tour of the Visual FoxPro 6.0 Application Wizard and Builder. The wizard created a framework for an application and the builder allowed you to add components to that framework.

The framework created by the wizard was used as the example for seeing all of the various non-visible manager classes. You examined the framework to see each of the manager objects described in the opening section.

To pull together all of the manager classes, see **Figure 24**.

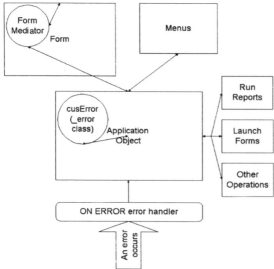

Figure 24. The big picture of the Visual FoxPro 6.0 application framework.

In Figure 24, you can see all of the manager operations together. This diagram is a composite of the diagrams you saw in the individual discussions of each manager operation. You can see that the application object is at the center of all activity in the framework. Every other component in the system uses the application object to provide the services it needs. This centralized control allows the framework to handle the entire housekeeping of the system because it is aware of everything that happens.

The application object knows about every form that exists, and every menu and toolbar created. It is aware of all errors that occur and the environment in which they occur. The application object knows what data session the forms are using, it can determine the status of any data session, and the tables open there. Essentially, the application object is the "grand poohbah" of everything that happens inside the system.

In the last section of this chapter, you saw a number of methods for making modifications to the framework. In the examples, you saw new behaviors introduced, and existing behaviors changed.

You also saw that some methods of modifying the behavior of the framework are more desirable. Modifying the classes in the framework library was the least desirable of the four methods shown: direct modification of the framework classes, subclassing, decorator classes, and mediator classes.

You may choose to use the framework created by the application wizard for your work, you may choose to create your own framework, or you may use a third-party framework. Regardless, the contents of this chapter should give you a head start on understanding the nature and design of an application framework.

Chapter 14
Developer Tools

Any craftsman's output can be improved by having good tools at hand. The Visual Fox-Pro development environment includes some very good tools. There are times, however, when the developer needs something more than what comes in the box. When that time comes, you can draw upon many of the third-party products available, or even whip up your own tool on the spot. This chapter looks at the tools that have helped make me a better, more productive developer.

Tips for effective use of the native VFP developer tools

Before FoxPro 2.0, developer tools were almost entirely third-party tools. Code generators and documentation utilities for the various Xbase variants were common. The only alternatives were those that individual developers created for themselves. The most common were some variant of a screen or report "painter" that would allow the developer to lay out data-entry screens or reports, then automatically generate the code to reproduce it. FoxPro 2.0 introduced the idea of storing the specifications for screens, menus, reports, labels and the entire project in FoxPro tables. Along with that idea was introduced a set of tools for visually designing and managing program elements by interacting with these meta tables—the Project Manager, Report Writer, Screen Builder, and Menu Builder. These tools had become, for the most part, ones that most of us could use as our primary development environment.

Visual FoxPro 3.0, with some minor name changes, continued to make these tools available. However, the native VFP 3.0 tools lacked some important capabilities, most notably in the Form Designer. As a result, many developers and third-party tool vendors immediately cobbled up some tools to speed form design and layout in particular. VFP 3.0 also provided two new tools: the Class Designer, to allow visual creation of the object classes introduced with VFP 3.0; and the Class Browser, which provided some additional class library management capabilities.

Visual FoxPro 5.0 corrected many of the omissions of VFP 3.0. Features that made it easier to lay out form elements, and to simultaneously set the properties of multiple controls, pretty much eliminated the need for home-grown and third-party tools that had been used to provide these capabilities in VFP 3.0. The VFP 5.0 code editor introduced some significant features, including syntax coloring and the ability to execute a block of code from within the editor. Visual FoxPro 5.0 also introduced a wonderful set of debugging tools that we'll examine in detail later in this chapter.

Visual FoxPro 6.0 expands on the Class Browser to include functionality that Microsoft terms a "Component Gallery." This functionality frees the developer from categorizing components only by where they are stored, and allows us instead to group them by function. VFP 6.0 also introduces a new debugging tool, the Coverage Profiler.

Anyone moderately experienced with Visual FoxPro is usually fairly comfortable with the native Visual FoxPro design tools, so I shan't waste a lot of time and space to recap their use. However, I would like to touch on a few techniques that I've either been slow to adopt, and wondered afterward, "Why haven't I been doing this all along?" or techniques I've discovered on my own that you may find useful.

The next section discusses creating your own development tools, and the chapter closes with a discussion of commercial third-party tools.

The project manager — use for file and class management

Most components of a project are not represented by a single file. Because the project "meta-data" is stored as Visual FoxPro tables, each table has an accompanying memo file. The actual data, too, consists of multiple files on disk for each entity listed under the data heading in the Project Manager. Thus, when you select a program element you are selecting all files that "contribute" to that element. For instance, when selecting a form, you are selecting both the .SCX and the .SCT memo file. If you select a database container, you're selecting the .DBC, .DCT and .DCX files that together make up the database container. If you right-click on an item listed in the Project Manager and select "Rename," you will rename all files associated with that entity. Contrast this with doing the same thing in Windows Explorer, where you re-name each file individually. You then have to deal with the error that occurs when you try to open the project and it can't find the original file. Similarly, clicking the "Remove" button in the Project Manager acts on all files associated with the selected item. If we respond to the "Remove from project or delete from disk?" message box by requesting the "Delete" option, all related files are deleted, and the reference to the deleted element is removed from the Project Manager.

There is a potential trap in renaming a class library. When adding a class instance to a form, subclassing a class, or including a class in a composite class, the class library that contains the class is included along with the class name. Consequently, renaming the class could make a class or form that uses a class contained in the renamed class library inoperable. Fortunately, the Project Manager issues a warning to this effect when renaming a class library. Unfortunately, neither the Project Manager nor the Class Browser is so helpful when renaming a *class*, so you must exercise due care when renaming classes. In fact, you can hose yourself up very nicely by renaming object classes. The Class Browser seems to attempt to resolve references to a class within the same class library, but in the current VFP 6.0 build I'm working with, it seems to be broken. It successfully changes the class name in the reference, but has a problem with the classlib reference. Don't despair if you get into trouble when changing class names, or the location or names of class libraries. A utility discussed later in this chapter (in the section on creating your own developer tools) will save the day.

Along with "Menus" and "Text Files," there is an "Other files" group listed under the "Other" tab in the Project Manager. This is often used for .BMP or .ICO files that you want to include in the project. However, you can also list other files that you want to access easily from within the VFP IDE. These might include a Visio class diagram, a "to-do" list in a Word .DOC file, or a vendor's documentation in an HTML Help (.CHM) file (.HLP-style help files apparently can't be opened via the Project Manager).

You can use the Class Browser (discussed later) to move or copy a class from one class library to another. However, I only just recently realized that dragging and dropping a class from one classlib to another *in the project manager* will *copy* the class. This is handy when you want to modify a class but don't want to experiment with your production class. You can copy it to another classlib to play around with it.

Form Designer tricks

Layout tricks

One Form Designer trick was completely unknown to me until a "newbie"—who'd only been using the Form Designer for a few months—showed me something he'd discovered. (Probably through something arcane, like reading the documentation! I don't know about you, but the longer I use a tool, the less inclined I am to dig into the help file and online docs. Big mistake.) The Form Layout toolbar has three buttons that size the selected controls to the same height or width or both. These buttons use the largest control as the "reference" in this operation. As a result, I relied on the menu options, which offer the choice of using the largest or smallest as the reference control, until this fellow showed me that pressing the Ctrl key when clicking the toolbar button would size all of the selected controls to the *smallest* control in the group. Clicking on any of the alignment buttons to align top, bottom, left or right edges will align the controls using the topmost, bottommost, leftmost or rightmost control, respectively, as a reference. However, the Ctrl key again will alter the behavior of these buttons. Holding the Ctrl key and clicking on the "Align Right Edges" button will align the right edges but use the leftmost object as a reference.

Another formatting trick is to rely on the Form Layout toolbar buttons that align the control centers. I can never keep straight the two menu prompts for aligning centers ("Align horizontal centers" and "Align vertical centers"). No sooner do I think I've got it straight, than I select the wrong one. The trouble is that the menu prompts are just plain wrong. They should be either reversed from their actual actions, or read "Align horizontal centers vertically" and "Align vertical centers horizontally." The good news is that the pictures on the Form Layout toolbar buttons are hard to screw up. A frustrating behavior of these layout commands is that the controls will both be moved to a common center. I often want to align the center of Control A with the center of Control B, leaving Control B in its current position. The trick to getting this behavior is to align the controls' edges first, and then align their centers.

Instantiation order

The formatting options of "Bring to front" and "Send to back" are commonly used to determine which control is visually "in front of" another control. This permits placing a shape on a form on top of a label, then using the "Send to back" to move the shape behind the label so the label is visible. However, what you may not realize is that this formatting option works by changing the instantiation order of the controls. If you examine the form's .SCX file, you'll see that the order of the controls manipulated with "Bring to front" or "Send to back" is actually moved from one record to another to accomplish this. Normally the order in which controls are added to a form determines instantiation order. We can manipulate the tab order of the controls independently by using the TabIndex property, or interactively using the tab-ordering tools. However, this has no effect on the instantiation order of the controls.

This seems like a piece of trivial knowledge until you have two controls that need to be instantiated in a particular order. You'll find that using "Bring to front" and "Send to back" will allow you to fiddle with the instantiation order without being forced to remove and re-add the controls.

> My ever-vigilant technical editor raised an interesting question with regard to instantiation order. If you have a situation in which the instantiation order of controls is critical, doesn't this imply very tight coupling between the controls? As discussed in the chapter on forms, tight coupling is usually something to be avoided.
>
> The thing to remember is that the issue of tight coupling is best viewed in the context of reusability. A loosely coupled object is more self-sufficient and less sensitive to the environment in which it is used. This is of concern when we are creating a reusable object class. Once we are working with a form instance, the issue of reusability is no longer of concern. We know the environment in which we are operating, and can write code that is customized to that environment. This is true also in composite reusable classes. Each object can be tightly coupled with other objects within the composite class, because their encapsulation within a single container object ensures that whatever environment we require is being provided by the composite class.
>
> Instantiation order can also be critical to actually implementing loosely coupled objects. Consider an object that "registers" itself with a form when it is instantiated, storing a reference to itself to a form property. An object might do this to make it easier for it to receive messages from the form or other objects, which can reference the form property rather than relying on the name of the first object. Another object may need to communicate with the first, and needs to do so when its Init() code executes. The second class might be very loosely coupled, being able to perform some default behavior in the event that the first object does not exist. However, to realize the full benefit of the cooperation between the two objects, Object A must instantiate (and register itself) before Object B, so that Object B can send a message to Object A when it instantiates.
>
> Bottom line is that the "loose coupling" issue is indeed important with reusable objects, but tight coupling is expected in form and object instances and in the design of composite objects.

Form (.SCX) file corruption

There is a bug that has existed in the Form Designer ever since Visual FoxPro 3.0. Folks at Microsoft have observed this bug, so it isn't entirely in the imagination of those of us who have encountered it in the field. The reason it hasn't been corrected is that no one can consistently reproduce it. Don't you hate those? Anyway, this bug has bitten me a half-dozen times over the years. It wasn't until I had a co-worker who encountered this one on a regular basis that I stumbled on what appears to be a fix.

The behavior in question is the actual *swapping* of method code. The code you placed in method A will suddenly appear in method B, and vice-versa. The most common place this seems to occur is between the BeforeOpenTables and AfterCloseTables event methods of the Data Environment. However, I've seen one case in which the entire set of form-level methods was scrambled. Although it takes a while to figure out why your form is blowing up in your face, it isn't too big a deal to move stuff around and put it back where it belongs. The frustrating thing is that the next time you edit and run the form, it'll move the method code around *again*! If you examine the .SCX table, you'll see that the form source code is all stored in a single Methods memo field. When the Form Designer closes this file, the source code in the Methods field is compiled to pseudo-code and placed in the ObjCode memo field. This problem appears to involve something that actually takes the code from between one PROCEDURE...ENDPROC and moves it to another. How can this be?

The answer (I think) is that, contrary to our expectations, it is not a one-way relationship between the Methods field and the ObjCode field. To illustrate this, create a form, place some code in one of the methods, then close and save the form. Open the .SCX table, and examine the record representing the form (usually the third record—you'll see "form" in the Baseclass field). You'll see the code you just placed into the form method. Examine the Objcode field, and you'll see some gobbledygook that represents the compiled version of the code. While you're looking at ObjCode field, erase it—select the entire contents of the memo and hit the <Delete> key! Now, close the table and reopen the form in the Form Designer and examine the method into which you placed some code. It's empty, even though you didn't touch the contents of the Methods field. To verify that you didn't erase the wrong field, reopen the .SCX table and look at the Methods field. The code is still there, isn't it?

This leads to the fix I've discovered for the swapping-methods behavior. Open the form's .SCX file as a table, REPLACE ALL ObjCode WITH "", close the table, and then issue the command COMPILE FORM <formname>. This will remove all the object code and force Visual FoxPro to recompile all of the code in the Methods field. So far, this seems to do the trick. By the way, this trick also seems to be a generic solution for forms that seem to be "corrupted." I've had forms that the Form Designer refused to open. Purging the ObjCode fields and recompiling has on several occasions restored these forms to a usable condition.

The Class Browser

The Class Browser brings an important dimension to managing object classes and class libraries. The Project Manager displays a list of all classes contained in any class library included in the project. The class hierarchy to which a class belongs, and where the class fits into this hierarchy, is an important piece of information missing from this display. When confronted with a complex set of class libraries, whether your own or those for a framework that may be unfamiliar to you, the Class Browser is indispensable for coming to grips with the class structure.

If you examine a class library using the Class Browser, and one of the classes is subclassed from a class contained in another class library, this is indicated by the chevron character («). If you open the class library containing the parent class using the View Additional File button, the Class Browser inserts the class into the class hierarchy. **Figures 1** and **2** illustrate this.

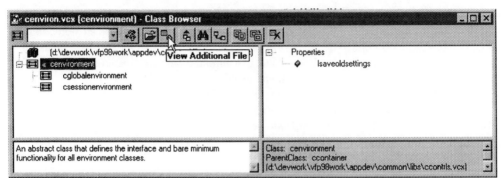

Figure 1. *The Class Browser showing the cEnvironment class in the CENVIRON.VCX class library. This class is subclassed from the cContainer class contained in the CCONTRLS.VCX class library. Note the View Additional File button.*

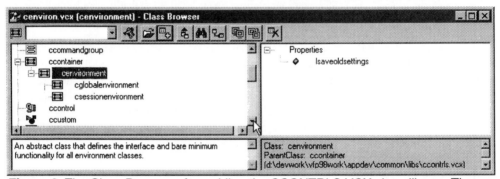

Figure 2. *The Class Browser after adding the CCONTRLS.VCX class library. The chevron character no longer appears next to the cEnvironment class. Instead, the cEnvironment class is shown as subclassed from cContainer.*

Another important feature of the Class Browser is allowing redefinition of a class or form. Occasionally I'll spend considerable time creating a class or form subclassed from class B and decide later that it should be subclassed instead from class A. The Class Browser allows me to change the parent class, provided that it's descended from the same baseclass object—you can't redefine an object subclassed from a custom control as a text box. Should this kind of redefinition be necessary, I've found that it can be accomplished using the HackVCX.APP tool discussed later.

The VFP documentation describes using the Class Browser to *copy* classes from one class library to another. The documentation's instructions as of this writing are incorrect. If you select a class in the Class Browser, drag the class icon that appears just to the left of the Class Type combo box and drop it on a second instance of the Class Browser, displaying a different class library will move the class from one classlib to another. To copy a class, press the Ctrl key before clicking on the class icon. This feature of the Class Browser is super for effectively organizing your class libraries.

You can rename methods in both the Class Browser and in the new Property/Method dialog. However, beware of doing so. If you have a subclass that uses this method, the method code in the subclass gets "lost" in the process of renaming the class.

Some of the things you can do in the Class Browser, such as renaming a class, or moving a class from one classlib to another, can cause a problem with forms that use those classes. The Class Browser can open form (.SCX) files as well as class libraries. If you have a class that you want to rename or move, load the forms that use that class into the Class Browser along with the classlib containing the class. When the class is renamed or moved, the Class Browser will update the references to that class in all the loaded forms.

The Report Designer—gaining printer independence

The Report Designer is a fairly straightforward tool, and hasn't changed significantly since FoxPro 2.5. I've never considered myself much of a report-writing whiz, but I have discovered something that is probably worth passing along.

If you create an application that involves report printing (and who doesn't?), you probably give the user some means of selecting a printer to use to produce the report. One of the easiest ways is to prompt the user for a destination printer using the GETPRINTER() function, then place the user's selection into a SET PRINTER TO NAME <printer name> prior to running the report. An alternative that provides more control over printing options is to use the SYS(1037) function that invokes the Printer Setup dialog. Either approach will work fine in your development environment. You can redirect a report to any printer installed on your workstation, both local and networked.

The problems start when your client or user tries to direct a report to a printer installed on *their* workstation. Often, no matter what they do, it'll end up going to whatever printer they have installed as their default printer. What the heck is going on?

As you might be aware, the Report Designer stores information in the report file about your currently selected printer when you create a report. This information is found in the first record of the .FRX table, in the Expr, Tag1 and Tag2 fields. An example is shown in **Figure 3**.

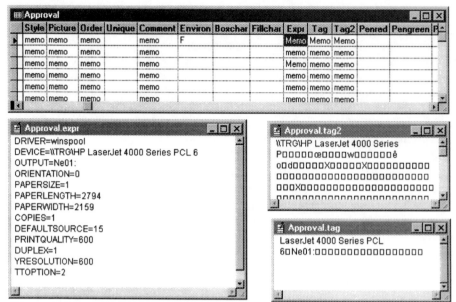

Figure 3. *The contents of the first-record Expr, Tag1 and Tag2 fields in a report's .FRX file. Note all of the information about the currently selected printer that is stored in these fields.*

Visual FoxPro will indeed respect the user's selection of a report destination made using SET PRINTER TO NAME or SYS(1037), but only if the printer specified in the report file is installed on the user's system. If the specified printer is not installed, output is always directed to the default printer. The way around this problem is to remove all information contained in these three fields before the reports are compiled into your application. Once this is done, the user is free to direct output to any installed printer.

As usual, there is more than one way to skin a cat. Some developers make a practice of installing report files as free-standing tables rather than compiling them into the application. Developers who follow this practice will often directly manipulate the contents of the EXPR field to change the selected printer, the number of copies, output trays, and so on. This is often accomplished through the printer control options of the COMMDLG control. If you require this level of control but still want to distribute canned reports compiled into the application, there is a middle ground. Any table (including power-tool meta tables like the form .SCX files and the report .FRX files) that are compiled into an application can't be modified, but can be USEd, and COPY TO'd. Thus you can USE an .FRX file, COPY TO <temporary path and filename.FRX>, manipulate the contents of the Expr field, issue the command REPORT FORM <temporary path and filename.FRX> and then erase the temporary file.

This report and printer behavior is observed with VFP 3.0, 5.0 and 6.0 under Windows 3.1, 3.11 and Windows 95 and NT 4.0. I haven't yet tested this under Windows 98, but would expect to see the same problem.

Over the years I've often watched developers struggle with reports that involve complex relations between parent and child tables. I've found that the easiest way to create reports is to run a query or open a view that creates a single, highly denormalized table. Don't be concerned that the customer name and address appears on all 246 records when you only want it to appear in the header. If you place the customer name in the header or footer band, that's the only place it will appear. All the grouping and aggregating functions of the Report Designer work just fine, and in fact, you'll have better luck getting consistent results and behavior by creating a single result set on which to base your reports.

The reason this works so well is that you can separate the creation of the result set from its visual representation. You are able to concentrate on getting a set of records that contain all the information you want to appear on the report, and in the order you want them to appear, and then concentrate on layout. With a good result set in hand, you can then concentrate on aggregating, grouping and laying out the information within the Report Designer.

The Visual FoxPro editor

With VFP 5.0 we finally got some cool editor features. I won't belabor them here—just right-clicking in the Editor window and playing with each of the options is all you really need to do. Beautify works quite well (although it hoses up my carefully formatted SQL statements), and is nice in a multi-programmer shop where half the developers prefer tabs and the other half prefer spaces for indenting. The Beautify option allows you to switch code blocks back and forth between the two indenting methods. Another new feature introduced in VFP 6.0 is the ability to set a breakpoint directly in the editor via the Context menu.

I think that many developers overlook the power of the syntax coloring options in the VFP editor. **Figure 4** is a screen shot of a code snippet in my editor. Even in black-and-white, you can easily distinguish the various elements of this code, although the background for the literals and strings look to be the same. **Table 1** shows the settings I use.

Table 1. My syntax color settings.

Element	Background	Foreground	Style
Comments	yellow	black	bold italic
Keywords	white	blue	bold
Literals	cyan	black	normal
Operators	white	red	bold
Strings	light gray	black	normal
Variables	white	black	normal

The bright yellow contrasting background, together with the black bold italic foreground on comments makes them jump right off the screen. The contrasting background on the literals and strings makes them easy to spot, too. This also has the added benefit of helping to spot mismatched string delimiters. Try these settings (or something similar) for a session or two, and I think you might be surprised how much more effective you are, particularly in complex chunks of code. You might want to change some of the colors—many dislike the cyan, but the specific colors are less important than the contrast they lend to different code elements. If you can come up with a color scheme that allows you to stand too far from the monitor to be able to read it, but still identify the operators, strings, literals, keywords, variables and comments, you've got a good color scheme.

Figure 4. *Be bold in getting some contrast into your code—use contrasting background colors so you can identify code elements from across the room.*

VFP debugging tools

Being able to decide what information you need and the ability to collect that information is the lifeblood of effective debugging. Toward this end, Visual FoxPro 5.0 finally gave us some serious debugging tools. The equivalent to the Watch window and the Trace window are all we had in VFP 3.0 and earlier. Both tools are much improved in VFP 5.0 and later, and are joined by some new tools and features that make debugging easier.

The debugging tools are available in two environments, selectable from the Tools|Options|Debug dialog. One is a "Debug Frame," in which the entire suite of debugging windows are made available using a top-level form that exists outside the Visual FoxPro desktop. The other is the "FoxPro Frame," in which individual debugging windows can be opened as needed and kept visible on the Visual FoxPro desktop while you run your code, do stuff at the Command window, or interact with a form. For what it's worth, I personally have no use for the "Debug Frame" option. I seldom need all of the windows at the same time, and if I can't watch or interact with my app and watch the debugging tools at the same time without Alt-Tabbing, then I'm not happy. There is one capability that comes along with the Debug Frame, and that is the ability to save and reload a configuration—a set of breakpoints and watch values. This is available only from the Debugging menu, which is part of the Debug

Frame. Should I ever need this capability, I will likely temporarily switch to a Debug Frame, load or save the configuration, and then switch back to the FoxPro Frame.

Watch window

Enter a value and watch it change. Set a breakpoint on its change. What could be simpler? Don't forget that you can *change* the value of a memvar or field in the Watch window. Also remember that you can drag and drop expressions from the Trace window or a code window into the Watch window. I always have a reference to _SCREEN.ActiveForm in the Watch window.

Trace window

There is nothing so illuminating as watching your code execute line-by-line. How many times have you had some piece of code that continues to misbehave, even after several cycles of tweak-run-tweak-run? Many times I've finally traced the code and *immediately* seen the error! Visual FoxPro's Trace window has some wonderful features, including the ability to place the mouse pointer over a variable or field and some simple expressions, and see the value. No need to place the variable or field name in the Watch window. It's a big time-saver to be able to execute, without actually stepping through a user-defined function or another procedure called from the routine we are tracing, by selecting "Step Over" from the Debugger toolbar or the Context menu. Likewise, it saves time to be able to "Step Out" of a procedure or function that we are reasonably sure is working as expected, so we can "cut to the chase" and get back to the calling routine.

One of my favorite execution options in the Trace window is the "Run to Cursor" option. You can scroll the Trace window and set a breakpoint, but you can also simply click the mouse pointer to place the blinking cursor on a line of code, then select the "Run to Cursor" option. Execution will continue until the indicated line is encountered, just like setting a breakpoint. This is useful for zipping through a FOR/NEXT or WHILE loop when you're only interested in the results of the loop rather than watching it run through each iteration of the loop.

It took me a long time to notice one feature of the Trace window. By right-clicking to bring up the Context menu, I can load a .PRG file and then use the execution options (Step Into, Run to Cursor, and so on) to immediately begin tracing the code. No need to set breakpoints. Unfortunately, you can't do the same with forms or objects.

Locals window

This window lists all objects and variables that are scoped to the currently executing procedure. At first, given the ability to just wave the mouse pointer over a memvar in the Trace window, the Locals window doesn't seem to be particularly useful. However, what's local? Most experienced FoxPro developers are very conscious of variable scope, but you will occasionally forget to declare a memvar local, and this'll bite ya in the butt. Looking at the Locals window, you'll see that a memvar has a value before it should, because it's not local to the calling routine, but PRIVATE—therefore, it's visible to the called routine.

The Locals window is also always there, so when you want to check a memvar or object that you forgot to place into the Watch window, you can just check the Locals window. When working at the Command window, too, particularly when creating objects and arrays, the Locals window is a real help.

As with the Watch window, you can change the value of a variable or field in the Locals window, but unlike the Watch window, you can't set a breakpoint.

Call Stack window

Using the Trace, Locals and Call Stack windows together puts an incredible amount of power in the developer's hands to examine every aspect of an executing program. The Call Stack window can help debug a complex situation, such as a form with methods that call other methods. I'm sometimes puzzled as to why a certain method is being called under certain circumstances, or uncertain which of several possible calls to a particular method is the one that got me where I am.

Figures 5 and **6** show just how powerful these three debugging tools can be. I set a breakpoint on the Requery() method of the example Time Card form used in Chapter 5. If you'll recall, this method was called through a cascade of events started with the change in a combo box. As you can see from Figure 5, the Call Stack window shows the entire chain of four methods that were followed to get to the Requery() method. The Locals window shows the currently scoped memvars (only the Time Card form), and the Trace window shows the currently executing code.

Figure 6 shows the same debugging session, but I've selected the next method up the calling stack, the uKeyValue_Assign method (note the • symbol to indicate the currently selected routine). The Trace window changes to show this code snippet and the Locals window changes to show the variables scoped to this piece of code. In this case there is only one memvar declared and in use, vNewVal. Note that the "fly-over" value display works only in the currently executing routine. You must rely on the Locals window to check the values of memvars in routines other than the one currently executing.

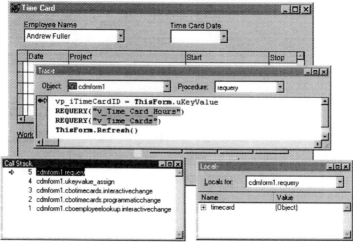

Figure 5. Tracing the Requery() method of the Time Card form discussed in Chapter 5. Note the position of the pointers in the Call Stack and Trace windows, and the contents of the Locals window.

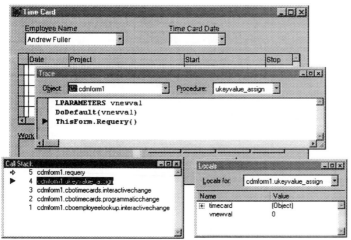

Figure 6. *Tracing the Requery() method of the Time Card form discussed in Chapter 5. Here I've selected the uKeyValue_Assign() method in the Call Stack window. Note how the code displayed in the Trace window and the contents of the Locals window have changed to display code and memvars scoped to the currently selected routine.*

Breakpoints dialog

Those of us who are slow learners have used (for far too long) the old techniques of setting breakpoints in the Trace and Watch windows. This will automatically add the breakpoints in the Breakpoints dialog. However, the Breakpoints dialog is much more flexible and efficient. You can easily set a breakpoint on a combination of conditions. As shown in **Figure 7**, using the Time Card form again, I can set a breakpoint for the Requery() method, but specifically for the TimeCard.SCX object, so that another object's Requery() method doesn't trigger the breakpoint. I can also set the breakpoint so that the execution is suspended only when the uKeyValue property is 3. Setting a breakpoint on a particular line of code in the editor or the Trace window will trigger the break every time that line of code is executed. The Breakpoints dialog will allow you to specify how many times the line of code is executed before triggering the suspension of execution, by using the Pass Count setting. You might be able to achieve these results by setting a breakpoint on a properly constructed expression in the Watch window, but the Breakpoints dialog is much easier. The Breakpoints dialog also allows you to establish a breakpoint and then enable or disable it as needed.

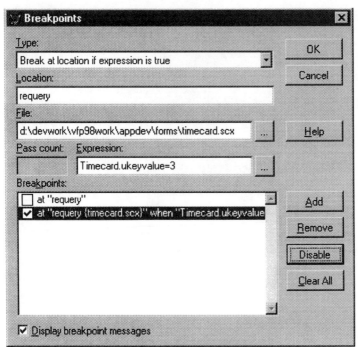

Figure 7. The Breakpoints dialog, showing a complex breakpoint condition—a combination of object, method and variable values.

Output window and Event Tracking

For years I've peppered my code with WAIT WINDOWs to identify when certain code segments are executing. The Output window and the DEBUGOUT command provide a little more flexibility when actually outputting variable, field or property values because you don't have to convert the values to the character data type as you do when using WAIT WINDOWs.

As I've climbed the Visual FoxPro learning curve, I've struggled with understanding the exact order in which events occur. Often events occur in an order that is contrary to what I might expect, and this misunderstanding can lead to some difficult debugging sessions. In Visual FoxPro 3.0, all we had to use was code in each event method that reported when it was being triggered. To address this problem I created a testbed form with special methods and properties for reporting on event firing.

VFP 5.0 introduced the Event Tracking feature. This tool reports the firing of selected events to the Output window. A little time spent with the Event Tracking dialog to confirm or clarify your understanding of the order in which events fire, or exactly when certain events fire, can save a lot of time when writing event-dependent code. When tracking a large number of events, it may be more appropriate to use the option of directing Event Tracking output to a file. **Figure 8** shows the Event Tracking dialog with several events selected. The results from launching the Time Card form with these settings are shown in **Figure 9**.

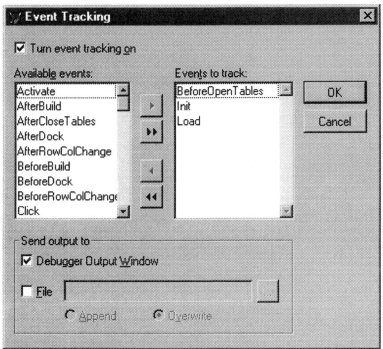

Figure 8. *The Event Tracking dialog. The BeforeOpenTables, Load and Init events have been selected for tracking.*

```
Debug Output
cdmform1.Load()
cdmform1.txtdate.Init()
cdmform1.cboemployee.Init()
cdmform1.dataenvironment.cursor2.Init()
cdmform1.dataenvironment.cursor4.Init()
cdmform1.dataenvironment.cursor3.Init()
cdmform1.dataenvironment.cursor1.Init()
cdmform1.dataenvironment.Init()
cdmform1.grdv_time_card_hours.column1.header1.Init()
cdmform1.grdv_time_card_hours.column1.text1.Init()
cdmform1.grdv_time_card_hours.column1.Init()
cdmform1.grdv_time_card_hours.column2.header1.Init()
cdmform1.grdv_time_card_hours.column2.cboprojects1.Init()
cdmform1.grdv_time_card_hours.column2.Init()
cdmform1.grdv_time_card_hours.column4.header1.Init()
cdmform1.grdv_time_card_hours.column4.text1.Init()
cdmform1.grdv_time_card_hours.column4.Init()
cdmform1.grdv_time_card_hours.column5.header1.Init()
cdmform1.grdv_time_card_hours.column5.text1.Init()
cdmform1.grdv_time_card_hours.column5.Init()
cdmform1.grdv_time_card_hours.column6.header1.Init()
cdmform1.grdv_time_card_hours.column6.cboworkcodes1.Init()
cdmform1.grdv_time_card_hours.column6.Init()
cdmform1.grdv_time_card_hours.column7.header1.Init()
cdmform1.grdv_time_card_hours.column7.text1.Init()
cdmform1.grdv_time_card_hours.column7.Init()
cdmform1.grdv_time_card_hours.column8.header1.Init()
cdmform1.grdv_time_card_hours.column8.text1.Init()
cdmform1.grdv_time_card_hours.column8.Init()
cdmform1.grdv_time_card_hours.Init()
cdmform1.lblcfullname.Init()
cdmform1.cboemployeelookup.Init()
cdmform1.cbotimecards.Init()
cdmform1.edtmworkdescription.Init()
cdmform1.lblmworkdescription.Init()
cdmform1.cmdadd.Init()
cdmform1.cmdcancel.Init()
cdmform1.cmdsave.Init()
cdmform1.cmddelete.Init()
cdmform1.cmdclose.Init()
cdmform1.csessionenvironment1.clabel1.Init()
cdmform1.csessionenvironment1.Init()
cdmform1.label1.Init()
cdmform1.Init()
```

Figure 9. The Debug Output window showing the results of opening the Time Card form with Event Tracking turned on.

Coverage Logging

If you ever have an unidentified performance bottleneck in an application, Coverage Logging may help you track it down. Coverage Logging allows you to specify a log file to which program execution information is written. You can specify the log file by issuing the SET COVERAGE TO command or by clicking on the "Toggle Coverage Logging" button in the Debugger toolbar. With Coverage Logging turned on, information on execution of any program elements is output to the specified log file. The file stores this information in a comma-delimited text format. VFP 6.0 added an additional sixth column to this output, the "Call Stack Level," which was not included in the output in VFP 5.0. **Table 2** shows the contents of a coverage log file, but abbreviates the filename to exclude the file path, which is normally included.

Table 2. *Contents of a Coverage Log file.*

Duration	Class	Procedure	Line	File	Call Stack Level
0.000	Cboemployees	Cboemployees.init	1	chap5.vct	2
0.080	Cboprojects	Cboprojects.init	1	chap5.vct	2
0.000	Cboprojects	Cboprojects.requery	3	chap5.vct	3
0.000	Cboprojects	Cboprojects.requery	5	chap5.vct	3
0.000	Cboprojects	Cboprojects.requery	9	chap5.vct	3
0.010	Cboprojects	Cboprojects.requery	12	chap5.vct	3

As you can see, cboProjects.Init() takes 80 milliseconds to execute, and line 12 of cbo-Projects.Requery() takes 10 milliseconds to execute. The other logged events take less than a millisecond to execute. This kind of information makes it easy to spot which lines of code are slowing things down.

Coverage Profiler

VFP 6.0 introduces a coverage profiler, invoked by selecting "Coverage Profiler" from the Tools menu. In order to use it, you must first produce a coverage log file. The Coverage Profiler takes this log file and does some very interesting analysis with it. Not only does it show the lines of code executed along with their execution times, but also how many times each line of code is executed. This is great for spotting the control that is being refreshed 1,746 times for every KeyPress. **Figure 10** shows the Coverage Profiler in use.

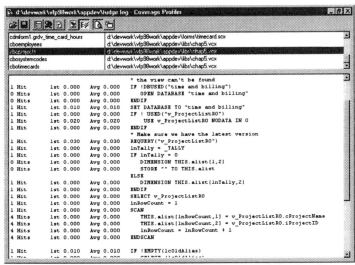

Figure 10. *The Coverage Profiler's analysis of the log file created while running TimeCard.SCX. Note the lines of code that show 0 hits, and the lines within the SCAN...ENDSCAN loop that are executed four times each. Note also that the profiler shows not only the time to execute the line of code the first time, but the average execution time when there are multiple hits.*

Microsoft has given Visual FoxPro developers more debugging horsepower than we've ever had. For more ideas about how to put these tools to use see the Debugging appendix.

One final note on debugging tools doesn't relate to a tool at all, but is something to stand up and cheer about. I'm sure we've all been faced with the Access Violation or Illegal Operation error that brings our app crashing down around our ears. Until VFP 6.0 you were forced to step through your code one line at a time until you could spot the line of code that was triggering the error. I'll discuss ways to attack this particular problem in Appendix Five. However, in VFP 6.0 Microsoft has given us a new error message box that is raised when an access violation or illegal operation occurs. This message box identifies the module and line number where the error was triggered. We can't trap this information in an error log file as we can other errors. However, if this information can be noted during development or in production, it can save a lot of work in tracking down and correcting the problem.

Roll-your-own tools

No matter how powerful the tools that come in the box, there are always times when we need or want something a little extra. Visual FoxPro stores much of the "source code" we create in FoxPro tables. Since working with FoxPro tables is what we do all day long, this makes it very easy for us to whip up our own utilities. Some of these are quite impressive and have been turned into commercial products. However, a lot of us are hackers at heart and love making our own tools. My first published article was about a tool that took advantage of the fact that a .PJX file is simply a table. Written for FoxPro 2.0, it searched the project directory tree for files that weren't found in the project, and gave the developer the opportunity to examine and archive or delete the extra junk that had accumulated in the project's space. (See Cleanup.SCX later in this section for a tool that could be modified to do this with VFP applications.) Another published article covered a much more sophisticated tool I created for doing a global search-and-replace within a project. I still run into folks today who are using it.

If you haven't done so, I'm hoping that the two simple examples here encourage you to build your own tools when needed. You'll often find tool creation to be one of the more challenging and educational activities in your career as a developer.

SearchAll.PRG

How often have you tried to open a form or report or some other power-tool meta table using the power tool, only to be faced with a cryptic error referencing some element that you thought you'd removed? Sometimes the error refers to a specific line of the source-code file, making it easier to find the problem, but often you're not so lucky. Sometimes a piece of information is buried in a large application data file. It might be some "dirty" data that is causing a problem. Other times it might be a value that you suspect is seldom, if ever, encountered, and you want to search the entire table for the value.

SearchAll (see the source code in Listing 14-1) loops through the entire table, including all the fields, looking for matches between a search string and the contents of any character and memo fields encountered. In addition to the first two arguments, specifying a search string and the table name, there is an optional third argument that allows SearchAll to report the contents of one of the table fields. This utility falls into the "quick-and-dirty" category. It's just a program—there is no interface and no slick installation program.

Running SearchAll with the following line of code:

```
DO searchall WITH "Expense","comboclass.scx"
```

Yields these results on the VFP desktop:

Record 4 Field PROPERTIES
Record 5 Field PROPERTIES
Record 5 Field METHODS
Record 5 Field OBJCODE

Running SearchAll with the optional third argument also reports the name of the object in which the search string was found:

```
DO searchall WITH "Expense","comboclass.scx","objname"
```

Record 4 Field PROPERTIES   - objname: Cbosystemcodes1
Record 5 Field PROPERTIES   - objname: Ccommandbutton2
Record 5 Field METHODS   - objname: Ccommandbutton2
Record 5 Field OBJCODE   - objname: Ccommandbutton2

You could just as easily search a 500,000-record data file such as an "orders" table that had some corrupted data somewhere in it. If you had determined that the corrupted data involved null characters (CHR(0)), you could search the entire table for the corrupted records by using:

```
DO searchall WITH CHR(0),"CustOrder","cOrderNo"
```

While SearchAll.PRG is written to search for a character string, you could easily modify this program to be a little more flexible, and allow you to search for logical, date, datetime, or numeric values.

Listing 14-1. *SearchAll.PRG—a utility program to locate a character string anywhere in a table.*

```
LPARAMETERS tcString, tcTable, tcReportField
LOCAL lcString, lnFields
lcString = UPPER(tcString)
IF NOT USED(tcTable)
  USE (tcTable)
ENDIF
SELECT (tcTable)
lnFields = FCOUNT()
LOCATE
SCAN
  FOR i = 1 TO lnFields
    IF TYPE("tcReportField") = "C"
      lcReport = "Examining " ;
        + ALLTRIM(TRANSFORM(EVALUATE(tcReportField),"")) ;
        + ": " + FIELD(i)
    ELSE
      lcReport = FIELD(i)
```

```
      ENDIF
      WAIT lcReport WINDOW NOWAIT
      IF (TYPE( FIELD(i) ) = "C" OR TYPE( FIELD(i) )= "M") ;
          AND lcString $ UPPER(EVALUATE(FIELD(i)))
        ? "Record " + LTRIM(STR(RECNO())) + " Field " + FIELD(i)
        IF TYPE("tcReportField") = "C"
          ?? " - " + tcReportField + ": " + EVALUATE(tcReportField)
        ENDIF
      ENDIF
    ENDFOR &&* i = 1 to FCOUNT()
ENDSCAN
```

HackVCX.APP

A big step up from SearchAll is Rick Schummer's HackVCX.APP. It's still a very simple application in principle, but Rick has taken the time to put a nice interface on it. In fact, that's what this little baby's all about. As I mentioned in the sections on the Project Manager and Class Browser, you can hose yourself up pretty thoroughly by renaming classes and class libraries. Sometimes just trying to change your directory structure or moving a project to a different drive can cause problems. One of the worst messes to try to clean up is when you take over a project that used VFP baseclasses to construct everything and you want to jack up each form and slip your foundation classes under it.

You can address these problems by opening each affected form or class library as a table, then browsing and hacking each object class and class library reference to get them all pointed to the right classes in the right places. Given the fact that much of this information is stored in memo fields makes this a bit of a pain in the ol' butt-ola.

HackVCX to the rescue. Nothing fancy, but it makes fixing these kinds of problems a lot more bearable because it exposes all the memo fields in a .VCX or .SCX file in edit boxes. Rick originally wrote this as a demonstration of an SDI form, but I found that changing the ShowWindow property from "2– As Top-Level Form" to "0 – In Screen" gave access to the Cut and Paste options on the System menu.

Note in **Figure 11** the "Compile SCX?" check box. When checked (the default), the Classlib or Form file is recompiled when the form is closed.

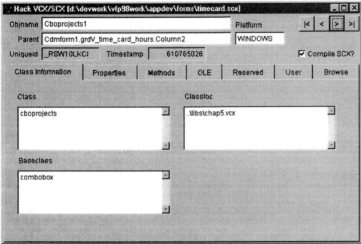

Figure 11. HackVCX—a handy tool for editing an .SCX or .VCX file.

Cleanup.SCX

Taking roll-your-own tools to another level yet is Jim Booth's Cleanup.SCX. A single-form tool, its purpose is to accommodate those who must transport an entire project development directory from one machine to another, either via e-mail or a space-limited medium such as a SyQuest EZ-135 drive or an Iomega ZIP drive.

During development, many of the meta tables increase in size, simply as a result of your editing existing features. As modifications are made, records in the tables are deleted and new ones added. Someone at Microsoft wisely figured out that this is easier than editing an existing record. This is why the Database Designer has a "Cleanup Database" option, and the Class Browser has a "Clean up class library" toolbar button. Both of these operations pack the meta tables. Taking up additional disk space in a project directory tree are .BAK files for edited program files and modified .DBF files, .FXP files from compiled programs, .TBK files from modified tables with memo fields, and .MNP and .MXP files from generated and compiled menus. All this "stuff" can make the difference between getting the entire project onto a single Zip disk or not.

Jim's utility walks the directory tree starting from its startup directory, compiling a list of all folders it finds and whether or not a particular folder contains any Visual FoxPro files. This information is displayed in a TreeView control. As shown in **Figure 12**, you can then determine which directory to process, whether to process subdirectories, and which types of files to process.

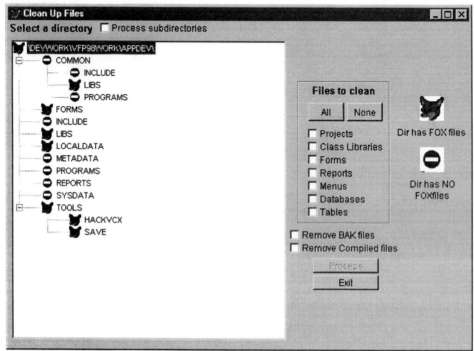

Figure 12. *Cleanup.SCX, a tool to recover disk space within a project directory tree.*

This utility has some wonderful example code. Take a look at the Init() and PopList() methods for an example of how to instantiate an ImageList control, set its properties to a list of images, instantiate a TreeView control, and populate its nodes, all programmatically. Note that you'll need to have both the TreeView and ImageList controls installed on your machine in order to use this tool. If you didn't elect to install these ActiveX controls during your Visual FoxPro installation, you can do so later by restarting the VFP Setup program, selecting Add/Remove components, and then selecting these two controls from the list of ActiveX controls that ship with Visual FoxPro.

Cleanup.SCX also (both in its PopList() and CleanThem() methods) shows how to handle recursively called methods and walking a directory tree.

You can modify how this tool works or what it does. For instance, you could modify it to walk a directory tree from the current directory, rather than the directory in which Cleanup.SCX is installed. You could use Cleanup.SCX as the basis for an application that would examine a project file, and then walk the directory tree looking for files that are on disk but not included in the project. These files are candidates for archiving or removal from the disk to recover disk space.

Third-party developer tools

The third-party tool and add-in market has always been fairly active for Xbase developers. With Visual FoxPro's migration away from its Xbase heritage toward object orientation and a place within Microsoft's Windows DNA architecture, and the demise or significant decline of competing products such as Visual dBase and CA Visual Objects, the market is not what it once was. However, there is still a wealth of significant products that can make you more productive or effective as a Visual FoxPro developer.

I want to make a distinction between developer tools and application add-ins. Some products are intended to be included in your applications and tend to provide some additional, usually commonly requested, functionality. Query building, report generation, data encryption, and internationalization are common examples of the kinds of functionality an add-in product provides. ActiveX controls are also included in this category. Add-ins do indeed speed the development process, but do so by substituting someone else's code for your own. The tools I examine here are two that have contributed greatly to my productivity in creating my own applications by enhancing the development process, rather than providing plug-in functionality.

Both products discussed below relate to the foundation of our development efforts, and indeed for the final application—the database. I use both products and have found that, while they both assist in database management and design, they have different spheres of operation and are highly complementary. While I do briefly describe their features, this is not an exhaustive review of either product. Both have been reviewed in *FoxTalk* and *FoxPro Advisor*.

Xcase

Xcase, from RESolution, Inc., is a database-design CASE tool. The standard edition is designed to work solely with Visual FoxPro databases and tables, while the professional edition works with Visual FoxPro databases, the Visual Basic/Access Jet database and a number of other database servers including SQL Server and Oracle. It should be noted that Xcase will also work with FoxPro 2.x tables.

Xcase is a two-way tool. You can create a model in Xcase, and from that model create a VFP database. If you have a Visual FoxPro database, you can "import" that database into an Xcase model, make changes to it, and then update the VFP database with the changes you've made in the Xcase model. If you make a change in a VFP database for which you have a Xcase model, you can then update the Xcase model with the changes made to the database.

The exception to this is views. The Xcase view designer is far superior to the VFP View Designer in creating and maintaining views. Changes to the database structure are automatically reflected in the views maintained in Xcase. Views automatically inherit the properties of the fields of the tables on which they are based, including captions, default values, and (unfortunately) rules. However, I'd rather have all the features migrate rather than none. The folks at RESolution very wisely (in my opinion) decided that their time was better spent working on more important features than the challenging task of parsing SQL commands and winnowing out all of the view properties from a Visual FoxPro database. You can maintain VFP database views in Xcase, but you cannot create or make changes to views in the VFP database and then update the Xcase model with these views. The practical effect of this limitation is actually beneficial. I've found it more convenient to maintain read-only views in a viewscript program. The reason is that it's often far easier to write, debug and test a view while in the Visual FoxPro development environment, than it is to create the view in Xcase, update the VFP database from the Xcase model, and then test it back in VFP. Because of the limitation in migrating views from the VFP database to the Xcase model, Xcase in effect ignores views that are added to the database that don't exist in the model. You can freely add views to the database without fear that they'll be overwritten when you update the database from the model.

Xcase allows you to establish a standard of using a surrogate key for all tables. When establishing a relation by visually connecting two tables, the primary key of the parent table is automatically migrated as the foreign key of the child table. Primary and foreign keys are automatically indexed. You can select any entity and display a list of incoming or outgoing relations. Relations can be named. The conventional Cascade/Delete/Restrict/Ignore Referential Integrity rules can be established for all relations, and Xcase can generate Xbase-style RI code, similar to that created by the VFP RI builder. Xcase RI code also provides for two additional options for RI enforcement, one which assigns a default foreign key value to orphaned child records, and another that assigns the primary key value of a default parent record to the foreign key fields of orphaned records—sort of an "automatic adoption" behavior.

One of the most powerful features of Xcase is the concept of "domains." In Xcase, a domain is a user-defined data type. For instance, if I decide that my key fields will be system-generated, six-character fields, and define the domain of these fields as "Key," I can create a table. Instead of specifying the field type and length as C(6), I can simply specify the type as "Key" and be done with it. I can also associate a whole host of default values for a defined domain, including caption, rule, default value, comment, rule text and about 20 others. To see the beauty of this system, consider being halfway through designing a database of 80 tables, using this Key domain all along to define primary and foreign key fields. If you decide that this type of key won't work for some reason, without Xcase you're doomed to spending several hours going back and redefining all primary and foreign key fields. With Xcase you simply redefine the key domain and this change cascades throughout the model.

Visual FoxPro provides its own database design tool, called (not surprisingly) the Database Designer. This tool works fine for a small database, but quickly reaches its limits to visually represent a database schema as the database grows in size and complexity. To graphically illustrate this point, **Figure 13** shows a database that I am currently involved with. Don't be dismayed if you can't make any sense of this illustration. This is a screen shot from Xcase that shows the entire database. Zoomed out as it is, nothing is legible, but you can get some feel for the complexity of the database from the numerous lines representing the persistent relations between the tables. Note that this picture would be even more illegible if it included the overloaded codes table that is related to virtually every other table in the system, with as many as 50 relations to a single table.

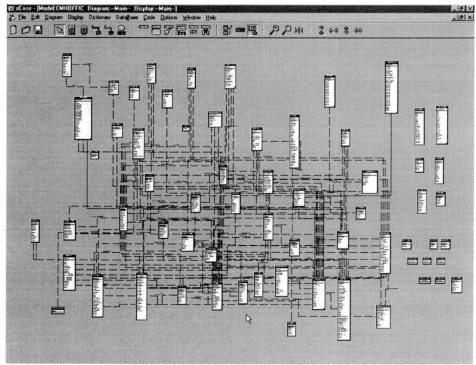

Figure 13. *A complex database as it appears in Xcase*

If Xcase couldn't improve on this mess, it wouldn't be worth much. **Figure 14** shows an example of Xcase's *zoom window*, which displays a magnified view of the area under the mouse pointer.

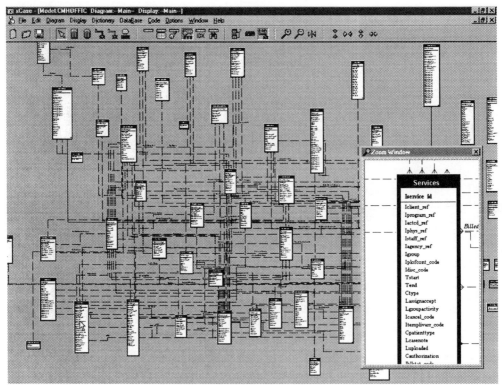

Figure 14. *Xcase's zoom window acts like a magnifying glass that coincides with the mouse pointer. Note the mouse pointer over the Services table in the lower left-hand corner.*

Even better, you can define and name multiple displays, each of which can zero in on a subset of the tables in the database, as shown in **Figure 15**.

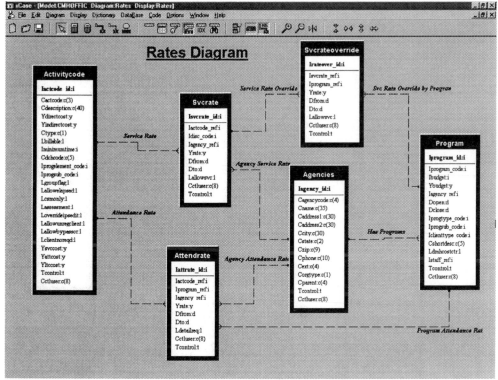

Figure 15. *A named display within Xcase showing one segment of the entire database.*

The Xcase displays are conventional entity-relationship diagrams. You have complete control over the cardinality of the relation types, such as one-to-one, one-to-none-or-many, or many-to-many. In this display, the table names, field names, field types and sizes and relations are all displayed. There are several options for how the entities are displayed. You can include only the entity names or their descriptions. You can display only primary and foreign key fields. You can choose to display field types and sizes. You can set colors for foregrounds, backgrounds and text styles. In Figure 15, if any child tables related to the AttendRate and SvcRate tables were included, the color of the relation lines would match the background colors of the parent tables. Field descriptions can be displayed instead of their actual names in the tables. This is useful during the initial design stages when you're working with a client or end user. You don't have to explain your naming convention for fields because everything is displayed in terms understandable to the client.

Xcase provides full support for all features of Visual FoxPro, including default values, captions, DisplayClass and DisplayLibrary properties, rules, triggers and comments.

Another feature of Xcase that I particularly like is the ability to "browse" the tables that store the entity, field, index, relation and view information. This makes it easy to ensure that all address fields are consistently named cAddress, and that I haven't used cZipCode in some tables and cZip_Code in others. **Figure 16** shows one of these "browsers." (I placed this word in quotes because Xcase uses the term *browser* to refer to a different, customizable form that displays information about database elements.)

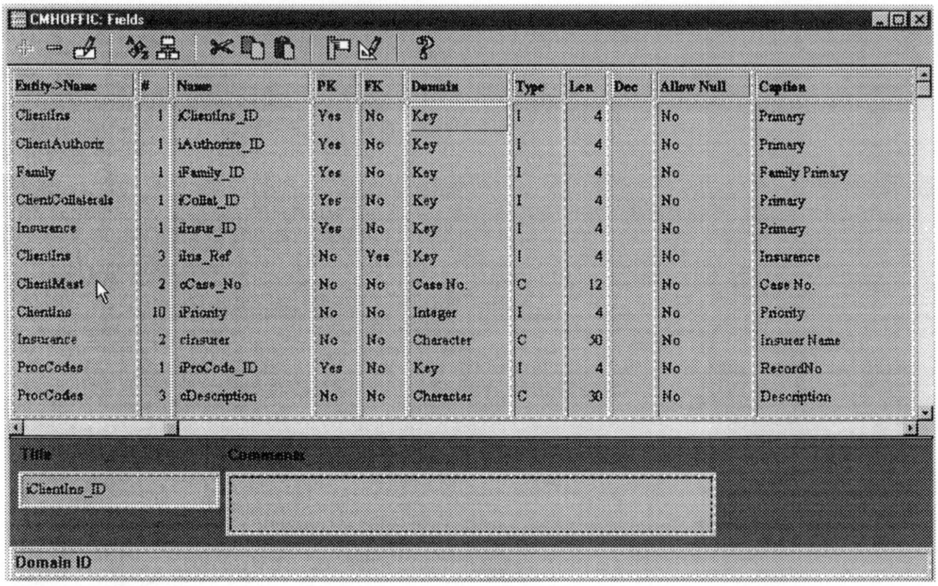

Figure 16. *An Xcase browser showing the fields for a multiple tables.*

Each of the browsers can be sorted according to several different fields. It's even possible (if none of the predefined indexes do the job and within certain limitations) to define your own index expressions.

The professional edition of Xcase is helpful when migrating a local-data application to a client/server architecture. Even if you have no immediate need to design a client/server application, the professional edition allows you to view the actual data in the database using ODBC.

There are a couple of reasons that I find a CASE tool like Xcase so valuable.

Software development is an iterative process. CASE tools help you stand back and look at the "big picture" and do a much better job of getting things right on the first pass. With Xcase, you can fiddle and tweak and move and rename and change the way things are laid out, and get a very good feel for how the entire database fits together. But this isn't the only strength of this kind of tool. I find it hard to imagine any database that is "cast in stone" once the coding starts. During development, various problems or shortcomings of the database design will become evident. Often the time and effort involved in making a change prevents the developers from doing it. Xcase won't make changing the code any easier, but it will certainly make modifying the database much easier. As an example, consider the use of domains mentioned above. This kind of capability allows sweeping changes to be made in a matter of minutes instead of days, and therefore encourages developers to make changes to the database design as soon as the need becomes apparent, rather than saying "We're too far along now to make such a change."

Many development efforts are a little short on documentation. I'm as guilty as anyone else of not adequately documenting systems I've created. Xcase allows you to document the database in the process of creating it. When the project is finished, you can spend a little time adding some graphical and explanatory elements to the displays, and print out an entire book of diagrams and reports describing every aspect of the database.

For a database like the one used in the samples for this book, Xcase would be a bit of overkill, although it does a very nice job of documenting even a simple database. But it becomes indispensable when working with a database like the one in Figure 13, with more than 60 tables and hundreds of relations. Without Xcase, I'm afraid my coworkers would have long ago found me under my desk, drooling and babbling and playing with my fingers.

Stonefield Database Toolkit

If Xcase's strong suit is database design, SDT's strong suit is database maintenance. As I near completion of a development project, database modifications become less frequent, and I can concentrate on the maintenance issues that need to be addressed when the application is in production.

SDT 5.1 works with both VFP 5.0 and VFP 6.0, and can be used as a much superior replacement for the VFP Database Designer. It provides outstanding support for views, migrating table field properties to the view fields and keeping the views "in sync" with the tables when the table structures are changed. You can set a flag on those views that must be maintained in code, so that you don't inadvertently try to load a complex view into the View Designer. Unlike Xcase, SDT wisely excludes field-level rules from the table properties that are migrated to views.

One of the thorny problems involved with maintaining a database is updating a client's or user's database when it's necessary to make structural changes. You code and test against the "master" database, but then you need a way to make the client's database look like yours. SDT includes a utility program to update a client's database based on changes you've made to the "master" database, simplifying the process of updating the client site.

SDT has some important maintenance capabilities that begin to blur the line between a developer's tool and an add-in. The updating feature is designed to be included in your application to facilitate changes to the database structure. SDT also includes distributable object classes that allow packing and re-indexing tables more reliably than the native PACK and REINDEX commands.

The structure of each database must match the structure as described in the database container. Sometimes during development, in the process of modifying table structures and moving things around, these two structures can get "out of sync." Attempting to open a table under these circumstances will trigger an error to the effect that the database container and the table structure don't match, and VFP won't open the table. The VALIDATE DATABASE RECOVER command is intended to fix this situation, but can do so only by removing the table's information from the database container and removing the back-link from the table to the DBC. This destroys all default values, validation rules, relations, triggers, and so on, that may have existed in the DBC. This is not an optimum solution, and even if it were, the VALIDATE DATABASE RECOVER command cannot be used in the runtime environment. SDT can successfully resolve this problem *without* destroying any information in the process.

SDT does its magic by storing information about the database's structure in a set of "metadata" tables through a technology known as DBCX II. This technology begins by describing the database structure, picking up where the database container leaves off, most notably by storing complete index and index expression information—something sorely lacking in the database container. DBCX II also provides an opportunity to create any kind of extended property for both tables and individual fields. For instance, if you want to create a two-line heading for use on reports, one that is different from the Caption property stored in the database container, you can create two text-type properties for your table fields, called cReptHead1 and cReptHead2. Once you've defined these as field properties using SDT, you can then establish the report headings for each field in the database. I've used SDT for this purpose, as well as setting flags on tables that can't be packed, or setting security properties that determine what fields can be seen by which users.

SDT can also automatically produce documentation, completely describing your tables as well as their structures, indexes, and extended properties.

Historically, many people have been critical of the .DBF file structure, calling it "fragile" and therefore unreliable. In my opinion, improvements to FoxPro and Visual FoxPro over the years make Visual FoxPro files as stable and reliable as a file-based database system can be. Using a UPS (Un-interruptable Power Supply on all file servers and regular routine maintenance, which includes re-indexing all tables on a regular basis, I have never personally seen a single case of file, header or memo pointer corruption in a FoxPro or Visual FoxPro database. However, there is another layer of complexity once you introduce the database container. While in my experience the database container is not at all fragile, in a production environment the DBC and its features are prone to getting snarled up in the development environment because of the unspeakable things we do to them in the process of writing applications. I spend a great deal less time struggling with this kind of problem by using SDT to maintain my database during development.

Invest in your toolbox

Whenever a friend or acquaintance gets married, I always try to take the groom aside and explain to him an unwritten clause in the marriage contract: For every "Honey-Do" project that The Wife comes up with, The Husband gets to buy a new tool. Hang curtain rods? Sure! But the job can't be done without that nifty new 15-amp hydraulic curtain-rod installation tool with the power plaster-dust collection system.

Some of us are tool freaks, and that seems to carry over into our work as developers. Some developers get as much or more satisfaction from creating development tools as we do actually creating applications. Some enjoy it so much that they begin producing tools for others, either as freeware, shareware or commercial products.

If you haven't already, I'd like to encourage you to try your hand at creating some tools of your own. You'll find that doing so often extends your knowledge of Visual FoxPro more than working on an application, and will make you a better developer in the process.

If you're not inclined to build your own tools, be sure to check the file libraries in CompuServe's VFOX and FOXUSERS forums, and on the Universal Thread. You're likely to find some wonderful tools that other VFP developers have created and which you might find useful.

Give some consideration to the many tools advertised in *FoxPro Advisor* and found in the Resource Guide that came with your copy of Visual FoxPro. Post a message in the VFOX forum or the Universal Thread and ask others if they've used these tools and whether they find them useful. Be advised that you should be careful when evaluating folks' responses, since their way of working may be very different from yours. A recommendation from any one person may or may not be meaningful to you if your philosophies of application development are different.

The important thing is, whether you make, borrow or buy your tools, that they can be important to your productivity and the quality of your product, and deserve as much attention as you devote to any other aspect of your professional development.

Appendix One
Glossary

Abstract Class	A class whose design intends that it never be used to create an object. The class exists just for subclassing.
Abstraction	The process of describing a complex problem in simple terms.
Access Method	A method that fires whenever the property it is associated with is accessed. These methods are named <PropertyName>_Access.
Alias	A name assigned to a work area when a table or cursor is open in it. Sometimes confused with a table's name, which is the file name on the disk. Tables can be open in work areas that have an alias that is different from the file name.
Assertions	The statement, in code, of various rules that must be met in order for the code to continue. Visual FoxPro uses the ASSERT command to provide this functionality. Assertions should be used to warn programmers of unexpected situations during development. The SET ASSERTS ON/OFF command will turn on and off the processing of the ASSERT commands.
Assign Method	A method that fires whenever the property it is associated with is assigned a value. These methods are named <PropertyName>_Assign.
Black Box	A routine that requires no knowledge of its implementation details to use it.
Builder	A program in Visual FoxPro that modifies objects at design time. Examples are the Grid Builder and the Application Builder. Builders are reentrant. Visual FoxPro allows you to create your own builders.
Business Domain	The set of rules and constraints that are related to the nature of the business for which an application is being developed.
Business Domain Experts	The people within a client's organization who best know the workings of the business. These people can tell you about the business domain.
Business Logic	The code that enforces the business domain. This code can be part of the user interface, part of the database rules and triggers, or in a separate object altogether.

Business Object   An object that enforces the business logic.

Business Rules   The set of rules that determines what constitutes valid data in the
                       business. These rules, along with any non-rule constraints, make up the
                       business logic.

Candidate Index   A Visual FoxPro index that prevents duplicate values from getting into
                       a table. A table can have more than one candidate index. Candidate
                       indexes are available to both free tables and tables included in a
                       database container.

Candidate Key   A relational database design element. This is a field or set of fields that
                       uniquely identifies a specific instance of an entity, but is not used as the
                       primary key.

Cardinality   The numeric aspect of a relationship, that is, two tables may be related
                       in a "1 to 1" relationship, or in a "1 to 0-#" relationship, or a "1 to 1-#"
                       relationship among others. In other words, the "one to many"
                       relationship can be further defined to indicate whether a child is
                       required for each parent and even the number of children required.

Cascaded Delete   Deletion of all child records with a foreign key value matching the
                       primary key value of the parent record being deleted.

Cascaded Update   Changing a foreign key value in a child table to the new value just
                       established in a parent table's primary key.

Cascading   When modifying a class's code, encountering the requirement to make
Modification   modifications to code that is called from the originally modified code.
                       This cascading of modifications can be two or more levels deep.

CASE   Computer Aided System Engineering. CASE tools are applications that
                       assist in designing and coding applications.

Child Cursor   A cursor, view or table that is the target of a relation. The label child is
                       dynamic, meaning a particular pair of tables might have table1 as child
                       at one point and table2 as child at another point.

Class   The blueprint for an object. A class of an object defines the nature of
                       the object and includes method and event code definitions along with
                       property values.

Collection	A property of a container object that holds references to the contained objects. Collections are similar to array properties except that the array functions do not work with them.
Compiler Directives	Commands that affect how the compiler will compile code. `#DEFINE` is an example of a compiler directive. All compiler directives in Visual FoxPro begin with the # symbol.
Composite Class	A class that is built by combining multiple classes using one of Visual FoxPro's container base classes to hold the other classes. A form defined as a class is an example of a composite class.
Compound Key	A primary or candidate key that uses more than one field in its definition.
Concrete Class	A class design that is used to create objects. The antithesis of the Abstract Class.
Contracts	The rules that a framework places on the components of an application. For example, if the application object requires that forms call its RegisterForm method from their Activate event, that would be a contract between the application object of the framework and the forms.
Coverage Analysis/ Code Profiling	Coverage analysis and code profiling are two methods of testing your code. Coverage analysis tells you what lines of code have been executed and what lines have not been executed. This allows you to design tests that execute all of the code to avoid shipping a product with untested code. Code profiling tells you information about how long each line took to execute. This allows you to identify those lines of code that are adversely affecting the system's performance. Visual FoxPro 6.0 has the Coverage Profiler utility to give you both Coverage Analysis and Code Profiling.
Cursor	In relational database design, refers to the **CUR**rent **S**et **O**f **R**ecords.
Data Buffering	Holding data in a memory buffer. Visual FoxPro gives us control over that memory buffer with its buffer modes.
Data Centric Interface	A user interface that is a direct representation of the underlying data structures.

Decorator	A design pattern that adds additional responsibilities to an object dynamically. Also known as a wrapper class (from *Design Patterns*, Gamma and Helms et al, Addison Wesley, 1995, Reading, MA. ISBN: 0-201-63361-2).
Default Data Session	Either data session number 1, which is the data session of the command window, or the data session of the calling object. A form that is set to the default data session will use session 1, unless it was called as a modal form from another form, in which case it will use the data session of the calling form.
Delayed Instantiation	Waiting until the last minute to create the objects inside a container. Example: using proxy objects on non-visible pages in a page frame to create the content of the page when it is first accessed. Proxy objects are defined below.
Delegation	Passing responsibility for an operation from one object to a different, more appropriate object.
Design Time	As opposed to run-time, this is the time you are modifying code or otherwise working on the development. For example, a form is in design-time when you have it open in the Form Designer for editing.
Developer's Interface	The set of methods, arguments for those methods, and properties that a class exposes to the developer.
Dirty Buffer	A data buffer that contains pending changes which have not yet been written to the files or reverted.
Domain	The entire definition of something. The term *domain* is used for many different things in relational database design. There are field domains, table domains, database domains, business domains, and so on.
Domain Constraints	Limitations placed on what constitutes validity for the item to which the domain applies.
Early Composition	Building composite classes in the class design at an early level of the subclassing. An example would be a container class that has buttons added to it from the Visual FoxPro CommandButton base class. The buttons in the container class would have code in their click events to cause various behaviors. *This is not a desirable design* because it complicates further specialization of the container class through subclassing.

Encapsulation	Maintaining everything that an object requires to do its job within that object. Perfect encapsulation is a goal to strive for that is seldom reached.
Event Queue	The event messages waiting to be processed. In event-driven software, like Visual FoxPro, messages are received from the user, the operating system, and other things on a regular basis. When these messages arrive while the system in a state that prevents responding to them, the messages are "queued" up to be handled at the next opportunity.
Foreign Key	A field or group of fields in one table that identifies a record in another table.
Framework Aware	An object that is capable of behaving correctly within a set of framework contracts.
Goal Centric Interface	A user interface whose style and presentation is centered around the user's goals. The most difficult style for the developer to design, yet the smoothest style for users.
Hungarian Notation	A naming convention invented by a Hungarian programmer that includes a full definition of variable name prefixes, abbreviations, suffixes and many other things. In the FoxPro community, there has been a fairly common naming convention that is derived from Hungarian Notation.
Include File	A text file that contains compiler-directive statements. The file is used by placing a #INCLUDE directive in a program that refers to the particular Include File.
Inheritance	The inclusion of all or some of the definition of another class in a class definition. Generally used to further specialize the behavior of a class. For example, you might create a command button class named MyButtons, and then create a class that is derived from MyButtons named MyNavButtons. The MyButtons class is called the *parent* or *super* class, and the MyNavButtons is called a *subclass*. MyNavButtons will inherit all of the properties and behaviors of MyButtons.
Instantiate	To create an instance of a class as an object. When you create an object from a class you are instantiating the object.

Internal Consistency	Ensuring that the full set of data for a record is consistent within itself. For example, if there is a table named *employees* and there are two fields named MaritalStatus and SpousesName, internal consistency would preclude filling the SpousesName field when the MaritalStatus is single.
Intersecting Table	A table that describes the intersection of two other tables in a many-to-many relationship. See "Many to many relation" in this glossary for more information.
Iterative Development	An approach to application development that uses iterations in the process. The whole application is constructed by building subparts of the application, one at a time, and returning to the design phase for each subsequent part. Allowing fact discovery to occur during a development phase, which takes the developer back to an earlier design or analysis phase to make changes in those aspects of the application.
Key	1. A field or set of fields that is used to maintain a relationship between data in two different tables. 2. The expression on which an index is based.
Late Composition	The opposite of early composition. This class design approach dictates that all objects contained in a container class be fully defined as independent and separate classes before they are placed into the container class. Building the container class as the last step in the class hierarchy just before the class is used to instantiate objects.
Local Variable	A memory variable that is local to a procedure. Local variables are visible, that is, available for reading and updating, only within the procedure that declared them. The LOCAL declaration command creates local variables. Local variables cannot be addressed either in procedures called from the creating procedure or in procedures above the creating procedure in the program calling stack.
Loose Coupling	Minimizing the constraints placed on two objects or procedures in dealing with each other. Loose coupling allows the objects or procedures to interact with minimal knowledge of each other. Tight coupling, the opposite of loose coupling, requires that the two objects or procedures are aware of each other's inner working details in order to interact. Loose coupling is another goal to strive for that can never be fully reached.
Macro Expansion	See "Macro Substitution"

Macro Substitution More accurately called *macro expansion*, it is the process of expanding a character variable so that the variable's contents are seen as literal text by the system. For example:

```
lcCommand = "DIR"
&lcCommand
```

The & is the macro expansion operator. In the above example the variable is assigned the value of "DIR", and the &lcCommand line is equivalent to using **DIR d**irectly.

Manager Classes Classes that are designed to handle certain operations within a system. For example, a Form Manager is used to manage forms, that is, to launch them, track them, and provide services to them.

Manifest Constant A compiler-directive constant value. Manifest constants are defined using the #DEFINE compiler directive. They are essentially a search-and-replace operation for the compiler to do before compiling the code.

Many-To-Many Relation A relationship, in a relational database, where many records in one table are related to many records in another table. An example would be invoices to inventory items, where any one invoice could have many items sold, and any item could be sold on many invoices. Database languages do not handle this type of relationship; it needs to be resolved into two one-to-many relationships. The resolution is to create an Intersecting Table. In the invoice-to-inventory example, that intersecting table might be called InvoiceLines, where any one invoice might have many lines but any line might be associated with only one invoice. Also, an inventory item might be sold on many lines but any one line might sell only one item. Therefore, there are two one-to-many relationships.

Mediator An object that encapsulates how a set of objects will interact. A mediator promotes loose coupling by preventing the mediated objects from referring to each other directly (from *Design Patterns*, Gamma and Helms et al, Addison Wesley, 1995, Reading, MA. ISBN: 0-201-63361-2).

Memvars A generally accepted abbreviation for "memory variables."

Modal The state of a window that prevents access to other windows and to the system menu and/or toolbars.

Modeless

A system design that expresses no mode of operation. For example, forms that allow the user to edit data without clicking an Edit button to start the process are called modeless. Although they are not really modeless, only the process of changing modes is concealed from the user.

Modes

A state of an object such as editing, adding, viewing, and so forth. These modes of operation may be explicitly requested through user interaction with controls, or they may be automatically handled by the internal event handling of the object. For example, a data-entry form might be in edit mode or viewing mode. If the user is required do something before editing is allowed, the form is called *moded*. If the form shifts into edit mode when the user changes a value of the data, the form is called *modeless* (even though internally it has clear modes of operation).

Name Expression

Visual FoxPro allows you to use expressions where it expects to see the name of something, like a file or field. You do this by enclosing the expression in parentheses, as in USE (lcTable) or REPLACE (lcField) WITH Value.

Naming Convention

A standard used in naming things. The Visual FoxPro help file has naming conventions for variables, objects, fields and so on.

Nested Join Syntax

Building a multi-table (more than two) join condition in an SQL SELECT command by first listing all the JOINs followed by all of the ONs in a last-in, first-out manner. For example:

```
SELECT Table1.Field, Table2.Field, Table3.Field ;
   FROM Table1 JOIN Tale2 ;
        Table2 JOIN Table3 ;
        ON Tbale2.KeyField = Table3.KeyField ;
      ON Table1.KeyField = Table2.KeyField ;
   ...
```

NODEFAULT

A command used in method and/or event code to prevent the default Visual FoxPro behavior from occurring. For example, the default behavior for a KeyPress event in a text box is to change the value of the text box to reflect the key pressed. You can process the keystrokes yourself in the KeyPress event, and if you don't allow Visual FoxPro to affect the value of the text box you can issue a NODEFAULT command to stop that behavior.

Nonmodal

A window whose state allows access to other windows and the menu and toolbars is said to be a *nonmodal* window.

N-Tier Design	A design approach that divides various system operations among distinctly different actors. The N in N-tier can be three or more. For example, a 3-tier system design may have one tier for the user interface, one for the business logic enforcement, and a third for database storage and retrieval.
NULL	The absence of value. A distinct value that represents the unknown state.
Object	"An object has state, behavior, and identity; the structure and behavior of similar objects are defined in their common class; the terms instance and object are interchangeable." —*Grady Booch*
Object Based	An application-development approach that uses objects but is limited in the class design aspect.
Object Oriented	"System of Components which encapsulate data and function, inherit these things from other components, and communicate via messages with one another." —*Edward Yourdan*
One-To-Many Relation	A relationship, in a relational database, where one record in one table is related to many records in another table. An example would be the relationship between customers and invoices. One customer may have many invoices, but any one invoice belongs to only one customer.
Optimistic Philosophy	A multi-user system design approach that doesn't check for user data collisions until it tries to save an edit session. It is called *optimistic* because the design expects that there will seldom be any conflict when it tries to save the edit.
Ordinality	See Cardinality.
Orphaned Records	Records in a table in which the foreign keys refer to parent records that do not exist in the parent table.
Parameter Object	An object created for passing values to another object by passing an object reference of the parameter object.
Parameterized Views	Local and/or remote views that include replaceable parameters in the filter conditions.
Parent Class	The class from which a subclass derives its definition. Also called a *superclass*.

Parent Cursor	A cursor, view or table that is the source of a relation. The label *parent* is dynamic, meaning a particular pair of tables may have table1 as parent at one point and table2 as parent at another point.
Persistent Relations	Relations between tables and/or views that are permanently stored in the database definition. These relations are descriptive of the relational design of the database and persist from one run to the next. These relations are not necessarily the only way that the items can be related in the application. In Visual FoxPro, persistent relations are created in the database container, and are used as default relations and by referential integrity enforcement code.
Pessimistic Philosophy	The opposite of the Optimistic philosophy. A multi-user system design that ensures the ability to write the data before allowing the user to edit that data.
Polymorphism	The ability of an operation to apply to several types. There are two types of polymorphism, Inherent and Ad Hoc. Inherent means that operations are inherited by every subtype, and Ad Hoc means that different operations of different types have the same name. Polymorphism, a feature of object-oriented development systems, allows for the creation of interchangeable class definitions.
Primary Index	A Visual FoxPro index type that prevents the addition of duplicate values of the index expression to a table. A table can have only one primary index. Primary indexes are available only for tables that are included in a database container.
Primary Key	A field or group of fields that unambiguously identifies a specific record within a table. The primary key, or any part of it, cannot have a value of NULL.
Private Data Session	An encapsulated set of work areas and environment settings. A private data session can open tables and set environment settings without affecting, or being affected by, other data sessions.
Private Variable	A memory variable whose scope of visibility is the procedure that created it and those procedures called from the creating procedure. Private variables are hidden from procedures higher in the calling stack. They are released when the creating procedure terminates. Memory variables are, by default, private in scope in Visual FoxPro. You can ensure that a private variable exists for a specific procedure by using the PRIVATE declaration, which will hide any existing variables in higher level procedures with the same name as the declared variable.

Process Centric
Interface

A user interface design that centers on the various processes in that
system. The least desirable of the three user interface designs (process,
data, and goal centric).

Profiling, Code

See Coverage Analysis/Code Profiling

Program to
Interface

An approach to application development that hides the implementation
details of the objects or procedures. This design requires that the
calling code only know the name of an object method or a procedure
and its parameters and return value in order to use that item. There is no
need for knowledge of how that method or procedure operates to call
the method or procedure and use its services.

Programming by
Exception

An object-oriented programming language design where writing any
code in a subclass's method will override inheritance of the parent or
superclass method. Visual FoxPro is a "program by exception"
development language. Writing any code in a subclass method in
Visual FoxPro will prevent the superclass's code from executing. To
get the superclass's code to run after writing code in the subclass's
method, you can use the `DoDefault()` function.

Proxy

Provides a placeholder or surrogate for another object or set of objects
to control access to that object or set of objects (from *Design Patterns*,
Gamma and Helms et al, Addison Wesley, 1995, Reading, MA. ISBN:
0-201-63361-2).

Public Variable

A memory variable that is scoped from the time of its declaration as
public until it is either expressly released from memory with the
`RELEASE` command or the Visual FoxPro run session ends. The `PUBLIC`
declaration command is used to create public variables. Public
variables should be avoided as much as possible. These variables
frustrate encapsulation and promote tight external coupling, both of
which cause a system to be more difficult to enhance and maintain.

Reentrant

The ability of an operation to be reentered without detriment to the
previous run of that operation. In Visual FoxPro, builders are reentrant
and wizards are not.

Referential
Integrity

The set of rules that describes the relations in a database and their
integrity maintenance.

Registry

A file in the Windows 95 or Windows NT operating system that holds
system information descriptive of the applications installed and the
OLE classes available, among other things.

Regular Indexes	The simplest and most common type of indexes available. There is no uniqueness enforcement, allowing multiple entries in the index for the same index expression value.
Relational Database	A database that is comprised of multiple tables, which each store information about a single person, place, thing or concept. These tables are related to each other, by shared values, to produce information that none of the tables can provide alone.
Relationship	A fact about or an association between two entities in a relational database design.
Restricted Delete	Check to see if there are any child records, and if so, prohibit the deletion of the parent record.
Restricted Insert	Check to see if there is a record in the parent table whose primary key value is the same as the foreign key value for the record being inserted. If there is, allow the insert; if not, prohibit the insert.
Restricted Update	Check to see if there are any child records, and if so, prohibit the update.
Run-Time	As opposed to design-time, this is the time when a program component is running. For example, when you issue DO FORM to run the form, it will be in run-time.
Rushmore	Visual FoxPro's optimization technology. This technology uses indexes to increase the speed of resolving filters and queries. Rushmore can optimize the expressions associated with the FOR clauses and the WHERE clause of the SQL SELECT command.
Scaffolding	A testing and debugging technique that allows you to easily test code execution. The word *scaffolding* is derived from the building industry, where scaffolds are used to allow workers to reach areas that they would not otherwise be able to reach. Software scaffolding is similar in that it allows the execution of code that would otherwise not function properly. Two types of scaffolding are commonly used. The first is often called stubbing, which means a lower level routine is stubbed, or dummied, so that a higher level routine can be tested. For example, you might write a stub function that displays a wait window and call it from your menu system so that you can test the menu without writing all the code that the menu will call.
	The second type of scaffolding is when you encounter a control or some code that is not functioning properly. You can build a dummy

form to hold the control or code and test it in a controlled environment. Once you have it working in the dummy form, you can copy it into the actual form, knowing that the code tested in the scaffold form is functioning properly. This is helpful in limiting the number of variables that are affecting the behavior.

Self Relation

An association between records within the same table. For example, an employee table might contain a field named ManagerID that points to another record in the same employee table.

Sequential Join
Syntax

Stating the JOINs in an SQL SELECT statement in a JOIN ... ON ... JOIN ... ON ... sequential manner. For example:

```
SELECT Table1.Field, Table2.Field, Table3.Field ;
  FROM Table1 JOIN Tale2 ;
       ON Table1.KeyField = Table2.KeyField ;
       Table2 JOIN Table3 ;
       ON Table2.KeyField = Table3.KeyField ;
  …
```

Source Object
(Drag and Drop)

The object where a drag operation begins.

Sovereign
Application

An application that requires the user's undivided attention and therefore can take over the screen display and system resources during its operation.

Specialization

The ability of an object to inherit operations and attributes from a superclass with possible restrictions and/or enhancements.

Subclass

A class definition that inherits some or all of its behavior and settings from another—parent or super—class.

Super Class

A class that is used in the creation of one or more subclasses.

Surrogate Primary
Key

A field added to a table's structure that has no meaning or purpose other than being the primary key.

Target Object
(Drag and Drop)

The object on which a drop operation occurs.

Temporal Relations

Relationships created in forms, reports, or program code. These relations may be consistent with the persistent relations defined or they may be different. Temporal relations have no permanence and are lost when the system ends (they are volatile).

Transaction

The ability to group a set of table operations into one, all or none, operation.

Transient Application	The opposite of a sovereign application. An application that does not require the user's full attention. Utility applications like calculators or Rolodex applications fall into this category.
Triggering Operations	The most generalized form of business rule, encompassing domains and key business rules as well as other types of attribute business rules. The rules that make some sets of data correct and others incorrect. Do not confuse triggering operations with trigger events.
Triggers	A set of table events that are automatically called when certain operations occur to the table. Visual FoxPro provides three triggers: Update, Insert, and Delete. These triggers are often used for writing the referential integrity enforcement code.
Unique Indexes	Unique indexes are similar to regular indexes, in that they don't enforce uniqueness on the expression. However, they do store only one reference in the index for each unique value of the expression.
View	A virtual table that contains information from other real tables in a database system. The data source for a view in Visual FoxPro may be local Visual FoxPro DBF tables, or remote tables from a database server or some other database management system.
Volatile	Exists only at run-time and is lost on exiting a working session. Memory variables and temporal relationships are volatile, while table fields and persistent relationships are non-volatile.
White Box	An object-oriented design that requires some knowledge of the internal implementation details in order to use a component. A framework designed to be enhanced through subclassing is called a *white box framework.*
Wizard	A utility program that will create some system component. Unlike builders, wizards are not reentrant, meaning that rerunning a wizard will overwrite any existing component with the newly created one.
Xbase	A generic term used to refer to all of the programming languages that have evolved from the dBase II dialect.

Appendix Two
Relational Database Design

At the root of all things in application development is data storage. If the data is stored correctly, the possibilities for dealing with that data are boundless. If the data is stored incorrectly, it will limit the possibilities and cause unnecessary complexities in handling the data. Designing databases and tables is a science of its own. Some good tools are available to verify that a data design is sound. In this appendix you will discover these tools and learn how to apply them to your work.

What is a relational database?

A relational database is a set of tables, each holding fields and records that are related to each other with primary and foreign keys. The definition of a relational database system also describes the operations that can be done to those tables. C. J. Date has compiled a set of relational myths in his paper, "Some Relational Myths Exploded," published in *InfoMIS 4* Number 2 in 1984. These myths will help you to understand what a relational database is by reviewing what it is not.

Here are some excerpts from C. J. Date's book, *Relational Database Selected Writings* published by Addison Wesley (1986, ISBN:0-201-14196-5). The excerpts come mostly from Chapter 6, "Some Relational Myths Exploded."

Myth #1:   *"A relational database is a database in which the data is stored as tables."* This myth shows a misunderstanding of the division between the physical and logical database designs. Tables relate to the physical storage of the data on disk, while relational database design is focused on the logical structure of data without regard to how the design will be physically implemented. Any database management system (DBMS) that forces the designer to deal with the physical storage of the data does not meet one of the basic rules of relational databases— that the designer needs only to deal with the logical data design and should not be concerned with how that data is physically stored.

Myth #2:   *"A relation is just a flat file."* A relation should not be regarded as just a flat file table, but rather as a disciplined table. A table where all records are of the same type, fields have no meaning in their order from left to right, the records have no particular order, every field is single valued, and the records have a unique identifier.

Myth #3:   *"The relational model is just flat files."* Dr. Date says, "The relational model is the theoretical foundation on which systems are built." The relational model does not consist of a data structure alone. It includes three components: the structure, the operations done to that data, and the integrity definitions.

Myth #19:   *"The relational model is just theory."* Granted, the relational model is theory, but that's not a weak point. It is the sound theoretical framework that gives the relational model its strength. Dr. Date, when speaking about the people who claim that the relational model is impractical due to its theoretical underpinnings, says, "My own position is exactly the opposite; systems that do not have some solid theoretical base are usually very difficult for anyone to understand."

Myth #20:   *"Relational databases require 'third normal form.'"* If a data design is relational, then the tables within that design are *normalized* in that every field is single valued; repeating groups are not allowed. This rule is the first normal form; the reason it is called *first* is that there are other high levels of normalization. The second normal form requires that a table be in first normal form, third normal form requires that the table be in second normal form and so on. While these higher normal forms are desirable and designers should spend time attempting to comply with them, Dr. Date says, "Relational systems do not require any level of normalization other than first."

Myth #25:   *"Third normal form is a panacea."* Third normal form can be simplified to the idea "Only one place for each fact." While this is a desirable goal for database design, it also has a downside. Religiously adhering to third normal form generally creates many small files. These many files can have a detrimental effect on performance. In addition, third normal form by far does not deal with the entire set of issues related to relational database design.

The database design process

Designing relational databases is not done in a vacuum. It requires more than a thorough understanding of the design principles. The design process is just that—a process. It is a complex process at best.

It is necessary to meet with users to discover and document the business requirements of the data. The user interface for the system has to be fleshed out so that its impact on the data design can be determined. The following sections discuss various parts of the relational database design process.

Getting the information from the client

Analysis is the information-collection phase of designing a database. During analysis, you want to gather as much information as possible about the data that a business works with. This task requires cooperation between you and the client. You will need the help of the client's best people in order to figure out all of the nuances of the business data.

It helps if you can keep the conversation on the business and its needs and keep the client away from the computer application you will be developing. For one, the application will be a vague idea at this point in its development and the client will likely want to dive into detailed design. They will grill you on the details of the forms and the detailed content of the data. You will be asked about this detail at a time when you know little or nothing about the data requirements. You are very likely, at this early stage, to make statements about the application that you will later regret having said.

Keeping the client focused on fact-finding is not always easy. It requires that you suppress the temptation to "brag" about your great ideas and thoughts. You must be in full control of the conversations if they are to be efficient in gathering the information that you need. You, not the client, must be the one asking the questions.

You must find a way past the management to talk to the actual daily users of the data. The management knows what they want the requirements to be, but the users know what the real requirements are. Management manages and users do. This difference is not a small one when you are searching for the details of how the business works. Keep in mind, also, that the users will live with your application. Management will only pay for it. As the source of the dollars, management will want to give input to the system design; however, you'll find the real lowdown on how things *must* work in talking with the users.

Initially, keep the conversations as informal as you can. Take copious notes on everything that is said. You may even consider taping these conversations and having them transcribed. It is from the information gathered in these first conversations that you will build your first data design.

Your first design is sure to be off the mark. It is sure to go through multiple revisions before you and the client agree that the data design covers the needs of the business. In order for the client to give you useful comments, you need a method of describing the data design to them. You should schedule multiple meetings with the client during this data-analysis phase. At each meeting after the first, you should come prepared with a paper describing your conclusions from the previous meetings. You may even want to send the paper to the client before the next meeting to allow them to read it. The first order of business at each meeting should be to review that paper so you can immediately note the changes. You want to get the changes right away so you don't continue down a dead-end road if your conclusions are out in left field somewhere.

You will need to allocate some time to instruct the client in reading and using the diagrams you use in your data design. At some point, the written prose describing the data design may become encyclopedic in size, so using diagrams will become a much more efficient method of describing the design. If the client is conversant with the diagrams, you will have a much easier time of reviewing the design together.

Designing the database
During the phase described above, you will be designing table structures. You will identify the major tables needed and begin to lay out their field definitions. It is important, at this point, to realize that you are building a relational database design and not the actual tables you will implement in Visual FoxPro.

You do not want your design to be affected by any constraints or limitations of Visual FoxPro or any other database manager. You want the design to be relationally sound. Leave the implementation until the implementation. Doing things this way allows you to discover facts about the data design that might be lost within the limitations of the implementation tool. For example, I know of a Visual FoxPro system in use today that contains one table that exceeds 64 gigabytes of data. But I thought Visual FoxPro's limitation was two gigabytes for any file. It is, and that's the beauty of this data design stuff. The relational table I mentioned is stored in multiple DBF files through what is called data partitioning. The developers of this system did their analysis and design the right way—they designed the relational model before beginning to implement that model. The design called for one table to hold that particular data. The developers kept the relational design, in that they implemented one virtual table composed of multiple disk files.

The major goal in the table design is to get the individual data points (fields) into the correct tables. The design should also contain a description of how the data in these tables are related to each other. The relations you are getting at here are not necessarily the relations you will create for any given report or form in the system. These relations are descriptive of the business nature of the data. For example, in the business schema a customer has invoices, so you would describe the customer-to-invoice relationship with customer as parent and invoice as child. However, in any given form or report you might set the relationship the other way. The relationships you build here are the ones that will influence the referential integrity constraints you will state later.

You should review the table designs with the client to ensure that you do not omit details. The earlier you review the table designs, the more likely that any changes will be easy to implement. The more often you review the design with the client, the more likely it becomes that the design will work for the application.

In the book *Handbook of Relational Database Design* by Fleming and von Halle (Addison Wesley, Reading, MA, 1989, ISBN: 0-201-11434-8), the authors describe 25 "rules" of relational design in 549 pages. While I recommend the book, it is not very realistic to expect that you, or anyone, will be able to quote the 25 rules and their definitions. That is why this book is called a *handbook*—like any handbook, it is meant to be referred to frequently during the design process.

Fleming and von Halle, on page 20 of the *Handbook of Relational Database Design*, provide a set of criteria for defining an optimal logical database design. They ascribe six qualities to this optimal design:

- *Structural validity*—consistency with the way the business defines and organizes information
- *Simplicity*—ease of understanding even by unskilled people (e.g. by users or by non-systems professionals)
- *Nonredundancy*—inclusion of no extraneous information; in particular, representation of any one piece of information exactly once (this may be a subcriterion of simplicity)
- *Sharability*—not specific to any particular application or technology; thereby usable by many
- *Extensibility*—ability to evolve to support new requirements with minimal effect on existing base
- *Integrity*—consistency with the way the business uses and manages information values

Structural validity is the quality of having the data design match the way the business sees its information. In doing this, you create a design that is capable of dealing with changes in the business over time. If your design is a true model of the business, anything that happens in the business theoretically can happen in your data design.

Simplicity might seem to be an irony. Most folks think that a relational design is complex and difficult to understand, let alone to build. However, they are wrong. Exactly the opposite is true. A truly optimal relational database design achieves a level of simplicity that allows non-database professionals to understand it. By following the principles of relational design, you will be simplifying, not complicating, your data designs.

In achieving a fully nonredundant design, one place for everything and everything in its place, you remove a number of possible problems. Only redundant data can be inconsistent—if a value appears in only one place, there is no possibility for that value to be inconsistent.

By creating a solid, logical data design before addressing any specifics of the tool being used to implement that design, you are creating a data design that can be used by many different tools. Documenting that logical design will allow you to reuse it later for a different implementation. For example, you might design a database system to be implemented fully in Visual FoxPro. Later, it might become necessary to move that application's data to Microsoft SQL Server or Oracle. Having a solid, logical design available will certainly make that change easier.

You reach extensibility through the other qualities in the list. Structural validity, sharability, and nonredundancy all contribute to the extensibility of the design.

Integrity of the design ensures that the data will function within the scope of the business for which it is built. The next section discusses the idea of integrity in more detail.

Determining the referential integrity rules

Referential integrity rules are totally influenced by the nature of the business. These rules are even called *Key Business Rules* in the field of relational database design. The name Key Business Rules derives from the fact that these rules are business rules that govern how to handle the integrity of the relationships between keys, both primary and foreign.

For example, you have a client who needs a system built to track their sales activity. You design a Customer and an Invoice table. You realize that the relationship between customer records and invoice records is very important and that you must protect that relationship. The integrity protection avenues available to you for enforcing this protection are cascade or restrict. In dealing with the deletion of customer records, you can either cascade the deletion to the invoice tables, or restrict the deletion in the customer table when there are invoice records for that customer.

Either one of these approaches will protect the relationships. However, I think if you check with the controller at the client, you will find that they are quite uncomfortable with randomly deleting invoice records because some user hit a button in the customer form. The business rules determine the method you use to protect the referential integrity.

The process of normalization

There is a set of rules that you can use to test your design for structural soundness. That is the process of normalization. With normalization, you successively examine each table and its fields for structural redundancies and inconsistencies. This definition may seem quite academic. In plain English, this means that you review the design of each table in turn and apply a set of rules to the table that will remove any data redundancies. These rules will also remove any inconsistencies in the data. If you think about it, you can only have an inconsistency if there is more than one item involved. Therefore, by definition, you will remove inconsistencies by removing redundancies: no redundant data, no inconsistent data.

The following sections present each normal form (set of rules) and provide an example for that form. The examples used here are designed to clearly present the normal form issues. The flaws in these examples will be obvious for the particular normal form being discussed. Your database designs will most likely require more careful examination to discover any rule violations.

Let's take a moment to discuss why you should be concerned with normalization at all. There are four basic goals to the normalization process:

- *Minimize the space required to store the data.* By removing redundancies, you cause the data to be recorded in only one place, thereby reducing the space required.
- *Minimize the possibility of data inconsistencies.* As stated above, if there are no redundancies then there can be no inconsistencies.
- *Minimize possible update and delete anomalies.* By not requiring that updates occur in more than one place for a particular piece of data, you prevent any update anomalies. By ensuring that all data in the fields of a table is dependent on the primary key for that table, you ensure that deletions can be handled in terms of any effect on related tables.
- *Maximize the stability of the data structure.* This goal is not referring to stability in terms of file damage. It is referring to the ability of new functionality being introduced to a system without requiring that the data structures be changed. For example, assume you were hired to build a system for a client to track the hourly sales at the client's six stores. The client told you that these stores are open for eight hours a day. You might design a table like the one in **Figure 1**.

Hourly Sales

| Store # |
| Date |
| Hour1 |
| Hour2 |
| Hour3 |
| Hour4 |
| Hour5 |
| Hour6 |
| Hour7 |
| Hour8 |

Figure 1. An example of the table design for hourly sales.

This design may work fine in the current business environment. However, what happens if the stores stay open for more than eight hours a day or some stores have different hours than others? These questions point out the flaws in the design in Figure 1. **Figure 2** presents a different design for the same system.

Hourly Sales

```
┌──────────────┐
│ Store #      │
│ Date         │
│ Hour         │
├──────────────┤
│ Sales        │
└──────────────┘
```

Figure 2. *A better design for the hourly sales table.*

To understand why the second design is better, consider one question: What is the first table recording in one record? The first design records one day's sales for a store in each record. The second records one hour's sales for a store in each record. The requirement was to record hourly sales, so the second design must be better, since it does what was required, while the first design was recording something altogether different.

What happens if the owner decides to open his/her stores for more hours during the holiday season? The second design requires no modification to the data to handle this change. The first design would require changes to the table design to accommodate the new hours. This is referred to as *data structure stability*, the ability to add features or functionality to a system without changing the data design. In essence, if you succeed at modeling the business in the data design, then, theoretically, anything that could happen in the business can also happen in the database.

In the following sections describing the rules of normalization, each rule is presented in boldface, followed by a discussion of each rule and appropriate examples.

First normal form
Reduce tables to first normal form (1NF) by removing repeating or multi-valued fields to another, child, table.

This rule states that there shall be no multi-valued fields in any table. What does it mean by multi-valued fields? **Figure 3** shows a design for a customer table.

Figure 3. *A customer table design.*

Figure 3 lists a number of fields. If you ask yourself the meaning of each of those fields, you will discover something interesting. Company name is the name of the customer. Address is the location of the customer. Contact1 is the name of a contact person at the customer. Contact2 is the name of a contact person at the customer. Wait, is there an echo in here? No, but the fields Contact1 and Contact2 both have the same meaning, or domain. They are both the same data type and length, and they share the same set of valid values. That means they are the same field. In fact, the contacts at the customer represent a multi-valued field within the customer table.

How do you fix this and make this table design comply with the first normal form? **Figure 4** shows how.

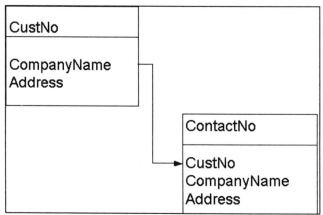

Figure 4. *The resolution of 1NF in the customer table.*

Here we comply with the first normal form rule by removing the two fields Contact1 and Contact2 from the Customer table and creating a new child table for contact information. The new table is related to the Customer table on the value of the common CustNo field. There is more to this normal form than meets the eye. Referring back to Figure 3, what would happen if the client got a new customer that had five contact people? How would the Figure 3 design handle a customer with only one contact person?

The answer is that the design cannot handle a customer with more than two contacts, and for those customers with only one contact there will be wasted space in the table. The second design, seen in Figure 4, can handle a virtually unlimited number of contacts for any customer. The second design does not waste space for any customer.

Second normal form

Reduce 1NF tables to second normal form (2NF) by removing fields that are not dependent on the whole primary key.

2NF deals with each field in a table and its dependence on the primary key for its value. This normal form is really involved in situations where the primary key is composed of more than one field. To better understand the rule, refer to **Figure 5**.

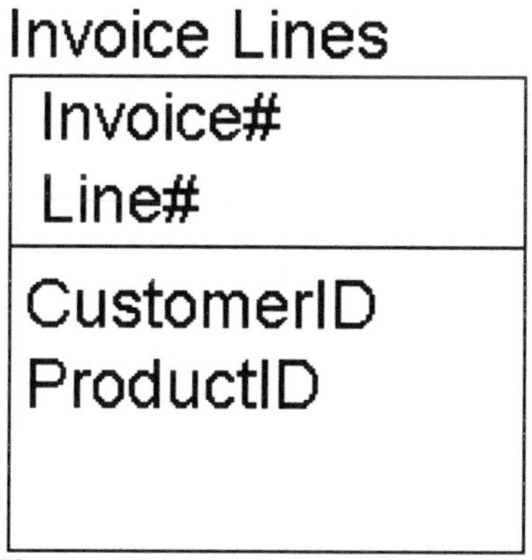

Invoice Lines

| Invoice# |
| Line# |
| CustomerID |
| ProductID |
| |

Figure 5. An invoice line item table design.

In the table in Figure 5, ask yourself if each of the fields below the line is dependent on all of the fields above the line for its value. For ProductID the answer is yes, you need to know both the Invoice# and the Line# in order to determine what product is being sold. However, for CustomerID you only need to know the Inoivce#—the Line# has no effect on the CustomerID. Therefore, the CustomerID is not dependent on the *whole* primary key of the Invoice Line table.

How do you resolve this situation and put this table in second normal form? **Figure 6** shows you how.

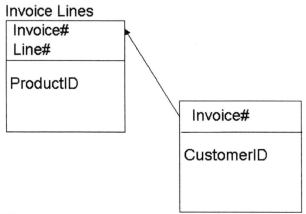

Figure 6. *The resolution of second normal form for the Invoice Line table.*

In Figure 6 we have moved the CustomerID field out of the Invoice Line table and into the Invoice table, which is the parent of the Invoice Line table.

Third normal form
Reduce 2NF tables to third normal form (3NF) by removing fields that depend on other, non-key fields (other than candidate keys).

Third normal form deals with fields that are dependent on other fields that are not part of the primary key. It states that all fields within a table *must* be dependent on the primary key and only the primary key for their values. **Figure 7** shows a table that is not in third normal form.

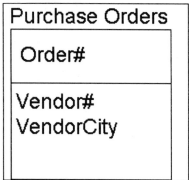

Figure 7. *A purchase order table that is in violation of the third normal form.*

In the table design in Figure 7, you need to ask yourself if either of the fields below the line is dependent on anything other than the primary key (the fields above the line). Yes, the VendorCity is dependent on the Vendor# field. You may ask why this design got past second normal form. It did so because the VendorCity is dependent on the primary key. If the Order# changes, the VendorCity is as likely to change as the Vendor#. However, the VendorCity is also dependent on the Vendor#—that is, if you change the Vendor# for any purchase order, the city is likely to change.

The resolution of third normal form for this table is seen in **Figure 8**.

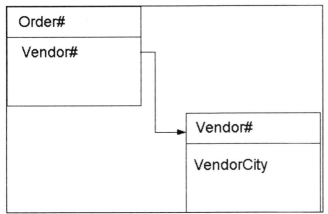

Figure 8. The third normal form applied to the purchase order table.

We resolve the design in Figure 7 to third normal form by moving the codependent field, VendorCity, to a parent table. Figure 8 shows the resolution, where the VendorCity is in the Vendor table.

Boyce Codd normal form
Reduce 3NF tables to Boyce Codd normal form (BCNF) by ensuring that they are in 3NF for any feasible choice of candidate key as primary key.

This normal form applies only when there is more than one candidate for the primary key of a table. If you are using surrogate primary keys as described earlier in this book, then you will always need to apply Boyce Codd normal form. **Figure 9** shows a table design with multiple candidates for the primary key.

Figure 9. An employee table design with three candidate keys.

In the table design of Figure 9, there are three candidates for the role of primary key. EmpId, Clock#, and SocSec# all can fill the role of primary key because they are unique for each employee, they are required before an employee can report to work, and they identify the employee's record in the table.

Figure 9 shows that the EmpId field has been assigned as the primary key for the table. You would have already ensured that the table is in third normal form using the EmpId field. Boyce Codd normal form states that the table must also be in third normal form for each of the other candidate keys as primary key. The resolution of third normal form requires that you go back and apply first, second, and third normal forms using Clock# as the primary key, and then using SocSec# as the primary key.

Fourth normal form
Reduce BCNF tables to fourth normal form (4NF) by removing any independently multi-valued components of the primary key to multiple new parent entities.

This one is a mouthful! Actually, it really isn't that complex. The rule applies to primary keys with two or more fields involved. Remember, back in the book earlier, when Steve and I talked about surrogate primary keys? We both said it was a very good idea to use them. Well, now you might begin to see why. If you are using surrogate primary keys, your primary keys are *always* only one field. If your primary keys are only one field, Boyce Codd normal form is the end for you. Both this normal form and the next one apply only to compound primary keys.

Okay, so much for the sermon. Now on to understanding fourth normal form. The rule says that you don't want a primary key that is composed of two or more fields where those fields might have multiple values independently from each other. **Figure 10** shows a table with this problem.

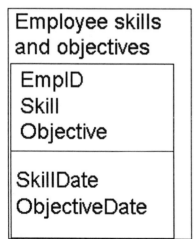

Figure 10. A table that is in violation of fourth normal form.

The purpose of the table in Figure 10 is to record information about employees, their skills and their objectives. To appreciate the problem with the design, you need to look at sample data. **Table 1** shows some sample data from the Figure 10 table.

Table 1. *Sample data for the table described in Figure 10.*

Employee	Skill	Objective
Jones	Accounting	More money
Jones	Accounting	Masters degree
Jones	Public speaking	More money
Jones	Public speaking	Masters degree

Notice that four records here represent each of two skills and two objectives. The real problem, though, comes when Jones gets the masters degree. How many records need updating for that one event? Two records need updating if Jones gets the masters degree.

The problem is worse when you consider what needs to happen to the data if Jones doesn't get the masters but gains a skill in auditing. To reflect that new skill requires the addition of two records, one for audit and more money and one for audit and masters degree. God forbid that after becoming an auditor Jones decides to set an objective to become a VP; that would require the addition of three records.

This violation of fourth normal form will only increase in complexity over time. How do you resolve the design? **Figure 11** shows you the Figure 10 design after resolving fourth normal form.

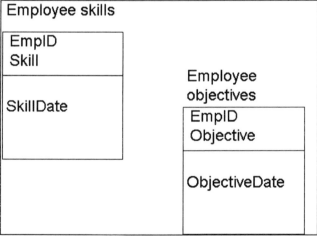

Figure 11. *The table design from Figure 10 after applying fourth normal form.*

The resolution is to get rid of the employee skill and objective table, and create an employee-skill table and an employee-objective table. Notice that there is no relationship between the employee-skill table and the employee-objective table. The lack of a relationship indicates that skills and objectives are independent from each other, reinforcing the fact that the original design was a violation of fourth normal form.

Fifth normal form

Reduce 4NF tables to fifth normal form (5NF) by removing pair-wise cyclic dependencies (appearing within composite primary keys with three or more component fields) to three or more new parent tables.

This normal form rule is a mind bender and a tongue twister—try reading it aloud three times fast. The point of this rule is less complex than the definition would lead you to believe. There are two important elements to this rule. The first is that the primary key must contain three or more fields. The second is the reference to pair-wise cyclic dependencies.

If your table has a primary key with one field, then Boyce Codd normal form *is* fifth normal form. If your table has a two-field primary key, then fourth normal form *is* fifth normal form.

Essentially, fifth normal form describes a situation where a primary key has three or more fields and those fields are interdependent for their values. We'll use a three-field primary key to explain the rule.

Consider a table that has FieldA, FieldB, and FieldC as the components of the primary key. If you determine that FieldA is dependent on the combination of FieldB and FieldC, then you are heading toward a fifth normal form problem. This is the pair-wise part to it all: Any one field is dependent on the other two (pair). If you continue with the fields and find that FieldB is dependent on the combination of FieldA and FieldC, and that FieldC is dependent on the combination of FieldA and FieldB, you have met the cyclic part of the rule. No matter which of the three fields you consider, it is dependent on the other two. This is a pair-wise cyclic dependency.

Figure 12 shows a table with this problem.

Figure 12. *A table design in violation of fifth normal form.*

The table in **Figure 12** records information about buyers, the vendors they buy from, and the products they buy from those vendors. The primary key is composed of the buyer, vendor, and product. The cyclic pair-wise dependency is that, in order to determine a buyer, you need to know the vendor and the product. To know the vendor you need to know the buyer and the product, and to know the product you need to know the buyer and the vendor. Hence, there is a pair-wise cyclic dependency in the primary key.

So much for the theory—why should you care? **Table 2** shows sample data from the table in Figure 12.

Table 2. Sample data for the buying table.

Buyer	Vendor	Product
Mary	Jordache	Jeans
Mary	Jordache	Sneakers
Sally	Jordache	Jeans
Mary	Liz Claiborne	Blouses
Sally	Liz Claiborne	Blouses

Asking a couple of questions will help you to see the problem. What happens if Liz Claiborne starts selling jeans? You need to add two records to record that fact, one for Mary and one for Sally. What happens if Liz Claiborne starts selling sneakers and Sally starts buying sneakers? Again, you cannot record this situation in only one record; you must add two to the table. As the data grows, the problem compounds.

Figure 13 shows the resolution of this table into fifth normal form.

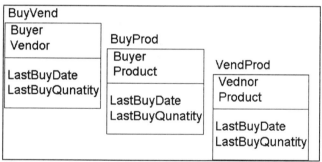

Figure 13. The buying data design resolved into fifth normal form.

You resolve the table to fifth normal form by dumping the errant table and replacing it with three or more new tables, each having two of the fields used in the primary key of the original as its primary key.

Denormalization

Wait a minute, you just went through all of these normal forms and now we're going to talk about denormalizing? Yes, we are.

The important thing to notice is that we don't mention denormalization until the data design is fully normalized into fifth normal form. This is because each normal form is important. At each step in the process, tables that were missing might be discovered. Data fields can be moved into the correct tables. Internal primary key problems are resolved. Too much improvement to ignore.

Once the design is fully normalized, you can afford the luxury of considering other factors about the system's use of the data. For example, the tables in **Figure 14** are fully normalized to the fifth normal form.

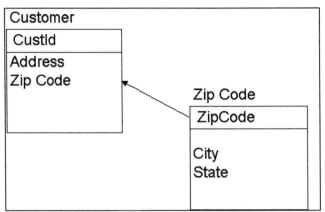

Figure 14. *A third normal form-compliant design for customer address data.*

The Zip Code table was discovered at the third normal form. We realized that the city and state fields were dependent on the zip code field; the zip code field is not part of the primary key, nor is it a candidate key. This caused us to create the Zip Code table and to relate the information in that table to the customer table.

Now consider a pragmatic issue about the system. The customer table is expected to hold more than 10 million records. The client prints mailing labels for all customers every Thursday to do their direct-mail advertising. In our testing, we found that it takes, on average, 0.001 seconds to print a label from a single table and that it takes 0.01 seconds to print a label from a two-table relation. A difference of nine thousandths of second is not much. Multiply that nine thousandths of second by 10 million and do the math—this is a difference of 1.04 *days*. The 10 million label run from one table will take 2.78 hours, while the two-table version will take 1.16 *days*. There is very powerful temptation to put the city and state data back into the customer table, and denormalization is the process of doing that.

Would you eliminate the Zip Code table from the design? No, this table serves a purpose in limiting the possible inconsistencies with the city, state, and zip code. The Zip Code table will still be recognized as the primary source for the city and state values. You would simply duplicate the values in the customer table.

Figure 14 shows the customer table after denormalizing.

Figure 15. *A denormalized customer table design.*

The important point here is that it should not be an easy decision to denormalize. In doing this you have introduced redundant data into your design. Redundant data means the database will occupy more space. It also means there is a possible point of inconsistency, that is, a situation where the city and state in the customer table don't match the city and state values from the Zip Code table. To deal with this you will need to use code to ensure that the customer records are updated when the city or state fields of the zip code record change. However, in the example, the performance difference was so drastic it dwarfed the consistency and storage issues.

When you decide to denormalize the data, be sure to document it well. If you don't, you run the risk of someone following you on the project and fixing the normalization, which, of course, will break the label run.

In the above description of denormalization, keeping the Zip Code table was recommended. The Zip Code table becomes the single source for city and state information. The data from the Zip Code table is used to populate the city and state fields in the customer table.

To take another example, consider a customer record with a field named Balance. This field is derived from the total of the invoices minus the total of the payments for that customer. You denormalize from third normal form so that the display of the balance on the customer data entry form doesn't require processing all the invoices and payment for each customer. However, you would always use the detail tables to produce reports, and any discrepancy between the details and the balance field would have the details overwrite the balance field.

I once posted this information on the CompuServe FoxForum and got the following question in response: "Why do database programmers always feel that the detail is accurate and the summary is inaccurate? Isn't it possible that the summary was updated and the detail record supporting that summary failed to be written to disk?"

Yes, that is possible, and my reply was this: "Database developers should be concerned with consistency and not accuracy. If we can provide consistent balances in all reports, then an accountant can find the inaccuracy and correct it. If we are not consistent, and one report has one total and another report has a different total, no one can figure out how to correct it. Consistency is the responsibility of database developers, accuracy is the responsibility of accountants."

Summary

Relational database design is a critical aspect of application design. The decisions you make while designing the database will impact all aspects of the application. In this appendix, you studied relational databases by first seeing what they are not, in the myths from C. J. Date.

You then saw the criteria for an optimal logical data design from Fleming and von Halle. The point was made that a truly good relational design is simple and can be understood by non-database professionals.

Referential integrity was found to be a business issue rather than a database issue. You saw that the business rules will dictate the methods you use to protect the integrity of the relationships in the data.

You worked through all six normal forms. You saw that, contrary to the popular myth, third normal form is *not* "good enough." The three normal forms beyond third normal form have specific situations in which they apply. Boyce Codd applies when there is more than one candidate for primary key. Fourth normal form applies when the primary key is composed of two or more fields. Fifth normal form applies when the primary key is composed of three or more fields.

The last issue discussed was denormalization, the process of backing up from fully normalized design in order to meet some other, non-database design, requirement.

We recommend you read the *Handbook of Relational Database Design* from Fleming and von Halle, and *Relational Database Selected Writings* from C. J. Date.

Appendix Three
Suggested Readings

Gamma and Helms et al. *Design Patterns Elements of Reusable Object Oriented Software.* Addison Wesley, Reading MA, 1995. ISBN: 0=201-63361-2.

Donald A. Norman. *The Design of Everyday Things.* Doubleday, New York, NY. 1988. ISBN: 0-385-26774-6

Martin Fowler et al. *UML Distilled Applying The Standard Object Modeling Language.* Addison Wesley, Reading, MA. 1997. ISBN: 0-201-32563-2

Edward Yourdan. *Death March The Complete Software Developer's Guide to Surviving "Mission Impossible" Projects.* Prentice Hall PTR, Upper Saddle River, NJ. 1997. ISBN: 0-13-748310-4

Steve McConnell. *Code Complete.* Microsoft Press, Redmond, WA. ISBN: 1-55615-484-4

Michael J. Hernandez, *Database Design for Mere Mortals.* Addison Wesley, Reading, MA. 1997. ISBN: 0-201-69471-9

Savannah Brentnall. *Object Orientation in Visual FoxPro.* Addison Wesley, Reading, MA. 1996. ISBN: 0-201-47943-5

Edward Yourdan. *Object-Oriented Systems Design An Integrated Approach.* Prentice Hall PTR, Englewood Cliffs, NJ. 1994. ISBN: 0-13-636325-3

Alan Cooper. *About Face The Essentials of User Interface Design.* IDG Books, Foster City, CA. 1995. ISBN: 1-56884-322-4

Bruce F. Webster. *Pitfalls of Object-Oriented Development.* M&T Books, New York, NY. 1995. ISBN: 1-55851-397-3

Martin and Odell. *Object-Oriented Analysis & Design.* Prentice Hall, Englewood Cliffs, NJ. 1992. ISBN: 0-13-630245-9

Fleming and von Halle. *Handbook of Relational Database Design.* Addison Wesley, Reading, MA. 1989. ISBN: 0-201-11434-8

C. J. Date. *Relational Database Selected Writings.* Addison Wesley, Reading, MA. 1989. ISBN: 0-201-14196-5

Bowman, Emerson, and Darnovsky. *The Practical SQL Handbook Using Structured Query Language.* Addison Wesley, Reading, MA. 1996. ISBN: 0-201-44787-8

David A. Taylor, Ph.D. *Object-Oriented Technology: A Manager's Guide.* Addison-Wesley, Reading, MA. 1990. ISBN: 0-201-56358-4

Wirfs-Brock, Wilkerson, Wiener. *Designing Object-Oriented Software.* Prentice-Hall 1990. ISBN: 0-13-629825-7

Steve McConnell, *Rapid Development.* Microsoft Press, Redmund 1996. ISBN: 1-55615-900-5

Whil Hentzen, *Building Visual Studio Applications on a Visual FoxPro Foundation.* Hentzenwerke Publishing, Milwaukee 1998. ISBN: 0-9655093-5-4

Granor and Roche, *Hacker's Guide to Visual FoxPro 6.0.* Hentzenwerke Publishing, Milwaukee 1998. ISBN: 0-9655093-6-2

Markus Egger, *Advanced Object Oriented Programming with Visual FoxPro 6.0.* Hentzenwerke Publishing, Milwaukee 1998. ISBN: 0-9655093-8-9

Rick Strahl, *Internet Applications with Visual Foxpro6.0.* Hentzenwerke Publishing, Milwaukee 1998. ISBN: 0-9655093-9-7

Appendix Four
Debugging

The ability to debug is a skill that transcends any particular application or any particular programming language or environment. It's important to recognize debugging as a separate skill set that needs as much attention as learning the latest programming languages and tools. Effective debugging requires the proper mind-set, a methodical attention to detail, and a desire to really debug your application, and not just "fix" it.

Again, I encourage you to read what Steve McConnell has to say about debugging in *Code Complete*. He presents many interesting points that are supported by research into the programming and debugging process. This appendix concentrates on my perspective on debugging, and concentrates on what I feel is the most significant cause of inefficient debugging.

One of the activities that has most improved my debugging skills is beta testing Visual FoxPro. Beta testing involves not just *finding* bugs, but proving to the development team at Microsoft that the bug exists. A beta tester must document what they think they've identified as some anomalous behavior. Bug reports are submitted by a) describing the steps to reproduce the observed behavior, and b) describing what behavior was expected, and if not readily apparent, *why* they expected something different from what they have observed.

Some beta testers take a very methodical approach and explore each feature of the product in detail. They test each command, function, interface element, help file entry, object property, event and method, and catalog aspects of the product that do not behave as expected, or that do not behave in a manner consistent with the product documentation. I prefer to beta test by actually creating applications. Testing the product in a manner that stresses not only the individual components, but stresses them *in situ*, where the interaction of the components (and my understanding of their behavior) are tested, can reveal problems that wouldn't otherwise become apparent. The downside to this type of beta testing is that you might have a complex form, class or program that you've been working on for several days. The development team requires a concise set of instructions to reproduce the problem, so my first step is to try to reproduce the behavior. I'm never certain, at first, whether the behavior I'm observing is as a result of a problem with the product, or a problem with my implementation. Often, I'm unable to reproduce the behavior, and I'm forced to go back and look at what else may be causing the problem.

Whose coding error is it?

After attacking a particular bug for hours without making much (if any) success, beware of falling into the trap of suspecting a bug in the! This is more often than not a dead end. We all know that virtually every piece of commercial software has shipped with *some* bugs in it, and a product as complex as FoxPro is no exception. The reality of programming is that *everyone*, with the exception of the lucky folks that write microprocessor microcode, can, sooner or later, run up against someone else's bug. Assembly language programmers have to deal with microcode bugs. "C" programmers have to deal with bugs in the Windows API and the "C" compiler they're using. Programmers using high-level languages (like FoxPro) have to deal with all the foregoing and their own compiler's bugs.

However, it's important to note that during beta testing, for every confirmed bug that I report, I would estimate that there are at *least* a dozen other suspected bugs that I never report. The reason is that in attempting to distill the behavior to its essence and to reproduce it, I discover the error is with *my* code, and *not* Microsoft's. Yeah, my code may be much more bug-prone than that of some others. However, if I'm getting a 6-to-1 ratio between my bugs and FoxPro's while it's in *beta*, then the ratio has to climb *much* higher once the product is released. Statistically, there is always a much better chance that unexpected behavior is due to an error in my code than to a bug in FoxPro, and my time is going to be much better spent working on that assumption. A suspected bug in the product you're working with should be the absolute drop-dead last suspicion that should cross your mind in the process of debugging an application.

Even if I do find a bug in a released version of FoxPro, this doesn't mean that I've solved the problem. The problem is still in my lap, and it's up to me to deal with it. My users won't be real happy if development ceases while I wait for the next revision to "clean up" the bugs in the current version (and introduce a few new ones along the way). Remember that the devil you know is preferred to the devil you don't know.

Learning to debug is not a finite process. As development tools evolve, I'm continually having to refine my debugging techniques to take into account new language features. Prior to Visual FoxPro 3.0, I never had to suspect omission of "**This**" or "**ThisForm**" from a line of code.

The Scientific Method

The Scientific Method is a $20 phrase to describe what is simply a logical way of attacking a problem. I was fortunate in that I had an outstanding science teacher in grade school that pounded the Scientific Method into my head at a young age. It's something that can be applied to almost any kind of technical problem, whether it's auto mechanics, plumbing, electronics or computer programming.

The Scientific Method is a logical series of steps taken to come to an understanding of some phenomenon. In daily life it's usually applied to some phenomenon of *mis*behavior. The car won't start, the toilet won't flush, the fuse blows, or in the case of a piece of software (in technical jargon), "it's broke". Many of us follow the steps of the Scientific Method without knowing that that's what we're doing. The steps are these:

1) Gather data or make observations to describe the phenomenon

2) Form a hypothesis (sometimes called a SWAG or Scientific Wild-Assed Guess) that attempts to explain the data or observations

3) Set up a test (sometimes called an "experiment") to determine the validity of the hypothesis.

4) Perform the test and again make observations and gather data.

5) Refine the hypothesis to accommodate the observations collected in the experiment.

6) Set up another test to test the new hypothesis

And so on...

Steps 4 through 6 are repeated as many times as necessary, until what eventually emerges is a hypothesis that is confirmed by a reproducible test.

In the scientific community this process is repeated ad nauseum for decades, if not centuries, until eventually someone notices that no one has come up with a test for a particular hypothesis that contradicts the hypothesis. At this point the hypothesis is elevated to the status of a *Theory*. In the scientific community a theory is something that may be accepted (for the time being) as Truth in the formation of other hypotheses describing related phenomena.

Fortunately for programmers, we don't have to be this rigorous. We just have to get the darn thing working, and reasonably close to the promised delivery date. But while we're not after Cosmic Truth, this process is exactly what is needed to track down a bug in our applications.

Sometimes the process is trivial:

Observation: FoxPro ceases executing with a "Data type is invalid for this property" error on the following line of code

```
ThisForm.Caption = .NULL.
```

Hypothesis: I goofed when typing in the code.

Test: Change line of code to

```
ThisForm.Caption = ".NULL."
```

and run the form

Observation: No error, form caption reads ".NULL."

Conclusion: I have to quit writing code at 3 A.M.

Again, the important point is that the Scientific Method is really something that we've done intuitively all our lives. We apply it instinctively, almost by reflex - observe (read error message, look at code), form hypothesis (surmise that typo or undeclared variable, or untested condition etc., etc., caused the error) and test hypothesis (correct and re-run). Where some developers fail in applying this technique is that they reach a point where they step out of this cycle short of the point where it may begin to yield results. They yell "FoxPro has a bug", or take it to their co-worker/resident FoxPro guru, or post a message in an online forum or newsgroup. Rather than continuing with the scientific method until they find the bug, they admit defeat prematurely, and thereby delay getting to the root of the problem, fixing it, and getting on with getting the deliverable in a deliverable state!

In much of our debugging, the procedure is as trivial as in the example above. We quickly form a hypothesis, and verify this hypothesis by doing nothing more than looking again at a section of code that we intended to perform some function. On re-examination, we discover that its logic was flawed, or there was a typographical error, or we made an assumption about the state of something that turned out to be a bad assumption. We then test by correcting the discovered error, and re-run the code.

Data gathering

Where I most often see developers get into trouble in debugging is through trying to identify a bug with insufficient information. It's important to know *exactly* and *in detail* what is happening before you can form a reasonable hypothesis to test. The initially observed behavior is often what the developer uses to try to form a hypothesis, and just as often the initially observed behavior is woefully inadequate.

As an example, consider a developer who uses a Drop-Down Combo Box for the first time, bound to a table field. The behavior the developer initially observes is:

"I type a value into the control, but the bound table field isn't updated to reflect what I've typed".

The developer needs to immediately begin asking (and answering) a string of questions:

1. Is whatever the developer is using to check the field's value working? E.g., if the field is being displayed in a TextBox, is the TextBox being refreshed?

2. Is the ControlSource of the ComboBox set properly?

3. Is the control's DisplayValue property changing to reflect the user's entry?

4. Is the control's Value property changing to reflect the user's entry?

By answering these questions, the developer begins to limit the scope of the problem to that portion of the chain from user's fingers to table field that is not performing as expected.

Thus the first step in attacking some non-trivial debugging scenario is to ask questions to define *exactly* what is happening. If you don't know what's happening, you can't even begin to explain (and correct) the behavior you're seeing. A good analogy is a doctor's diagnosis of a patient's complaint. Sometimes the doctor can make an immediate diagnosis, but in many cases, the doctor could either have a tentative diagnosis, or be completely in the dark as to the nature of the patient's ailment. Either way, the first thing the physician does is to ask questions and order tests.

Without asking questions about a bug, a developer is like a doctor trying to treat symptoms rather than the underlying disease. Don't confuse the behavior with what is causing the problem. The behavior is only one of many clues.

Doctors have all kinds of diagnostic tools and procedures to diagnose a medical condition. We have Visual FoxPro's debugging tools. These tools allow us to answer just about any question we might have about how our programs are running, so we're limited only by our ability to ask questions.

Frankenbach's postulate and random fixes

One of my least favorite situations is the situation in which some misbehavior of my application miraculously cures itself. When this happens, I really begin to wish that I employed some kind of version-tracking scheme, even if it were only the habit of backing up my work every hour or so. I never know if the demon has been exorcised because of something I changed, because of a change in some environmental factor, or perhaps the shoemaker's elves had at it while I was at lunch.

When a bug disappears, I know that a clue to understanding the problem has just slipped through my fingers. If I had a copy of this piece of the application that exhibited the undesired behavior, I could compare it to the current version (that works correctly), and hopefully find out what was wrong with the first version. Developers that take advantage of such fortuitous "debugging" are on a narrow ledge. My friend David Frankenbach observes that "Bugs that go away by themselves have a nasty habit of coming back by themselves".

Sometimes it is helpful with something that really has me stumped, to deliberately trigger this "automatic debugging" by semi-randomly changing some piece of the puzzle. Changing the instantiation order of form objects, the RowSourceType or RecordSourceType of a list object or grid, changing from a filtered table to a local view, changing a button with a bitmap to one with a textual caption, anything that may *logically* have a bearing on the problem (it's important that what you change isn't *completely* random). However, should one of these changes result in the desired behavior, this alone is insufficient to consider it "debugged", because this addresses the symptom, not the illness. If you succeed in getting something to work by making random changes to your code, as Steve McConnell puts it, "you're not learning anything, you're just goofing around".

It is also important from the standpoint of maintainability to build as much consistency into our applications as possible. Randomly changing things until they work works against consistency. If my style of programming suggests that combo boxes used to select foreign keys be populated by a SQL SELECT statement, then this technique should be used consistently throughout the application. If, in order to get something working right, the pattern is changed for some controls, I'm causing myself two problems. First, I don't know why in certain cases the SQL SELECT RowSourceType approach didn't work, and wonder whether all of the other controls that use this RowSourceType will continue to do so in all circumstances. Second, 90% of my foreign-key-selecting combo's will use SQL SELECT's, and the other 10% (at apparent random) will use arrays. Once the application is into the maintenance phase of its life cycle, this inconsistency could make maintenance more difficult than necessary.

In the normal cycle of applying the scientific method to debugging an application, each time a set of observations is gathered, it's time to form a new hypothesis that attempts to explain the observations. There are times however when we just come up empty, and honestly haven't a clue as to why we're getting the behavior we're seeing. Making a change in a component that is logically relevant, but may be chosen at random is an attempt at generating a new set of observations when we run out of hypotheses to test. But it is important to realize that the *purpose* of this exercise is to generate a new set of phenomena to observe. I'm not interested in just fixing the darn thing from a functional standpoint (curing the symptom), but to fix it by tracking down the bug and squashing it. The "just change something" approach improves our chances of finding the bug by adding to our collection of observations so that we can formulate a new hypothesis to test. A related point is to change *one thing at a time*. Otherwise, we can never be sure which of several changes changed the observations.

Reproducing errors

Isolating an error can sometimes be accomplished by attempting to reproduce the behavior, just as is done during beta testing. Whether you are successful at reproducing the behavior or not, you've gained extremely valuable information about the bug.

Testing routines in an environment other than the one in which they normally operate often requires "scaffolding". This is creating a wrapper of some kind that allows testing of the routine in isolation from its environment. If it behaves differently within the scaffolding, then the scaffolding is an imperfect simulation of the routine's normal environment. Determination of the variations between the scaffolding and the normal operating environment will provide a clue as to the nature of the problem.

If you are successful at reproducing the behavior, you know that you've narrowed the scope of the problem - you've eliminated all of the things that *might* have been causing the unwanted behavior. If you fail to reproduce the behavior, then you know that the problem doesn't lie quite where you thought it did, and you can now focus more productively on the part of the application that *might* be causing the problem. You have a list of factors that are contributing to the problem, and a list of factors that are not, and you can then proceed to move more factors from column "A" to column "B", until you've distilled the situation to its nub.

Relating this back to the scientific method, in error reproduction you look on the original buggy portion of your application as an "experiment" that demonstrates the behavior. The scientific community devotes a great deal of effort to "replicate" the results of other researchers' experiments. In this way, the conclusions of the original researchers are tested, and either confirmed or contradicted. Likewise, trying to reproduce the unwanted behavior in a "pristine" environment performs the same function. You're asking "is my conclusion about where this problem is originating correct?", and then devising an experiment to test this.

It is in this question-asking step that the native debugging tools come into play. Proper use allows the developer to drill down into the application and come to a more complete understanding of the situation, and provide clues to the next step in zeroing in on the bug, and stomping that sucker! However, you have to ask the questions, and ask the right questions in order for the debugging tools to serve their purpose. You may not ask the right question immediately or even on the second or third pass. Sometimes you ask an endless series of questions for hours before you understand exactly where things are coming apart.

The more difficult bugs are those that appear under some circumstances but not others. The Call Stack and Locals Windows can help determine what is different about two circumstances that you think are the same. The most difficult bugs are those that appear seemingly at random. Again, careful examination of the situation using the debugging tools can lead to some idea as to where the problem lies.

Different Families of Bugs - The Good, The Bad, and the Ugly

I would love to set out a roadmap, or good methodology for debugging applications, but try as I might, I can't distill the process into a series of steps. There are so many different kinds of bugs and misbehaviors that our applications exhibit, that the best I can do is to stress the importance of applying the Scientific Method, having the proper mindset (it's *my* code that has the bug), and being creative and willing to think "outside the box". In fact, outside of the broad framework of the Scientific Method, it is best to use different approaches to solving a problem, rather than a slavish adherence to a rote procedure.

Still, there are certain broad categories of bugs that we can be aware of, and think about how we can approach them. Keep in mind that none of these categories are mutually exclusive. A particular piece of anomalous behavior can fall into several of these categories.

The Crashing Variety of Bugs

There are two types of "crashing" bugs. There are those of the GPF variety that result in an "Access Violation" in Windows NT or a "This program has performed an illegal operation" error in Windows 95. The other is the type we're most familiar with, the kind that triggers some kind of Visual FoxPro error that halts execution. This latter type is usually a bit easier to track down than others are, because the FoxPro error message gives us an important starting point to figure out what the problem might be. This doesn't always point to *exactly* where the problem lies, but will at least give us a clear clue. In my opinion the worst of these is some variant of a "syntax error" in a lengthy SQL statement. I sometimes find myself pleading with FoxPro, "Can you *please* be a little more specific"? VFP 6.0 does do a better job of this, highlighting syntax errors. However, there are some limitations on what it can tell you when it hits a "data type mismatch" while executing a query.

If careful examination of the command doesn't get you out of trouble, a good technique is to start cutting parts out or simplifying clauses or expressions until FoxPro stops complaining. Once you get whatever is left to run successfully, examine the piece that you last removed or modified to see what the problem is. It helps if you structure lengthy expressions making liberal use of line-continuation characters:

```
SELECT <field>, ;
    <field>, ;
    <field>, ;
    <field>, ;
  FROM <table> JOIN <table> ;
      ON <expression> ;
    JOIN <table> ;
      ON <expression> ;
    JOIN <table> ;
      ON <expression> ;
  WHERE <expression> ;
  ORDER BY <field> ;
  GROUP BY <field> ;
```

Or:

```
IIF( <expression> , ;
```

```
IIF(<expression, ;
   <expression>, ;
      <expression>), ;
<expression>)
```

This makes it easier to a) spot an error or b) make a modification to try to correct the problem.

The GPF category of crashing bug is frustrating because there is something happening that is in some ways completely out of our control. It's Microsoft's fault. However, we do have to deal with it, and we do have some ways to avoid the problem. Fortunately these seem to be quite rare, and are getting rarer with each Visual FoxPro release.

In my experience, GPF style crashes most often result from manipulation of objects – accessing or setting object properties, passing object references, instantiation of objects, destroying objects etc. While it may seem at first that there's nothing we can do to solve this type of problem, I've yet to find a problem with this type of crash that I wasn't able to fix. In every case, there has either been a bug in my code that was doing something strange, or I was able to accomplish what I wanted to do by doing things a little differently. Recently I had a form that was consistently crashing when launched from another form, but would run just fine by itself. It turned out that I was passing a reference to the calling form that was being mis-handled, and the reference was being destroyed when the memvar holding the reference went out of scope. Why? I dunno, but when I cleaned up my code so the reference was properly stored to a property of the child form, everything worked fine.

The new feature of VFP 6 that tells you exactly where the GPF is being triggered is a big help. But realize that this tells you what line of code is *triggering* the crash, which is in turn a clue to what is *causing* the crash – two different things. Look at the objects that are somehow related to the triggering line of code, and start to think about what you can change that might have some effect on the crash. If you change something and it still crashes, but at a different point, you might be on the right track.

Sometimes simply doing things in a different order – instantiating object "B" before object "A" - or in a more direct (or indirect) manner does the trick. Instead of manipulating object properties directly, call a method of the object to perform the task. Store object properties to memvars and then work with them instead of referencing the object properties directly. There is no pat answer, and this type of problem will sometimes really challenge your creativity. The bottom line is that if you change one thing at a time, and test, and change something else, and test, you'll eventually get around the problem. Make a mental note of what works, and as time goes on you'll find that you'll begin to get a better feel for what might be causing things to "go south" the next time around.

Bugs due to inadequate product knowledge

No one knows all the details about FoxPro, or any other development tool, so this is one we all come up against time and again. We think we understand how a particular control, function, method or command works, use it in the manner we think is correct, and then learn how things *really* work when our application doesn't work in the manner that we expect.

The important mindset here is to always assume we don't *really* know how things work. It's only when we take this mindset that we'll find those areas where our knowledge is inadequate. This is an important point. Always try to be aware of the assumptions you are making about FoxPro commands, functions and methods during a debugging session.

Bugs due to unexpected triggering of events

In FoxPro 2.x, we had few events to deal with. Code was executed more or less in a nice, neat linear fashion. In Visual FoxPro, things get out of hand much more easily.

It's easy to assume (since I designed this beast) that when I do *this* to *this* control, that *this* method code gets executed. When something strange happens, I start looking at that method code, and tracing it, and checking the value of memvars, object properties, record pointers and so on, trying to discover what's going wrong. What I may be ignoring is that another event is occurring before or after the event that I'm explicitly triggering, and as a result some additional code is being executed before or after the code I'm examining so closely!

There are also circumstances in which we assume certain events will always occur, and write our applications based on this assumption. For instance, I've fallen into the trap of assuming that whatever form control has focus, that it will always lose focus eventually, and that the control's Valid and LostFocus events will be triggered. This is certainly true when the user is navigating from one control to another in the form, even when the user closes the form using the Close button or the "Close" option on the form's control menu. However, because focus is never transferred to a Toolbar, the current control on a form never loses focus when the user decides to close a form by clicking on the "Close" button on a toolbar!

Bugs due to erroneous assumptions

This category of bugs can apply to almost any debugging scenario - we assume the darn thing is going to work, and it doesn't! But at a more granular level, we need to be aware of assumptions we are making when we write code, and then when we encounter problems, to immediately examine or re-evaluate all assumptions inherent in the situation.

Assumptions regarding the state of the environment, range of values for memvars and object properties, parameter values and data types, possible values to be evaluated by a FOR clause, a DO CASE structure, a DO WHILE structure, an IF or IIF() statement. This is the old advice about garbage in, garbage out. As long as I keep assuming that I don't have garbage in, I can't find the piece of garbage that's breaking my app.

The benefits of debugging

The usually accepted benefit of debugging an application is to get it working right. As such, few (if any) developers look forward to debugging. But it is in a large part through encountering bugs, tracking them down, and successfully fixing them that we grow in both our knowledge of our chosen development platform, and in our skill as developers. Experience and effective debugging leads to a decline in the incidence of bugs.

Authors who write about development products and have a book in the bookstores weeks or months after a new development product ships learn all they need to know by using the product. They inadvertently create bugs, track them down and fix them. They don't have any books or reference works to draw upon, but at a certain point, neither do the rest of us. I can guarantee you that no matter how many books on Visual FoxPro you have lining your shelves, you're going to run into bugs that are not addressed in any "how-to" or reference work. So you're on your own, as usual, and the better you are at debugging your applications, the better you will become at being a knowledgeable, creative developer, and at avoiding bugs in the future.

Using VFP 6.0's Debugging Tools

On many occasions I've seen developers slavishly stepping through dozens of lines of code using the Trace window, trying to locate where something is going wrong. The trace window is indeed a powerful tool, but should be brought into play only when you've localized (or at least think you've localized) the problem to a specific piece of code. Most of the additions to the suite of debugging tools made in VFP 5 and VFP 6 assist us in doing this kind of localization.

Where is the problem?

I may have a data bound ComboBox that is blank, not displaying what I assume to be the correct value after navigating to a new record. I could open the trace window and start stepping through the navigation code, watching the ComboBox at each step. However, this might involve stepping through a hundred lines of code, checking values of various memvars, field values and object properties along the way. I may indeed spot the problem, but if I don't, I may repeat the process several times before I spot it.

However, if instead I form some hypotheses about the *immediate* cause of the observed behavior, and begin testing those hypotheses, I'll proceed in a much more orderly, and more linear fashion to a resolution of the problem.

Note in the preceding paragraph that I stressed the "*immediate* cause of the observed behavior". To find out how we got to where we stand, we must efficiently retrace our steps. This means starting from what we observe and figuring out what events could yield this observed behavior. Focusing on a solution to the problem without understanding it will often result in spending far more time than necessary trying to guess at the cause, testing our guess, then making another guess.

In this example, there are several things that could be causing the observed behavior:

- The combo box hasn't been refreshed, leaving the Value Property out of sync with the field specified in the ControlSource property.
- The List property of the combo box does not contain a value that corresponds to the current Value property, which results in a blank DisplayValue
- The List property contains a value that does correspond to the current Value property, but the corresponding value is a string of spaces or the empty string.
- The value of the field specified in the ControlSource contains a value other than what I'm expecting

As you can see from this list, there are a number of values that can be checked to test the four stated hypotheses. The DisplayValue, Value and List properties, as well as the value of the field specified in the ControlSource can all be examined using the Watch window, the Locals window. Using the SYS(1270) function to create an object reference to display in the Watch or Locals window can often make things a little easier, particularly when the object in question is deep inside a container hierarchy.

Which of the 4 hypotheses above turns out to be correct then leads to another set of questions, and another set of hypotheses. Let's assume that the last item in the list above, "The value of the field specified in the ControlSource contains a value other than the one I'm expecting" turned out to be the case. My new hypotheses are then:

- The record pointer isn't positioned on the record I'm expecting to be on
- The value of the bound field isn't what I expect it to be
- Something has changed the value of the bound field to something other than what I'm expecting

Again, I can observe certain values in the Watch and Locals window, including the RECNO() or a primary or candidate key field, and the value of the field of interest, and perhaps including the value returned by GETFLDSTATE() if I suspect something is changing the field's value.

After problem localization, bring in the Trace window

This process is identifying a chain of events that are connecting a problem with my code to an observed behavior. Thus far I've determined that the ComboBox, its List property and it's relation to its ControlSource are all working properly. I haven't yet identified the root cause. Assuming that I discover that the record pointer is on Record 11 and not record 8 as I was expecting, I can then set a breakpoint on the change in the RECNO() or set a breakpoint for when RECNO() = 11, run the form, and execution is suspended and the trace window is opened when that condition is met.

Occasionally a hypothesis revolves around whether or not a particular method is getting called. In the past I've used WAIT WINDOW to spit up a message when a particular method is called, or to output a certain value. The DEBUGOUT command and Output window is preferred to WAIT WINDOWs as they don't require that all output values be converted to characters, and the Output window can show an entire series of DEBUGOUT commands. I can also execute a DEBUGOUT command conditionally, so that it is only executed when certain conditions go out of expected bounds.

In addition to setting breakpoints and using DEBUGOUT to alert me to the execution of certain code modules, the Call Stack window is often an invaluable tool. I expect methods and functions to be called under certain circumstances, and not others. Sometimes a method gets called under circumstances that I didn't intend, but unless I know what method called it, I don't know whether it's being called when I expect it to be called or not. The Call Stack window shows exactly how I got to the module I'm currently examining in the trace window, and I can even traverse back up to the calling method or function to determine what circumstances caused the current module to be called.

The point to all this is to quit looking at code and tracing code until you have a pretty good idea where in your code the problem might lie. Use the tools that you have to check values to test your hypotheses, and trace code only after you know what the likely source of the problem is.   I'm not discouraging use of the Trace window as the initial debugging tool. If I have a 12-line FOR...ENDFOR loop that isn't working right, the Trace window will often yield an immediate fix, as it forces me to examine each line of code in turn. There's something magical about the Trace window. Something that I'll gloss right over in the code editing window will stand up and yell at me from the Trace window. Likewise, I'm not advocating a pedantic step-by-step debugging process in every case. Sometimes I immediately know where I've made a mistake and just go in and fix it. Usually I know what kind of mistakes I tend to make over and over again, and I'm usually pretty adept at spotting the symptoms of one of my usual mistakes.

Performance problems

Coverage Logging and the Coverage Profiler are tools that I don't use anywhere near as often as the Trace, Watch, Locals and Output windows. However, any time you have some kind of performance bottleneck, do not even begin to try to fix the problem until you create a coverage log and use the Coverage Profiler. Optimizing a part of an application can require a lot of work and a fair amount of creativity and can often tax your programming skills to the max. I hate to expend this kind of effort on the wrong part of the problem.

I recently had occasion to examine a form that was performing very poorly when moving to a new record set. My first thought was that the view query needed to be optimized. However, I fortunately ran a coverage log and used the Coverage Profiler first. It showed that there was indeed probable room for improvement in the query, but also showed that some controls were being refreshed dozens of times, and may of these controls contained code in their refresh methods. As I've often done, this programmer had figured "I'll do another Refresh() just to make sure" at several points in his code, forgetting that there was a single Refresh() call made at a critical point in the foundation form class, making all of the other calls to the form's Refresh() method redundant. Adding some indexes to optimize the query improved the performance significantly, but another 50% improvement was achieved by eliminating the redundant Requery() calls. This would have gone unsuspected (and unaddressed) without use of the Coverage Profiler.

Usually, the general location of the performance bottleneck is pretty obvious. As a result it isn't necessary to create a Coverage log for more than is absolutely necessary, which also makes the Coverage Profiler much faster when it analyzes the Coverage log.

If, for example, I have a Requery() method on my form for retrieving a new set of records, I'll place the following in the Requery() method:

```
SET COVERAGE TO requery.log
<Rest of Requery() code>
SET COVERAGE TO & Closes the log file and sets coverage "OFF"
```

While doing this means that I have to remember to go in and remove the SET COVERAGE TO code, I'll log only that code that I suspect is the problem area, making the Coverage profiler much faster, and making it easier to examine the resulting output.

The hard ones

There are three categories of bugs that present unique problems to the VFP developer, but it is possible to overcome them:

- Major crashes – "Access Violations" or "Illegal Operation" errors – Generically known as "GPF's"
- Event Order and Timing problems
- VFP bugs

Major Crashes

The first category, the "Major crash" was a real pain with VFP 5. The first challenge was finding what triggered the crash, the second was what to do about it. Fortunately, VFP 6 has eliminated some of the headache with the first challenge. VFP 6 will now report the executing module and the currently executing line of that module when an "Illegal Operation" or "Access Violation" occurs. Unfortunately you get this information only if your code is executing when the crash occurs. If it's VFP's internal code that is executing, such as when an object is being instantiated or destroyed, it just crashes, and you're back to square 1. In this case you have to resort to using the Trace window to step through your code until whatever happens happens, and you have some clue to what is contributing to the crash.

Whether you have VFP 6's helpful "dump", or are able to narrow down the problem to a particular action using the Trace window, you are still faced with the problem of how to correct the problem.

In my experience, these types of crashes are almost always caused by some kind of object manipulation:

- Instantiation of an object
- Setting an object property
- Reading an object property
- Destroying an object
- Storing an object reference
- Clearing an object reference

The bad news is that the crash doesn't always coincide precisely with one of the events described above, but may be triggered by some ancillary operation related to an object. The good news is that fixing the problem doesn't require a real deep understanding of what's happening. This is fortunate as we don't have the tools to go in and debug Microsoft's code. I've had very good results with simply doing things a little differently. Sometimes its something as simple as changing the order in which I do things. I'll change the order in which properties are set, or in which objects are instantiated or destroyed. Sometimes something apparently trivial like storing an object reference to a memvar before storing it to another object property. Sometimes if I'm having trouble when passing an object reference from object to object, I'll instead figure a way to allow an object to grab a reference to another object as needed, rather than by storing a reference to the object.

If this feels like "voodoo programming" you're right. It's just a matter of fiddling with your code until it does things a little differently, so that the problem isn't triggered. For what it's worth, I find these kinds of problems much more prevalent during development than during execution of production code.

Event Order and Timing Problems

The introduction of Event Logging in VFP 5 provides a tool to easily determine the exact order in which events occur. This is usually sufficient to solve most problems in this area. However, I occasionally stumble across a situation where things don't quite occur in the expected order. For instance, if you have a control bound to a form property, and call a method in the InteractiveChange() of the control that references that form property, you may be surprised to find that the form property has not yet changed to reflect the new value of the control when the method called from the InteractiveChange() executes. This is an example of situations in which things seem to be happening "too fast" in one area relative to another, so that something else isn't yet up to speed, and things don't work as we expect. If this sounds really vague and fuzzy, that's because it is.

There are two techniques that I've found that can be tried to get around these problems. The first, and which is tailor-made for the situation described in the preceding paragraph is to explicitly assign the control's value to the property specified in the ControlSource in the InteractiveChange() event method before calling the method that relies on this value. The second technique is one of those things that I'll throw into a piece of code when my guts tell me that there may be a timing issue that is causing the problem. This trick I learned from Doug Hennig, and seems to have something like a 25% success rate in fixing something that feels like a timing issue.

The trick involves putting a "pause" into the execution of some code, by putting an INKEY() command into your code, with an interval argument specifying how long the code should pause. For example, a line that reads INKEY(0.1) will pause for a tenth of a second before proceeding.

VFP bugs

"What?" you say? "VFP has *BUGS*?"

Yup, but they get fewer and less onerous all the time. Sometimes they're real subtle and only one developer in a thousand will see a particular bug, but when you hit one, it's in your lap and there's no one else around to help you figure out how to solve it.

If I could offer advice on how to work around every VFP bug you're likely to encounter, I should probably go to work for Microsoft. To be honest, I don't run into too many of them, but I've hit a few.

One of the worst was a problem I ran into on a VFP 5 application in which a grid would very consistently try to position the record pointer on a non-existent record when a) the RecordSource was a view, b) all of the records in the view were newly-appended records and c) the user pressed the <PgDn> key. I couldn't wait for VFP 6 to ship, so I wrote code in the KeyPress() event method to process the keystroke and issue a NODEFAULT under these circumstances. Not pretty, but it worked.

Many of the little bugs I do encounter seem to have something to do with repainting forms. Just recently I ran into a situation where a simple call to a ListBox's Requery() method would cause the ListBox to appear as if there were two items selected, even though only one item was in fact selected. I've also observed this in a ListBox where the MultiSelect property was set .F. In neither case was the ListIndex property or the value of the control changing.

The solution was to use the LockScreen property to force repainting of the form after all manipulations of the ListBox were completed. Since this discovery, I've gone back and tried this trick (with some success) to solve other problems that appeared to be related to improper repainting of the form.

Beyond these tips, I can only say that VFP will seldom expose an infelicity that is insurmountable. First, try to isolate the behavior to confirm that it is indeed a problem with VFP and not with your code. Remember, 99% of the bugs I think I've found in VFP turn out to be due to my own ham-handedness. Second, once you've discovered a problem that seems to be in the VFP code itself, use some creativity to solve the problem. Yes it might be (and probably *will* be) a kludge, but document it as a work-around and put it in. If it works, you're home free.

Index

About the Authors

Jim Booth

Jim Booth is a Visual FoxPro developer and trainer. He has written articles for the major FoxPro journals and has spoken at conferences in North America and Europe. He was a co-author for "Visual FoxPro Unleashed" published by Sams. Jim has been the recipient of the Microsoft Most Valuable Professional Award every year since the award was first presented in 1993.

Jim wrote chapters 2, 3, 4, 8, 10, 12, and Appendices One and Two. Both authors wrote chapter 7.

Steve Sawyer

Steve Sawyer is President of the Detroit Area Fox User Group, a Microsoft Support MVP, and a Microsoft Certified Professional. He is co-author of "The Pros Talk Visual FoxPro 3" (Microsoft Press 1996), and is a frequent contributor to both FoxTalk and FoxPro Advisor. He is a contributing editor at Advisor Publications, editing the monthly "Tips/Tricks/Traps" column in FoxPro Advisor.

Steve wrote chapters: 1, 5, 6, 9, 11, 13, 14 and Appendices Three and Four.

Steven P. Dingle, Technical Editor

Steve Dingle is an independent consultant specializing in custom FoxPro applications development since the early 90's. He is a Microsoft MVP (Most Valuable Professional) and also a Sysop for the FoxPro related forums on CompuServe (VFOX and FOXUSER).

How to Download Source Code, Sample Files, And .CHM files

Several additional resources are available to you from Hentzenwerke Publishing's website. They include: source code referred to in the book, sample data sets, and the .CHM file of the entire book.

To download the files:

1. Go to our website:

   www.hentzenwerke.com

2. Click on **Books** and follow the prompts.

As a protection to your investment (and ours!), there is a password scheme in place to prevent the downloading of these files without purchasing the book.

**You will need to have the book with you
in order to download the files!**

Note: The .CHM file is covered by the same copyright laws as the printed book. Reproduction and/or distribution of the .CHM file is prohibited.